THE BRITISH ARMY
IN MESOPOTAMIA,
1914–1918

THE BRITISH ARMY
IN MESOPOTAMIA,
1914–1918

Paul Knight

McFarland & Company, Inc., Publishers

Jefferson, North Carolina, and London

LIBRARY OF CONGRESS CATALOGUING-IN-PUBLICATION DATA

Knight, Paul, 1970–
The British army in Mesopotamia,
1914–1918 / Paul Knight.
p.   cm.
Includes bibliographical references and index.

ISBN 978-0-7864-7049-5

softcover : acid free paper ∞

1. World War, 1914–1918 — Campaigns — Iraq.
2. Great Britain. Army — History — World War, 1914–1918.
I. Title.
D568.5.K58 2013   940.4'09567 — dc23   2013021574

BRITISH LIBRARY CATALOGUING DATA ARE AVAILABLE

On the cover: Sir Frederick Stanley Maude's troops entering
Baghdad, March 1917; British flag © 2013 Shutterstock

Manufactured in the United States of America

*McFarland & Company, Inc., Publishers
Box 611, Jefferson, North Carolina 28640
www.mcfarlandpub.com*

Table of Contents

Introduction

When, in 2005, I served with the British Army in Camp Abu Naji, Al-Amara in Maysan Province, Iraq, I was astonished and somewhat embarrassed to learn that the British Army had fought there in 1915. I had a Ph.D. in history (admittedly not in 20th century Middle Eastern history) and thought I had a good grasp of British history, but here was a whole chapter I had no knowledge of.[1] From where I was, the next major town up the Tigris was Kut, which had played a pivotal role in the first half of the First World War, also something I knew nothing about.

I was not alone in my ignorance. Most people in Britain are unaware that Britain was even in Mesopotamia during the Great War. I would joke that the reason for this was that there were no Australians in Mesopotamia, so they have not made any films to complete the trilogy of Gallipoli and Palestine/Syria. If one adds in David Lean's 1962 film *Lawrence of Arabia*, then the campaigns against Turkey along the Red Sea and Mediterranean are well covered in the public mind.

Yet it was these failures on the Western Front, in Gallipoli and in breaking out of Egypt which drove the planners in Mesopotamia to overreach themselves, resulting in failure and tragedy on a scale unknown in the history of the British Army. It also forced the British Tommy and the Indian sepoy to fight in conditions worse than the worst of the Western Front. The prospect of failure at Gallipoli pressured the planners to advance on Baghdad when they were clearly unprepared. The failure at Gallipoli released battle-hardened divisions for service in Mesopotamia to seal the fate of the garrison at Kut. To relieve Kut, divisions newly arrived in that theater, were thrown into the battle, piecemeal, without their supporting units, across a narrow front, in the middle of winter, with rivers flooding out of their trenches and the logistics chain failing to cope, against entrenched Turks supported by modern machine guns and artillery. For these men, there was no friendly French canteen a few miles behind the lines, or the prospect of leave in Britain.

The Arab Revolt and Allenby's much-vaunted capture of Jerusalem in 1917 both happened after Maude's capture of Baghdad in the spring of 1917. The Tigris Corps was a whole campaigning season ahead of Allenby and Lawrence. The Tigris Corps also lacked a pre-war British base (such as Egypt) to operate from, or friendly Arab tribes to support it.[2]

The situation around Kut, above, is only one part of the story. The original purpose of the 1914 landing was to secure the Royal Navy's oil supply from Persia (Iran) and to secure Britain's political allies in the Persian Gulf. This was arguably the most successful "descent on a hostile coast" of the war.

Success brought "mission creep" in order to secure the base. The terrain could be as challenging as the enemy: waterless deserts; flooded plains too deep for the army, not deep enough for the navy; Arab tribes who looted and murdered indiscriminately; midday temperatures exceeding 110F.

Into Mesopotamia arrived young, ambitious generals. The heat and demands of command meant that the old did not last long. Charles Townsend was arguably the most successful allied general of 1915. When General Maude took command of the Tigris Corps, he and his team were younger than those at a comparable formation on the Western Front. Maude rebuilt a shattered army and launched a modern, methodical, well-supported campaign to drive the Turks out of what is now Iraq.

Part of this process (which was commenced before Maude took command, but was greatly sped up under him) included the first modern infrastructure development in Mesopotamia. The soldiers fought amongst the ruins of great civilizations. The British Army built modern port facilities in Basra and brought in port management. Railways and roads were built. Agriculture was encouraged. Aerial photography allowed the first maps to be produced. Public health, education and veterinary facilities were provided. The legal system was reviewed, with Arabic made the official language. Taxation was overhauled and the revenue of the religious institutions charities was used for that purpose rather than pilfered. The colonial rule of the Turk was replaced by the colonial rule of the Briton. The records of the British administrators themselves will, undoubtedly, paint a rosy picture of their results. Nevertheless, it is without doubt that the likes of Sir Percy Cox and Gertrude Bell, who dedicated many years of their lives to Mesopotamia, were committed to the improvement of Mesopotamia, the creation of modern Iraq, and the first Arab government in Baghdad in centuries.

The great controversy of Mesopotamia is whether or not the campaign was needed in the first place. Pre-war German war plans aimed to raise rebellion in the Muslim colonies of the Western Allies, which would tie down European troops who would otherwise be better employed in Europe against Germany. This plan was not realized on the scale envisaged, but Mesopotamia did achieve this objective. Ultimately, two army corps, some 250,000 men and 100,000 casualties, would be committed. The British commitment of manpower reached five times that of the Turks. It was a massive drain on manpower, material, shipping and money which could have been employed elsewhere.

The other question that needed to be answered was, what was it all for? Even in 1918, there was no answer. The Royal Navy's oil supply and Britain's Arab allies had been secured years before. It was as if a great military machine had taken on a life and purpose of its own, unrelated to the wider war aims.

So this was the Mesopotamia campaign. In this book, I have attempted to focus on the war as it affected the soldier. By definition, it has to be an account of the battles, as these were the great seismic shifts of the period. My interest, though, is how the conditions affected the man: the heat, the lack of water, the breakdown of logistics, the unreliability of the Arabs, the mirages, the dust, the flooding, the winter cold. How do you navigate at night in a featureless terrain without reliable communications or maps for a dawn attack? How were these overcome? Or were they overcome? Campaigning was restricted to the rivers until mechanized transport released those shackles. This meant that the Turks knew where the attacks would fall. Artillery spotters could not observe the enemy due to the mirage and the lack of vantage points. Artillery spotting by airplanes became essential but took time to bring the airplanes into theater and perfect the necessary skills. The absence of maps plagued both the Turks and the British. Pilots making sketch maps in flight hardly provided ideal material with which to launch a divisional attack, but it provided the British generals with an advantage over the Turks. In time, accurate maps would be produced.

By the end of the campaign, with all of these developments falling into place, the all-arms battle was developed. Aviation spotted for the artillery to support the infantry's attack. It was finally possible for a flanking force to traverse the desert and cut off the Turkish retreat, capturing whole formations. Aviation harassed the retreating Turks. Lorried infantry and armored cars raided quickly and deeply, adding confusion to the Turkish commanders. Maps accurately plotted enemy positions. Lorries brought forward water to refresh the attack. General Brooking's great success at Ramadi in 1917 was essentially the same plan as used by Townsend at Kut two years before. The difference was that Townsend lacked the information (maps, radios, aviation) and the logistical support (infantry transport and water resupply) for his plan to succeed—his men were simply too exhausted to follow up their victory, and the Turks were able to escape to fight again at Ctesiphon. The Turks did not escape from Ramadi.

1

The Turkish Question

The outbreak of war with the Ottoman Empire (Turkey) in 1914 ended a general European policy to which all the major Great War belligerents subscribed: to maintain the integrity of the Ottoman Empire, in Asia at least.[1] This policy originated with Napoleon's Egyptian expedition which threatened the security of British India and Russia through the prospect of a Franco-Turkish alliance.[2] In the 1820s, European governments (including Russia, the self-proclaimed guardian of Orthodox Christians in the Ottoman Empire) had initially, at least, supported the Ottomans during the Greek revolt of 1821–1832.[3] The main 19th-century aberration from this general policy was the Battle of Navarino (1827) where an Anglo-Franco-Russian fleet defeated a Turko-Egyptian fleet to secure eventual Greek independence. It was also, incidentally, the last all-sail naval engagement. With less than a year to go before the Sarajevo assassinations which sparked off the Great War, Sir Edward Grey, the British foreign secretary, reiterated this policy:

> The cardinal factor of British policy, which is based upon considerations not merely local, is to uphold the integrity of the Turkish dominions in Asia.[4]

This statement was a reiteration of the 1901 Anglo-Ottoman accord which aimed to preserve the status quo. The problem was, what was the status quo? The British public in 1901 may have become used to a global map with increasing areas of pink, but there were still a number of "white spots" on the map — terra incognita — and Ottoman Arabia was just one of these areas. Leonard Woolley (who would excavate Ur in Iraq after the war) and T.E. Lawrence (of Arabia) excavated in the Sinai while Gertrude Bell (who would devote her later life to the creation of Iraq) excavated in Syria and Palestine. Others traveled, like Gertrude Bell who traveled by horse from Syria to Baghdad in 1909 or Captain W.E. Shakespear who crossed Arabia in 1914, only to be killed by a stray bullet while an observer to a desert battle between Arab tribes. Lawrence heard tales of Shakespear later in the war: "[The Ageyl] began to tell me long stories of Captain Shakespear, who had been received by ibn Saud in Riyadh as a personal friend, and had crossed

Arabia from the Persian Gulf to Egypt; and had been at last killed in battle by the Shammar." While Lawrence's role in the Arab Revolt is well known, Bell is less well known than she deserves to be — her main cinematographic moment is in the 1997 film *The English Patient* where, pouring over a "Bell" map, soldiers hope that *he* was right. In November 1915 she was informed by the director of naval intelligence that her presence had been requested in Cairo where, as Major Miss Bell, she became the first female officer in British military intelligence. So groundbreaking was she that there was no uniform for her, and she wore civilian clothes throughout. Coincidentally, as British interest in the region grew, so too did Ottoman paranoia that the British had more interest in the region than just filling in the "white spot."[5]

The reasons for this European policy were not entirely philanthropic, although some were. Initially, the aim was to assist in the defeat of Napoleon, which eventually occurred near Damascus.[6] In the years after 1815, a war-weary Europe demanded stability. Nationalist ideas had been unleashed by the French Revolution, and again after the 1848 Revolutions. The creation of nationalist movements demanding their homelands was undesirable for major European heads of state who presided over multi-ethnic empires: a precedent set in one empire would soon spread. This explains the European support offered to the Ottomans against its own (Christian) nationalists. The European statesmen predicted, with a high degree of accuracy, the chaos and disruption to their "World Order" which would follow the breakup of the Ottoman Empire in the Balkans and the Middle East. These statesmen saw that the best means of containing these forces was by maintaining the Ottoman Empire. Looking at the modern Middle East, these statesmen may well have said, "We told you so."

Further European support came when Constantinople (Istanbul) itself was threatened in the Oriental Crisis of 1840. Mohammed Ali, an Ottoman soldier of Albanian birth, was appointed *vali* (governor) of Egypt in 1805, in the aftermath of Napoleon's invasion, and seized effective control in 1820. The loss of Egypt was a major blow to Ottoman prestige even if Mohammed Ali always acknowledged the Sultan's overlord-ship. In the late 1830s, Egyptian armies occupied the Levant and in 1840 threatened to occupy Constantinople itself. European intervention forced Mohammed Ali to back down. Mohammed Ali established the dynasty of kings who would rule Egypt until the 1952 revolution.

In the Crimean War (1853–1856), the French and British empires aided the Ottoman Empire against the Russian Empire; the European powers also sided with Constantinople against the creation of an independent Romanian state in the 1870s.[7] In June 1875, rebellion broke out in Bosnia-Herzegovina. Ottoman forces failed to quell the uprising, and the following spring, Russian-inspired revolutionaries were prepared to act. The Ottomans, however, responded with their own weapon — the *bashi-bazouks* — the "damaged heads." These were paramilitary forces who were unleashed on the population while the Ottoman army watched on. There are only estimates of their victims, between 3,000 and 30,000. Eighty towns and villages were burned to the ground, and some 200 more were sacked.[8] Invariably, those most vulnerable and least able to protect themselves would have suffered most, while those in armed rebellion would have put up a defense. There are parallels with events in the Balkans of the 1990s. The Russians intervened in their self-appointed capacity of protectors of Christianity in the Ottoman Empire, and despite meeting unexpectedly stiff resistance at Plevna in modern-day Bulgaria, they reached San Stefano before an international conference was called. San Stefano was sufficiently close to Constantinople to be the site of the modern-day Istanbul international airport. European powers did not approve of Ottoman massacres in the Balkans, but neither did they want to see Russian access to warm waters. Russian conquests were surrendered, and the pattern of modern Balkan states began to appear which separated the Russian and Ottoman territories. Britain's price for saving Constantinople was Cyprus and the Suez Canal, a price which the Turks would not forget or forgive.

Even Britain's "temporary" occupation of Egypt in 1882, under the anti-imperialist premiership of William Gladstone, began as an attempt to restore the authority of the khedive (hereditary governor) and financial stability to maintain Ottoman integrity.[9] Although it is beyond the scope of this book, the post–1918 Turkish state was not without its allies amongst the great powers. France and Italy supported Turkey in the Greco-Turkish War of 1919–1922. Lloyd George, the British prime minister, supported the Greeks, but Winston Churchill, with his responsibilities for reducing the defense budget of Britain's newly acquired mandate territories, saw the benefits of a pro–Turkish policy in stabilizing the new Middle Eastern world. By 1922, the Greek army and population had been driven out of Asia Minor, ending millennia of Greek presence — Constantinople had been the Greek center of the Eastern Roman Empire until 1453.

Several European powers also saw benefits to maintaining

Ottoman territorial integrity as a means of limiting the expansionist ideas of their European neighbors. Britain in particular saw the Ottomans as halting Russian expansion southward, which would eventually threaten India. Rudyard Kipling's "Great Game" was the Central Asian cold war of the Victorian Era. Charles Townshend, who would lead the 6th Division's 1915 advance on Baghdad and into captivity from Kut in 1916, was a junior officer on the North West Frontier. He gained fame and renown for his part in the Siege of Chitral in 1895, in what is now Pakistan. The background was a murderous familial regicidal tendency which destabilized the region. British troops were marched for weeks for the relief while the Russians waited and watched for an opportunity that could be exploited.

In the decade before the outbreak of the Great War, the Ottoman Empire saw an acceleration in the loss of peripheral territories. In 1908, the Austro-Hungarian Empire annexed Bosnia-Herzegovina. This territory had been administered from Vienna since 1879 (although still under nominal Ottoman suzerainty) as part of the 1878 settlement which saved the Ottoman capital from Russia. In the same year, Crete also announced it was joining Greece, and Bulgaria became fully independent. In 1911, the Italians invaded the territories of Tripolitania, Fezzan and Cyrenaica (now Libya), which lay between the French in Algeria and British in Egypt. Captain Mustafa Kemal fought against the Italians and would go on to found the modern Turkish state as Ataturk. This war saw the first use of aircraft and dirigibles for aerial bombing, as well as armored cars. The Italians also occupied the Dodecanese Islands, against the wishes of Austro-Hungary, which feared destabilizing the fragile regional balance between Greece and Serbia.

In 1912–1913 and again in 1913, two Balkan wars were fought. The first effectively ended Ottoman rule in Europe outside of the limited, modern Turkish state and created an independent Albanian state. The second Balkan war was primarily a squabble amongst the victors, and the Ottomans took the opportunity to regain some lost possessions. On both occasions, the new, small, upstart Bulgarian state approached as close to Constantinople as the Russians had in 1878, a war which led to the ultimate independence of Bulgaria. Russia had its own designs on Constantinople and certainly did not want Bulgaria getting there first: Russian amphibious landings were prepared in support of the Ottomans against Bulgaria. A third Balkan crisis, in 1914, would plunge Europe into world war.[10]

Although Britain was uninvolved in the Balkan Wars and innocent of any losses suffered by the Ottomans, Indian Muslims prayed and raised money to support the Ottoman war effort while in Cawnpore rioters battled with the police who opened fire.[11] The scenario where the Muslim world reacts violently to perceived anti–Islamic threats and insults in Europe is by no means a modern phenomenon.

From the 1790s, the Sultans had an amazing ability to attract major European powers to bail them out of internal and external calamities. As often as not, Ottoman failings were the reason behind those calamities. In the case of Egypt in 1882, not only were the destabilizing issues primarily of Egyptian making, but both Constantinople and Cairo failed to take advantage of European offers to enforce political and financial stability. Constantinople also failed to take advantage of offers which would have recovered authority in Egypt lost to Mohammed Ali 40 years before, another calamity averted by European intervention.

By the late 19th century, Britain and France were starting to lose their special relationship. Following the disastrous 1878 war which saw Russian troops advance to San Stefano, British Prime Minister Benjamin Disreali and German Chancellor Bismarck negotiated a settlement which saw the Russians withdraw and return much of the conquered territory. However, Britain's price was Cyprus and the Suez Canal, followed by the 1882 occupation of Egypt. France, on the other hand, was buying out British railway interests in Anatolia in the 1880s and ran the first Orient Express from Paris in 1889. The French also took over managing the nearly bankrupt Ottoman public finances. Most damaging to Franco-Turkish relations was the 1894 Franco-Russian treaty: this damaged their position in Constantinople no less than Britain's 1882 occupation of Egypt.[12]

The Armenian Genocide of 1915 remains an infamous and controversial event. It is still officially denied in Turkey. This was not the first rebellion by or genocide against the Armenians. In 1894, following an uprising, an estimated 50,000 Armenians were killed. In a final act, in August 1896, armed Armenian nationalists seized the Ottoman Bank in Constantinople. A further 5,000 were killed. Sultan Abdul Hamid II became "Abdul the Damned" across Europe.[13]

Thus, the "Sick Man of Europe" was aided by her neighbors only to, ironically, outlive three of them, Russia, Germany and Austro-Hungary, if only by a year or less.

The "Young Turk" movement was founded in 1869 in response to collapsing Ottoman authority and contained many leaders of modern Turkey, including Mustafa Kemal—Ataturk—and Enver Pasha. A military coup in 1909 replaced Sultan Abdul Hamid II with his malleable brother, Mehmed Reshad V.[14] The Young Turks were displeased with the lack of military support which had been received from their European allies during the dismantling of their Balkan possessions. They did, however, accept that all and any assistance would be essential to modernize the Ottoman military to stem and, if possible, reverse the losses. There had been a German military mission in Constantinople since 1882, first under Colonel Koehler until his death the following year, and then his replacement, Lieutenant Colonel von der Goltz, who became a Turkish field marshal and died in Baghdad shortly after the British surrender at Kut in 1916. The German military mission was strengthened in 1913, under General Otto Lindeman von Sanders. The British Rear Admiral Arthur Limpus headed a similar British naval mission.[15]

German Unification and the Ottoman Empire

Imperial Germany was a relative latecomer to the imperial European scene. Germany was not unified until 1871, and that followed a decade of wars against Denmark, Austria and France. Kaiser Wilhelm I and his chancellor, Otto von Bismarck, were preoccupied with securing the new German state. This policy included friendly relations with their eastern neighbor, Russia, the only significant neighbor not to have been recently defeated by German arms.

Wilhelm died in 1888 and was succeeded by his son, the second German emperor of that name. The new Kaiser had been deformed from birth, with a withered right arm which prevented him gaining the military glory he so desired. Instead he designed elaborate military uniforms. Probably due to his deformity, Wilhelm II despised his imperial cousins, in particular George V, the king-emperor. Wilhelm and many other German nationalists considered that Germany needed overseas colonies to maintain its growth or, they feared, the new state would wither and die in the face of the other imperial powers. However, Germany was late on the scene. There were relatively few potential colonies remaining, and, infuriatingly to the advocates of German overseas imperialism, few Germans were interested in settling and developing those territories. There was one "place in the sun" remaining which could provide Germany with the space and resources to match British India—Ottoman Turkey. After all, weren't Mesopotamia and the Near East the birthplace of civilization, full of ruins of their former greatness? What did Africa (with the exception of Egypt) have to offer in comparison to the European empires which had carved it up? Surely, with German engineering and organization, they could revive farming and commerce in the region and produce a market for German goods. Thus, in the decades to come, Wilhelm would toy alternatively between becoming a kaiser sultan to place him on a par with the king emperor, or evicting the British from India and bringing about the collapse of the British Empire. For the modern reader, in retrospect, this sounds not unlike *Lebensraum*, but there was also the medieval "settlement in the east"—*Ostsiedlung*.

In the autumn of 1898, Kaiser Wilhelm II undertook a grand state tour of the Ottoman Empire. The agenda, ironically, was organized by Thomas Cook, the famous British provider of Mediterranean holidays to this day. At the end of the tour, in an infamous speech, Wilhelm announced that "His Majesty the Sultan and the 300 million Muslims scattered across the globe who revere him as their Caliph, can rest assured that the German Emperor is, and at all times will remain, their friend." There were over 100 million British Muslim subjects from India to the Gulf, Egypt and across Africa. In 1920, Churchill wrote, in relation to the settlement in Iraq which he was striving to achieve: "We are the greatest Mohammedan power in the world. It is our duty, more than any other Government, to study policies which are in harmony with Mohammedan feeling."[16] That sentiment was equally relevant in the years before 1914. Bearing in mind that so many of the world's Muslims lived not under the Kaiser or the Sultan, this statement raised eyebrows in European diplomatic and royal circles — what, exactly, were his intentions towards the Queen Empress's subjects? *Punch* magazine quipped, "*Deutschland uber Allah.*" An unlikely myth of *Hajji Wilhelm* was born: that the Kaiser had converted to Islam and undertaken the *hajj* (pilgrimage) to Mecca, a city into which only Muslims are permitted.[17]

Thus, Abdul the Damned and global Islam had a friend in Europe, despite the fate of the Armenians and despite the overlordship of many Muslims by the kaiser's cousins. Whatever could he be after?

John Buchan, the creator of Richard Hannay, wrote *Greenmantle* in 1916 and set it amongst the intrigue of Islamic jihad, German designs in the Near and Middle East and the Russian capture of the supposedly impregnable Ottoman fortress of Erzerum. It was the son of the spymaster, Sir Walter Bullivant, staggering, mortally wounded, into Brigadier General Delamain's tent outside Kut with vital clues which set Hannay and his friends on the road through enemy territory to Erzerum. Sir Walter's explanation to Hannay of German designs and Islamic fanaticism spoke of real concerns in the war years: "The Syrian army is as fanatical as the hordes of the Mahdi. The Senussi have taken a hand in the game. The Persian Moslems are threatening trouble. There is a dry wind blowing through the East, and the parched grasses wait the spark. And that wind is blowing towards the Indian border. Whence comes that wind, think you?" Buchan, through Sir Walter, also considered that the kaiser would surrender European territorial gains to retain access to the East through Mesopotamia.[18] In the years before and during the war, such theories were not without substance.

Archaeology and exploration went hand in hand with commercial exploitation. The most famous British exponents of this were Gertrude Bell and T.E. Lawrence, but amongst the Germans were Max von Oppenheim of the banking dynasty who traveled widely around the Near East and North Africa from the 1830s and the academic Kurt Prufer, the dragoman at the German consul in Cairo appointed in 1907 who was believed to arrange for Muslim volunteers to fight the Italians in 1911.[19] British authorities suspected that not a few of these were subsidized by Berlin. Between 1899 and 1906, the small German export firm of Robert Wonckhaus opened offices around the Gulf— Bahrain, Bushire (now Bandar-e Bushehr), Basra, Mohammera (now Khorramshahr) and Banda Abbas. Also in 1906, the Hamburg-Amerika Line, more famous for

transatlantic liners, opened a line between Germany and the Gulf, undercutting the British costs and servicing ports unvisited by British liners. German banks also appeared to challenge the British-owned Imperial Bank of Persia. In 1904, to counter this growth of German interest in what had been considered to be a "British lake," a political agent was dispatched to the region, Major Percy Cox, who would have a long, and controversial, career in the region.[20]

One individual whom Cox would meet in 1909 was Wilhlem Wassmuss, German consul to Bushire, but, according to the British authorities (and correctly), the center of anti–British scheming in the region. Cox described Wassmuss:

> In private life he was well liked by ourselves and the British community in general. On the other hand, as a consular colleague, I found him somewhat troublesome and truculent to deal with, inclined to make up for lack of tact ... by recourse to threat and bluster.

In 1915, Wassmuss would re-appear, as the "German Lawrence."[21]

Kaiser Wilhelm II made two state visits to the Ottoman Empire, in 1889 and in 1898. On the first visit, the kaiser had ascended to the throne the year before, and, the trip was undertaken against the advice of his chancellor, Bismark, whose pro–Russian foreign policy since unification in 1871 had tried to avoid unnecessary foreign entanglements in the Balkans and beyond while the borders of the new state were consolidated. This was not in keeping with the worldview of the new kaiser. Bismark would lose his office the following year.[22]

In 1893, the German-Russian Reinsurance Treaty was allowed to lapse, permitting the Franco-Russian defensive alliance and, ultimately, the triple alliance of the Entante Cordial of 1907 including Great Britain. Thus the battle lines for 1914 were drawn up.

During the second state visit, the kaiser rode into Jerusalem on a black charger, more like a conquering hero than a tourist.[23] The contrast between the kaiser and Allenby in 1917, who was a conquering hero but did not play that role for fear of portraying himself a Crusader, is significant in how the parties saw themselves and the future of their nations. Even Jesus Christ entered Jerusalem on a donkey.

On 30 July 1914, the kaiser would demand that England "must ... have the mask of Christian peaceableness torn publicly off her face.... Our consuls in Turkey and India, agents etc., must inflame the entire Mohammedan world to wild revolt against this hateful, lying, conscienceless people of shopkeepers."[24] Poor, perfidious Albion.

Germany and Jihad— Bringing Down the British in India from Within

In 1900, the British Empire was the most populous Muslim state in the world. Despite the hereditary position of the Ottoman sultan being the caliph of Sunni Islam, the actual number of Muslims within the Ottoman Empire was fairly small.[25] The huge areas of mountain and desert did not encourage dense settlements, while many of the more populated areas, such as along the coasts, were multi-cultural. There were significant Greek populations along the Anatolian coast, particularly at Smyrna (Izmir) and Christian Armenians in the Caucasus. The Balkan possessions, which were slowly lost in the decades before 1914, were predominately Christian, but with large Muslim populations. As the Ottoman Empire contracted, with the loss of non–Muslim provinces and the genocides and ethnic cleansing of non–Muslim populations of the war years and beyond, the concentration of Muslims in the empire increased. The modern perception of a Muslim-dominated Middle and Near East is a post–1920s creation. The world in 1914 was far more cosmopolitan.[26]

The Russian, French and Italian empires also all had substantial Muslim populations. Germany, by comparison, had only a few Muslim subjects, which could be conveniently ignored. In some future war for global dominance which Germany must fight and win to obtain its rightful position in the world, these vast, disgruntled, Muslim populations could be encouraged to rise in rebellion. At the very least, the threat of colonial uprisings would require large numbers of European troops to be stationed overseas to suppress their Muslim subjects and, by implication, could not be deployed in Europe against Germany. Given the racial attitudes of the time, a European soldier was worth several times a "native" soldier, even amongst the so-called "martial races." Furthermore, the native populations were a great source of manpower for the allied war effort. If Germany could prevent this resource from being tapped effectively, it would again adversely affect the allied war effort. Religion and colonial oppression were two tools used to create this discourse. With these elements in place, Germany's armies would march, against greatly reduced opposition, to victory. Although these anti-colonial rebellions never materialized on the scale hoped for, the desired effect was achieved when Britain deployed troops in significant numbers against the Ottoman possessions. After the war, German general Eric von Ludendorff observed that "the stiffer the Turkish defense in Palestine and Mesopotamia, and the larger the force absorbed in the English effort to achieve their object, the more our burden in the West would be lightened."[27]

For the British Empire, there were two key weak points — India and Egypt. India's North West Frontier (today roughly the Pakistan-Afghanistan border), was notoriously unstable, as Townshend found at Chitral. The emir of Afghanistan, Habibullah, was paid by Delhi to keep his tribesmen on his side of the border. The British had already suffered two major defeats to incursions to Kabul (1839 and 1879) and had decided that bribery was a far safer policy than risking further imperial defeat and humiliation for another territory which nobody wanted. In 1915, £800,000 was deposited in Indian banks or invested in London. This was the unspent portion of Habibullah's subsidies.[28] Whether this was to secure the emir's long-term cooperation or to provide a pension fund in the event that the anti–British majority in his court decided to remove him is unclear. Possibly both.

From the German perspective, the main problem with Afghanistan was the physical and geographical remoteness of the country from Europe. This isolation would be increased if there was a general war with Russia as well as Britain.

The other nation to be traversed en route to fermenting Indian revolution was Persia (Iran). Part of the 1907 Anglo-Russian Convention (see below) was the division of Persia into Russian and British spheres of influence, with a narrow, neutral band in between. Naturally, this greatly offended the Persians who had not been consulted. This unintended side effect of settling Anglo-Russian antagonisms provoked the Persians, and the pro–German Swedish officers of their gendarmerie — ironically funded by the British. If Germany could exploit Persian anti–British and anti–Russian sentiment, Persia could bridge the Ottoman Empire to Afghanistan en route to India. As with all of the politics in the region at the time, as the reader has probably already identified, you have to conveniently ignore the 1911 agreement whereby Germany recognized the Russian interest in Persia.[29]

The second British weakness was Egypt, with the strategically vital Suez Canal. If Egypt could be occupied by the Ottomans or Germans, or at least the canal closed (as it was in the 1950s and 1970s), it would sever Britain and the European battlefields from huge parts of the empire, primarily India, but also Australia and New Zealand. Egypt in 1914 was nominally part of the Ottoman Empire, as in the days of Mohammed Ali, and was ruled by the khedive with British advisors. It would not be necessary for the Ottoman army to conquer Egypt. Simply to reach the Suez Canal and remain there would be enough in order to close it while tying down many British divisions who would otherwise be deployed to fight in Europe. Alternatively, an anti–British rebellion in Egypt would have the same effect.

That was the plan, at least.

India

It would be naive to think that the German ideas of anti–British rebellion across the empire lacked substance. The story of pre–1914 political assassinations by oppressed minorities focuses on Sarajevo while the story of Indian independence is largely that of Mahatma Gandhi and the Second World War. There were anti–British elements in India before 1914. In 1909, there was a failed assassination attempt on the viceroy, Lord Minto. In 1912, there was another unsuccessful attempt against his successor, Lord Hardinge, and Sir William Curzon Wyllie, aide-de-camp to the secretary of state for India, was assassinated. The perpetrator was tried in the Old Bailey, executed, and buried in Pentonville Prison, London, until the body was repatriated to India in 1976. The assassin, Dhingra, was, however, a Hindu and was unlikely to appreciate either a Muslim or German emperor replacing a British one.[30]

Further anti–British activities were planned closer to the heart of the British establishment by the Hindu manager of a hostel for Indian students in London. Vinayak Savarkar was called one of the most dangerous men India had produced. He wrote a highly inflammatory history of the Indian Mutiny which was published in Holland and bound in the cover of Dickens' *Pickwick Papers*. Savarkar was arrested in 1910 and exiled to the Andaman Islands.[31]

Monsoon failures and the resultant famines in the Punjab forced Sikhs to migrate to Southeast Asia and the west coast of Canada and America. San Francisco found itself the center of a revolutionary movement, which the German counsel encouraged. A British India policeman, William Hopkins, was dispatched to monitor it. While the United States may have had no love for the British Empire, given their mutual history, in segregation America there was no desire to support a movement which called for the general massacre of Europeans.[32] Unlike Germany, America was not such a fertile ground for rebellion. Punjabi emigrants returning from the United States rioted on 29 September 1914, resulting in loss of life to both rioters and police. German agitators in America were believed to be at the heart of the troubles.[33]

Egyptians, despite being occupied far more recently than India by the British, and despite being far more closely linked to the Ottoman Empire, both geographically and culturally, did not seem to be particularly keen on jihad either. Even when the Turkish army, with German support, reached the Suez Canal in 1915, there was no general uprising. No matter how anti–British the population may have been, there was no desire to replace a relatively benign British rule (which permitted dissent and espionage from within) with the harsh rule of Constantinople.[34] So, for example, in 1906, a dispute arose between Cairo and Constantinople for the Aqaba border region. Although the actions of Lord Cromer, as consul general and effective ruler of Egypt from 1882 until 1907, were pro–Egyptian, and the acquisition of the Aqaba (in modern-day Jordan) would benefit Egypt, the Egyptian nationalists (and Indian Muslims, for that matter) favored Sultan Abdul Hamid's claim. It mattered little that the Royal Navy protected the hajj pilgrims from British-controlled ports and on British ships.[35]

The Berlin-Baghdad Railway

One of the more significant ramifications with the kaiser's interest on all things Oriental was the Berlin-Baghdad Railway. In its ultimate form, it would link Hamburg on the North Sea with Basra (initially intended to be Kuwait, but British political

agents got there first).[36] Most of the European leg of the railway was already built: the famous Simplon Orient Express as used in Agatha Christie's *Murder on the Orient Express* and Ian Fleming's James Bond novel *From Russia with Love*. Baghdad is 2,000 miles from Constantinople and was, in 1900, an imperial backwater of 150,000 inhabitants; it no longer held the mystique of *1001 Arabian Nights* except in the mind of nineteenth century dreamers who had never been there.[37] Basra is a further 500 miles and, as the British would find in 1914, totally lacking in facilities to handle modern shipping.

However, a 2,500-mile railway across the Anatolian mountains and Arabian deserts was precisely the sort of project which inspired fin de siècle industrialists: railways crisscrossed North and South America, Africa, India and Russia; huge engineering projects were the marvels of the world; canals cut though land masses to make shorter and safer journeys, like the Suez, Kiel, Panama and Caledonian. Why shouldn't Germany fund, build and run a railway to the Gulf? It was predicted to cut three days off the sea journey via the Suez Canal and bypass the Royal Navy.[38]

The German-planned railway was not the only scheme to be sold in Constantinople. French railways were driving inland from the Aegean coastal towns like Smyrna (Izmir) while a British-backed scheme planed a railway from Alexandretta (Iskenderun) direct to Basra. This route would avoid the challenging Taurus Mountains. By this time, the sultan was disinclined towards the British or French, the former having taken his richest province, Egypt, while the latter were occupying the Maghreb.[39] The sultan also feared a coastal route which would be vulnerable to naval attack, despite being cheaper to build and, by running through populous and commercially active areas, more likely to return a profit. Meanwhile the Russians vetoed any route through eastern Anatolia as threatening their border region. A German railway through the mountains seemed to be the only way forward. The concession was signed in 1899, aiming to be completed in eight years and granting German prospectors a monopoly on prospecting 20 kilometers either side of the railway. The Berlin Museum contains the archaeological finds discovered during the building of the railway.[40] By 1914 the railway had not yet penetrated the mountains of eastern Anatolia. The railway was not necessarily feared by the British. In 1899, Lord Curzon became viceroy of India and considered that the railway and German influence would strengthen the Ottomans against Russia. In the context of the pre–1907 Great Game politics, the ending of Bismarck's pro–Russian policy was no bad thing. A strengthened Ottoman Empire, with German assistance, would provide a stronger bulwark to Russian expansion towards India, which was in Britain's favor.[41]

By 1907, the Great Game was over, and there was the first modern arms race. The new German fleet was primarily a short-range weapon. Short range from the Baltic and North Sea bases meant a direct threat to Great Britain. The Royal Navy, by comparison, had a global reach. The German threat to Britain would be realized in 1914 but appeared in popular fiction in the years before — Erskine Childers' *The Riddle in the Sands* (published in 1903) was the first modern spy novel, and John Buchan's *The Thirty Nine Steps* (1915) was set in the summer of 1914.

Germany also had plans for economic expansion through the Middle East to the Persian Gulf, which Britain had long considered a "British lake." The East India Company had first arrived to trade for pearls in the 17th and 18th centuries, and later the Royal Navy undertook anti-piracy and anti–gun running operations. Navigation aids and wireless systems were being introduced. The coastal chiefs were at peace with one another and with their subjects.[42] Between the 1870s and the eve of the First World War, Britain was involved in resolving the border between the Ottoman and Persian empires; the inhabitants of these disputed regions were often unaware where their allegiances lay. An Ottoman-Persian commission with Anglo-Russian moderation finally completed its task as war broke out in Europe and the commissioners scattered to their respective homes; G.E. Hubbard's account, *From the Gulf to Ararat*, is a fascinating account of the region on the eve of war.

Hubbard left Marseilles for Mohammera in southwest Persia in November 1913 and, having reached Mount Ararat on the Russian-Ottoman-Persian border, passed though Constantinople just before war was declared. His account is that of an empire about to disappear and is all the more poignant for that. Despite having the luxury of peacetime travel, he described the Shatt-al-Arab as "a great, broad river ... but the palm groves on either side cut off from view most of the country beyond, and what there is to see of it is mostly dismal-looking swamp" and a "lifeless scene, and the only moving things in it are the occasional flocks of wild-fowl." Basra "is a rather mean and dilapidated town," the Ashar is the port for smaller vessels, but "the big ships lie anchored in mid-stream opposite a long line of substantial brick buildings where the European merchants live and do business." Mohammera's streets were "filthy beyond the power of description, but as all the European bungalows, including the bank and the club, lie along the river-bank, one goes everywhere by water, as if one were in Venice, and so avoids their horrors." The *belem* he describes as a fascinating boat, a cross between a canoe and a punt with a little gondola added. For part of the journey, the party was accompanied by Captain Arnold Wilson, who would serve in Mesopotamia as a political officer from 1914.[43]

Oil

Odd as it may seem from the perspective of the modern world dependent on oil and familiar with the great reserves below the Middle Eastern sands, Mesopotamia did not factor at all. Even in the years after 1918, when Churchill was trying to provide a political and military (i.e., cost-saving) solution to Iraq, oil was not a factor, although there was a growing awareness of the potential in the 1920s. When Churchill did mention oil, it was as a military rather than economic asset. It would be the 1950s before oil revenue became significant for Iraq. Persia was the only oil-producing Middle Eastern nation until 1927.[44]

Oil did play an indirect role in Mesopotamia's fate. In 1901, William D'Arcy, a Briton who had made a fortune from gold in Australia, obtained a concession from the shah of Persia to drill for oil in the southwest of the country. In 1908 he struck oil near Ahwaz on the River Karun, 100 miles upstream from the Shatt-al-Arab. A pipeline took the oil to a refinery and storage tanks on Abadan Island in the Shatt. The Anglo-Persian Oil Company was born (APOC, later British Petroleum and now BP). By 1914, APOC was a major oil exporter, and, anticipating a move from coal to oil, the Admiralty (under Winston Churchill in his capacity as first sea lord) persuaded the British government to buy a controlling share.[45] Incidentally, the German navy also toyed with a similar change of fuel but could not without guaranteed sources of oil.

Despite Churchill's initial enthusiasm for the APOC project, he was willing to abandon the company:

> There is little likelihood of any troops being available for this purpose. Indian forces must be used at the decisive point. We shall have to buy our oil elsewhere. The Turk also can be dealt with better at the center. I have told Lord Crewe that Europe and Egypt have greater claims than we have on the Indian Army.[46]

The End of Peace

As late as mid–October 1914, Britain, France and Russia were still hoping and trying to maintain Ottoman neutrality in the general European war which had already broken out, in the face of extreme provocation which would have provided a *casus belli*. The traditional view is that the Ottomans were dragged, unwillingly, into the war by German bullying. However, there were those in the Ottoman government, in particular Enver Pasha, who decided to embark on an imperialist war to regain lost possessions in the Balkans and Caucasus, but not, ironically, Egypt.[47]

The *casus belli* for the Entente's declarations of war can be given as being about pairs of ships, not oil at all: the *Reshadieh* and *Sultan Osman I* being built in Britain, the *Goeben* and *Breslau* in the Mediterranean, and the *Emden* and *Konigsberg* in the Indian Ocean.[48]

In the summer of 1914, two dreadnought class ships were being built in Britain for the Ottoman Navy, the *Reshadieh* and *Sultan Osman I*. These had been paid for by public subscription with the aim of recapturing the lost Aegean Islands.

With Europe sliding into war, Churchill, as first sea lord, raised the question of seizing both ships and then compensating Constantinople. This action was agreed on 31 July 1914, but no action was taken until 3 August, the day after war was declared on Germany (although not Turkey, yet). It should be noted that Churchill was the only Turkophile member of the cabinet at that time, despite the anti–Turkish nature of the seizure, and would remain so — after the war he opposed Lloyd George's pro–Greece anti–Turkish policy, which was not conducive to good Anglo-Arab relations across the newly acquired territories.

There were good precedents for seizing the ships. The British government was justifiably concerned about delivering two modern warships to a nation whose future intentions were unclear. The British government was also entirely within its rights to do so, and Chile's *Latorre* would also be commandeered, although, of course, Chile was not a belligerent party. A pro-German press in Constantinople took advantage of this affront to the national dignity, even after Britain offered generous terms to Constantinople which included renting the ships for the duration of the war and then refitting or replacing (in case of their loss) them after the war.[49]

The ships were renamed HMS *Agincourt* and *Erin*, fought at the Battle of Jutland, and were broken up in 1922 to comply with the tonnage limitations under the Treaty of Washington.

Meanwhile, the German battlecruiser *Goeben* and light cruiser *Breslau* entered the Dardenelles and remained, with the permission of Constantinople, in violation of the 1871 Treaty of London, under which neutral nations should intern ships from belligerent nations for the duration of the war. The Ottoman authorities got round this by announcing that they were purchasing the two ships, although without the prior knowledge of the German authorities, and renamed them *Yavuz* and *Midilli*. The ships even retained their German officers and crews (although now wearing the fez). With war declared against Germany, British Admiral Limpus was in the unenviable position of commanding German ships with German crews. The fictional "purchase" of the *Goeben* and *Breslau* was an example of Ottoman manipulation of the belligerents for their own advantage.[50]

Another pair of ships, the *Emden* and *Konigsburg*, were operating in the Indian Ocean, and there was a fear that she would make for the Persian Gulf to disrupt oil supplies. The Royal Navy increased its presence in the Gulf with the deploying of the old battleship *Ocean*, who would later be lost at Gal-

lipoli. Concerns were raised when the (still officially neutral) governor of Basra objected to the presence of British warships in the Shatt-al-Arab, which he had never done before. The *Emden* cruised around the eastern Indian Ocean, bombarded Madras and took 30 prizes before being run aground following the Battle of Cacos with the more powerful HMAS *Sydney* on 9 November 1914. The *Konigsberg*, meanwhile, was blockaded in the Rufiji Delta in modern-day Tanzania from October 1914 until destroyed in July 1915.

Back in the Shatt-al-Arab, on 28 September, a Royal Navy sloop, HMS *Espiègle*, and a Royal Indian Marine ship, *Dalhousie*, entered the Shatt, while another sloop, HMS *Odin*, patrolled the entrance. The *Espiègle* sailed for the Persian town of Mohammera at the mouth of the Karun River while the *Dalhousie* sailed for Abadan. The governor of Basra ordered *Espiègle*'s departure with a message reading, "Please you leave the Shat before 24 hours." In response to this, *Espiègle* moved from the Shatt into the Karun River and Persian territory. Ottoman guns were positioned opposite Mohammera, and the British consul was informed that unless the ships left within eight days, they would not be allowed to.[51]

With general war being waged in Europe, the Indian army was directed with supporting the war effort in France, Egypt and East Africa. Four expeditionary forces were initially dispatched. Of these, Force "D," based around the 16th Indian Infantry Brigade commanded by Brigadier General Delamain embarked with orders for Egypt. Once at sea, secret orders were opened which redirected him to Bahrain to secure the Persian oil supply. There his brigade was also in a position to act against the Ottoman Empire should Constantinople act in a belligerent manner.[52]

The final acts of the peace came from the Turks. The Ottoman navy with their ex–German ships entered the Black Sea on 27 October and the following day fired on Odessa and Russian ships. The German ambassador to Constantinople insisted on written instructions from Enver Pasha so that "it will be impossible to charge us with having pulled Turkey by guile into a war she did not want."[53]

On the same day, Bedouin columns were identified 20 miles inside the Egyptian border. The British Egyptian authorities complained. Constantinople replied that it did not recognize the border with Egypt.[54] The British army withdrew to the Suez Canal to establish a more defensible position.

On 3 November 1914, Indian Expeditionary Force "D" arrived at the mouth of the Shatt-al-Arab.

2

Securing the Oil, October 1914–April 1915

In an era before air conditioning and ice-making machines, the Persian Gulf was not a hospitable environment for Europeans. The unsuitability of the climate was one reason given by Churchill to withdraw the army in the 1920s. Even today, for the expatriate workers in the glass and steel metropolises which have sprung up along the southern shore in the last generation, or for the Coalition soldiers in Iraq, the mid-summer heat does not encourage venturing outside. Midday temperatures reach 57C/134F; anything metallic burns to the touch. The northerly wind, the *shamal*, bores down over the deserts and superheats the atmosphere. Sunglasses protect the eyes from the searing winds as much as from the sun's glare. In these temperatures, the air is dry, unless there is an unexpected downpour when the water sits on the surface of the sunbaked mud. The evaporating rain adds humidity to the discomforts.[1] But at least the rising daytime temperature resolves one other persistent plague in Iraq: flies. When Allah created Hell, it is said that he was not satisfied, so he created Iraq and gave it flies.

Iraq is not unbearably hot year round. Spring and autumn are cool and can be pleasant. Winter can be very cold, and the British Special Forces patrol codenamed Bravo Two Zero suffered during January 1991.[2] Winter brings rain. Around the twin rivers, the Tigris and Euphrates, where most of the population lives, flooding makes land travel impossible. Low-lying alluvial floodplains become inundated. Even without the regular flooding, the riverside areas are crisscrossed by dykes, canals, ditches and bunds which delay or channel movements. At a time where there were no railways and few roads, riverine transport was the most important. But, at the height of summer, water-levels fall. This limited the draft of ships which could be used on the undredged rivers — ships ran aground and journeys were delayed.

Fortunately, the British Empire in 1914 was blessed with troops from her Indian Empire, and British soldiers who were acclimatized through long service.[3] This avoided the need for acclimatization for troops straight out of Europe. Lieutenant Colonel J.E. Tennant, RFC, described the rising temperatures

as he sailed from England to command the Royal Flying Corps in Mesopotamia: the saloon was an inferno; soldiers volunteered to help the stokers; the ship's doctor who died of heatstroke; soldiers defending Egypt bathing in the Suez Canal at 1 A.M. to cool down; sweat dripping from his head down into his socks. The journey was 22 days to Bombay to acclimatize, then onwards to Mesopotamia. Muscat was a "god-forsaken looking spot" yet "picturesque and medieval," without any shade. Gertrude Bell in a paper on Muscat's internal politics described the Royal Navy's pre-war suppression of arms smuggling in the Gulf as a boon for the sheikh, as his rebellious subjects were unable to access weapons to use against him, which is hardly a glowing recommendation of his government. General Townshend, en route to Mesopotamia to take command of the 6th Division, was more polite than Tennant about Muscat. For him, it was "a tiny town ... with a quaint old Portuguese fort." At Bushire, Persia, Tennant's vessel met HMS *Juno* with 40 heatstroke cases. Basra, he found, was hot and humid, which sapped all impulse and desire. The humid heat "hangs heavy on the lungs," everything is saturated, ink runs on the paper, matches will not light. Basra port was in fact a creek, the Ashar, and there were no modern dock facilities. Surrounding the port were creeks and lagoons to support the date palms; the Arab saying was that the Baswaris had their feet in water and their heads in Hell.[4]

Wilson described Basra in the first winter of occupation, for those who only knew the port which was developed by the British authorities:

> In considering the very rapid growth of a somewhat elaborate form of administration at Basra, and later elsewhere, it must be borne in mind that the necessity of establishing a sanitary system approaching European standards was imperatively forced on us by military needs. The force arrive in winter, in a wet year; the desert was a sea of mud; the date-groves were fetid morasses; the few elevated areas were for the most part occupied by reed huts and surrounded by refuse heaps, which were tolerated by the local population, but which would have been fatal to raw troops. Billeting had to be resorted to on a

large scale, which necessitated an elaborate sanitary organisation.[5]

This was a land without the amenities enjoyed by the Coalition troops in Iraq post–2003, such as they were, and without the luxury of the modern Gulf cities. A generation after Tennant, Harry Hopkins, special advisor to U.S. president F.D. Roosevelt, impolitely observed that "the Persian Gulf is the arsehole of the world, and Basra is eighty miles up it."[6]

It was into this environment that the British government requested a "demonstration" from the Indian government. While at Muscat, Tennant commented on the casualties sustained defending Britain's friend against hostile Arabs:

> Little did the British public, more immediately affected by the greater wars, realise how forgotten British officers were dying in nameless fights, or rotting with fever in distant outposts, "unknown, uncared-for, and unsung."[7]

The Ottoman Army in Mesopotamia

Mesopotamia was a military backwater and a long way down the list of priorities for the reforming (and daydreaming) of the Young Turks in Constantinople. Initially the Fourth Army Inspection Area based in Baghdad, it was rechristened Iraq Area Command and eventually 6th Army. There were two corps in the area, XII and XIII. Each corps should consist of three regiments of three battalions, with a strength of 8,000 to 9,000 rifles. This was about half the strength of an equivalent British unit. XII Corps was composed of the 35th and 36th Divisions, while XIII consisted of just the 37th, with the 38th still in the process of being formed, so having only six of nine battalions. These units were largely recruited from the local Arab population, who (with similar racial prejudices to the British in India) were considered to be of inferior quality to Turkish soldiers. Indeed, Townshend described the 38th Division as

> a unit much under strength and composed largely of locally enlisted Arabs, drilled by Turkish officers and instructors on the same principle as our Indian battalions, but certainly not so good as our Indian troops, and indeed more or less unreliable.

Furthermore, some units were dispersed as frontier guards and so lacked the opportunity for formation training. The soldiers were desperately short of personal equipment as well as modern equipment like artillery. The other Turkish division in Mesopotamia was the 35th. To this can be added the 23rd Turkish Regiment which had been sent to the area nine months previously as a punishment. The 6th Army commanded some 13,000 troops. In 1914, around Basra, there were some 4,700 to 5,000 men with 18 artillery pieces and just three machine guns. Al-Fao itself, the only place where the British could land,

there were less than 400 men with just three artillery pieces to resist the landing.[8]

The Army in India, 1914

In an age when communications and transport were considerably slower than today, the Indian government held responsibility for certain imperial commitments. Under the Commission of the Administration of the Expenditure of India in 1900, these areas were determined as Egypt, Persia and the Gulf, Afghanistan, Central Asia, Siam, and East Africa, although throughout the war, Egypt was not part of India's remit. The reader should note that India in 1914 was larger than the modern state; it included Pakistan, Bangladesh and Sri Lanka (Ceylon). With some 76,000 British and 159,000 Indian soldiers based in India in 1914, it was natural that India would be a base for "Eastern" expeditions until further forces could be sent from Britain. The Indian government was based in Delhi (or Simla during the summer months) and was headed by the viceroy, Lord Hardinge of Penshurst.[9] He and his government were subordinate to the British government in London. The viceroy's "opposite number" in London was the secretary of state for India, the Marquis of Crewe (also referred to as Lord Crewe).[10]

The Army in India had only come into being in 1903.[11] Previously, there had been a mix of troops from the three "Presidencies" (Bombay, Madras and Bengal) and various "Princely" forces. The army was in no means a "national" one: India was an empire — the Raj — in its own right. India and the army reflected the multitude of states, peoples and religions there. The army was composed of conventional divisions and brigades, each brigade consisting of three Indian and one British battalions. There were also Imperial Service Troops which were raised and paid for by various princely states, officered by Indian gentlemen and trained by the Army in India. An Imperial Service Cavalry Brigade composed of the Hyderabad, Mysore and Patiala Lancers would depart India in late 1914 and serve in Palestine.[12]

The "Army in India" Committee of 1912 defined the duties of the army as:

1. Maintaining internal security and tranquility;
2. Dealing with frontier states and tribes which may be hostile;
3. Hold its own against an outside power until reinforced from Home.[13]

Each Indian battalion was officered by 13 British and 17 Indian officers. Battalions were a microcosm of the Raj in military. The British officers commanded the battalion and double companies, adjutant, quartermaster, signaling, scout and transport officers. Indian officers commanded companies and half companies (with the outbreak of war, British Army–style companies and platoons were adopted), with the rank of *subadar* and *jemadar*. The senior Indian officer, the *subadar major*, had additional duties, and a *jemadar* acted as an Indian adjutant. Cavalry regiments contained 16 British and 17 Indian officers, with a *risaldar major*, three *risaldars*, four *ressaidars* and nine *jemadars* in similar positions to those in the infantry. With the complex nature of race, religion and caste, different battalions and even companies within the same battalion were raised from different groupings. Depending on one's viewpoint, this either fostered competition, which was desirable in a military unit, or reinforced divisions to prevent a repeat of the Indian mutiny. Either way, the effect in a protracted war (unlike the border and internal security duties normally undertaken) was that feeding arrangements and the provision of replacements were excessively complicated. Even promotions were fraught with difficulties as an Indian from one group could not command soldiers of another group. Clearly, in a modern war fought at great distances from the home base, such idiosyncrasies were anachronisms, yet to fail to pay close attention could, and did, adversely affect morale and military effectiveness. Add to that the religious element of Muslim Indian soldiers fighting against the sultan in a holy land, and you can begin to understand the worries of British India's administrators and generals.[14]

In total, there were 39 cavalry regiments, 138 infantry battalions and 12 mountain artillery regiments, but only 3 engineer regiments, organized into nine divisions and three independent infantry brigades. In addition, India supplied a division for Burma and a brigade for Aden. In contrast with today, in 1914 Aden was one of the three largest ports east of Suez and an important coaling station vital to the shipping lines which connected the empire and fed the war effort. The British battalions would be rotated for tours of imperial service. The one anomaly was that there were no Indian field artillery regiments: the shadow of the Indian Mutiny was a long one.

Although the Indian Army was organized into divisions for expeditionary warfare, the army's role remained internal security and border warfare. Consequently, although an Indian division was structurally similar to a British division, the Indian division would be "lighter." An Indian division would also have only a third of the guns provided to a British one.

The mountain artillery regiments were well suited for border warfare in the North West Frontier or suppressing rebellions, but they would be of limited value against entrenched positions. There had also been funding restrictions, and the most visible representation of this is the photographs of Indian infantry using the old 1903 leather equipment when British infantry had moved onto the Mills web equipment. Some regiments were still equipped with old Long Magazine Lee Enfields even within the same brigade, as when the 16th Brigade first landed in Mesopotamia. The Indian Army also contained less medical services, less machine guns and less communications equipment when compared with a British equivalent formation. It was assumed, throughout the empire, that Britain would make up any shortfalls in equipment in time of war. Unfortunately, in 1914, Britain required all she could produce for her own defense.[15]

As part of the imperial commitment to the outbreak of world war, India prepared several Indian Expeditionary Forces. Initially titled A though to G, the IEFs would serve on the Western Front, Gallipoli, the Suez and East Africa as well as Mesopotamia.[16] It should be noted that not all within the Indian government were keen to send troops to Europe. With the prospect of Turkey entering the war came the prospect that the sultan, as the nominal leader of all Muslims, would call a jihad; the viceroy did not want to face inflamed Muslim sentiments along the North West Frontier with his best regiments fighting in Europe.[17]

The Royal Navy

The Royal Navy had a long-standing presence in the Persian Gulf on anti-piracy duties, in particular to protect the Indian merchants who traded in the region for dates, still the region's largest export in 1914.[18] The senior naval officer was Commander Cathcart Wason on HMS *Odin*, but with the outbreak of war, Commander Wilfred Nunn, commanding HMS *Espiègle*, was ordered to the Gulf, and Nunn took over as SNO.[19] Nunn would hold this position throughout the war (with the exception of when HMS *Ocean* was present), and he would retire as a vice admiral. Both vessels were sloops, armed with four-inch guns, which would be, in the earliest months of the war, the heaviest British guns available. As most of the army's operations would be along the major waterways, naval gunfire support would be essential. Indeed, the army had the greatest difficulties where it was not able to call upon naval gunfire.[20] The sloops were also equipped with modern, efficient wireless systems. The Indian Army lacked the most modern equipment, and so these modern pieces of telecommunications were essential as the army moved further and further up the Tigris.

The naval presence would be reinforced steadily throughout the war, with Royal Indian Marine vessels and river steamers commandeered from India, specially designed river gunboats from England and whatever was available locally. The Ottoman gunboat *Marmaris* would eventually be captured and reflagged. There were local Arab craft and the steamers of Lynch Brothers, a British company which had operated in the region for some years and which knew the river and conditions well. Lynch Brother's steamers were armor plated even in peacetime against random sniping.[21]

The Royal Navy would not have the rivers entirely to themselves. The *Marmaris* has already been mentioned. The German Hamburg-Amerika line had a presence which, when the

Berlin-Baghdad Railway was completed, would have competed more directly with British-India trade. The navy also believed that the German ship *Emden* would be sold to the Ottoman Empire and operate out of Basra. The *Emden* raided widely in the Indian Ocean in the early days of the war when it was the most hunted ship in the world, until being beached to avoid sinking on 9 November 1914.[22] The waters of Mesopotamia did not always cooperate either. Seagoing vessels could reach Qurna at the head of the Shatt-al-Arab without difficulty. During the summer months, however, the water levels of the rivers fell, which restricted the size of vessels that could navigate them, and the constantly shifting sandbanks slowed down vessels that did attempt the passage.

The port of Basra was lacking in modern facilities, despite being the outlet for all of Mesopotamia, and of great antiquity — this was the port of departure of Sinbad the Sailor and was probably visited by the writers of the Psalms: "These men see the works of the Lord and His wonders in the deep."[23] The "port" was in effect a creek, the Ashar. Oceangoing vessels had to be unloaded by *mahailas*, local craft. The Germans had build a small wharf at Ma'qil for their railway supplies, three miles upriver from Basra, but unconnected to Basra except by water or by a detour into the desert. The surrounding land was intersected with creeks and covered in date palms and would be inundated every high tide and for months at a time during the floods. Although this would, in time, be rectified, at great expense, to provide modern facilities necessary to support a major campaign, Basra was not a great option for a naval base.[24]

Odin had been stationed in the Shatt-al-Arab to protect the oil, and remained despite Ottoman pressures to leave. With the arrival of *Espiègle*, the two captains conversed, and then the *Odin* sailed out of the Shatt while *Espiègle* sailed upriver. *Espiègle* communicated with the Ottoman fort at Al-Fao, who thought she was the *Odin* returning. *Espiègle* did nothing to correct the misunderstanding.[25] *Espiègle* anchored off Mahommerah, in Persian waters, but received a deputation which informed Nunn that the entire river was Ottoman and that belligerent warships were not allowed to enter. In response, *Espiègle* sailed up the Karun River, very definitely inside Persia, and waited. When Nunn asked his superiors for instructions, he was informed that *Odin* had been ordered outside the three-mile territorial limit. Meanwhile, an Ottoman battery was established on Dabba Island, opposite the mouth of the Karun, which would have blocked *Espiègle* in Persia "for the duration." Another position was established opposite the oil refinery at Abadan, where an artillery piece could have done some very serious damage.[26]

Espiègle's enforced isolation was tightened by the unreliability of the Persian telegraph system and attempts to block the Shatt-al-Arab by sinking ships. The crew, in their tropical white uniform, attempted to dye it khaki, with varying degrees of success, and added steel-plate and sandbag protection. Nunn was concerned about the possible arrival of the *Emden*, which

outgunned anything the Royal Navy operated in the Persian Gulf, so it was on his recommendation that the old battleship HMS *Ocean* was deployed to the region. *Ocean* would sink the following year when supporting operations at Gallipoli.[27]

Thus, when war was declared with Turkey, there was a significant Royal Navy presence in the Persian Gulf and Shatt-al-Arab. *Espiègle* slipped out of the Karun at midnight, passed the sleeping gunners on Dabba Island and landed a party which cut the Al-Fao–Basra telegraph. This marked the first hostile act of the war against the Ottoman Empire.[28]

Basra

The 6th (Poona) Division, of which the 16th Indian Infantry Brigade was part, moved to Bombay in preparation for shipment to Europe. The division sailed from Bombay on 16 October 1914.[29]

After three days at sea, Brigadier General Sir W.S. Delamain, commanding the 16 Brigade, opened sealed orders. The brigade, escorted by HMS *Ocean*, was designated Indian Expeditionary Force "D" and was directed to Bahrain. Their mission was to occupy Abadan Island, in Persia, and secure the pipelines and oil fields. In the event that war was declared, IEF "D" was to occupy Basra and would be reinforced by the remainder of the division.

ORBAT (Order of Battle)[30]:

16th Indian Infantry Brigade
- Brigade Headquarters
- 2nd Battalion, the Dorsetshire Regiment
- 20th Duke of Cambridge's Own Infantry (Brownlow's Punjabis)
- 104th Wellesley's Rifles
- 117th Mahrattas
- Brigade Troops:
  - 1st Indian Mountain Artillery Brigade
  - 22nd Company, Miners and Sappers
  - Section, 34th Divisional Signal Company
  - 125th Field Ambulance
  - 12th Mule Corps
  - 13th Mule Corps
  - Supply Column
  - Field Post Office
  - Ordnance Field Park

Delamain and his force arrived at Bahrain on 23 October 1914. Today, Bahrain provides the visitor with all of the modern amenities which could be asked for. In 1914, things were less clear-cut. Although there was a long-standing relationship between Britain and Bahrain, the arrival of the British Army (although the Royal Navy was a common sight in those waters) on their shores was a matter of some concern. IEF "D," both man and beast, remained on board iron ships for a week while water, meat and fuel began to run short. It was also believed that the large Persian community was pro–German. After a week, practice boat drills (diplomatically kept well away from the shore) were conducted, with great entertainment provided by those Indian troops who were not used to either boats or the sea.[31]

It must have come as a great relief when, on 30 October, Delamain was informed of the actions of the former German ships, *Goeben* and *Breslau*, in the Black Sea. IEF "D" arrived off the Shatt-al-Arab on 3 November. The 16th Brigade was supported by *Ocean*, *Espiègle* and *Odin*, together with the Royal Indian Marine, *Dalhousie*, and four armed launches: *Mashona*, *Miner*, *Carmsir*, and *Sirdar-i-Naphte*.

The bar at the mouth of the Shatt was swept for mines, and the force, less *Ocean* which drew too much water, entered the Shatt on 6 November. *Odin* bombarded the Ottoman fort on the Al-Fao Peninsula. A mixed force landed to occupy the fort consisting of British and Indian infantry, *Ocean*'s Royal Marines, a naval shore party, Maxim machine guns, and a section of mountain artillery. Opposing the 16th Brigade were two battalions from the 26th and 112th Regiments in Basra; at Zubair another battalion of the 112th Regiment; and in the area of Zubair, Al-Fao and Kuwait, two regiments of the 113th and 114th. The defending force totaled some 3,600 infantry.[32]

Espiègle had remained in the Shatt-al-Arab. It was expected that the arrival of a British invasion force would be the signal for Ottoman troops opposite Abadan Island to fire at the oil facilities. *Espiègle* positioned herself to fire on the Ottoman positions, without running the risk that any Ottoman overshoots would damage the oil facilities. When IEF "D" entered the Shatt-al-Arab, the Ottoman troops opened fire on *Espiègle*. For the sailors, after all of the maneuvering, the war was finally on. With four-inch and three-pound guns, Maxim machine guns and even rifles issued to spare sailors, the Ottoman position was silenced for the loss of two wounded sailors. The Battle of Abadan was a victory for the Royal Navy. The following day, *Espiègle* sighted the transports and escorts of IEF "D."[33]

IEF "D" sailed on, passed Abadan Island and started to land at Sanniyeh, a point three miles north of the island, and nine miles south of Mahommerah. Without docking facilities, it would take two days to unload.[34]

An Ottoman attack was repulsed on 11 November, thanks in part to accurate intelligence from the sheikh of Mohommera. The attack was launched at 0530 hours, and a double company of the 117th Maharattas, with two machine guns, held the attack. The 20th Infantry, with mountain artillery support, counter-attacked. When dawn permitted, the heavier guns of the sloops joined in and inflicted further damage.[35]

On 13 November, Lieutenant General Sir Arthur Barrett with the remainder of the 6th Division arrived to begin their laborious unloading.[36]

ORBAT (Order of Battle)[37]:

16th Indian Infantry Brigade
- 2nd Battalion, the Dorsetshire Regiment
- 20th Duke of Cambridge's Own Infantry (Brownlow's Punjabis)
- 104th Wellesley's Rifles
- 117th Mahrattas

17th Indian Infantry Brigade
- 1st Battalion, the Oxfordshire and Buckinghamshire Light Infantry
- 119th Infantry (the Mooltan Regiment)
- 103rd Mahratta Light Infantry
- 22nd Punjabis

18th Indian Infantry Brigade
- 2nd Battalion, the Norfolk Regiment
- 110th Mahratta Light Infantry
- 120th Rajputana Infantry
- 7th (Duke of Connaught's Own) Rajputs

Divisional Artillery
- X Brigade RFA
  - 76 Bty. RFA
  - 82 Bty. RFA
  - 63 Bty. RFA
- 1st Indian Mountain Artillery Brigade
  - 23rd (Peshawar) Mountain Battery (Frontier Force)
  - 30th Mountain Battery

Divisional troops
- 33rd Queen Victoria's Own Light Cavalry
- 17 Co. 3rd Sappers and Miners
- 22 Co. 3rd Sappers and Miners
- 48th Pioneers

The following day, the 16th Brigade undertook reconnaissance towards Basra with the *Odin* and later the *Espiègle* advancing parallel. Ottoman positions at Saihan were identified about four miles from the British base. Thick date palms restricted the naval gunfire as they prevented accurate spotting of the fall of shells. The brigade cleared the Ottoman positions with heavy fighting, and the whole force retired to Sanniya.[38]

On the same day, HMS *Lawrence* joined the flotilla. She was an armed paddle steamer used by the political service and was now manned by the Royal Navy with four four-inch and four six-pound guns.[39]

General Barrett advanced on Basra early on 17 November during a thunderstorm which turned the terrain into a morass of the glutinous mud typical of the region. The advanced guard identified enemy positions at Sahil which was attacked by the 18th (left) and 16th (right) Brigades, with a gap for supporting artillery fire. The cavalry covered the left flank, and the Royal

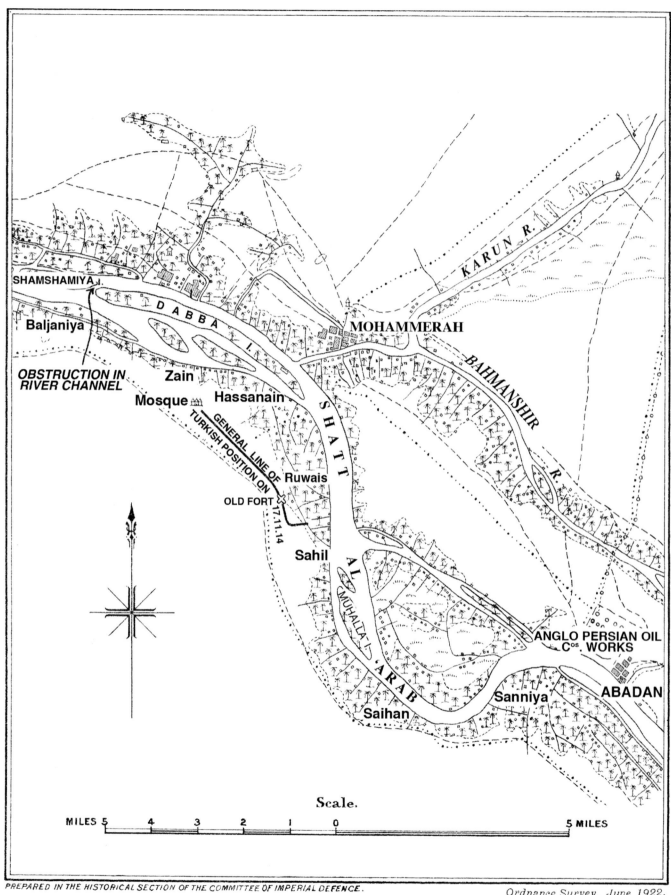

SHAMSHAMIYA I.

Baljaniya

OBSTRUCTION IN
RIVER CHANNEL

Zain

Mosque

Hassanain

DABBA I.

SHATT

KARUN R.

MOHAMMERAH

BAHMANSHIR R.

GENERAL LINE OF
TURKISH POSITION ON
17.11.14

Ruwais

OLD FORT

Sahil

AL MUHALLA I.

'ARAB

Saihan

Sanniya

ANGLO PERSIAN OIL
Cᵒˢ. WORKS

ABADAN

Scale.

MILES 5   4   3   2   1   0   5 MILES

PREPARED IN THE HISTORICAL SECTION OF THE COMMITTEE OF IMPERIAL DEFENCE.

Ordnance Survey, June 1922.

Operations on the Shatt Al Arab, November 1914

Navy covered the right. At about midday, the main enemy position was identified as a mud fort, which the 18th Brigade was deployed to attack. Accurate artillery fire assisted until the effects of a mirage meant that targets could no longer be identified. Accurate mapping became critical because the combination of flat, featureless landscape (relative to, for example, Britain, where the officers originated from — Baghdad, although 500 miles from the sea, is just over 100 feet above sea level) with the mirage distorting what few features there were made navigation extremely difficult.[40] The situation was saved by naval gunfire from the river, and the infantry charged over 400 yards of open ground, at which point the defenders fled.

However, the British suffered 353 casualties, including four Sapper officers, whose skills would be desperately needed in the watery landscape in which the division would be operating.[41] Lieutenant Spackman, regimental medical officer of the 48th Pioneers, set up his regimental aid post with a medical assistant and a dozen stretcher bearers, with which he attended to about 100 casualties who walked, crawled or were carried to him.[42]

The British forces camped in place for two days while stores were brought forward. The flotilla carried out reconnaissance of Dabba Island as far as Balzaniya and determined that would be the next Ottoman defensive position. They also skirmished with the *Marmaris*. By securing the mouth of the Karun, they were also able to release ships owned by the Lynch Brothers and the oil facilities which were used to assist the invasion forces. The Lynch Brothers had operated in Mesopotamia for many years and were familiar with the rivers. Their knowledge and support would be invaluable in the years to come.[43]

Meanwhile, the Turkish commander and *vali* of the province, Subri Bey, attempted to block the Shatt-al-Arab by sinking four vessels, including a German liner, the *Ekbatana*. They were chained together, but unfortunately, as the liner sank, it broke free and swung round to lie parallel to the shore. The resulting gap, known as Satan's Gap, maintained access to the open sea, but for a long time to come, all shipping to and from Basra would have to navigate this partially submerged bottleneck, which further frustrated the logistical supply chain. Attempts to refloat her failed, and she was left to bury herself in the river mud over time until she was no longer an obstacle.

Modern ***bellum*** **and marsh, taken from a road laid on a bund, near Basra, summer 2007. Even today, the terrain is flat, exposed and prone to flooding. Once flooded and covered with reeds, there were sudden increases in depth caused by the creeks. At Shaiba and for Townshend's regatta, similar poles and *bellums* were employed (author's collection).**

Espiègle sailed up to examine the gap and in the process drove off the *Marmaris* and silenced the guns on the opposite bank.[44]

General Barrett had not realized the extent of his victory at Sahil. It was the sheikh of Mohammerah through his contacts within Basra who informed the British that the town had been abandoned and was being looted by the inhabitants. *Espiègle* and *Odin* sailed into Basra and confirmed large-scale looting and burning. The looting was not limited to Basra. According to Wilson, "Forty-eight hours after the Turks had left, not a single Government building outside Basra possessed doors or window-frames." The presence of blue-jacketed Royal Marines restored order at the customs house and other government buildings. Wellesley's Rifles and the 117th Mahrattas arrived later on board the Lynch Brothers' steamers. As the troops moved into the city and restored order, they noted that neither the property of British merchants nor the English Club had been looted, and Nunn and his party rewarded themselves with a lager for their troubles. The Lynch Brothers' boatyard was untouched, which provided naval facilities unavailable elsewhere in the city. Supplies for the Berlin-Baghdad Railway were also found, which would be useful in a country where almost all building and engineering materials had to be imported.[45]

Basra had been entered, unopposed, on 21 November 1914, making it the first Axis town to be occupied during the Great War. Following a flag-raising ceremony in Basra, accompanied by a salute from the Royal Navy, Sir Percy Cox, the political advisor, issued a proclamation to the townspeople:

> The British government has now occupied Basra, and though a state of war with the Ottoman Government still prevails, yet we have no enmity or ill-will against the population, to whom we hope to prove good friends and protectors. No remnant of the Turkish administration remains in this place. In place thereof the British flag has been established, under which you will enjoy the benefits of liberty and justice, both in regard to your religious and secular affairs.[46]

Those sentiments would be echoed by later occupying armies and their political masters.

W.C. Spackman, the 48th Pioneer's RMO (Regimental Medical Officer) commented that the "rougher" types disapproved of the quick arrival of British authority as they hoped to profit from the chaos; he noted the gallows which were used to reestablish order. On the other hand, the large Jewish, Armenian and Chaldean Christian communities appreciated the safety to their property and lives which came in the wake of the British arrival, and the prospect of profitable trade. Spackman also commented on the cosmopolitan nature of the city of 60,000: Ethiopians and Somalis provided the heavy labor; Arabic, Persian, French, Turkish, English and Italian were all spoken.[47]

Basra had been occupied with relatively few casualties and without any undue problems. Initially, the main problem seems to have been the surprise, and even resentment, of the British soldiers' bare knees. The political response of the Arabs in the Basra *vilayet* and of the Persians were potential causes of concern. With a British presence in Basra, the sheik of Mohammerah, in whose territory the oil was located, was reassured. The need to preserve "face" amongst the regional powers would be a constant political factor in all operations. For the time being, the local Arabs seemed content to sit out the war. Cox and his administrators attempted to establish an administration, despite the destruction of many civil records. The merchants of Basra, as citizens of an enemy state, could not trade with the British, but Cox circumvented this by issuing passports of "Occupied Territories of Mesopotamia."[48] With its mercantile tradition which included an Indian merchant community, there were those in the town who saw the benefits of British rule (against Turkish rule) and the opportunity to benefit through trade with the British Empire and by supplying the soldiers. However, outside the town, where these benefits would not be enjoyed, the population was more ambivalent. To be fair, this was not a problem peculiar to the new British administrators; Ottoman rule had rarely been established outside the main population areas, and they had 500 years in which to get it right.

Accommodating the troops in Basra was a problem. When Townshend arrived, he found that his 16th Brigade had been flooded out of its tented cantonment and had to be accommodated in houses in the town. Householders were evicted from properties to provide accommodation, and although fair rents were paid, this was a major bone of contention between the town and military. Ominously, in anticipation of the attack on Basra, Barrett had requested a hospital ship from India. The ability of the British authorities to transport casualties to where adequate treatment could be administered would become a scandal. For now, with short distances, limited troop numbers and small engagements, the medical facilities were able to cope — by February 1915, there had only been 25 deaths attributed to disease.[49]

Qurna and the Garden of Eden

Indian Expeditionary Force "D" had successfully completed its mission. If events had been different, the Basra garrison might well have sat out the war as another insignificant backwater, surrounded by the enemy, unable to advance against the enemy, of questionable worth, tying up manpower and resources, with many dying from disease and in small-scale raiding, yet unable to be withdrawn.

This was not to be IEF "D's" fate. The main driving force behind this was Sir Percy Cox, who had his own ideas about how the campaign should develop. As soon as he was settled in Basra, just two weeks into the war against Turkey and 70 miles from the coast, he was advocating marching on Baghdad, 500 to 600 miles away. Baghdad was of no political or military significance. There were three Ottoman *vilayets* or provinces in what is now Iraq: Basra, Baghdad and Mosul. Although the three provincial capitals varied in size and importance, none of them held any seniority over the others. Baghdad, like Jerusalem, held an attraction because of its historical and religious connections. Furthermore, Cox was a career Indian politician, and prior to that an Indian Army officer, so he should have been well aware of the limitations of the Indian Army for attempting such a task.[50]

Cox telegraphed the viceroy saying that given the ease of success in Basra, "After earnest consideration of the arguments for and against I find it difficult to see how we can avoid taking over Baghdad" (23 November), and he was encouraged in by the sheikh of Kuwait on the 25 November: "Your victories have delighted me; next, please God, you will take Baghdad and what is connected with it." However, Cox's "arguments" in his telegram of the 23rd focused on the political dimensions and did not touch upon the logistical difficulties which would be critical in the years ahead.[51]

Cox may or may not have been aware that the Baghdad question had been raised by the viceroy to the secretary of state for India. The matter would require some serious consideration. The Russians were operating in the Caucasus. There were hostile Arab tribes around Baghdad. It was unlikely that the Turks would have sufficient troops to defend the city. General Sir Beauchamp Duff, commander-in-chief in India, did at least recognize the potential disaster which could overtake an overstretched force.

Lord Crewe urged caution too: "In the absence of extensive power to reinforce we must not cut more cake than we can eat."[52] This was November 1914. The war in Europe, which was the main focus, had entered the trenches. There was no reason not to expect a return to movement in the spring of 1915. The expected breakthrough and subsequent defeat of Germany would end the war. In this scenario, Basra was a sideshow. We now know that those dreams would be dashed in March 1915 at Neuve-Chapelle, which many Indian Army divisions participated in.

However, Lord Crewe did authorize an advance to Qurna. This town sits where the Tigris and Euphrates joined to form the Shatt-al-Arab. A third river, the Shwaiyib, joined the waterway from the east five miles south of the town. Qurna is the legendary site of the Garden of Eden. Even today, the Tree of Knowledge grows in the center of the town. There were advantages to the occupation. It would provide "defense in depth" for any Ottoman counter-attack on Basra from the north, and it did represent a more direct and shorter route to the oil fields. However it did also represent the next step towards Baghdad, which, although not meeting the aims and objectives of Cox, was the most he could achieve in the winter of 1914–1915.[53]

On 25 November, *Espiègle* and *Odin* and other vessels sailed up the Shatt to locate the nearest Turkish forces and found them 40 miles away at Qurna, including the *Marmaris*.[54] They returned to Qurna on 3 December with a reinforced flotilla and troops: 104th Rifles, 110th Marahattas and a company of Norfolks with half a company of Sappers and Miners, and artillery in support. The flotilla consisted of two warships, two armed river steamers mounted with field guns, and three armed launches. *Espiègle* and *Lawrence* came within range of Qurna, and an artillery duel ensued. They were supported by other vessels once they had released their lighters of troops and supplies.[55]

The soldiers disembarked on the north bank of the Shwaiyib and charged Turkish trenches at Muzaira'a during which they captured 60 soldiers and two field guns. During this attack, the British experienced a peculiar feature which would plague their operations in the future: the mirage.[56] What had appeared to be a substantial trench system was, in fact, only a single line. The Turkish survivors withdrew into the date palms which were planted along the river banks and were eventually evacuated across the Tigris into Qurna from where they fired into the date palms now occupied by British troops. The Tigris here was about 200 yards wide.

At this point, the river was too shallow for the sloops to advance further. *Odin* had a damaged rudder from the earlier reconnaissance but remained to provide artillery fire support. The smaller armed launches were too lightly armored to progress against the Ottoman fire: *Miner* was holed in the engine room beneath the waterline and only made shallow water

from where she could be recovered and repaired through the heroism of stokers Jones and Lacy, both of whom were decorated. Unable to advance further in the face of rifle and artillery fire from Qurna, the British withdrew to their landing place. During the night, the Turks took advantage of this situation and reoccupied their original positions.[57]

A plan was developed whereby, to negate the fire from Qurna, the 110th Infantry would force a crossing north of Qurna, out of sight of the town. Reinforcements were requested. On 7 December, the Norfolks (right) and half of the 120th (left) attacked the reoccupied Turkish positions at Muzaira'a while the 110th conducted a turning movement to the north of the village. The 120th were temporarily checked in their advance, but reinforced by a reserve company from the 7th Rajputs and closer naval gunfire support (*Espiègle* was dragged through mud to close in), the Turkish positions were carried by the bayonet. The British and Indians advanced to the riverbank where they established a firing line until dusk, when they withdrew to Muzaira'a. During the dueling between the navy and the Turkish artillery in Qurna, *Shaitan* was hit on the bridge by a shell, killing the captain, Lieutenant Commander Elkes, RNR, and disabling the rest of the crew so that she was withdrawn from the battle to refit.[58]

The following day, the 104th carried out a reconnaissance three miles up the Tigris and selected a crossing point. Three Indian soldiers successfully swam the river with a line and used that to tow a rope across, which was then used to haul a small dhow backwards and forwards. By the time the Turks realized what was happening, the 104th had crossed in sufficient numbers. Meanwhile, attacks with naval gunfire support retook the Arab villages and Ottoman positions abandoned the day before. The 104th Rifles were also able to cross the river using boats from friendly Arabs. That night with the army bivouaced opposite Qurna, the flotilla carefully navigated the river to get closer to the town.[59]

However, at midnight a steamer with all of its lights on left Qurna and sailed for the main body. Onboard was a message of surrender from Colonel Subhi Bey, the *vali* of Basra, commanding the Turkish 38th Division. On 9 December, 35 officers, 1,000 men and 7 guns surrendered, but in the night several units had slipped away, including the Osmanjik battalion commanded by Lieutenant Colonel Sulaiman Askari Bey, commander of all Turkish forces in the region.[60]

Qurna did not live up to its biblical image. Like Basra, Qurna was effectively an island with the low-lying "land" inundated by the floodwaters. The town was a collection of dirt tracks and mud-and-reed huts. The *Official History* (and all other writers) records the observations of one British soldier: it would not take the biblical flaming angel with a flaming sword to keep him out of Eden. The British soldiers did pay homage to the biblical connections by naming features appropriately: Adam's Walk and Temptation Square were but a couple.[61] Nor was Qurna a popular garrison location. As an island, with Ottoman troops occupying four further islands in the in-undated world, the water level was two feet higher than the British camp. The floodwaters were normally 3 feet deep, but over the irrigation channels it could be as deep as 20 feet. Reeds provided the only cover. They could be five feet tall but were commonly two feet tall, so they offered no protection from fire.[62]

Lieutenant Spackman was based at Qurna and while there he makes light of a serious and persistent problem — thieving Arabs. While trying to find the latrine one night, he realized that his confusion was caused by the theft of the latrine tent! The sentries noticed an offending trio making off with the said tent and opened fire, with several bullets passing close to Spackman and one striking a tent pole, bringing his tent down upon his head while he attempted to make himself respectable. While his fellow officers made light of the situation afterwards, the serious side of the escapade was the death of a regimental shoemaker and two other sepoys wounded, and the bayoneting of one of the thieves. This problem is a reoccurring theme, and not just limited to wartime. Hubbard recounts several audacious thefts, including the bedclothes of the chief Indian surveyor, a "portly" gentleman of 18 stone, while he slept.[63] On a lighter note, Spackman and his fellow officers had the opportunity to go hunting and fowling, on the pretext of training the sepoys how to use the local boats in the marshes. Again, this is a recurring theme in accounts of the campaign and speaks volumes of the expectations of the day that officers campaigned with shotguns. And it was not an activity in which the author was able to participate during his service in Iraq. On another occasion, Spackman was able to picnic and drink beer alongside the Baswaries and watched as *belems* of young men and women in their finest clothes courted. How the times have changed![64]

Despite the surrender of the 38th Division, there were Ottoman forces which could threaten Basra, one on each of the rivers. At Nasariya on the Euphrates was Lieutenant Colonel Sulaiman Askari Bey, and at Kut on the Tigris, Mehmet Fazil Pasha, with the 35th Division and Arab cavalry units. Bey's force also included Arab tribesmen, and he tried to encourage other tribes to rise up against the British invaders. For now, though, those tribes preferred to remain independent in their actions and take advantage of whatever opportunities came their way. Bey was ordered to attack Basra by War Minister Enver Pasha.

The River Karun to Ahwaz, Persia: Defending the Oil

Early in 1915, anti–British sentiment was being stirred up in Persian Arabistan by German agents and by the expected calling of a jihad by the sultan. Rumors were rife, and it was put about that Kaiser Wilhelm had undertaken a pilgrimage to Mecca and was styling himself Haji Wilhelm Mohammad,

Protector of All Muslims. The sheikh of Mohammerah was not loved by his subjects and was unable to prevent the oil pipes from being attacked. Pro-German elements even seized branches of the British-owned Imperial Bank of Persia and emptied their vaults for the anti–British cause. The telegraph system was hijacked to prevent its use by the Allies.

The chief German agent in the region was Wilhelm Wassmuss, who had served as the German counsel to Bushire. He spoke Persian and was familiar with local politics. He was able to recruit several local tribes against the British and attempted to capture the British counsel in Bushire. The attack was driven off by Indian soldiers. In response, Royal Marines and Indian soldiers occupied Bushire, destroyed the main settlement and cut down the date palms in retaliation. This would not be the end of British involvement in southern Persia, and in order to secure Mesopotamia, the oil and other regional interests, more British and Indian troops would be tied up there.[65]

Following reports of disturbances in Ahwaz, Brigadier General C. T. Robinson, commander Royal Artillery, was sent up the River Karun with the 4th and 7th Rajputs plus 30 men from each of the 2nd Dorsets and 33rd Cavalry, and two mountain guns. Robinson found a large force of Turks and Arabs northwest of Ahwaz and planned to attack their camp. The guns opened fire at 6,000 yards, but the Turks and Arabs advanced, threatening to encircle Robinson and forcing him to retreat. In the process he lost both his guns. The force was lucky to return to Anglo-Indian lines, with the assistance of reinforcements from the 33rd Cavalry which rode out to cover the retreat on 3 March.[66]

Lieutenant Staples, 11th Rajputs, wrote a fascinating account of this engagement:

> Well at 2am on 3rd March we were marched out, a force of less than 1,000 men All told to make "reconnaissance in force".... We had two field guns & two mountain guns. About 6 am we got to a place about 3 miles from the Arab Camps & it got light, so we wished them good morning by plumping shells into the Camps. We watched the Arabs with our glasses come buzzing out like a disturbed wasps nest & thought they were going to run away. We all felt sorry for them when we saw the shells bursting on them — However they didn't run away but produced green, red & white banners exactly the same shape as those used in May processions at Greenwich.... They also had a very large number of mounted men ... galloped round both our flanks & some got on to hills between us & our Camp.... Then they proceeded to advance upon us from three sides simultaneously & very rapidly & rifle fire soon started. We were all ordered to retire, which we proceeded to do. The enemy closed in upon us in rear with wonderful rapidity & stuck to our rearguard (with which I was most of the time) the whole way back to camp keeping an average distance of 150 × [150 yards] from us. In this manner we drifted back the eight miles or so to camp. We had to make the rear guard retire at a walk, to steady the sepoys, as we dared not let them double. Personally I never expected to get

back to camp as we were being pelted with bullets from never less than three sides all the time & were cruelly outnumbered — Two things to my mind saved us — One (& the most important) was the surprising inaccuracy of the Arabs' fire. The second was that they never had the pluck to push us & cut us all down, which I am sure they could have done. They used to make spasmodic efforts to do so, but only about 50 men would start & gallop in on us, shouting — & as soon as a dozen or so were shot, they used to wheel off.... I got hit very early in the show, as we were retiring a bullet flopped between my feet, ricocheted up and through the inside of the ankle of my left boot, my sock and part of my puttie & made a small channel about an inch long on the skin over the ankle bone little more than a graze really thus [sketch of his foot and ankle]. It felt as if some one had thrown a stone & hit one & I remember a hop skip & a jump with a shout of "damn." I took a rifle then and had one shot with which I got an Arab, who never moved after he fell. My ankle didn't hurt much at first but it soon began to get very stiff & swollen & I had to draw my sword and use it as a walking stick & a very good one it proved. We continued like this through low hills till about 2 or 3 miles from camp, where the hills ended & there was an absolutely level plain. Just before the rearguard left the hills, the Turks brought up their guns & started shelling the main body the shells passing over us before they exploded.... The last bit across the plain I did with a detachment of the Dorset regiments (about 20 men under a corporal.... The shells continued to fly over us, but the Turks fortunately mistook a building with a mud wall round it for our Camp & proceeded to vigorously shell it.... They were not using shrapnel but what is called "Segment shell" which is much the same. Well we continued across the couple of miles of plain with the Dorsets whom we extended widely & fixed bayonets because we were followed at about 300 yards by swarms of their mounted men, who fired at us from the saddle with no effect. WE were also being enfiladed by a collection of their ragamuffins from a hill at long range, but they did no harm — about four times anything between 50 & 100 of the mounted scallywags plucked up their courage, snorted vigorously & galloped in to cut us down. We used to halt & face about & start firing when they got to about 200 yards & by the time they had got to 100 yards from us, they always had about 12 empty saddles & the rest would invariably wheel round & gallop off. The horsemen gave up chasing us about a mile from camp but all these halts to repel their charges and pick up wounded had made my ankle stiff that I could barely hobble, even with the help of my sword, so that I had to put my arm round the neck of a Dorset Tommy, he passed me on later to a sepoy, because he had to help a man who couldn't walk at all & Major O'Keeffe, our doctor, took me on for a bit & finally about ¼ mile from camp, Sheepshanks of the 12th Cavalry who was out there attached to the 33rd rode up & he & O'Keeffe heaved me on to Sheepshanks horse which I rode in, but I am glad to say I didn't have to be helped till the enemy's attacks ceased.... I never saw a European anything but absolutely cool & collected although I don't think any of them expected to live to see camp. The private soldiers were as steady as the officers & one felt glad one's skin was a white

one. The three doctors were magnificent — Major O'Keeffe Captain Arthur both IMS one very Irish & the other very Scotch & Capt McCreery RAMC — his father I believe in AMS. They were all three of them dressing wounds all the time under fire & helping wounded & I know little O'Keeffe was one of the last into camp.... When I got into Camp I had to be lifted off the horse — The boot being an ordinary Tommy's boot, they took off easily enough. "Saves a lot of trouble that" said the hospital orderly Tommy, when he saw that the bootlace was cut through by the bullet.[67]

The Battle for Shaiba

General Barrett decided to occupy Shaiba, 10 miles to the west of Basra. Shaiba was the nearest high ground which would not be inundated in the season flooding. This decision marked the beginning of a 90-year association between Britain and Shaiba. For generations until 1958, it would be known as RAF Shaiba and would play an important role in the early days of intercontinental air travel as one of the staging posts to the empire, in much the same way that coaling stations supported steamships. RAF Shaiba supported RAF Habbaniya, 13 miles west of Falluja, during 1941. The siege of Habbaniya during a pro–German military coup in Baghdad was Britain's first victory of that war and secured the supply of oil which was essential to conduct military operations.[68] After 2003, Shaiba would be revisited, in the form of Shaiba Logistics Base (SLB), which supported Coalition forces in Multi-National Division (South East). To that generation of British soldiers, SLB would be known as "Shaibiza" or "Shagaluf," after two popular Spanish holiday resorts, Ibiza and Magaluf.

For Barrett, Shaiba (like Qurna) offered a defensible position which offered "defense in depth" for Basra as well as quartering his troops away from the town, where the lack of accommodation was a problem. The disadvantage was that the inundation between the two locations made communications and resupply difficult, especially if Shaiba was attacked. Spackman and the 48th Pioneers were redeployed from Qurna to Basra in March 1915, and on to Shaiba on 5 April, a march of 18 miles through knee-deep water. The sepoys marched barefoot and so found the going easier than the boot-wearing British soldiers. Both suffered in the heat, which was already at 120F/40C without any shade and tormented by dust storms which were only abated when rain turned the dust to mud:

> This sandstorm was sheer hell. It blew all that night and all the next day. Our little tents were quite useless, cooking and eating was impossible, so that I spent most of the day sitting on the sand with my Burberry over my head, eyes red and throat and lungs choked up. All military activity was suspended on both sides.[69]

Barrett was justifiably concerned about the presence of Turkish troops in Nasariya. Just up the river from its jointure with

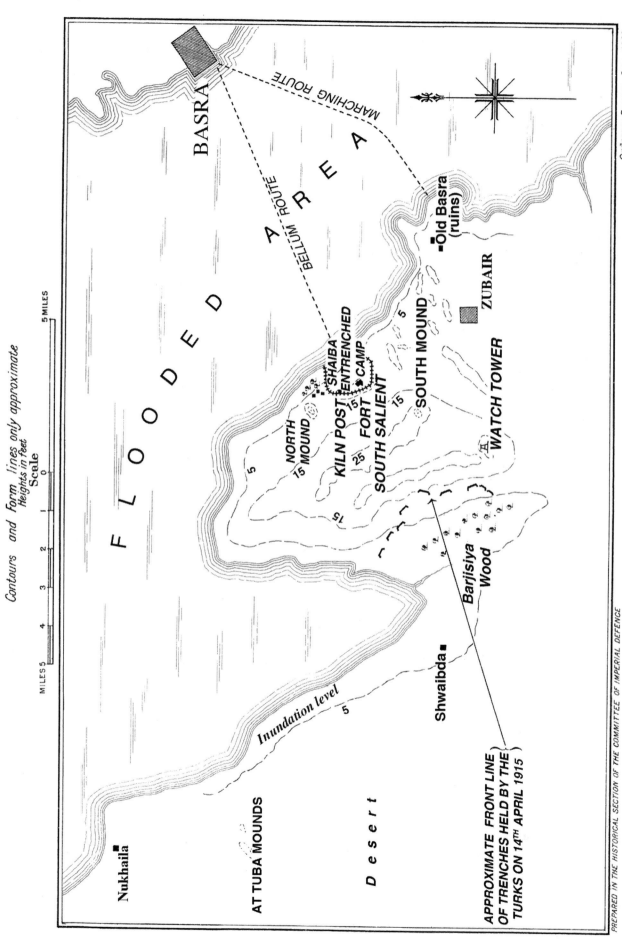

Contours and Form lines only approximate
Heights in feet
Scale

5 MILES

MILES 5   0   1   2   3   4   5

FLOODED AREA

BASRA

MARCHING ROUTE

BELLUM ROUTE

Old Basra (ruins)

ZUBAIR

SHAIBA ENTRENCHED CAMP

NORTH MOUND

15

KILN POST

FORT

SOUTH SALIENT

SOUTH MOUND

15

25

15

5

5

WATCH TOWER

Barjisiya Wood

Inundation level

5

Desert

Shwaibda

AT TUBA MOUNDS

Nukhaila

APPROXIMATE FRONT LINE OF TRENCHES HELD BY THE TURKS ON 14TH APRIL 1915

Ordnance Survey, June, 1922.

PREPARED IN THE HISTORICAL SECTION OF THE COMMITTEE OF IMPERIAL DEFENCE the Tigris was a huge seasonal lake, Hammar Lake. Beyond the lake was the town of Nasariya where Ottoman troops were concentrating for a move against Basra. An armed flotilla with infantry from the Norfolks and 7th Rajputs launched a pre-emptive attack. They shelled the camp and blocked the route south thus delaying the counter-attack and buying more time to fortify Shaiba camp.[70]

Shaiba camp was about three and a half miles in perimeter, with a *serai* known as Shaiba fort on its western edge. The perimeter was wired and entrenched. There were floods to the east, with the camp rising slightly to the west. The key features were the 60-foot tall brick kiln and the south salient just beyond the southern front.[71]

On the same day that the Ahwaz expedition returned to Basra, a reconnaissance force was dispatched from Shaiba northwest towards Nukhaila. The mixed cavalry and infantry force reached within four miles of their objective before being forced to withdraw due to the presence of Arab horsemen on their flanks. A second Arab force then attacked the British cavalry. The supporting infantry, struggling in the heavy sand and with their visibility obscured by dust, were unable to distinguish between friend and foe until the Arab horse almost stumbled into the infantry. Rifle, machine gun and artillery fire drove off the Arabs, and the force withdrew to Shaiba.[72]

Neither the deployment along the Karun nor the reconnaissance towards Nukhaila had gone well for the British. The initially optimistic observations on the abilities of the Ottoman forces in the region should have been revised accordingly. As a result, reinforcements were requested, to which the British government agreed and instructed the Indian government to send a further brigade. On 7 March 1915, the 33rd Brigade and a howitzer battery were embarked, which arrived in Basra on the 25th.[73] What had started out as a minor expedition was now growing. Further units were being readied in India in the event that they were needed: this would become the 12th Indian Division.

With two divisions deploying to Mesopotamia, it was decided to form II Indian Army Corps with General Sir John Nixon as its commander on 1 April 1915. Nixon was, like many senior commanders early in the war, approaching the end of his career. A cavalryman with a reputation for dash and leadership, who was not afraid to use uncontroversial methods nor willing to be hampered by administrative constraints, his instructions on leaving India were the same as those previously given to Barrett, but with one crucial difference: he was instructed to draw up plans for an advance on Baghdad. As we have seen, Cox was also an advocate of Baghdad, and so Nixon's presence in Basra would only have encouraged planning and advocating to this end:

> Your force is intended to retain complete control of the lower portion of Mesopotamia, comprising the Basra *Vilyates* and including all outlets to the sea and such portions of the neighbouring territories as may affect your operations.... 3. After acquainting yourself on the spot with the present situation you will submit:—(1) a plan for the effective occupation of the Basra *Vilyates*; (2) a plan for the subsequent advance on Baghdad.[74]

Nixon's first encounter after arriving in Basra was the long-expected counter-attack which commence on 12 April 1915 when some 4,000 Ottoman troops attempted to invest Shaiba camp from the east at Barjisiya Wood. The troops based in Shaiba were the three cavalry regiments of the 6th Indian Cavalry Brigade, the Bombay Engineers, and three British and ten Indian infantry battalions. General Fry commanded.[75]

The war diary for the 6th Cavalry Brigade for 11 April recorded that at 0750 hours, 800 horsemen were seen moving toward Barsijsiya Wood from Shwaibda, and another 1,500 to 2,000 beyond Shwaibda. The wood already contained an unknown number of enemy, and that afternoon a further 1,000 Arabs were seen in the vicinity of Shwaibda.[76]

To counter these moves, the 6th Cavalry Brigade was ordered to move at 0530 hours the following day (12th) towards Old Basra and az-Zubair, south of Shaiba, but as the advanced guard was departing, the orders were rescinded as it was believed that the enemy was preparing a large attack on Basra.[77]

The brigade remained inactive all day until 1600 hours when Major Wheeler, OC A Squadron, 7th Hariana Lancers, volunteered to attack the enemy positions. According to the regiment's war diary, Wheeler lead his squadron out of the camp past No. 8 piquet southeast about 1,500 yards. No 8 piquet was manned by members of "S" Battery, Royal Horse Artillery and a machine-gun section, both of which opened fire on the enemy. When Wheeler charged, the enemy fled their trenches, and the Lancers "got home with the lance." The combination of artillery, machine gun and lance did a great deal of damage to the enemy infantry. When enemy cavalry appeared from the high ground northeast of Old Basra, about 2,500 yards away, the lancers reformed and retired to the camp. The attack was accomplished for the loss of one man and one horse wounded. For this charge, Wheeler was awarded the Victoria Cross (VC), the first of 20 to be awarded to the army and three more to the navy in that theater by 1918. A dusk attack failed and then petered out. An attempt to keep the attackers at bay with a searchlight lasted just 15 minutes before it was put out of action.[78]

General Fry ordered the 6th Cavalry Brigade, with two guns and the 104th Rifles, to prepare to move the following morning, the 13th. The Turks attacked again about 0500 hours against the west and southwest of the camp, and at dawn (0545 hours), the first of the Turkish guns opened fire. It took about 15 minutes for the British artillery to identify and silence all but two long-range guns which outranged the British. The

Opposite: **The Battle of Shaiba, April 1915.**

Cavalry Brigade came under fire from palm groves which they pushed past, and at 0700 hours the 7th Lancers were ordered to charge several enemy positions, the major position being North Mound. The remainder of the brigade was held in reserve. In the face of heavy fire, the lancers took North Mound but were unable to hold it and withdrew. They were, nevertheless, able to get amongst an estimated 50 to 100 enemy with the lance again. Unfortunately, Major Wheeler, charging at the head of his squadron again, together with Jemadar Sudham Singh, were killed. In addition, 7 Indian soldiers were killed and 18 wounded and 36 horses killed.[79]

With the retirement of the 7th Lancers, the remainder of the brigade were withdrawn until 1150 hours. Infantry were ordered to retrieve abandoned enemy guns. The 104th Rifles cleared a length of trenches with the bayonet (for which they were highly commended by Delamain) while the 24th Punjabis retrieved the abandoned artillery with little opposition. The cavalry had the opportunity to charge fleeing enemy in the open, but the opportunity to inflict further casualties was missed as the force focused on the mission to retrieve the guns. The enemy had been cleared from west of the camp by 1430 hours, and the British withdrew into the camp by 1500 hours, where they passed a quiet night. There were, however, still enemy forces in positions to the southwest.[80]

When Private Bird of the Norfolks reached the North Mound as part of a brigade advance, he found Wheeler's body naked and mutilated beyond recognition, and that of the senior Indian officer alight and almost burned to a cinder.[81]

Lieutenant Spackman, with the 48th Pioneers, found himself rudely awoken by rifle fire on the morning of the 12th and spent the day in the trenches with the sepoys or tending to the wounded. The main feature in his location was the old fort, which was both the location chosen by the field ambulance and a target for the Turkish artillery, so the Pioneer's trenches received the "drop shorts." That night was "very unpleasant" as Turkish troops attempted to cut the wire and bomb the trenches. With dawn, the Turks withdrew, and the artillery duel resumed. Spackman considered that the Turkish rate of fire reduced considerably, which he attributed to lack of ammunition and water, and the midday heat. Back in the trenches, the best shots from the Pioneers were ordered to snipe at anyone who showed their head, while a machine-gunner from the Norfolks was able to get anyone who left the safety of the trenches with three or four shots.

Around midday, a truce was called by the Turks to treat the wounded who were exposed to the full heat of the sun. Spackman went forward, but after another RMO was killed, the truce ended abruptly. The Pioneers who had gone forward to protect the medical team put in a bayonet charge, followed by the medical team, which took them into sand dunes by the Turkish positions. From there, they were spotted by the British artillery who assumed them to be Turks and shelled them, until a British officer stood on the sand dune and waved his

pith helmet at them — not very military, but it served its purpose. From this position they were able to observe the bayonet charge of the 24th Punjabis onto the Turkish positions.[82]

Reinforcements were requested, which had to traverse the 10 inundated miles either by wading waste deep in water or by being poled in local *bellum* canoes. Supplies had to undertake the same tortuous journey. Local crews suddenly disappeared, so volunteers from the 20th Punjabis were called for. The water was so shallow in parts that the crews had to manhandle their *bellums*. Their progress was also opposed by hostile Arabs, and one convoy carrying ammunition had to return to Basra.[83]

On the third day of the battle, the 14th, there were still some 10,000 Turks with six guns in the vicinity of South Mound and Barsijiya Wood. At 0930 hours, the 16th Brigade led the advance, with the 18th Brigade in column on the left and cavalry on the right. In the middle of this hollow square were the artillery and headquarters units. They set out towards Old Basra and Az-Zubair where it was mistakenly believed that there were Turkish troops. At South Mound, Turkish positions at Barsijiya Wood were identified, and the column swung round to face them.

The British deployed with the 16th Brigade left and the 18th Brigade right, although the terrain prevented them from establishing a continuous front. The 16th Brigade deployed a square formation with the Dorsets and 24th forward with the 117th and the 119th in reserve. The 18th Brigade deployed the same formation with the Norfolks and 120th forward, the 22nd Sappers and Miners to the rear and the 110th rear but to the right. Around 1130 hours, the forward battalions crested a ridge and were engaged from a Turkish trench at 400 to 600 yards, with a second line 500 yards behind.

The heat was intense, and the colonel of one regiment noted the surreal nature of the battle: soldiers would be overcome by sleep for 10 or 15 minutes while their colleagues kept up a slow, deliberate fire. The absence of rapid fire made the whole engagement unreal, in contrast with the "Mad Minute" which characterized the 1914 actions in France. The battle was marred by extreme heat and mirages which prevented accurate observations. Spackman recorded the troops advancing and then disappearing into the dust. He also complimented one of the unsung heroes of the war, the "*bhisties*," whom he called the true Gunga Dins, for trudging back and forth with water skins to refresh the troops.[84]

Melliss ordered an advance at 1530 hours, and it was noted from about 1600 hours that the Turkish fire was beginning to slacken. Having closed in to about 200 yards from the Turkish trenches, a final bayonet charged secured the first line of trenches an hour later. White flags were observed in the second-line trenches, and troops began abandoning them. Exhaustion and a lack of artillery ammunition prevented the British from exploiting this retreat. It is believed that the Ottoman forces mistook a resupply column for Shaiba camp for reinforcement. The British troops were too exhausted to follow up this unexpected turn of events, but then they did not need too. The Ottoman troops did not stop retreating for 90 miles until they regained Nasariya. Their opportunistic Arab irregular allies now turned on them with murder and theft. Sulaiman Askari Bey, denouncing the faithlessness of his Arab allies, committed suicide.[85] The British cavalry brigade, watering its horses, were in no position to exploit the Turkish retreat, which no doubt saved them. The performance of the British cavalry was, not for the first time, found lacking: Melliss considered Kennedy, commanding the cavalry, as "a most incompetent person or gives grudging cooperation, I don't know which, but he is useless."[86]

The British victory had been a narrow one but a victory nonetheless. It had highlighted once again the difficulties of operating in Mesopotamia. Casualty evacuation and treatment and troop movements all had been hampered by the local weather conditions and the absence of reliable road networks. Spackman described casualty evacuation in better terms than any official report could:

> Pause to imagine being brought in, with other wounded with broken limbs or massive injuries, on a mule cart without springs, traveling for miles across rough desert under a burning sun. Imagine the pain and the thirst. That evening cartloads of dead and wounded Turks were brought in, the dead, dying and wounded all mixed up, the job of sorting them out being an appalling experience. No, there is nothing romantic, picturesque or glorious about the aftermath of a battle, with the maimed and wounded dying before your helpless eyes. Picture the squalor and the despair of the tired and overworked nursing staff struggling to give proper attention to each case. Such an experience is something to be seen, but then to try to forget.[87]

The reliance on water transport was again evident. However, unlike the operations against Qurna and Nasariya, which were combined operations undertaken with naval gun fire support, Shaiba was lacking in naval support. This pattern, whereby the British succeeded in combined operations but struggled when the army operated alone, was set out at Shaiba and on the Karun River. Captain Wilson speculated that this was the last battle to be fought without aerial reconnaissance. This in itself is worth a mention. When Maude rebuilt the army for his advance on Baghdad, aviation would be not only commonplace, but an integral part of "battlespace analysis" (aerial reconnaissance and photography for map preparation), supporting "shaping operations" (spotting fall of shot for the artillery and correcting their fire) and air-to-ground attacks with machine guns and bombs. For a general to fight a battle without having current information on what is happening beyond the range of his own eyesight is to link him to a byegone age. A subaltern today would expect to have greater tactical awareness through personal radios than was available at Shaiba.[88]

Yet the importance of the Battle of Shaiba, even if it was a close-run thing, should not be underestimated. Lieutenant General Sir George MacMunn, who would later become the inspector general of communications in Mesopotamia, wrote, "Some day, when the Lord of Hosts makes up His jewels, Shaiba, will be recognized as one of the decisive battles of the War, if not the world."[89] Success in arms encourages allies, or at least maintains the passive cooperation of the less committed parties. British failure at Shaiba would almost certainly have encouraged enemies into further aggressive acts. Any such

Wounded Turkish prisoners of war, attributed to the Battle of Shaiba, 1915.

diminution of British regional prestige would have also undermined the authority of Britain's allies and opened them up to attack, potentially ultimately unraveling the whole of British policy and interests in the Gulf region. This was precisely the situation which IEF "D" had set out to avoid.

Today, Shaiba is one of many forgotten allied victories of the Great War, similar to Tennant's musings on the fate of forgotten casualties of actions in far-flung fields.[90] When British troops returned to Shaiba 88 years later, it was possible to visit the huge monument in the desert to this victory. Its original position had been in Basra beside the Shatt. Rumor had it that Saddam Hussein wanted to dismantle the monument, but he found the task too daunting and left it in the desert. The author was never able to visit the monument but saw it in the distance while driving in convoys to and from Kuwait. Even at a distance, blurred through the heat haze which hung on the horizon, it rose from the desert, part monument to the dead, part Roman triumphal arch to victorious feats of arms.

Defending the Oil, Again

Winston Churchill, first lord of the Admiralty, and an original advocate of Mesopotamia, was now losing interest, and his attention was turning to Gallipoli as a means of breaking the Ottomans and aiding Russia. He was now considering Mesopotamia to be a waste of manpower and questioned why the navy could not buy its oil elsewhere. Forever mercurial, this habit which infuriated his generals as prime minister can be seen here in relation to his attitude towards the Eastern Question.[91] The navy, however, was concerned about fuel shortages and the impact on operations: 1915 would see the long-expected clash of the naval titans. The British public would be disappointed that it was not given a second Trafalgar, but thereafter naval operations would shift from sea battles to the less glamorous submarine warfare which came close to starving Britain into submission and would ultimately bring the United States of America into the war.[92]

An Ottoman force left the Tigris to attack the oil wells inside Persia, consisting of eight infantry battalions, eight guns and some 7,000 Arab tribesmen. To counter this, General Gorringe, who would command the 12th Division, entered Persian Arabistan. He found the local tribes to be either indifferent or hostile, and on one occasion two squadrons of cavalry were attacked, killing three officers. Gorringe reached Braika, 60 miles northeast of Basra, and then turned north to try and bring the Ottoman force to battle. He reached the town of Illa on the river Karkha. To cross this, his engineers had to build a bridge, no mean feat as the river was in spate, 250 yards wide, with steep banks and clinging mud; a gale blew throughout the task. With the river bridged, Gorringe crossed and advanced upriver.[93]

Gorringe, on the north bank, encountered the village of Khafajiya on the south bank, which belonged to the Beni Tamin tribe, and who were responsible for the mutilation of wounded British soldiers at Ahwaz on 3 March. To punish the village, Gorringe had to recross the river, which he did, and attacked the village without loss. The inhabitants were driven off, grain stores destroyed and 1,000 head of sheep and cattle seized as a fine.

Gorringe and his column returned to Basra with their prize and with the oil supply restored, but exhausted from the heat and without having seen a single Turk.[94]

The Oil Secured

Indian Expeditionary Force "D" had completed its task without major loss or setback. The army had performed well with limited objectives and cooperated well with the navy. Difficulties had been encountered. The local conditions were difficult, to say the least. The local population and remaining Ottoman forces were not going to allow Basra to be garrisoned peacefully. Yet, when reinforced with the 12th Indian Division and the activation of II Indian Corps on 1 April 1915, there was no reason not to believe that Basra, Shaiba, and Qurna could not be held, with occasional expeditions to "pacify" the inhabitants or defeat Ottoman forces.

The problems which would go on to plague advances against Nasariya and Baghdad were there for all to see in 1914–1915. It would become a scandal that they were not acted upon before undertaking more adventurous objectives. General Barrett would be replaced by Townshend. Barrett was considered too cautious, but ironically, that is what Mesopotamia required. The combination of Nixon and Cox driving Townshend on to greater glory would expose the inherent weaknesses to a critical extent. Cox himself would later admit that Barrett was probably the better candidate for addressing Basra's problems at the time and was against advancing, or at least advancing in a hurry.[95]

That was for the future. For now, Delhi could be pleased with the successful completion of limited objectives. It is perhaps worth pausing for a moment to contemplate "what if": what if IEF "D" had dug in and defended the oil without chasing glory up the Tigris? Well, it is likely that the Turkish Army and the Arab tribes would have raided the perimeter, resulting in a steady flow of fatalities. The Arabs within the occupied zone would have been unruly, knowing that the Turks would probably return at the end of the war, and they would be merciless to collaborators. There would have been no significant infrastructure investment. After the war, if Basra had been returned to the Ottoman Empire, it would have continued to be an under-developed provincial backwater whose sole significant export was dates.

3

Townshend's Regatta, April 1915–June 1915

Major General Charles Vere Ferrers Townshend arrived in Basra on 23 April 1915 to take up his post as GOC (General Officer Commanding) 6th (Poona) Division. He was a complex figure in his day, and he is a controversial character to this day: Chitral Charlie, the Victorian hero; Townshend of Kut who led his men into captivity and then abandoned them.

In the second quarter of 1915, Townshend was, without doubt, the man of the moment and the most successful British general serving anywhere in the world, if not the most successful general of any army on either side, anywhere in the world. No one else managed to advance so far, with so few casualties, repeatedly defeating his enemies, as Townshend did between Qurna and Ctesiphon.[1]

Townshend played a central role in the next phase of the campaign in Mesopotamia, so it is worthwhile briefly analyzing his career to date as his personality quirks go a long way in explaining what happened. Born in 1861 to a lower-middle-class family, Townshend was aware from an early age of his family's illustrious heritage. The 1st Marquis fought at Fontenoy, Dettingen, and was with Wolfe at Quebec. The current 5th Marquis was impoverished, and his successor, born in 1866, remained childless until 1916. If that line died out, the heir apparent was Townshend's father, so for all of his life until his captivity in Turkey, he held out for the title. Commissioned in 1881 into the Royal Marines Light Infantry, he was initially not even in the army, yet he was an ambitious social climber and networker. He was also a gifted entertainer. A banjo is a reoccurring item amongst his military equipment, and many contemporaries comment on his entertaining them with it. Naturally, he also cultivated a circle of theatrical friends with whom he was able to mix with ease. Posted to Egypt in 1882, he was there at the time of attempts to relieve "Gordon of Khartoum," although Townshend found himself garrisoning Suakin on the Red Sea, which was, by all accounts, filthy, unhygienic, boring and, probably most importantly to Townshend, away from the center of attention where he could get himself noticed and promoted.

Already Townshend had been examining other corps and services to transfer to, including the navy, the Indian Staff Corps and the cavalry. The act of transferring from one "cap badge" to another would naturally cause resentment from his fellow officers in the RMLI (Royal Marines Light Infantry), and also raise suspicions of Townshend's motives amongst the officers of the "cap badge" into which he was transferring. While there was nothing wrong with "transferring out" in itself, Townshend would use it repeatedly as a means of advancement, and in doing so, create a reputation which was not favorable.

Townshend also attempted to employ another tool to support his aim of transferring: he used his family connections to petition on his behalf and in doing so moved outside of the military chain of command. Again, while networking is not intrinsically wrong, Townshend would use his contacts shamelessly and his non-military connections time and time again, creating another unfavorable reputation. In time, his file would grow thick with petitions for advancement and postings which tried the patience of his friends and allies. For now, though, using his grandmother's contacts for a commission in the cavalry, with one of those ironies of the military system, he became one of three RMLI officers attached to the Egyptian Camel Corps!

Townshend would gain his first experience at the Battle of Abu Klea in January 1885, but the efforts were too little, too late: after 317 days of siege, Khartoum fell and Gordon was dead. Gordon became a great hero of Victorian Britain, and the Cult of the Besieged Hero would not have been lost on Townshend. Certainly he played upon it in his two subsequent sieges. For now, though, Townshend's campaign was almost over. He contracted enteric fever and subsequently dysentery and went home to England. However, Townshend did achieve two of his goals and in 1886 was transferred to the Indian Staff Corps and attached to a cavalry regiment, the Central Indian Horse (CIH). Three years of peaceful service later, Townshend was again itching for a change of scenery and petitioned the brother-in-law of the 5th Marquis, Redvers Buller,[2] to gain a position in the Egyptian Army. A transfer was arranged for Townshend.

Or maybe not. In 1891, Townshend was sent to Gilgit on the North West Frontier. Today, Gilgit is in the far north of Pakistan. Under "the Agent" of the Gilgit Agency, Colonel Durand, Townshend was to command the 1st (or Raga Pertab) Battalion of the Imperial Kashmir Contingent. Being 583 strong and still untrained, command would be demanding, but for the right character, it could be the making of him. Perhaps more importantly was his participation in the Hunza-Nagar Expedition, now yet another forgotten Victorian campaign but one in which three Victoria Crosses were won as part of the Great Game. Also involved in the campaign was Lieutenant Fenton Aylmer RE (Royal Engineers), who, as a general, would see his career ended for failing to relieve Townshend at Kut. Fenton was awarded the Victoria Cross and Townshend became military governor of Hunza and subsequently captain and then commanded 4 Squadron CIH.

In 1893, Townshend was appointed to command Fort Gupis, in the Hindu Kush of modern-day Pakistan midway between Gilgit and Chitral. Like Hunza and Nagar, Chitral was an unstable kingdom with murderous tendencies amongst the ruling family, caught in the middle of the Great Game and under the rapacious gaze of a neighbor. Townshend marched reinforcements to Chitral Fort and took command of the garrison where they were besieged from 3 March to 20 April 1895. The relief of Chitral up the Peshawar Valley was an achievement in its own right, but the establishment showed itself grateful to both forces. Townshend was "Mentioned in Dispatches" for the third time, promoted to brevet major and received the Most Honourable Order of the Bath (CB), upon which his biographer commented, "For a junior Captain, a CB was unprecedented."[3]

Townshend returned to England and rode the wave of public adulation which he adored. He dined with Her Majesty and the great and good of society — military, society, the nobility and the theatrical. While at home, he took a close interest in the affairs of the marquis, whom Townshend still had aspirations of succeeding. Then Townshend received an offer of a battalion in the Egyptian Army from General Sir Herbert Kitchener. The fact that the commander-in-chief offered the command of a battalion to a substantive captain who was not even under his command says something of Townshend's fame, but that fame can be a double-edged weapon.

Townshend arrived back in Cairo in February 1896, took command of the 12th Sudanese Battalion and began to cultivate the great and good of Anglo-Egyptian society. His timing was also fortuitous because, following the defeat of the Italians by the Ethiopians at Asowa on 1 March 1896, the Mahdists in the Sudan became more aggressive. Kitchener was urged by the British government to reconquer the Sudan, in part to relieve pressure on the Italians. Townshend's battalion participated in the expedition and fought at the Anglo-Egyptian victory at Ferkeh on 7 June 1896 and was "mentioned" for the fourth time, was promoted to brevet lieutenant colonel

and, when the campaigning resumed in 1898, received a fifth "mention" at the Battle of Atbara. Finally, Townshend commanded his battalion at Omdurman.

Here was an officer who was not without physical courage or the willingness to place himself in the middle of danger. He had also earned his promotions and awards and shown his ability to handle his commands well. But, having successfully led his battalion throughout the campaign and gained experience in major engagements, he resigned his command on 12 September 1898, to find himself unemployed although still an Indian Army officer. Townshend's bravery and ability were undoubted. Yet he seemed impervious to the negative effects that his attempts to manipulate the system for his own ends were creating. Eventually, he would have the regulations cited to him, but that would be a long time in the future. For now, his ambitions were tolerated, and even encourage. Townshend returned to England with three months' leave and set about arranging his next posting.

Townshend decided that a staff officer's post in India was his preferred next step on the career ladder. He sailed for India in 1899 and in July was offered a prestigious post, deputy assistant adjutant general, Punjabi Army, but was already considering alternatives, especially as the political situation in South Africa was deteriorating rapidly. In July Townshend wrote to Redvers Buller and, for good measure, General (later Field Marshal) Sir Evelyn Wood VC for alternative appointments, but in the end accepted DAAG. Yet despite the nature of this position, Townshend was in no hurry to reach India and, when he finally arrived, was informed that as such a post could not be held vacant, it had been filed and he should rejoin his regiment. Typically, Townshend was not to be deflected and went in person to petition Lord Curzon, the Viceroy, and second only to Her Majesty in the whole British Empire. Curzon supported Townshend and he was reinstated but, on arrival at Simla (the summer capital of British India), he received news of the death of the 5th Marquis and, as the 6th was unmarried and showed no intention of marrying, Townshend was naturally very interested. So interested, in fact, that he immediately applied for leave to settle the family affairs. Naturally this request was rejected, yet somehow he pulled strings and was on his way home again. Once home, not only did he write directly to Lord Curzon complaining about the difficulty of arranging leave, but also started pulling strings for a different appointment in South Africa. Indian Army Regulations were quoted to him in an attempt to get him to conform to the correct procedures.

Townshend arrived in Cape Town on 1 March 1900 to be informed that Ladysmith had been relieved after a siege of 118 days. Once ashore, however, confusion reigned, and no one knew what to do with Townshend. Kitchener again intervened and, by bypassing the chain of command, gained him employment with 1 Division. Further questions were asked about on whose authority Townshend was even in South Africa in the first place. Again, Kitchener intervened. Townshend found himself sent to 7 Division, where he was unwanted, and then offered an escort to General Robert's headquarters in Bloemfontein, only to be told he was too senior to fit in with the staff there. Ultimately, he became assistant adjutant general to the military governor of Bleomfontein and with it had his first experiences of staff work. He did not like it!

With the war entering its final phases, Townshend again started looking round for his next posting. He was still an officer in the CIH of the Indian Army but had expressed a desire to transfer to a British line regiment. Again, this was arranged, and a place was found for him in the Bedfordshire Regiment, a perfectly ordinary county regiment of the British Army. This was not what he had in mind, and he wrote directly to the secretary of state for war (in wartime!) to say that what he really wanted was something like the Irish Guards. Once again, officials far senior to him deemed to reply and act on his behalf. He was offered the Royal Fusiliers instead, which he believed was due to go to Cairo shortly. The Boer War had not been a great success for Townshend when many other "thrusters" had the opportunity to make a name for themselves. He also did not like staff work, even with the rank of colonel. On his return to England, he found that the 2nd Battalion, Royal Fusiliers, were not, after all, off to Cairo but were garrisoned in Dover. This is not what he had in mind at all.

After years of serving around the world and often being at the center of activity, or having his own command, Townshend found himself back at his substantive rank of major on garrison duties in a regiment of the line. He also did not get on with his commanding officer who thought that a period of regimental duties was just what Townshend needed. It wasn't, and Townshend immediately started looking round for a staff post again. This time, however, the patience of his supporters had worn thin, and he was told to stay put — he wanted regimental duties and he should at least complete his tour. Townshend would not take no for an answer. His commanding officer had also had enough of Townshend and had him transferred to the regimental depot at Hounslow Barracks, London — not exactly a career move, but it was a major's post and an independent command. After a year, Townshend arranged special leave to visit Canada to study likely America invasion routes and, coincidentally, follow the steps of his illustrious predecessor, Brigadier Townshend, who had fought with Wolfe at Quebec in 1759 for a biography Major Townshend was writing. On his return, he went straight to France to be hosted by a French infantry regiment (his wife was French), yet his prolonged absence did not seem to raise any eyebrows in the War Office. While in France, he met Lord Kitchener en route to India where he had been appointed commander-in-chief, and within a year Townshend was posted to India with the 1st Battalion.

Townshend's next step was to write directly to the adjutant general in India, Major General Horace Smith-Dorien, who in 1914 would command the British Expeditionary Force's II Corps at Le Cateau. Townshend pointed out that as a junior major, he was actually five years senior to his commanding officer, yet with the brevet system, he could hold the rank of lieutenant colonel, which could, and did, mean that a brevet officer could outrank his regimental officer by, for example, commanding a brigade containing his own regiment. The brevet rank could also be worn while serving on the staff. The potential for friction in this system is clear, and for an ambitious officer like Townshend, it gave grounds for pursuing his aims. Townshend was angling for a posting as Assistant Adjutant General (AAG), with the rank of full colonel. Initially, Smith-Dorien, as many before him, supported Townshend, but eventually Townshend had to be told that there were no vacancies for him and he would have to join his regiment, in Mandalay. When the battalion returned to the UK, to be posted to Parkhurst, Isle of Wight, this was, like Dover, not what Townshend had in mind (again), and he started petitioning (again). This failed, and he was posted back to Hounslow, which if it was not a "career move" first time around, certainly was not the second time around, but (again) he landed on his feet and was appointed temporary military attaché to Paris. This placed him close to his family and within the circle of the French army, which allowed him to cultivate connections on a European scale. The year 1906 saw him posted as second in command of the King's Shropshire Light Infantry in Fyzabad, India, with presumably yet another cap badge and, with the brevet system in operation again, commanding the Allahabad Brigade during the absence of the brigade commander for three months and finally as AAG to the 9th Division. In 1908, Townshend was promoted to substantive colonel and in 1909 was offered command of the River Colony District as a brigadier general, back in Bloemfontein.

Townshend would serve in South Africa until 1911, but after only five months in post, he took three months leave in the UK, during which he (again) angled for a command in the Mediterranean or the UK. With the creation of the Union of South Africa in 1911, his posting came to an end. In 1911, Townshend took leave in France, where he met, and formed a professional relationship with, General Foch, who was not yet the famous general he would become.

Following the Haldane Reforms to the volunteer part of the army, the Territorial Force (later the Territorial Army [TA]) was formed. Haldane, as secretary of state for war, intended that first-tour major generals were to command a Territorial division before commanding a regular division. Naturally, when informed of this, it was not what Townshend wanted, but Haldane was adamant and Townshend was selected to command the Home Counties Division. Five months later he was transferred to command the East Anglian Division. At least the location suited Townshend, as it included the family seat at Raynham Hall, even if the current marquis no longer lived there due to being financially impoverished. Townshend did not like the volunteer Territorials with their limited training — here was a man who had attended maneuvers of the French Army and now was dealing with having to adopt his training to incorporate his volunteers' entertainments or they would not attend training!

In June 1913, Townshend was posted to India to command the Jhansi Brigade as a brigadier general, and the following February he was offered the Rawal Pindi Brigade. With the international situation in Europe deteriorating — and clearly that was where careers were going to be made (again) — Townshend was pushing to return to Europe. This time, he was needed in India, and he would stay with the Indian Army. The North West Frontier became increasingly unstable as news of the Western Front reached the Raj. A "demonstration" was required and achieved its aims. Within the Indian Army, several regiments were "unstable," including Townshend's own 35th Sikhs. In a move which showed the good judgment and courage of the man, he bluffed the Sikhs into believing in his trust and faith in them — he chose that regiment to guard his quarters at night.

On 12 April 1915, Townshend would no doubt have been delighted to be informed that he had been appointed to command the 6th (Poona) Division.

If there is one man whose name is associated with Mesopotamia, it is, for better or for worse, Townshend. He fills the place held by Allenby in Palestine or Haig on the Western Front. There is no doubting his personal bravery. Many of his machinations to obtain postings around the empire were to put him in the center of military activities, which is where careers were made or lost — most noticeably the Boer War was a professional failure in that respect. Yet he failed to "play the game," with constant machinations to achieve favorable postings, often only to decide it was not what he wanted and then attempt to go back to his previous theater of service. The constant hopping between cap badges, regimental to staff duties, even services and armies, was tolerated (and only served to encourage him further) until eventually he was told to "shut up, put up and serve your time." For all his schemes and operational experience, he did not rise through the ranks particularly quickly. When posted to the 1st Battalion, Royal Fusiliers, he was senior in length of service to his commanding officer yet junior in rank.

He also had the "common touch" with his soldiers, which comes out with the handling of the 35th Shikhs, and most noticeably with the "Kuttites" during the siege. Yet he did not seem to get on well with the Territorials, and he disliked his sepoys in Mesopotamia.

He vacillated between being extremely professional and uninterested. Certainly he had no interest in regimental duties in provincial garrisons or staff duties. His immediate response to any new posting was to request extensive periods of leave. He knew his "art" very well and was well read on military history, especially Napoleon and the 1st Marquis — on the evening before leading the advance up the Tigris, Townshend dined with Nunn, who considered him to be "excellent company when one could get him off the subject of Napoleon" and said that he "discoursed at great length" about a victory of his ancestor. On that occasion there was no mention of the banjo.[4]

Townshend was probably a "ladies' man" who enjoyed the adulation as a hero of the Victorian age, and, with the wide range of supporters he managed to accumulate, it is difficult to imagine that he was a bore at dinner and parties. He also moved in theatrical circles, acquiring another circle of friends and supporters with which he corresponded. He was a keen attendee of the theater — at Fort Gupis in 1894, he had plastered the mud walls of his room with illustrations from Parisian theater and entertained his guests with French songs on the banjo. His theatrical flair manifested itself through his banjo, with which he entertained many over the years in obscure imperial backwaters; his literary flair manifested itself in his biography of the 1st Marquis and also, where it was perhaps less appropriate, in his petitions for advancement or postings. During and after the Siege of Kut, communiqués and self-justifying books proved further outlet.[5]

Here was a complex man, but then all men are complex, especially those who aspire for high office, and Townshend certainly did. He was not without his faults, but when properly motivated (i.e., when he wanted to do the job in hand), he could be thoroughly professional. He was not a "high flier," but there must have been something in the man which many in the political and military elite of late Victorian Britain into the early years of the 20th century saw and considered worthwhile to cultivate — why else would lords, generals, even the viceroy tolerate his impertinent and self-seeking correspondence, even accommodating his requests?

Break Out from Qurna: Amphibious Landings amongst the Marshes

Qurna, as already mentioned, was not a popular posting for soldiers of the II Indian Army Corps. It was surrounded by inundations on all sides, which were actually two feet higher than the level of the camp. In 1915 the floodwaters were reportedly higher than normal, and Spackman's 48th Pioneers worked hard to fight back the waters which breached the berms — they saved the hospital but found their brigade commander's tent in two feet of water.

The water level outside the town was generally 3 feet deep, but could be 20 feet deep over depressions, like irrigation ditches. In addition to persistent, although usually ineffectual, demonstrations by the local tribes (usually consisting of galloping towards the camp, firing off a few rifle rounds, and then retiring just as quickly), there were four Turkish positions about three miles north of Qurna. Each position was, like Qurna, an island of raised land in the inundation. On the left bank of the Tigris (such as it was) was One Tree Hill; although in a straight line from Qurna, it was the second-furthest position. On the right bank, running south to north away from Qurna and roughly parallel to the "river" were Norfolk Hill and One Tower Hill, with Shrapnel Hill and Gun Hill further north but also away from the river. Turkish artillery on One Gun Hill opened fire on Qurna on 19 March.[6]

To help clear the river, 400 rupees was paid for every mine recovered from the river. This helped clear the river and kept the local Arabs "gainfully employed" rather than causing mischief with Townshend's troops.[7]

Given the nature of the terrain which his army had to cross, Townshend decided that the only practical means of reaching the Turkish posts was to use the local Arab *bellums*—half ton canoes, 30 to 40 feet long, which looked cumbersome, although in fact they were slick on the move, but difficult to maneuver. Townshend selected his 17th Brigade for the attacks by *bellum*. Sixty were allocated to each battalion, and the soldiers set about familiarizing themselves with their new modes of transport. There were 328 *bellums* requisitioned, of which 96 were fitted with iron plates as a form of armor. The armor would be found to be an encumbrance which snagged when trying to pass through the reeds and would be removed during the day of the battle. Each *bellum* carried 10 men plus 125 rounds of reserve ammunition, two sandbags per man, one day's rations per man, and a waterproof sheet. A *bellum* is poled, like a punt, in shallow water but can be paddled like a canoe in deeper water. With the daytime temperatures starting to rise again, one can imagine the soldiers' fun and games which resulted from "training," the exasperation of their instructors and the amusement provided to the local Arabs.[8]

As well as the *bellums*, field guns, machine guns and field ambulances would travel on rafts and the Royal Navy would accompany. HMS *Espiègle, Odin, Comet* and *Clio; Shaitan, Lawrence, Miner* and *Lewis Pelly* acted as minesweepers (*Shaitan* and *Sumana* would sweep for mines with a chain dragged between them through the water); *Mejideh, Blosse Lynch* and *P-1;* four armed launches, two naval horse boats armed with 4.7-inch naval guns and several smaller boats: "Townshend's Regatta" was born.[9]

As a student of Napoleon, Townshend had a habit of comparing and justifying his actions with those of the Corsican who wanted to master Europe. When faced with devising a strategy for advancing north of Qurna, he was less than happy about the prospects of success. He considered a frontal assault to be costly and unnecessary and was opposed to the Napoleonic strategy. With Gorringe's 12th Division operating on the Ahwaz in Persia, Townshend suggested that he hold the Turks while Gorringe attacked from the east. Nixon, who at that point had not even visited Qurna, did not agree—he wanted to avoid violating Persian neutrality. So, a frontal assault it would have to be. Townshend also grumbled about the lack of artillery, the removal of his cavalry force (although they would not be much use in the floods) and the removal of his

18th Brigade to garrison Dirhamiyeh, southwest of Basra and, in Townshend's opinion, from where there was no realistic threat. He thought that a battalion would suffice. He also grumbled that it appeared that soldiers for all of the various duties to be carried out in Basra—military police, clerks, drivers—were drawn from 6th Division. Despite planning a methodical approach which attacked each objective sequentially and so provided maximum fire support to the attacking unit, Townshend was worried:

> Supposing the attack of the 17th Brigade was repulsed! It would be a veritable disaster, for it would be almost impossible for it to retreat. The labour of pushing and pulling the *bellums* through the thick reeds was immense, and progress painfully slow. All the wounded would be drowned ... the advance of the infantry in their flimsy *bellums*, struggling through deep water thick with reeds, to close with redoubts pumping shrapnel on them.[10]

Townshend's attack on the Turkish positions was launched at 0600 hours on 31 May 1915 across miles of flooded desert which offered no protection from the Turks or the sun—the temperature was reported to reach 100F. *Espiègle* carried Townshend and General Nixon, whose presence was unrequired but who nevertheless considered his presence necessary. The ships kept to the main channel and ahead of the *bellums*, whose crews found the work heavy going. They would have to dismount to push the *bellums* through the reeds where the water was shallow.

The 22nd Punjabis easily stormed One Tree Hill at 0630 hours, which was held by a garrison of just 20 who promptly surrendered. The Punjabis then dug in to set up their machine guns on One Tower Hill to "fire in" (with naval gunfire support) the Ox and Bucks and 119th Infantry. Turkish artillery at Abu Aran fired on the Punjabis inflicting seven casualties.

Norfolk Hill was the objective of the Oxfordshire and Buckinghamshire Light Infantry and the 119th. They were "fired in" by their machine guns and the 30th Mountain Battery. The first 600 yards was covered rapidly until they disembarked 100 yards from the island and waded ashore. Captain Brooke led the assault, being the first man into the redoubt, where he was killed. Five men were wounded. The garrison of 135 suffered 75 casualties before surrendering. The island was secured by 0730 hours, and, with a guard left to supervise the prisoners, the Ox and Bucks reembarked and rejoined the battle.

One Tower Hill became the object of the British artillery, naval gunfire and machine guns. The Ox and Bucks and the 119th were subject to very heavy, yet inaccurate, rifle fire, which was eventually suppressed by the British machine guns. When the island was stormed and secured by 0930 hours, the switchboard for firing the mines was discovered, together with the Turkish officer in charge.

Shrapnel Hill was the forth objective. The 103rd Mahrattas had approached slowly through the reeds under fire from the Turks, who could see their poles above the reeds. At about

0930 hours, the Mahrattas were a mile from their objective. But as soon as the *bellums* grounded and the Mahrattas jumped ashore, the garrison surrendered at 1100 hours.

One Gun Hill now became the target of all the British artillery and machine guns, and the garrison there surrendered by 1130 hours. All five objectives had been secured for minimal loss by midday.[11]

Meanwhile, General Nixon commanded two flanking actions. To the east, *Comet* and a 4.7-inch naval gun on a horse barge moved up the Shwaiyb and bombarded Ruta to disrupt the Turkish withdrawal. To the west, two more ships led by *Sushan* moved up the Al-Huwair (a tributary of the Euphrates) to divert the marsh Arabs from the main attack. Nunn commented that the left flank was "heavily engaged" by marsh Arabs who shot at the soldiers with everything from blunderbusses to stolen modern rifles.[12]

During the battle, another first occurred in Mesopotamia: the first flight by the Royal Flying Corps (RFC). Two aircraft had arrived by sea and been assembled. The inaugural flights had been delayed because it had proved difficult to find a long enough piece of dry ground to take off from. Captain Broke-Smith had arrived in Basra from Bombay on 9 April. An aerodrome was selected at Tanumah opposite Basra on the left bank of the Shatt-al-Arab. The initial pilots were from Australia and New Zealand and flew 70-hp Renault-powered Maurice-Farmans, which could reach 800 feet and 55 mph. To avoid confusion with Turkish airplanes whose insignia was a crescent in a circle, the British initially used a black stripe.[13]

The following day, 1 June, Townshend resumed the advance towards Abu Aran, a village en route to Ruta. After a bombardment of Baharan, the next "dry" feature upriver, to which the Turks did not reply, minesweeping vessels moved ahead of the regatta, accompanied by the Turkish mines officer captured the previous day who pointed out the location of the mines. Riflemen were placed on the bows to shoot at anything suspicious in the water, and when a large, wild pig was mistaken for a mine and shot, it made a welcome supplement to the campaign food.[14]

The infantry followed alongside the ships in the *bellums*. The RFC appeared again and dropped a message beside the *Espiègle*, which revealed that not only was Abu Aran empty (which explained why there was no artillery fire during the bombardment) but so too were Ruta and Muzaibila, and that the Turks were retreating up the river on anything which would float.[15]

At Abu Aran, Townshend ordered an advance to Ezra's Tomb. The smoke from the retreating steamers could be seen, but navigation was difficult: the Tigris meanders, and with the floodwaters, it was not easy to determine where the deep-water channel (the "river") was compared with the shallower floodwaters. The Regatta was, nevertheless, able to get within range of the *Marmaris* and a steamer, *Mosul*. The four-inch guns were fired to good effect and forced the Turks to cast off the lighters and *mahailas* (similar to a *dhow* in design for river use)

which they were towing. These were full of soldiers and other military stores and were captured at Ezra's Tomb. At Ezra's Tomb, Townshend left the *Odin* with his divisional staff to care for the prisoners. The staff was also to organize the remainder of the Regatta into appropriate formations and to send them onwards up the river. The 16th Brigade and the 30th Mountain Battery disembarked while Townshend advanced with the 17th Brigade.[16]

Townshend now boarded the *Espiègle* with Nunn and Cox and set off up the river accompanied by *Shaitan* and *Comet*. That evening, the ships came across a *mahaila* full of Turkish troops which had been cast off during the retreat. Nunn decided that with dark approaching, the ships should anchor and wait for the moon. The Turkish vessels were out of sight so the situation appeared safe. Once the engines were switched off, though, shouting could be heard. Searchlights were turned on to reveal more cast-off vessels full of Turkish soldiers and stores, and the half-sunk *Bulbul*, hit earlier in the day. Amongst the passengers were several Germans, who had made it ashore only to be robbed of everything and were almost naked; they were only too happy to surrender to Nunn.[17]

When the moon rose at 0200 hours on 2 June, the ships (*Espiègle*, *Clio*, *Comet*, *Miner*, *Shitan* and *Sumana*) set off once again and soon came across the *Marmaris*, aground and ablaze, having been hit by shells the previous day. Nearby was another steamer, *Mosul*, also aground and willing to surrender. With the river becoming too shallow for *Espiègle*, Nunn transferred his command to *Comet*, still with Townshend and Cox, and continued up the river accompanied by *Sumana*, *Shaitan* and *Lewis Pelly*, each towing a barge-mounted 4.7-inch gun. They saw no Turkish troops all day and anchored for the night at 1900 hours. During the night, a local sheikh arrived and hollered the Regatta. Townshend brought him aboard and served him coffee. During their conversation, Townshend "entrusted" the sheikh with secret information: 15,000 British troops were following and could he collect supplies to feed them? Of course this information was for the sheikh only, but Townshend was confident that it would soon be across the region.[18]

The following morning, the 3rd, *Comet* and *Shaitan* set off with the other vessels following. The villages were showing white flags, and there were shouts of welcome from the inhabitants. Clearly the secret information had not remained secret for long. Twelve miles short of Al-Amara, Townshend called a halt while he discussed what to do with the town. Via the *Comet's* radio he had been informed that an RFC flight over the town reported columns of Turkish troops moving into the town. There were also three steamers in the town taking on troops. This was a town of some 10,000 inhabitants and would have had its own troops in addition to those seen advancing there.[19] Townshend surveyed his own force: 41 officers and men all told. Nunn and Cox advocated pushing on. Townshend needed some convincing. What would the newspaper headlines make of a divisional commander being captured in an obscure

Arab town? It would be career ending, as indeed it was for him about a year later. But there are times when a commander just has to take a chance, and Townshend was certainly not one to miss out on the prospect of glory, or to wait while the rest of the Regatta caught up.

At 0945 hours, *Shaitan* and *Comet* set off for Al-Amara. *Shaitan*, commanded by Lieutenant Mark Singleton, went ahead. As he entered a long straight of the river through the town, Singleton spied a bridge of boats with Turkish troops crossing to embark on a steamer. The steamer also spied *Shaitan*, cast off, and tried to get through a gap in the bridge of boats and escape. *Shaitan* fired a warning shot and made for full speed, heading for the gap in the bridge of boats. Just beyond, the river makes a sharp left turn. *Shaitan* shot round the bend and confronted some 2,000 Turkish troops. No one fired a shot. About half a mile outside the town, *Shaitan* tied up, and Singleton accepted the surrender of six officers and about 100 men. The officers were invited aboard, disarmed, and returned to Al-Amara with the soldiers marching along the bank. They were joined by more armed Turkish troops, who simply surrendered. Back at the bridge of boats, the soldiers sat down outside a coffee shop. In this mad dash, some 2,500 Turkish troops had been routed, 11 officers and 250 men captured. *Comet* was still a mile south of Al-Amara. Singleton was awarded the Distinguished Service Order, and two members of the crew received the Distinguished Service Medal, CPO (Chief Petty Officer) Roberts, RNR, (Royal Naval Reserve) and Gunlayer Leading Seaman Rowe.[20]

When Townshend and Cox arrived, at 1330 hours, they met the governor and the commandant of the town, and a number of other Turkish officers, all of whom surrendered. Orders were given to collect supplies for the 15,000 British soldiers who were following. On the riverbank, Lieutenant Palmer, RN (Royal Navy), stood guard with two sailors, one marine and a dozen West Kents and Hampshires. A message was received that a battalion of the Constantinople Fire Brigade, an elite regiment of the Turkish Army, wanted to surrender. Palmer, with an interpreter, one marine and one seaman, and a huge amount of courage, marched off to receive the surrender of 400 fully-armed troops. After their arms had been stacked, Palmer marched at the head of the regiment, with the marine and sailor at the rear, to the river and onto a lighter, which was moored in the middle of the river under the guns of the two Royal Navy ships.

Further Turkish troops were pouring into the town. These were probably those identified by the RFC. They were not, as had been assumed, reinforcements heading to stabilize the situation on the Tigris but were retreating from Gorringe's expedition on the Ahwaz. Fearing that the meager British force would be overwhelmed, *Shaitan* sailed to the edge of the town and fired a few shells to scare off the Turks. Most fled away from the town, but, unperturbed, a group of 50 surrendered to the *Shaitan*. Yet the Turks kept trying to get into the town

to surrender. The local tribe was the Beni Lam, whose name keeps reappearing in accounts of Mesopotamia—like Hubbard's account from just before the war—and the Turkish soldiers were in fear of the Beni Lam's reputation. They did not want to fall into the Beni Lam's hands, which explains their enthusiasm to surrender.

Night fell in Al-Amara. A curfew was called, with the threat of being shot if anyone was seen on the streets. A searchlight was seen further down the river, but it halted for the night: the 16th Brigade reached Qalat Salih at about 0100 hours.[21] The group, for they can hardly be called an army, must have spent an anxious and restless night. However, the night passed uneventfully for them. During the night, though, the inhabitants caught on to the reality of the situation; Maxim guns were used to quieten the inhabitants. In the morning, looting began, but they were too late, and an hour after dawn, a company of Dorsets arrived. Order was restored with a few overhead shots. More British troops arrived during the day, and Nixon arrived in the evening.

Seventeen field guns, 2,000 prisoners together with arms, ammunition and several vessels were captured in Al-Amara.

Total British casualties for the whole of Townshend's Regatta were reported as 4 killed and 21 wounded.[22]

As an example of shear guts, derring-do, spirit, bluff and all of those other characteristics attributed to the British at the height of empire, the capture of Al-Amara must rank as one of the great exploits. The *Official History* described the actions of Singleton and his eight men thus: "Greater daring than that of *Shaitan* can hardly be imagined."[23]

Qurna to Al-Amara is about 60 miles as the crow flies; much further as the river meanders and the deep-water channel disappeared into marsh. No British general managed to advance that far in 1915. No British general in 1915 managed to conduct a divisional-level operation with so few casualties. In this action, Townshend had captured a significant enemy town and extended British control near enough to the edge of the Basra *vilayet* on the Tigris. Bear in mind that in 1915, what we think of as Iraq was three separate *vilayets*, unconnected. Al-Amara would also serve as a base from which to protect the oil fields. As we have seen, Turkish troops from there had retired to Al-Amara. There was every reason to halt at the edge of Basra *vilayet* without any loss of face; mission accomplished.

There were three problems with resting at Al-Amara. First of all, to complete the occupation of Basra *vilayet* required the occupation of Nasariya on the Euphrates. This attack would be undertaken by the 12th Division. Joining the Tigris and Euphrates was a canal, the Shatt-al-Hai, which was believed to be navigable. The Tigris end of the canal came out at Kut, the next major town up the Tigris, just over the border into Baghdad *vilayet*. By garrisoning both towns, they would be mutually supporting in the event of an attack on either. One successful campaign necessitated another. Secondly, through Townshend's success, there was no reason not to continue pursuing the Turks northwards while they were on the run. Thirdly, Baghdad remained a glittering prize — this city of great antiquity, capital of one of the world's great civilizations, and so it remained in the minds of military planners even if the 1915 city did not live up to those dreams — and in the minds of military planners amongst the failures and stalemates of 1915, a prize which was too glittering to ignore. Like the more famous capture of Jerusalem, Baghdad was a "great moral and political if not strategic prize."[24] Kut would be just one more little step towards Baghdad.

Al-Amara, 1915–2005

In 1915, Al-Amara was a relatively new town, founded in 1866 as the administrative center of that part of the Basra *vilayet.* Its climate was drier and so more comfortable than Basra and it became a more popular posting.[25] This is how Wilfred Nunn described the town on his arrival:

> We had arrived at quite a decent-looking town, which, situated on the eastern bank of the Tigris, to which it shows a long row of regular, well-built houses, is of symmetrical appearance and possesses a fine frontage to the river. Amara looks across the river towards groves of feathery crested palm-trees and scattered dots of houses along the western bank — the whole effect, under a blue sky, in brilliant sunshine, being very picturesque.

When Lieutenant Spackman arrived, in the wake of the occupation, he considered that the temperature was cooler, although still 100F and much less humid. The Jahala Canal, just north of the town, and away from the local ladies, was a popular bathing place. The open market provided all of the fresh fruit and vegetables he required — his duties included provisioning his regiment's officers' mess — and he was able to stand there and watch colorful caravans of Persians, Kurds, Bakhtiaris and Lurs trading with the Arabs, Jews, Armenians, Chaldeans, Sabeans and Greeks of Al-Amara. There was even a sect of devil worshipers! Trade along the Silk Road into Central Asia, or east via the Pusht-i-Kuh mountains, or north into mountains towards the Caucasus continued regardless of some European war which was intruding on their life.[26]

Lieutenant Colonel Tennant who arrived in 1916 to command the RFC in Mesopotamia described the town as being composed of the "regulation Arab houses of mud bricks" on either side of the river. He commented on the bazaar's fame for silverwork where Jews, Chaldeans, Arabs, Persians and Indians thronged. There were by then two miles of hospital tents along the river and even surrounding the gallows in a square. One of the Arab houses had been turned into an officers' mess where a cool whiskey and soda could be enjoyed on the veranda.[27]

Camp Abu Naji was established south of Al-Amara on the west bank. It was there that the British Army reestablished a base in 2003. The explanation for the camp's name given to the author was the camp of the "son of a good man," which did not translate correctly. Abu does mean "son of" in Arabic. In post-war Iraq, Gertrude Bell was friends with a "fruit and vegetable" grower named Haji Naji who, at the time of King Faisal's coronation, was sufficiently well connected to throw a party for Faisal, Bell and Kinahan Cornwallis, who had been appointed as Faisal's advisor. To be a fruit and vegetable grower of sufficient standing to host the king, one needed to be a significant landowner. "Abu Naji" in this context may have referred not to sons in a literal sense but to "adopted" sons of Haji Naji, a man of significant standing who was, in that sense, a "good man."

Al-Amarah in 2005, when the author served there, did not reflect the positive comments from 1915. The town had grown across both sides of the river and many of the palm trees had gone. The draining of the marshes may also have dried out the terrain. The previous year had seen a major campaign against the British forces when CIMIC (Civil Military Co-Operation) House in the town came under repeated attack and Private Johnson Beharry won the Victoria Cross.[28]

For John Simpson, the BBC reporter, in all of his visits to Saddam's Iraq, the only province he was not allowed to visit was Maysan, with Al-Amara as its capital. Camp Abu Naji had grown to house a full army corps but still failed to subdue the descendants of the Beni Lam who had terrorized the Turkish army in 1915. The camp known to the British soldiers was greatly reduced; all patrols out to the main road passed through ruins of the larger camp.

4

Nasariya, June–July 1915

From Qurna at the head of the Shatt-al-Arab, the Euphrates extends away to the west, through Hammar Lake to Suq-ash-Shuyukh, Nasariya, and away towards Syria and Anatolia. The river from Qurna to Hammar was referred to as the Old Channel; a newer canal, the New Channel, took a more direct route towards Basra.

Nasariya had been the base from which the 1915 Turkish counter-attack had been launched against Shaiba, so the British authorities at Basra had kept one eye in that direction, even as Townshend had raced up the Tigris. The British authorities had also been keeping one eye on the Karun River into Persia, which meant there was a constant pull on limited resources. It may have been possible to place a blocking force somewhere on the Euphrates at a safe distance to protect the camps at Qurna and Shaiba, yet easily accessible by water to resupply and reinforce. However, Nasariya attracted the interests of ambitious generals and politicians for two reasons. Firstly, from Nasariya the Shatt-al-Hai extended northwards to Kut on the Tigris. By occupying both of these towns, the garrisons could be mutually supporting rather than separated by hundreds of miles of desert. This assumption proved to be erroneous, as for most of the year the water levels were too low to be of any use and would run dry 30 miles north of Nasariya.[1] Secondly, Nasariya sat within the Basra *vilayet*. Delamain's original instructions had been to capture Basra. If these instructions were read as meaning Basra *vilayet*, rather than just Basra town, then it was necessary to send an expedition to capture Nasariya.

Not everyone considered such expansion necessary. Captain Arnold Wilson who served on Gorringe's staff as a political officer during the Nasariya operations considered that they had already conquered enough to be secure: "Basra was easily defendable, and once we held Amara and Qurna the narrow strip of land along the Tigris was unlikely to be the scene of serious fighting."[2]

While Gorringe had been operating on the Ahwaz, it had been down to the Royal Navy to blockade the Euphrates. It transported army detachments around the waterways and provided fire support on demand. The navy also explored the wa-terways towards Hammar Lake as far as Kabaish (or Chabaish) which was the limit of travel for the navy's sloops. On 28 April, the *Lewis Pelly* commanded by Lieutenant W.V.H. Harris found three improvised mines off El Huir Creek, five miles west of Qurna. Fortunately, they were all made safe before they could cause any damage.

On 5 May, *Espiègle* led *Odin*, and the river steamers *Salimi*, *Shushan* and *Massoudieh*, and accompanied by Arab tribesmen in *bellums* from the friendly sheikh of Medina. Their objective was the hostile village of Hallaf. It was a bloodless (at least for the British) "demonstration." Today, such collective punishment would be forbidden in military operations, and even at the time, there were those who doubted their effectiveness. The "demonstrations" did not deter Arab attacks, which plagued the British Army throughout its time in Mesopotamia, and so can be seen as a crude response arising from the frustration of being unable get along with the indigenous population. The allied Arabs returned laden with loot, with which they were evidently pleased. They were further delighted to be saluted by a blast from the ship's siren. It was not exactly the Spithead review, as Nunn observed, but then this was the essential nature of riverine warfare in 1915 Mesopotamia.[3]

On the 8th, another similar operation consisting of the same sloops and river steamers, plus 24 *bellums* of infantry from Qurna, was carried out against the village of Mazra, three miles west of Qurna. They returned to Qurna that evening having destroyed or captured 16 large *mahailas*.

The following day, the 9th, *Shushan*, commanded by Lieutenant Commander Cookson RN conducted a reconnaissance of the El Huir Creek to determine whether or not it was sufficiently navigable to be used for a flanking movement. She was equipped with two three-pounders and three Maxims, plus an additional complement of 30 men from the Ox and Bucks Light Infantry. The *Shushan* attracted considerable hostile fire from the local tribesmen hidden in the tall reeds at the edge of the creek. During this engagement, Cookson was severely wounded in the right side of the chest, and three soldiers received flesh wounds. Fortunately, *Shushan* had not traveled alone. *Clio* had anchored in the Euphrates near the mouth of the creek, and her four-inch guns were sufficient to dissuade the Arabs from following the *Shushan*.

Five days later, on the 14th, a reconnaissance was conducted through Hammar Lake to the Akaika Channel which led to Nasariya. It was discovered that a dam had been built across the channel which was covered by two Turkish launches. This dam was an integral part of the local irrigation plan and was not erected against the British. The launches fired at the Royal Navy's inquisitiveness, as did Arabs from the shore. The launches were outgunned and quickly withdrew. It was also understood that there were mines and sunken vessels beyond the dam.[4]

Intelligence reports considered that there were an estimated seven Turkish battalions with a few guns at Nasariya, which lay some 110 miles northwest of Basra and 90 miles from Qurna. These were supported by two British-built Thorney-croft launches armed with one-pound quick-firing "pom-pom" guns. These had already been encountered by the Royal Navy in the Akaika Channel where they were outgunned, but with the combination of bends in the river and trees, the launches could hide to negate the greater firepower of the British vessels. There were also the local Arab tribes, who could be counted on to oppose a British expedition, at least until the Turks were defeated.

A successful assault along the Euphrates could defeat the remaining Turkish forces, and, hopefully, through a show of British force, the local tribes would then become friendly, or at least cooperative, rather than aggressively anti–British. This in turn would provide "defense in depth" to cover the core of the British operations along the Shatt-al-Arab. Unfortunately, future events would prove that the Nasariya area became yet another intractable mire. The local Muntafiq Confederation was as problematic as the Beni Lam where around Al-Amarah. This was not a problem particular to the British: they merely inherited the hostility which had previously been reserved for the Turks. Ajaimi, the sheikh of the Muntafiq, remained pro–Turkish throughout the war.[5] The 1920 uprising would start there — the Shi'a religious centers of Najaf and Karbala both lie in this area.

Nasariya was also the site of Ur of the Chaldees, one of the many great archaeological sites with which Iraq is blessed. Ur may not be as familiar to the wider world as Babylon, but it has its own significance in the biblical world: Ur was the birth-place of Abraham. The first recorded use of the wheel and writ-ten laws have also been attributed to Ur. In 2007, the author was fortunate enough to visit Ur, which lay within the perime-ter of the former Iraqi Air Force base at Talil, then occupied by the U.S. military but with British, Australian and Romanian contingents. *Talil* is Arabic for "hills," and out of the flat Mesopotamian plain rises a ziggurat, a flat-topped pyramid. From the reconstructed summit, the author was reminded of the biblical story where Abraham took his son to the summit

of a mountain to sacrifice him to God when God, accepting Abraham's devotion, provided a lamb trapped in a bush as an alternative sacrifice. Mesopotamia, as the reader is by now well aware, is very flat, and there are no natural hills within sight of Ur. The sensation of being in touch with history, and more importantly a part of history which is so woven into Western culture, was all-pervasive. The first archaeological dig at Ur took place in the 1850s, but between 1922 and 1934, Sir Charles Leonard Woolley undertook the most systematic exploration in a joint British Museum and University of Pennsylvania funded project. One of Woolley's assistants at Ur, Max Mal-lowen, became Agatha Christie's second husband. Christie vis-ited the archaeological site, and so it is not surprising that in her 1934 *Murder on the Orient Express*, Colonel Arbuthnot ex-plained to Hercule Poirot that his unusual choice of traveling overland from India to Britain was to visit the ruins at Ur. Tennant, commanding the RFC in Mesopotamia in the mid-dle years of the war, would also try to visit the ruins (it is unclear from his account if he got there or not due to the un-expected arrival of a German aircraft), and Wilfred Nunn would observe the ruins as he passed in 1915. Nunn's crewmen were less appreciative of the archaeological marvel which they experienced at the king-emperor's expense and responded, "There's air."[6]

The author was fortunate enough to fly over the picturesque marshes to Talil. In 1915, the British Army would have no such luck. Whatever the difficulties with navigating the convoluted and erratic Tigris, the Euphrates was far worse.

On 10 June, Nixon had been asked by the Indian authorities for his plans to complete the occupation of the Basra *vilayet* as India was seeking London's approval. Nixon replied that he was planning for the occupation of Nasariya, which, together with Al-Amara, would complete that objective, although he thought that the occupation of Kut would strengthen his hold. On the 13th, the viceroy cabled Chamberlain in the India Office recommending the occupation of Nasariya. No reply was received. On the 22nd, the viceroy assumed London had agreed to the Nasariya plan and ordered Nixon to proceed. It was command and control by omission. Chamberlain's approval arrived on the 27th.[7]

The 30th Brigade, commanded by Brigadier General C.J. Melliss VC, from General Gorringe's incomplete 12th Division, was chosen for the expedition along the Euphrates:

1/4th Hampshires (from the 33rd Brigade)

2/7th Gurkhas

24th Punjabis

76th Punjabis

48th Pioneers (two double coys)

63rd Battery, RFA

30th Mountain Battery

Four 4.7-inch guns on horse boats

The author before the ziggurat at Ur, following in the tradition of Vice Admiral Wilfred Nunn, Lieutenant Colonel J.E. Tennant, Dame Agatha Christie, Sir Leonard Woolley and Sir Max Mallowan. The brick facade is modern, but the original core is visible above the modern brickwork. Summer 2007 (author's collection).

12th Company, Sappers and Miners

12th Signals Company (section)[8]

Melliss was deeply unimpressed with the prospects, as he wrote to his wife:

> This is a rotten show, I wish you could see the situation as I write. Imagine a large flat bottomed river steamer boat with a large iron barge on either side, all crammed with men ... packed like sardines. Now imagine a dozen of this sort of river steamer each towing two iron barges, all crammed with men. This is Gorringe's show to capture Nasiriyeh.... It was neither fun nor excitement nor war.[9]

At the time Melliss wrote this, the brigade was still on Lake Hammar, and although there was sporadic firing, they had yet to reach the Turkish defenses where the real fighting and discomfort would begin.

Whatever the hazards, if ever a determined general was needed to force through a victory on the Euphrates, it was Gorringe. Russell Brandon, writing in 1969, considered him to be

> the ideal man for a relentless slog. A big man, highly coloured, deeply tanned, officious and utterly without tact, he reminded those less insensitive than himself of an enormous he-goat, and allowed nothing — not Turks, Nurretin, counter-attacks, casualties, swamps, Marsh Arabs or deeply entrenched redoubts — to stop him.[10]

The 30th Brigade left Qurna at the height of summer — at 0400 hours on 27 June. Once again, Nunn and his reliable sailors escorted the army. The sloops *Espiègle*, *Odin* and *Miner* were unable to progress beyond Kabaish, so Nunn transferred to *Shushan*. With the *Muzaffi* and *Massoudieh*, these three stern-wheeled steamers were armed with 12-pounder, 3-pounder and Maxim machine guns. *Sumana* had two horse barges lashed to its side with 4.7-inch guns. These old stern-wheelers were of considerable antiquity and military experience, having originally been built for the 1884 Gordon Relief Expedition along the Nile to Khartoum, in which Townshend had served in the Egyptian Army. Some armor plating was added to these vessels, but this was limited so as not to increase their draft, which would further limit their passage through Hammar Lake.[11] Gorringe traveled on *Blosse Lynch* and was accompanied by *Mejideh* and *Malamir*. Each was armed with two 18-pounder guns from the Royal Artillery. Four barges accompanied the expedition, *T1* and *T4*, *Shuhrur* and *Shirin*, each pulling *mahailas*, or lighters, crammed with stores of all kinds. The mountain artillery was transported on *bellums*, which were taken along to provide the infantry with mobility in the flooded areas.[12]

The first stage of the journey was through 30 miles of waterways flanked by tall reeds to Kabaish, until the expedition reached the 15-mile-long Hammar. In June, the lake contained about five feet of water, falling to three feet as the summer progressed, although on occasion as little as 18 inches.[13] Ultimately, supplies would have to be transported by *bellums*, and even then they would have to be manhandled. The broad lake was dotted with small islands, some inhabited, with fishermen on *mashufs*, fishing nets in the creeks and water buffalo shoulder deep in mud and water. There was no chartered passage through the many shallows, and many boats grounded, only to be manhandled back into the deeper water. As time passed and the water level fell, there was a very real risk that the larger vessels would be trapped either side of the lake with the associated difficulties of resupplying, relieving or reinforcing any troops on the Nasariya side. These extra demands exasperated the chronic shortage of shipping which was already struggling to supply troops on the Tigris. Once again the British Army was at the mercy of the rivers. That this expedition was undertaken at the worst possible time of the year for the British Army shows the impatience of Cox and Nixon, and once again the burden would fall upon the Tommy and the sepoy. Birch Reynoldson described the conditions that were encountered, all of which would have been well known to Nixon before ordering the advance:

> Sickness of all kinds became rife, sun-stroke and heat-stroke were common, fever and dysentery and para-typhoid — ample warning was given to those responsible of the difficulties to be expected if they should ever have to deal with such a rush of casualties.... Probably seldom before have British, or, for that matter native, troops been required to fight under such terrible conditions of weather and climate, in a difficult country, against a resolute enemy.[14]

The alternative route, though the desert at the height of summer, would have been infinitely worse.

Gorringe's flotilla reached the Akaika Channel on the far side of the lake on 27 June 1915. Gorringe joined Nunn aboard *Shushan* at 1445 hours that afternoon to explore the dam, or bund, which effectively blocked the exit from the lake. Although the dam was some 30 feet wide at the top and built very strongly from sunken *mahailas*, logs, rocks and mud, Gorringe was in his element — he had been commissioned into the Royal Engineers — and for the next two days he reveled in the challenge, despite temperatures in excess of 110F. Nunn was dragged along to watch, although one feels he would have been more comfortable on board his steamer. During their initial inspection, one of the Thorneycroft launches appeared and started to shell the bund, pockmarking it. Gorringe announced that perhaps they should retire and started to walk back to the vessels, far too slowly for Nunn's comfort. Thereafter, Nunn's flotilla quickly returned fire to keep the launches out of sight. The adjacent villages were occupied, and the sappers set to work on destroying the bund.[15]

Captain A.R. Ubsdell, 2/66th Punjabis and ADC to Gorringe, described the situation:

> *Sunday June 27th.* We arrived at the other side of the lake at about 1 o'clock

Iraqi Marshes, Summer 2007

Scale

MILES 5 4 3 2 1 0 5 MILES

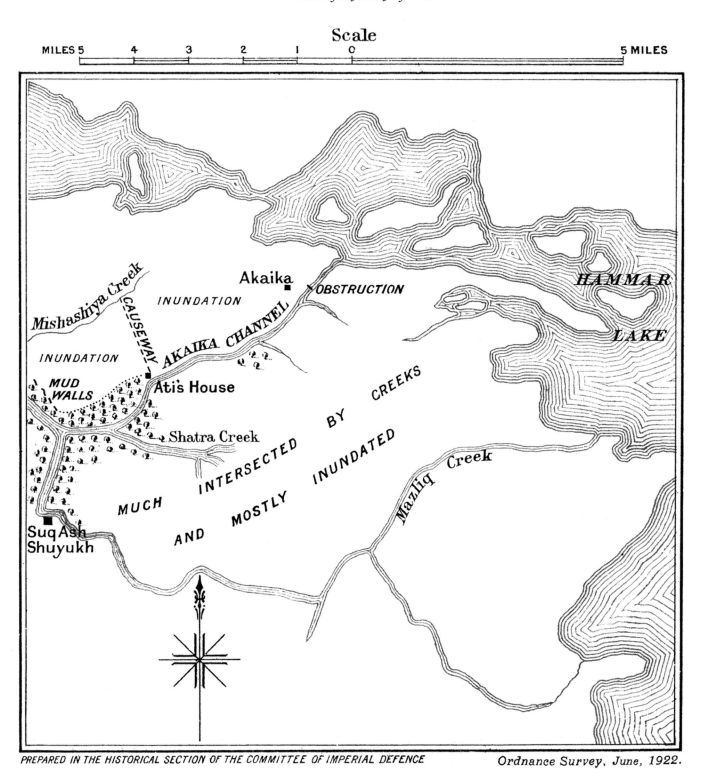

PREPARED IN THE HISTORICAL SECTION OF THE COMMITTEE OF IMPERIAL DEFENCE

Ordnance Survey, June, 1922.

Operations in the Akaika Channel, 27th June to 5th July 1915

& were just going into the Channel when the two gun boats sent back word that they had been fired on, & as we drew up to where they were, the enemy opened fire on us. They were pom-poms & came from the Two Thorneycroft boats the Turks have. They have built a big obstruction across the river just above where we are anchored, & just above that again there is a bend in the river hidden by a clump of date palms — Their two boats (each had two pom-poms) kept rushing round the corner & blazing off a few rounds & then returning behind the trees again — We blazed a few rounds at them with our two 4.7, which are being towed by the second of the two gun boats, but I don't think we did any damage — At 2 o'clock the G.O.C. & two or three officers went up to have a look at the obstruction to ascertain the best way of blowing it up. On their way back at about 4.30 they did it again. We were out of range really, although a few of the 1lb shells fell about 20 yards ahead of us — At 6.30 a party went off to blow the obstruction up. Some of the 48th & some 4th Hants went as pickets, while the S&M [Sappers and Miners] got things ready. They met with no resistance, but did not get the thing blown up at 12 o'clock as expected owing to the fuses not working properly.[16]

It would take a further two attempts and 60 lb of explosives to breach the bund. When a hole finally was blasted, the force of water pouring though was more than the steamers could manage, and once more the vessels had to be dragged through the passage. The water level was four feet higher behind the dam than in the lake. The *Shushan* was the first to attempt the passage. It took two regiments of men to haul her through the breach — Nunn called it a "cataract" — and then it required Gorringe on the bund with a megaphone to encourage the haulers while Nunn on the bridge encouraged his engineers. While *Shushan* was struggling, a *bellum* of sepoys approached too close to the cataract, were tipped into the creek and were swept past the steamer. Although the sepoys were in no real danger and were all collected by one of the small vessels accompanying *Shushan*, there was a great deal of shrieking which no doubt lightened the moment for the rest of the expedition! At the same time, the flow of water slackened and *Shushan* was dragged through.[17]

It would be 30 June before the expedition assembled above Hammar Lake. Only then did the campaigning begin in earnest. *Shushan* and *Massoudieh* with its two horse boats and 4.7-inch guns traveled on to conduct reconnaissance of the next length of the creek. Having anchored, the reconnaissance was continued on foot, which Nunn described as "a both interesting and exciting experience." They closed to some 600 yards of the Turkish positions from where Colonel Brown from Gorringe's staff sketched out the terrain. Aware that they were in and amongst hostile Arab territory, Nunn was relieved to be back on board and away without a shot having been fired.[18]

On the left bank stood a mud tower, nicknamed "Ati's House," which would be occupied on 4 July and used as the general's headquarters. From the top it gave a commanding view of the local terrain — swamp and marsh, intersected with creeks and high bunds, covered in date gardens and the serpentine waterway twisting away.[19]

The Turkish defenders had taken advantage of the time afforded them. Two thousand yards further on from Ati's House, the Shahtar Creek entered the channel from the right bank. Local informants told the British that this confluence was mined and covered by Turkish guns.

The advance resumed on 4 July. Escorted by the gunboats, the 76th Punjabis with a company of the 48th Pioneers and a section of mountain artillery captured Ati's House and a position on the opposite bank. A reconnaissance force followed a bund northwards to the Mishashiya Creek. They came under concerted opposition and so were unable find a suitable crossing which could have been exploited in a flanking movement. Meanwhile, the 2/7th Gurkhas crossed to the right bank and began advancing. They soon came across stout opposition amongst the water channels, walls and date groves from Arabs. By the evening they reached the Shahtar. The Turkish positions were on the far bank, so the Gurkhas dug in for the night where they were reinforced by the 1/4th Hampshires.

They advanced again in the early hours of the 5th. From their new position, they were afforded excellent positions to direct fire on the Turkish positions. On the opposite, left bank, the 24th and 76th Punjabis with their mountain guns resumed their advance with orders to get beyond the Turkish positions. Their objective was to cut off any Turkish retreat, including their shipping. Throughout their move, they were again engaged from beyond bunds by Arabs. The *Sumana* and *Shushan* also advanced to provide naval gunfire support and drew heavy gun and rifle fire. *Sumana* was twice hit by shells, one hitting her main steam pipe (she would eventually have to be sent back to Basra for repairs) and another passing down the middle of the dinner table while her crew were eating! Her captain, Lieutenant W.V.H. Harris, and two sailors were wounded in the engagement.[20]

The Punjabis and their mountain guns opened fire on the Turkish positions, who surrendered at about 1320 hours. One of the Thorneycroft launches had joined the fray but was able to retire upriver. The Punjabis crossed the river in *bellums* to take possession of a pair of Turkish guns. Meanwhile, on the right bank, the Gurkhas and Hampshires had continued their advance, forcing the Turks to retire until they fell back on their now captured battery, at which point they promptly surrendered. *Shushan* and *Massoudieh* moved forward sweeping for mines with the aid of a captured Turkish officer. They found just one, but having completed the sweep the remainder of the flotilla moved forward.[21]

Nunn concludes this stage of the operation with an assessment of the Turkish strength: about 300 Turkish soldiers supported by 2,000 Arabs with two guns and two launches. They had been further reinforced by 700 Turkish soldiers and another two guns from Nasariya. There losses, he estimated,

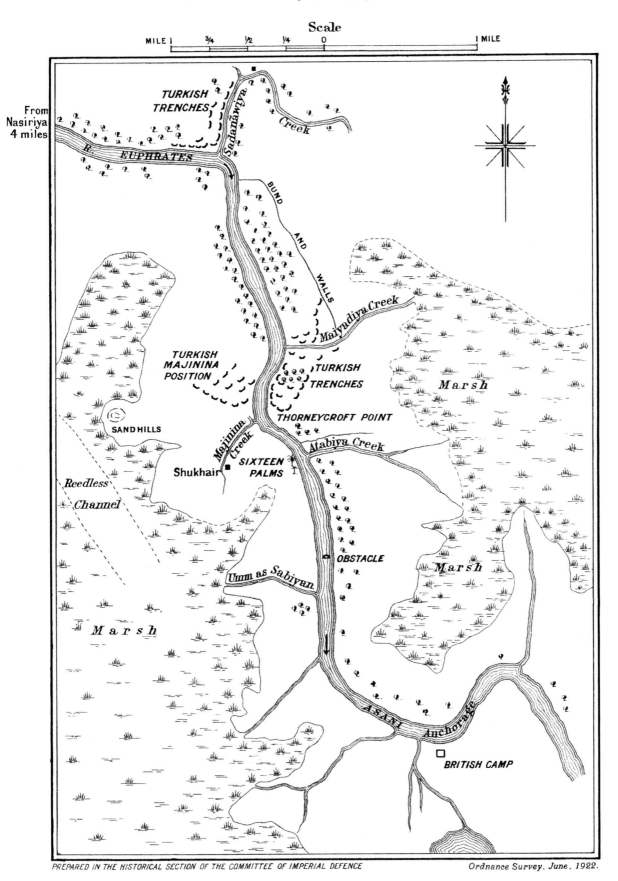

Scale

MILE 1   3/4   1/2   1/4   0   1 MILE

From
Nasiriya
4 miles

TURKISH
TRENCHES

Sadanawiya   *Creek*

R. EUPHRATES

BUND AND WALLS

Maiyadiya Creek

TURKISH
MAJININA
POSITION

TURKISH
TRENCHES

Marsh

SAND HILLS

THORNEYCROFT POINT

Majinina Creek

Atabiya Creek

Reedless

Channel

Shukhair

SIXTEEN
PALMS

OBSTACLE

Marsh

Umm as Sabiyan

Marsh

ASANI Anchorage

BRITISH CAMP

PREPARED IN THE HISTORICAL SECTION OF THE COMMITTEE OF IMPERIAL DEFENCE   Ordnance Survey, June, 1922.

Operations near Nasariya, 6 to 24 July 1915

were "considerable," with 91 soldiers and two guns captured. With the exception of the guns and launches, any estimates of numbers was, and remains, extremely subjective. He could be more accurate with the British losses: 109 military and three naval killed and wounded, the naval casualties being those three given for the *Shushan*, above.[22]

The following day, the 6th, Nunn took Sir Percy Cox aboard *Shushan* and *Massoudieh* down the Mazliq Creek to Suq-ash-Shuyukh which was occupied without any fighting. The town was already festooned with white flags, and the British delegation was met by Arab dignitaries when they stepped ashore, who were eager to surrender. Unfortunately, it was impossible to find yet another union flag to hoist over the town, although an old Indian political flag was located, and a flag-raising ceremony was conducted with sailors in the best uniforms that they could muster forming the cordon. This was a town of some 12,000 inhabitants and was the trade center for the local area — the name means "Market of the Sheikhs." There was no Turkish garrison in the town, but it was blessed by a branch of the Turkish telegraph network. Local intelligence here suggested that there were still 2,000 Turkish troops with four field and two mountain guns and two launches supported by Arab irregulars ahead of them. The 12th Division had some 1,900 effective soldiers.[23]

The division established a forward base at the Assani anchorage while the extent of the next Turkish defenses was established. Straight from the flag raising at Suq-ash-Shuyukh, Nunn pushed on up the Euphrates and was fired on from positions at the Majinina Creek. The next line of Turkish defenses was based around two creeks at Majinina and Maiyadiya extending left and right from the Euphrates, about four miles from Nasariya. Numerous bunds acted as dykes to control the waters. It was ideal terrain from which to defend, and large numbers of Turks could be seen preparing defenses.[24] To approach, the assaulting infantry would have to cross yet more creeks and swamps, with the moist 120F temperatures sapping strength while encouraging biting insects attracted by the prospect of blood, or just salt.

Two steamers, *Frat* and *Risafa*, and one of the Thorneycroft launches had been sunk about 3,000 yards south of these defenses, but the scuttling had been rushed and Nunn was able to take his flotilla around the obstacles. The remaining Thorneycroft launch was observed, and *Shushan* and *Massoudieh* moved forward to engage the enemy more closely. This drew Turkish artillery fire on the vessels, but they obliged the Thorneycroft launch to retire, thus claiming another small victory for the Royal Navy's riverine supremacy.[25]

Gorringe's first plan to assault the Majinina position was planned for the night of the 7 July with a force moving along the south bank of the Sabiyan Creek with supporting artillery and naval gunfire. According to Nunn's map, the Sabiyan extends due west from the Euphrates while the Majinina extended southwestwards and, presumably, became less of an obstacle to

cross than where it joined the Euphrates. Gorringe may have been able to flank the Majinina positions and avoid a frontal assault over a substantial water feature. However, it was found that there were an estimated 2,000 defenders, and Gorringe was forced to call for reinforcements from Basra. With yet another delay, stores were starting to run short. At the same time, shallow draft vessels which were urgently needed on the Tigris were diverted to ferry reinforcements up the Euphrates.[26]

While the expedition waited for reinforcements, the naval gunners learned a whole new branch of gunnery from their army colleagues — indirect fire. As the 4.7-inch guns on the horse boats were so low in the river, they could not see over the banks to fire directly at the enemy. The date palms further obscured their view. The army provided telephone cable and presumably some instruction on fire control. Lieutenant Commander Seymour served as the forward observation officer and got the hang of the procedures eventually, apparently not without some mishaps — "some of it, I must confess, rather exciting for our friends as well as foes!"[27]

The Turkish defense was not passive either. On the evening of 11 July a Turkish attack reached within 15 yards of the British positions before being repulsed.[28]

Captain Wilson was the sole Arabic-speaking officer in the division and participated in reconnaissance. On one such patrol, he observed two Turkish soldiers, apparently patrolling on the far side of a channel, whom Wilson shot, one in the shoulder and one in the back. He retired for reinforcements from another patrol which was towing a *bellum* of ammunition. They crossed the channel to find the pair of Turks:

> Presently we advanced and I saw, to my horror, that the Arabs had been busy. The two Turks I had shot lay on the opposite side, stripped naked and their throats cut. Incidents such as these afterwards came within the experience of practically all members of the civil administration employed in Mesopotamia outside the large towns: that they should have been able, nevertheless, to put some trust in the Arab tribes, and to gain their confidence in large measure, is an indication of the spirit that animated them.[29]

Melliss was now getting the fighting he wanted, although he was still not happy: "Wish it were in a less enervating climate, falling into deep swamps up to your neck in hot mud as I did several times the other day does not help one to command."[30]

Reinforcements arrived from Basra which occupied the left bank positions, freeing the 30th Brigade to cross the river in preparation for the forthcoming attack. The new arrivals were composed of half a battalion of the Royal West Kents, the 67th with part of the 90th Punjabis, the 44th Merwara Infantry and a section of the Hampshire's Howitzer Battery.

Gorringe's next plan of attack, timed for 14 July, was for the 12th Brigade on the left bank to fix the Turkish defenders while Melliss' 30th Brigade attacked on the right. Casualties and illness had already reduced the assaulting brigade to 1,500 men. Melliss, like Townshend before him, worried at the thought of his men assaulting in crowded *bellums*. Unlike Townshend's amphibious assault, Melliss' was not a success. Although the British had an advantage in artillery of two to one, the advantage was not brought to bear. Melliss would blame Gorringe's interfering in every aspect of the campaign for negating this advantage. Gorringe then reduced the attacking force from a brigade to a single regiment, the 24th Punjabis. When Gorringe ordered Wilson to guide the attack, Wilson refused. Wilson considered that the water was too high and that not enough reconnaissance had been done. In writing, he informed Gorringe that he would participate either as an officer attached to the Punjabis or as a political officer, but not as a guide. "Had [Gorringe] court-martialed me, I should not have blamed him, but he probably realized that my commission, which I was risking, was more to me than anything else." None of this bode well.[31]

Colonel Climo led his Pubjabis into the attack which closed to 200 yards from the Turkish trenches before being cut down. Repeated attempts to renew the advance failed, and the Punjabis were forced to retire under fire, never an easy task to achieve. Some 120 of 400 men were casualties. They tried to recover their fallen comrades, but as the Arabs advanced, the bodies had to be abandoned in the deep water. Knowing the Arabs' reputation regarding captured bodies, this was no easy decision to take. The whole failed operation took nine and a half hours in appalling conditions wading in water up to four feet deep. Of 8 British officers and 428 Indian other ranks, there were 56 killed and 91 wounded. All but two of the British officers were killed, which highlights the disproportionate risks undertaken by this small pool of specialist (and hard to replace) officers. On the right bank, the 76th Punjabis and 48th Pioneers were at least able to advance towards the Majinnia. In the process they captured the village of Shukhair and Sixteen Palms Post where the creek joined the Euphrates.[32]

Prior to the attack, Melliss wrote of the conditions being endured:

I am very glad Gorringe has seen the wisdom of asking for reinforcements and another brigade arrives tomorrow, rather 3½ battalions & 2 five inch howitzers, with this we ought to do the job without serious losses although I don't think it is by any means an easy one. They have a dreadful open field of fire in front of both their positions on the right & left banks & across their front on the right is a water channel 5 or 6 feet deep at a distance of 200 yards from their rifles, the plan of attack is for my brigade to make a turning movement in boats through the marshes round his right which will cut off his retreat from Nasiryeh & the other brigade to make a feint attack to attack his left. I dont like my job the men crowded up in boats offer a beastly easy target & if their guns get on to us we shant like it & we shall like it still less if our guns don't succeed in knocking the Turks out of some dry ground (islands) in the middle of the marshes which guard their right flank. However let us hope it will all pan out well & that we shall get to Nasariyeh & have some rest for we are all feeling tired out in this climate. My brigade is only the skeleton of one now 1500 men & lots of British officers sick & wounded Smithett 76th Punjabis wounded his 2nd in command sick Colonel Taylor & Colonel Haldane both invalided to India. The Hampshires are merely a scratch lot of 240 Officers and men, not a regiment. The 24th Punjabis is the only regiment of any strength Viz 577, the 76th only 350 7th Gurkhas 340. What do you think of that for a brigade? Yesterday & today I got into a hot fire, drawing quite unintentionally the whole fire of the enemy's positions guns, rifles & maxims. They are evidently jumpy & thought we were attacking them the reason yesterday was that I pushed out a couple of Gurkha companies through a strip of palm grove to make close reconnaissance of the enemy, as I was lying down with the scout line taking in their trenches though my field glasses they spotted me & opened a devil of a fire of course I had to order a withdrawal at once & luckily thanks to the many trees & their high fire we got back with only 1 man killed & the Gurkhas say they accounted for 5 Turks of a picquet in the palm groves which first opened fire on us.

Afterwards, Melliss wrote his account of his men's tribulations:

On the 14th my Brigade was detailed to make turning movement through the marshes against the enemy's right in order to seize a sort of island from which we could take the Turkish position in rear by gun and rifle fire, of course the movement had to be carried out with the men in native canoes (called Bellums) which hold about 10 men and are poled or paddled through the marshes which vary in depth from 2 to 4 feet and sometimes of water with clay or mud at the bottom. I had made my arrangements to carry this out when the GOC (Gorringe) changed the plan and said he would prefer the movement to be carried out by one battalion only and detached the 24th Punjabis for it supported by four guns of the mountain battery. Alas with disastrous results — the 24th by canoeing through the night arrived by dawn some 1000 yards from the island in the marshes and proceeded to advance against it on foot through the mud and water of the marshes, all went pretty well (although the men were exhausted with the heavy wading) until they got within 200 yards of the island when their attack was blasted by hot fire from trenches held by the Turks, our poor fellows were shot down right and left trying to charge the positions Majors Cook Norton, Capt Leslie Smith were shot dead, Lieut Haverfield mortally wounded Lt [blank] killed missing or captured & he had to retire. Then old Climo made a gallant attempt to save the situation & got together a few officers & men & advanced again, his adjutant poor young Birbeck was shot dead & a number of his party killed or wounded & he had to retire. The casualties were over 123 out of some 400 men, only Climo 1 subaltern & 1 Dr left. Many missing, no doubt wounded men who fell into the water & were drowned. You may imaging how we of the 30th Brigade felt for Climo & his regiment. All those good fellows we have know in Suez all gone. Climo is left with 2 subalterns, young Pim, whose chubby face had grown quite old looking & Rind the Qtr Master. Pim was at Shaiba & this last affair. How I wish now Gorringe had not altered his plans.[33]

Gorringe was now feeling the pressure too. With strong enemy positions to his front and falling water levels to his rear, Nunn considered that his position was "most unenviable," which can be read as a classic line of British understatement.[34] Unless the division advanced and took the Turkish positions, defeating them in the process, he risked being cut off from Basra with an active enemy to his fore. Then there was the position of the local Arabs, which as usual could best be described as indifferent, with the potential for hostility to both Turk and Briton alike. Gorringe desperately needed reinforcements to make good his losses, let alone to give him parity of numbers with the Turks.

The arrival of reinforcements was slow as the crossing of the Hammar became more and more frustrated. They did not arrive until the 19 and 20 July. The 18th Brigade arrived with the remaining half battalion of the Royal West Kents together with a section of a heavy artillery battery and another section of the Hampshire Howitzer Battery. Two modern BE2s arrived which at least gave Gorringe aerial supremacy and accurate intelligence. Unfortunately the Turks were also reinforced, and increasingly numbers of Arabs were congregating away to the northeast. Although they would not play a direct role in the fighting on the Euphrates, their presence was ominous in the event of any British defeat or withdrawal.[35]

A third assault was planned for 24 July, but the night before there was a Turkish attack. Nunn, at general headquarters (GHQ), noted how bullets aimed at the front-line trenches hit the date palms around him, ripping off big branches and hurling them onto the ground. He moved his bed away from a hole in the wall. The horse-boat-mounted 4.7-inch guns were now registered on enemy positions, and the procedures of the forward observation officers had been refined, even if Turkish fire did repeatedly break the telephone lines. *Sumana* had returned from her repairs in Basra to add her weight to the forthcoming attack.[36]

The attack would be carried out by Brigadier General K.E. Lean's 12th Brigade which had followed the 30th, and so had not been ready for operations until 13 July. It consisted of the following:

- 2nd Queen's Own Royal West Kents
- 44th Merwana Infantry
- 67th Punjabis
- 90th Punjabis

The preliminary bombardment began at 0430 hours (although see below for 0500 hours), and a cool breeze made the weather slightly more bearable. The 12th Brigade, lead by the Royal West Kents, left their trenches on the left bank, north of the Atabiya creek, to cross the open ground described previously by Melliss. The Turkish defense of "Thorneycroft Point" was vigorously executed until about 0640 hours when they exhausted their reserves and fell back. The exploits of the Royal West Kents were recorded:

At 5 A.M. on the 24th the bombardment opened. It was a heavy one ... by Mesopotamian standards and the guns made good practice, but when the time came for the advance the Turks were by no means shaken and put up a stiff resistance. The leading companies went over the top at 5:30 and pushed rapidly forward. As the date-palms concealed the advance of our infantry from the artillery it was arranged that the left flank of the advancing troops should carry a conspicuous yellow flag to mark the progress of the advance.... On reaching the edge of the date-palms in front of the trenches the leaders came under a very heavy fire, which for a moment checked the attack. But Major Kitson and the supports were close behind, and as they came up the leading companies pushed on with them. "It was the most magnificent sight," wrote an officer of the 90th Punjabis, "to watch those fellows going up under the terrific fusillade from their front ... in spite of the casualties, just as if they were on a monoeuvre parade. As soon as they got up to the trenches they wheeled round to the right, so we had to stop our fire for fear of hitting them.... They got in with their bayonets and all we could see from where we were was Mr. Turk running as if he Devil himself were after him." ... However, while the right companies were firing at the Turkish loopholes and keeping down the rifle-fire of the defence, Nos. III and IV on the left had pushed on unchecked. Here there was a little more cover and, led by Major Kitson, they had got in all mixed up together and carried the Turkish trench.... Directly Nos. III and IV got in on the Turkish flank and began to work to the right, Nos. I and II sprang up again and swept over the trenches opposite them, a company of the 90th Punjabis following close behind. A good many Turks were bayoneted there and then, many were taken, and the remainder bolted to their left."[37]

When 12th Brigade were seen entering the Turkish trenches, the 30th Brigade across the river advanced to the Majinia Canal. To cross this, *Sumana* towed an armored barge with engineers and bridging equipment which was intended to be grounded in the canal where high, steep banks would protect the engineers while they constructed a bridge for the assaulting troops. *Sumana's* actions did not go unnoticed. She received 87 bullet holes between her bow and funnel and had her steam pipe fractured again. The sappers in the barge fared equally badly, and a third of them became casualties.

An hour later, the bridge was still unsuitable for use. For once, fortunately, the unique topography of Mesopotamia played into the hands of the invaders. Most of the creeks and canals were not tributaries of the major rivers but extracted water to irrigate the surrounding land. The grounded barge served to cut the canal from the Euphrates, and the water level began to fall until the infantry could cross unaided.[38]

Arnold Wilson gives a different version of events. The night before the attack, he swam the creek to determine how deep it was. At points he found it to be four feet six inches deep; at others he could not feel the bottom with his foot. He did not want to dive for fear the splashes would be heard. He then let the current carry him up the creek until his foot found the bottom again. There he got out of the creek and started to make his way back to camp. He was cold, exhausted, wearing only his shirt, having lost his "rubber shoes" in the creek, but made it back to safety where he wrote his report for Gorringe and then slept. Gorringe appreciated Wilson's efforts, as Gorringe disliked frontal attacks, so information about how wide his flanking movement would have to go was essential.[39]

At about 1000 hours, the Hampshires and Gurkhas crossed the canal, driving home with the bayonet. The Turkish trenches had thin overhead cover from the sun only, but not sufficient overhead protection from fire. Bayonets could be thrust downwards, and a fusillade of bullets returned. The 76th Punjabis moved in support to their left while the *Shushan* and *Massoudieh* supported from the river to their right with gunfire. *Muzaffri* also supported with a battery of Maxim guns. The Turkish defenders withdrew, and as the pressure was maintained the Turks had no opportunity to reform and establish further defenses. However, the Turks were able to disengage and withdraw to fight another day.[40]

The pressure was maintained as far as the Sadanawiya Creek, which the 12th Brigade reached at about 1300 hours. The 30th Brigade advanced to a parallel position across the Euphrates. Gorringe moved forward to assess the situation aboard *Mejidieh* on which were mounted two guns from the 63rd Field Battery, RFA. Their shrapnel shells no doubt did serious damage amongst the Turks who would not have had the opportunity to construct adequate overhead cover. Nunn recounted one of his sailors, sitting on the deck without any protection, "playing a Maxim down their trenches." However, the Turks were not beaten yet, and their artillery fire prevented *Shushan* from advancing forward of the positions occupied by the two lead British brigades. After two hours, the Turks again showed signs of withdrawing from this position. The 30th Brigade crossed the Sadanawiya and occupied the former Turkish positions, and it was there, utterly exhausted by the exertions in over 110F of humid heat, that they halted.[41]

Melliss was critical of Gorringe's failure to bring up the reserves by steamer and defeat the Turks once and for all. However, as Townshend found, cutting off and destroying a Turkish force in the field was an elusive objective. Colonel Bowker, commanding officer (CO) of the Hampshires, blamed the failure to pursue the Turks on their own artillery, which prevented the attackers from definitively closing in. Nunn adds that *Shushan* and *Muzaffri* joined with the advance, the former advancing up the river while the latter landed its Maxim guns on the recently vacated Turkish positions. However, as the Turks were fresher than his Hampshires following their attack, it made little difference to Bowker, as the Turks were able to retreat faster than the attackers could follow them, especially as they appear to have discarded all of their equipment. The six guns in the Maiyadiya creek position were also abandoned.[42]

Gorringe retired to dinner and bed following a successful day's advance and was not seen until 1000 hours the following day. Meanwhile, Nunn, ever energetic and at the fore, conducted a reconnaissance as far as Nasariya, sinking the last of the Thorneycroft launches in the process. However, this was not before the *Shushan*'s age began to tell. The 12-pound gun's recoil with its temporary mounting began straining the port deck. The gun was moved to the starboard side, but the old vessel (one of those built for the Relief of Khartoum the previous century) was straining under the violent recoil. Nunn found the town abandoned, festooned with white flags and being looted by the Arabs, although a volley of fire from the barracks indicated that the Turkish troops were unaware that they had in fact lost the battle. They appear to have slipped away later that day. Nunn retired to a safe distance. The following morning a *mashuf* of Arab elders approached *Shushan* and asked to come aboard. They were fearful of the British reprisal for having been fired at after the white flag had been raised. Diplomatically, Nunn explained how the British had come not to fight the Arabs but to expel the Turks, but that the sheikhs had to maintain order in the town until Gorringe arrived. Nunn found Melliss, who provided 50 Gurkhas and two Maxims to support the *Shushan* and *Massoudieh*, and returned to take possession of the town by raising the Union Jack. The response of the townspeople was muted.[43]

Gorringe and the main body marched into Nasariya and suffered accordingly in the heat and a sandstorm. The fatigue of the previous days' activities was beginning to catch up now that the excitement and adrenaline were wearing off. Navy rum was offered to the soldiers who would have appreciated its medicinal effect. No doubt they also felt much better when they were informed of the king-emperor's telegram of congratulation stating, "The splendid achievements of General Gorringe's column in spite of many hardships and intense heat fills me with admiration."[44]

Nasariya was not a healthy posting, despite being a relatively modern town, not unlike Al-Amara, with well-built masonry houses; broad, well-lit streets; and large blocks of Turkish government offices. Nasariya was the center of the *sanjak* of Muntafiq in the Basra *vilayet*. The Turkish military commander had also performed the duties of the civil administrator in an area where the powerful Muntafiq Confederacy did, and would, prove troublesome. There was already a hospital full of Turkish wounded, apparently unattended. However, the medical care provided to the British and Indians was not much better. Many had to endure the journey back to Basra on the metal decks of barges. This was a foretaste of the complete collapse of medical facilities which would be experienced on the Tigris.[45] Arnold Wilson observed the state of the medical treatment and evacuation. It would be a miniature of the crisis which would swamp the fighting along the Tigris the coming winter:

> After the battle, as after the preceding engagement, I spent some hours assisting in the evacuation of the wounded. I was horrified at what I saw, for at every point it was clear that the

shamefully bad arrangements arose from bad staff work on the part of the medical authorities, rather than from inherent difficulties. The wounded were crowded on board to lie on iron decks that had not been cleaned since horses and mules had stood on them for a week. There were few mattresses.[46]

Curiously, Wilson mentioned horses and mules, yet none were recorded as traveling with the expedition. *Bellums* were used for transporting the mountain guns. There were no opportunities for horses and mules in and amongst the swamps and creeks of the Euphrates. Indeed, the Quetta Staff College's *Critical Study* makes the point that "no animals could be employed: consequently the fighting troops had to do all the handling of stores, guns and ammunition." Wilson's statement would suggest that the decks had not been cleaned since they were used on the Tigris before being sent to the Euphrates.[47]

Nunn and his flotilla pushed up the Euphrates to Samawa, another 71 miles. The Turkish police and garrison had fled on hearing of Gorringe's victory. The sheikh greeted Nunn and asked them to take over control of the town, but on returning to Gorringe, who sought further instructions from India, no further advance above Nasariya was permitted. One 28 July, all but a small naval contingent with *Sumana* were withdrawn to Kabaish, with the greatest of difficulties crossing the Hammar, and then again when navigating the larger sloops down to Basra. *Sumana* was withdrawn a week later for future operations on the Tigris. While Nunn had been operating on the Euphrates, the Admiralty had reorganized operations in the region. The Persian Gulf and Mesopotamia Divisions were separated, with Nunn commanding the Mesopotamia Division. This covered all operations north of Fao at the mouth of the Shatt-al-Arab. Further instructions were for the naval personnel to proceed to Ceylon (Sri Lanka) to rest at the navy's hill camp, Diyatalawa, in rotation. Nunn left Captain C. Mackenzie of the *Clio* as senior naval officer while he took *Espiègle* to Ceylon, the crew to rest and the sloop for a refit.[48]

With the capture of Nasariya, Indian Expeditionary Force "D" had completed its task. Basra *vilayet* was occupied, with garrisons at key points on both the Tigris and Euphrates. There was defense in depth against any Turkish counter-attack which would have to force its way through Indian Army divisions with Royal Naval support, which had proved to be far superior to anything which the Ottoman Empire had been able to field.

Delamain's instructions had been completed to the letter, even with the wider reading of Basra as the *vilayet* and not just the port. Chamberlain at the India Office in London wanted Nixon to sit tight within its defensive boundaries. Mesopotamia was, after all, a sideshow, and London had many more important theaters where there were more pressing demands for men and material.

However, the campaign in Mesopotamia was taking on a momentum of its own, with Nixon happy to encourage such momentum. The 6th Division on the Tigris was near Ali-al-Gharbi. Kut was only four miles beyond the border of the *vilayat* and, it was argued, would link to Nasariya via the Shatt-al-Hai. On 27 July, Hardinge argued that occupying Kut was now a strategic necessity, for the oil, the lower reaches of the Tigris and for Nasariya, and doing so would materially reduce the garrisons required to hold Basra.[49] Hardinge knew exactly how to tempt Chamberlain into allowing yet another advance on the Tigris.

5

Kut, Ctesiphon and Back to Kut, April 1915–November 1915

Ctesiphon, known to the Turks as Salman Pak, lay just 20 miles outside of Baghdad but marked the high-water mark of Townshend's advance up the Tigris. It is a site of great antiquity, like many in Mesopotamia; the massive vaulted brick-built hall 85 feet long was built by the Sassanid King Chosroes (or Khosrau) I after A.D. 541. It was also believed to be the burial place of the Prophet Mohammed's barber, Salman Pak, which made it holy land for Townshend's Muslim soldiers. Townshend would instruct GHQ to use Cetsiphon, not Salman Pak, so avoid undermining Indian Muslim religious sentiments. First, though, Townshend and the 6th Division had to get there.[1]

While Gorringe fought through the swamps of the Euphrates, the 6th Division had idled the summer away in the sweltering heat of the Mesopotamian summer, and Townshend had convalesced in India. The debate about a further advance to Kut was only authorized on 6 August 1915. In July, Chamberlain, Hardinge and Nixon had debated the merits of the advance. Nixon was confident he could supply a division based at Kut. Chamberlain's concern was for the navy's oil, but he made it clear that there were no reinforcements. Hardinge argued that from Kut a division could secure the oil, the Tigris and, via the Shatt-al-Hai, Nasariya and the Euphrates. However, there were requests to "borrow" the 28th Brigade from Aden for the offensive, and thereafter it would be returned. The 28th Brigade had been sent from Egypt to Aden expressly to prevent the Turks from overrunning that vital coaling station which supported the imperial maritime communications that were essential for the war effort. Once Aden was secured, it was required back in Egypt. Unsurprisingly, the brigade was not made available. On 5 August, Hardinge telegraphed Chamberlain to formally propose the advance to Kut and made a point of noting that Nixon was unaware of discussions about the 28th Brigade — Nixon would have to plan within the resources he had to hand. By reply on the 6th, the advance was authorized. The summer heat, however, had not been kind to

the British forces — the 1/4th Hampshires had only 115 effective soldiers. The Tigris was at its summer low, which restricted the size of ships that could be utilized, further exasperating the shipping shortages in the theater.[2]

The 6th Division began to concentrate, but it would be 20 August before this could be completed. Townshend's return to the division on the 28th raised morale as it indicated a return to activity, and no doubt more victories. His orders were for "the destruction and dispersal of the enemy, who, according to the intelligence already furnished you, are prepared to dispute your advance; & the occupation of Kut, thereby consolidating our control of the Basra vilayet." The division was concentrated at Ali-al-Gharbi with the navy in support as ever, although on this occasion it was commanded by Lieutenant Commander Cookson. Townshend set off on 11 September to Sannaiyat where he halted and sent the ships back to Al-Amara for more supplies and artillery. The river was at a seasonal low, and he was 300 mules below establishment for land transport. The few Turkish troops who were encountered withdrew without much resistance. It would be the 16th before the division reached Sannaiyat, eight miles south of the Turkish positions. Shortages of transport delayed the move. The infantry marched for two days, but even by setting off at dawn and halting at 0830 hours, 101 men fell out sick.[3]

The advance was now accompanied by aircraft, which provided Townshend with accurate information about Turkish dispositions especially between the river and various marshes in the area. The Suwaikiya marsh was the largest in the region and would form Townshend's right boundary about six miles from the left bank of the Tigris. Townshend was able to establish his division in that area. The Suwada marsh was the largest marsh facing Townshend, about two miles wide and situated about two and a half miles from the river. Between the river and the Suwada marsh lay "Horse Shoe Marsh" with a frontage of about a mile. This was believed to be an oxbow lake where a loop in the Tigris had been left isolated when the main river eroded a new channel. The Ataba Marsh, another two and a half miles beyond the Suwada had a frontage of about two miles. Townshend faced a frontage of eight and a half miles within which there were three marsh features which were "no-go" to his troops and which occupied some five miles of the frontage.

Trench systems reminiscent of the Western Front were built over the previous months between the river and Suwada Marsh (and Horse Shoe Marsh), which incorporated the 20-foot high banks of an ancient canal, known as the Es-Sinn Banks. Beyond the Suwada Marsh towards, but not all the way to, the Ataba Marsh were more trenches with three redoubts, named by the British North, Center and South. The weak point in the Turkish defenses was the gap between the North Redoubt and the Ataba Marsh which was drying out faster than the Turks could build trenches. There was a gap of just 300 yards, but this was where Townshend decided to strike. The Tigris was blocked by a boom. On the right bank, there were further Turkish emplacements, culminating in a redoubt which would become known as the Dujaila Redoubt the following year.

With the flat surrounding terrain, defensive positions on top of the banks offered excellent fields of view and of fire. The defenses included wire entanglements and land mines, with communication trenches to the rear, underground bunkers, pumping engines for drinking water, river quays for resupply, and well-prepared brick and mortar gun positions. Water jugs were placed at regular intervals in the trenches. To the front, ditches with sharpened stakes added another line of defense. A boom closed the river. These positions were held by the Turkish 35th Division. Across the river, the Turkish 38th Division created further entrenchments. Turkish forces were estimated at 6,000 men with 38 guns, under Yusuf Nur-ud-Din (Nureddin Pasha). Both divisions consisted of six battalions, while four more were held in reserve with the cavalry, camalry and Arab horsemen. Townshend, with his eye on the historical, likened the defenses to Wellington's Lines of Torres Verdas.[4] It would appear that the impetus which Townshend had created in the spring, pushing the panicked Turkish troops up the river, had been lost; the rout was over, and digging in commenced in earnest. To their rear, reinforcements were also arriving, in the shape of the 51st Division and a new division, the 45th, being raised in Baghdad from border guards and gendarmes.[5]

Townshend established his headquarters at Nukhailat on the 26th, four miles south of the Turkish positions. He commanded some 11,000 men with 28 guns and 40 machine guns. A bridge of boats and an observation tower were built in the featureless terrain. Brigadier Delamain crossed the Tigris and set up a camp to give the impression that this was the main British force. The Turks took the bait and shelled the deception camp, despite attempts across the river to encourage the Turkish fire and give away their positions: Captain Reynardson said that even sitting, in full view, on an anthill, reading the *Times*,

he was not a tempting enough target for them to fire at him.[6] The 103rd Mahrattas advanced two miles as if taking up positions for an attack against the 38th Division. On the 23rd, in another demonstration, but under cover of darkness, Delamain crossed the river ready for the attack.

Townshend's plan of attack for 28 September was intended to be a battle of annihilation with a force getting behind the enemy and cutting off their line of retreat. The plan required three columns:

- Column B, the "minimum force": General Fry's 18th Brigade would demonstrate before Turkish positions between the river and the Suwada Marsh, including the Horse Shoe Marsh, to persuade the Turks that this is where the attack would come from.

- Column A: General Delamain commanded a smaller column of (one and a half battalions) with a company of sappers and miners, and three batteries each of two Maxim machine-guns, whose objective were three Turkish redoubts between the Suwada and Ataba marshes.

- Column C, under General Hoghton was based on his 17th Brigade reinforced with two more battalions from the 16th Brigade, four Maxim machine guns, two armored cars[7] and the cavalry. His objective was to pass in the 300-yard gap between the North Redoubt and the Ataba Marsh and attack the redoubts from the rear.

Delamain's column set off at 0200 hours, crossing the Tigris by the bridge of boats which shifted the "principal mass" from the right bank to the left bank. Nur-ud-Din, meanwhile, sent troops in the opposite direction. He made for Clery's Post at the point of the Suweida Marsh closest to the British lines. There, Hoghton's column, C, detached to pass round the North Redoubt.

Hoghton's column had the farthest to travel after leaving Delamain's in position. When the sun came up around 0600 hours, it was clear that the compass bearings he had been marching on were inaccurate (they had been compiled from aerial reconnaissance), as they marched at night through featureless terrain, and he was out of place — instead of passing inside the Ataba Marsh, he was passing around the outside of it. Rather than retrace his steps, Hoghton continued around the outside of the marsh to bring his column behind the Turkish positions. Unfortunately, the fine dust was too much for the artillery, necessitating a detour further north and a longer delay. He then ran into a Turkish reserve battalion, which was cleared by a bayonet charge by the 104th Wellesley's Rifles, capturing 111 Turkish soldiers and an officer. Delamain, meanwhile, was waiting on Hoghton.[8]

It was 0820 hours before Delamain could see Hoghton's force on the horizon behind the Turkish positions. Hoghton's detour had exhausted the telephone cable which he carried — seven miles' worth — and the two commanders had been out of touch for some time. Neither column was equipped with

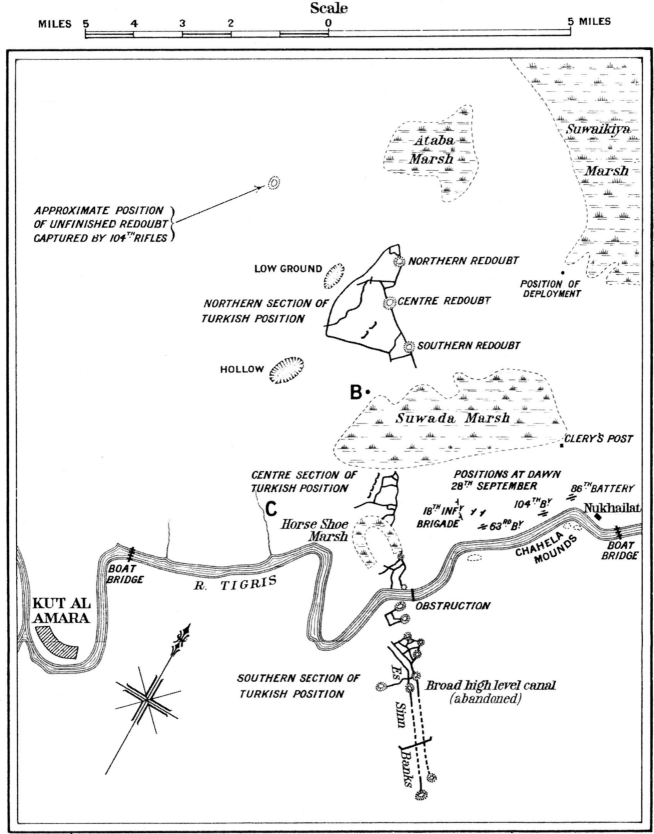

Battle of Kut, 28 September 1915

one of the two wireless sets carried by the division. These sets were located with Townshend and Nixon, although for the battle, Nixon joined Townshend on the observation tower and so the two sets were unused. Delamain ordered the attack on the North Redoubt. The Turks resisted strongly, and it was only with assistance from Hoghton's troops attacking from the rear that the redoubt fell. Delamain's men then turned to fight their way through the trench system to the Center Redoubt, but by now a strong wind had whipped up the dust, obscuring the view of the artillery observers and depriving the infantry of artillery support. The redoubt was carried, as was the South Redoubt by 1245 hours.

Having secured the Turkish northern position, Hoghton's force combined with Delamain's, and together they continued the advance by turning left to close on the river. The advance was hampered by their casualties. The troops had been marching and attacking since 0200. Their water bottles were long since empty as no source of resupply had been found during the march. Ammunition was running low and, to top it all, the dust made the going slow and difficult. When the column halted for a rest at about 1530 hours, they came under fire from Turkish guns near the Tigris. Finally, as they approached the river, they came under fire from a Turkish battalion brought across the river and occupying a dry nullah. They were cleared with a bayonet charge, but with this final exertion the column was spent and collapsed where they were, or made for the river, maddened by thirst. The Turks withdrew.[9]

General Fry's "demonstration," meanwhile, which was successfully convincing Nur-ud-Din that he was the main attack, was waiting for Delamain to get behind the Turk's center position before attacking. He planned to attack three up (7th Rajputs, 120th Infantry, 110th Mahrattas with the Norfolks in reserve) with field artillery and naval gunfire support. The brigade encountered problems common in Mesopotamia. Firstly, there were inaccurate maps, which meant that that Horse Shoe Marsh was more extensive than expected, which hampered the advance. Secondly, the flat terrain prevented the artillery from observing "fall of shot" which reduced their effectiveness. Fry's brigade also bivouacked just beyond the Turkish positions.

With the army spent, Townshend looked to the navy to strike a further blow against the Turks by clearing their boat bridge, which they undertook. However, they soon came under fire from both banks and discovered the boom across the river. The boom consisted of a *mahaila* and two barges connected by a steel hawser. Cookson brought *Comet* alongside the *mahaila* with the intention of cutting the hawser so that the boats would swing clear on the current. Given the amount of fire which the *Comet* was attracting, the task of cutting the hawser was extremely dangerous. Cookson took an axe and swung over the side of *Comet* but was mortally wounded in the process and died on the deck of his ship: Townshend considered that "he found that he could not send a man over the ship's side to cut away the obstruction because it meant certain death, so he

took an axe and went himself." For his action, Cookson was awarded a posthumous Victoria Cross.[10]

The following day, the Turks slipped away, abandoning their positions.

Townshend's assessment of the battle was that

> the battle of Kut-al-Amara can be said to have been one of the most important in the history of the British Army in India. There had been nothing of its magnitude either in the Afghan war or the Indian mutiny. For it was fought against equally well armed and of equal numbers to ourselves. In addition we ejected them from a very strong and up-to-date position, commanding ground as open and flat as a billiard table.[11]

Lieutenant Spackman's regiment, the 48th Pioneers, did not participate in the battle, but he was able to visit the Turkish positions afterwards and described them:

> Riding in, I had a close look at the vacated enemy trenches. They were well-sited and protected by a deadly ditch filled with barbed wire, with machine-gun posts placed so as to be almost invisible from the front. A direct assault would certainly have resulted in the attackers suffering terrible casualties. I was amused to see a few of the ancient muzzle-loader guns with, alongside, piles of authentic cannon balls, in hidden emplacements trained across the river.[12]

Townshend had planned the Battle of Kut, as it became known at the time (later it would also be referred to as the First Battle of Es-Sinn, as there would be a Second Battle of Es-Sinn during the Relief of Kut), to be a master stroke, capturing the Turkish 35th Division in a well-coordinated and well-planned right-flanking move which Napoleon would have approved of. Townshend and his division had obstacles to overcome which Napoleon and the *Grand Armee* did not have: like the lack of artillery observation positions, extreme heat, lack of water, dust and modern entrenched positions. It was perhaps too much to consider, as Townshend, in his normal self-publicizing, theatrical manner, that Kut should have been one of the great battles of the war. Townshend was fortunate that his theater gave him the scope to maneuver as he desired — how would he have managed on the Western Front with artillery barrages and frontal attacks?

He was right in saying that Kut was a turning point. The failure to destroy the Turkish 35th Division allowed it to withdraw, regroup and eventually take part in his destruction at Kut. It also meant that the 35th Division would harass the 6th Division as it advanced to Kut town.

Kut town was not as popular as Al-Amara. The 12th Division's under-strength 30th Brigade would be based there as line of communications troops.

Kut was still a victory, if not as complete as Townshend would have liked. Delamain's deception camp on the right bank convinced the Turks that that was the direction of attack, and then slipping across the river to attack on the left bank was a master stroke. Hoghton's task of encircling the Turkish positions was a sound one to "bag" a whole division. Could it have been accomplished if Hoghton had not become lost, forced into a diversion through soft ground, delayed by running into a Turkish position which had to be assaulted and then, combined with Delamain's force, commanding exhausted and dehydrated troops? Possibly. But he did not. The 35th Division escaped to fight another day.

The Battle of Kut cost 1,233 British casualties, of which 94 were killed, but for the casualties it was a long way back to the base hospital at Basra. The Turkish losses were some 4,000, including 1,153 prisoners, plus 14 guns and other stores of material and ammunition.[13] While the British losses were nowhere near as light as during Townshend's Regatta, they were still very favorable in terms of the Western Front and only added to Townshend's reputation as the most successful British general of the year. The downside was that the casualty-clearing system was starting to stain due to the distance from Basra. For every subsequent battle he fought, even if the casualty figures remained the same, Townshend would find it increasingly difficult to remove his wounded. This should have been clear to both him and Nixon, and adequate procedures should have been put in place before any further advance was contemplated. In fact, this situation was contemplated as part of the advance on Baghdad, and a solution was arrived at, even if it turned out to be ultimately (and indeed negligently) flawed.

The pursuit of the retreating Turkish troops up the river lacked the vigor of Townshend's Regatta. The water was lower, and the British forces were less well organized following the battle. Lines of communications were also becoming stretched — the 12th Division were the line of communications troops, which meant that there were no reserves in theater. Kut was 120 miles from the sea and surrounded by Arab tribes whose past record showed that they were willing to fall upon the defeated army, whichever side that may be. Indeed, the British did not have to wait to be defeated to be attacked. Fifteen *mahailas* carrying coal and oil for the steamers were attacked and sunk on the Tigris.[14] The further up the river Townshend advanced, the more desperate the situation would become if he suffered a reversal. The pursuit followed the Turks another 60 miles, halfway to Baghdad, as far as Aziziyeh, before calling a halt.

Battle of Ctesiphon

The decision to advance on Baghdad became a highly controversial one in the light of subsequent events. In fairness to those who ultimately made the decision, it was much debated by telegram between London, Delhi and Basra. What form should the attack take? Occupation or raid? What size of force would be needed to seize the town? What size would be required to hold it against the inevitable Turkish counter-attack? And could either of these forces be adequately supplied and reinforced? Indeed, was it even necessary to go to Baghdad?

It was expected that the occupation of Baghdad would allow a link-up with Russian forces in Anatolia or Persia, thereby cutting off the land route to India via Afghanistan. This would secure India from *jihad* which was a persistent concern in Delhi. It was also becoming clear by the autumn of 1915 that the Gallipoli landings had stalled. The prospect of admitting defeat and evacuating the peninsula was looming. The capture of Baghdad would offset the loss of prestige associated with failure at Gallipoli. The Egyptian front remained static. Meanwhile, the pro–Allies Greek premier, Venizelos, fell from power; Persia was unstable; there were concerns on the North West Frontier; there was a renewed German offensive against Serbia; and Bulgaria was joining the war on Germany's side. However, the prospect of capturing Baghdad and then loosing it to a Turkish counter-attack could not be contemplated.

At the end of August, Nixon stated in an "appreciation" that one division could occupy Baghdad, but it would require two to hold it, for which he would require an additional cavalry brigade and two of infantry. As the Turkish forces had been undertaking an orderly retreat to their new positions at Ctesiphon since June, the opportunity to "stampede" the Turks all the way from Qurna to Baghdad had been lost. Townshend expressed his concerns to Nixon on 3 October: "If I may be allowed to express an opinion, I should say that our object up to the battle of Kut has been the consolidation of the Basra *vilayate* and occupation of the strategic post of Kut" and went on to clarify the dangers which would be encountered by a force driven out of Baghdad and forced to retreat amongst hostile tribes. The following day, Chamberlain requested Nixon's plans now that, owing to the navigational difficulties, the prospect of "catching and smashing" the enemy had passed. On the 5th, Chamberlain raised the political consequences of being forced out of Baghdad. At this time, Nixon was informed that as there were no prospects of more reinforcements, there would be no advance on Baghdad. It was established that Nixon had sufficient forces to take Baghdad but not to hold it, and Nixon himself informed London and Delhi that the navigation difficulties on the Tigris had been overcome. With this information, on the 9th Chamberlain informed Hardinge that Nixon should maintain his present position but be prepared to advance on Baghdad — news of reinforcements would follow. The news was passed to Nixon on the 10th, and on the 11th Townshend issued a "divisional order" to that effect. On the 15th, Chamberlain informed Hardinge that two Indian divisions in France were being considered for Mesopotamia. However, as there would be delays in getting them to Basra (not least of the problems were the German U-boats and shipping shortages), it would not be safe for Nixon to advance on Baghdad until the divisions had departed Egypt. Despite the clear difficulties and delays in moving two divisions to Mesopotamia, Hardinge telegraphed Chamberlain on the 23rd to say that the Indian Staff considered that Nixon could advance on Baghdad and seize it, holding it long enough for the two new divisions to arrive. Delay ran the risk that the Allied withdrawal from Gallipoli would release divisions in Mesopotamia, and there were Middle Eastern political questions which could be resolved by occupying Baghdad. Chamberlain was given until the 25th to answer; otherwise Hardinge would order Nixon onto Baghdad. Chamberlain's reply of the 23rd gave the green light:

> Nixon may march on Baghdad if he is satisfied that force he has available is sufficient for the operation. Reinforcements will take time owing to relief and transport arrangements, but two divisions will be sent as soon as possible.

But one is left with the feeling that he was forced into action by India. Lord Kitchener certainly was not in favor of the advance. He was concerned with the defense of Egypt, and indeed now that the evacuation of Gallipoli was a realistic prospect, the release of Turkish divisions threatened Basra, Aden, Egypt or Salonika.[15]

The decision to take Baghdad had more to do with the international situation, in India, in the Balkans, in Gallipoli. On those grounds, taking Baghdad was a perfectly logical next step. However, two very important considerations were not adequately analyzed. Firstly, the logistics, which Nixon gave the impression were not a problem for the operations in mind. This was clearly not the case. Secondly, it was always assumed that British arms would take Baghdad. The "nightmare scenario" envisage by the politicians was for Baghdad to be captured and then lost to a Turkish counter-attack. With two more divisions en route, there was a gamble over who would arrive first, British or Turkish reinforcements, but this was a gamble which Chamberlain, Hardinge and Nixon were prepared to take. What was never considered was the situation in which the advance on Baghdad was repulsed. And why should it have been? British arms had been victorious so far. Well, yes, they had, but it had been far from a walk-over, and Chamberlain knew that the "stampede" following Qurna had been halted. Kut had been a success, but not without its difficulties. Each subsequent battle would see the 6th Division more and more tired, and further and further away from Basra, whereas the Turks were retiring on their internal lines and had months to prepare positions to defend Baghdad. The failure to consider this eventuality is the point on which the tragedy which became Kut began to unfold.

General Nixon was ordered by India to advance on Baghdad on 24 October 1915. Townshend was less than enthusiastic — the Turks were better organized than at the beginning of the year, and his troops were weakening through casualties, exhaustion and lengthening supply lines — but the campaign was gaining a prestige all out of proportion to its military significance. He was riding a wave and could not get off.

The division was also tired and under-strength, which impacted on moral. Townshend described his men to the viceroy: "These troops of mine are *tired* and their tails are *not* up, but slightly down." The three British battalions, which were considered to be the core of the division, were greatly under-strength — the Dorsets were down to just 297 fit for service — and the quality of recruits did not inspire Townshend. Perhaps even more worrying was the attitude of the Indian soldiers. Delamain thought that in the Battle of Kut, his Indians had fought on the whole "without spirit," although one battalion had fought particularly well, and suffered 45 percent casualties in the process. There were concerns whether the Shi'a Muslim soldiers would fight in the Shi'a Muslim holy places, of which Ctesiphon was one — reputedly the burial place of Salman Pak, the barber of the Prophet Mohammed. Townshend was dissatisfied with the quality of Indian reinforcements — he mentioned a "widespread unwillingness" to advance against the holy place — but this view was disputed by Captain Wilson, although he was forced to concede that one Indian battalion was returned to Basra because of the high desertion rates.[16] Yet for now, they were still riding on Townshend's good luck so far, and as Spackman put it, it was only towards the end of the siege of Kut that his soldiers began to question his abilities.[17]

Even the prime minister, Asquith, in public at least supported the advance when, on 2 November 1915, he told the House of Commons:

> General Nixon's force is now within measurable distance of Baghdad. I do not think that in the whole war there has been a series of operations more carefully contrived, more brilliantly conducted, and with a better prospect of final success.

Yet in private, the previous March he had been questioning what exactly Britain was doing there:

> Grey [the foreign secretary until 1916, famous for saying, "The lights are going out all over Europe"] and I ... both think that in the real interests of our future the best thing would be if at the end of the War we could say that we had taken and gained nothing, and this not from a merely moral and sentimental point of view. Taking Mesopotamia, for instance, means spending millions in irrigation and development with no immediate or early return. Keeping up quite a large army in an unfamiliar country, tacking every kind of tangled administrative question worse than we have ever had in India, with a hornets' nest of Arab tribes, and even if that were all set right having a perpetual menace on our flank in Kurdistan.[18]

Asquith had succinctly summed up the predicament of not only his government but also many others in the century to come: what are we doing here and how do we get out? There was no policy for either, yet Asquith could no more call a halt to the only successful campaign of 1915 than Townshend could.

Back in Mesopotamia, on the night of 27/28 October, a

night attack was launched from Azaziyah on the Turkish forward position at Al-Kutuniya, eight miles away. The Turks were surprised in the early morning and they retreated. Once again the cavalry failed to cut off their retreat. The Turkish positions were destroyed and the British withdrew to Azaziyah.[19]

Reinforcements and supplies were brought up the river to Townshend, but with falling water levels, the larger ships could no longer make the journey. It was not until 18 November that Townshend occupied Zor, 15 miles above Al-Kutuniya, and then to Lajj on the 20th where the division concentrated. Over half of the shipping capacity was required for grain, fodder and firewood, and the *shamal* lasted for longer than usual which delayed the *mahailas* which sailed up the Tigris.[20]

Nur-ud-Din had not been idle. He had been reinforced too. The 38th and 45th Divisions occupied the front line with the 51st in the second line. He now had an advantage over Townshend in men at least, and his hand was shortly to be strengthened further. Townshend requested from the RFC a reconnaissance flight to Baghdad to see what was happening there. The commander of the RFC detachment, Major Reilly, volunteered. Ctesiphon did not lie under his flight path, but he noticed changes to the defenses in the distance and changed course to investigate. Unfortunately, his engine was hit, and he was forced to make an emergency landing where he was captured by Arab tribesmen. Even more unfortunately, he had a sketch map of the river and British dispositions. Not only was this the first reliable information which Nur-ud-Din possessed about the British; it was also the only map available at Turkish headquarters. According to a Turkish account reprinted in the *Official History*, Reilly's crash was "taken as a happy omen that the luck of the enemy was about to change." Not only was Townshend deprived of Reilly's discovery, but the following day, two further aircraft were put out of action, leaving him with just one. He had lost his air superiority.[21]

Things were not all going Nur-ud-Din's way. The British War Office was aware of an additional 30,000 Turkish troops dispatched from Anatolia to the Mesopotamian front. Nixon was not unduly worried because he fully expected to be in Baghdad before they arrived. Perhaps, regardless of where Townshend was, he should have been more worried at the thought of the 6th Division, battered and exhausted in Baghdad, with only the weak 12th Division to support, provide reserves, secure the rest of the occupied territories and secure the lines of communication. The Turkish reinforcements were commanded by Khalil Bey, uncle of the Turkish war minister and, given the nepotism at the top of the Turkish government and military, he could be expected to take over from Nur-ud-Din.

More worrying and disturbing for Nur-ud-Din was news, also known to the British War Office, that the German General von der Goltz was en route to take command of the Mesopotamia campaign. Nur-ud-Din was not impressed, and he informed the Turkish high command:

> The Iraq Army has already proved that it does not need the military knowledge of Goltz Pasha.... The idea of sending a non–Muslim general to Iraq, which has a Muslim population and where we declared a Holy War, is remarkable.[22]

The Turkish defenses were centered on the famous arch and incorporated the remains of other ancient structures, most noticeably what the British called the "High Wall." The front line was some 12,000 yards long, from near the river, running roughly northwards. There were fifteen redoubts in all, with the northernmost point being defended by two redoubts, identified by Townshend as "Vital Point" (VP). The southernmost part of the defenses lay in a loop of the river which meant that any attack would have to either cross the river or pass in front of the trenches before they could be attacked. There were further trenches across the river.

The second line of defenses lay some 6,000 yards to the rear and was less extensive. There was also a potential weakness because to the rear, at about 1,000 yards, the Tigris ran parallel to the trenches. If Townshend could successfully execute the sort of movement he attempted at Kut, he could trap the 51st Division against a bend in the river with only a bridge of boats for them to escape over. That bridge would be vulnerable to the Royal Navy. The defenses extended across the river on the right bank.

In between the two lines of defenses were artillery positions. The terrain overall was the same flat, exposed, scrubby plain which offered ideal fields of view and of fire for the defenders.

At Ctesiphon, the Turkish forces consisted of some 18,000 infantry, 400 cavalry (the Iraq Cavalry Brigade) and two regiments of camelry. There were also 52 artillery pieces, 19 machine guns and several thousand Arab tribesmen. Nixon's staff underestimated the opposition: 13,000 men with 38 guns. Townshend, who, as we will see during the Siege of Kut, was lax about numbers, thought there were only 10,000 to 11,000 men and 30 guns.

- 35th Division — 3,800 rifles
  - 103rd Regiment — three battalions
  - 104th Regiment — two battalions
  - 105th Regiment — two battalions
- 38th Division — 3,100 rifles
  - 112th Regiment ⎫
  - 113th Regiment ⎬ — three battalions each
  - 114th Regiment ⎭
- 45th Division — 6,300 rifles
  - 3rd Regiment ⎫
  - 141st Regiment ⎬ — thee battalions each
  - 142nd Regiment ⎭
- 51st Division — 5,800 rifles
  - 7th Regiment ⎫
  - 9th Regiment ⎬ — three battalions each
  - 44th Regiment[23] ⎭

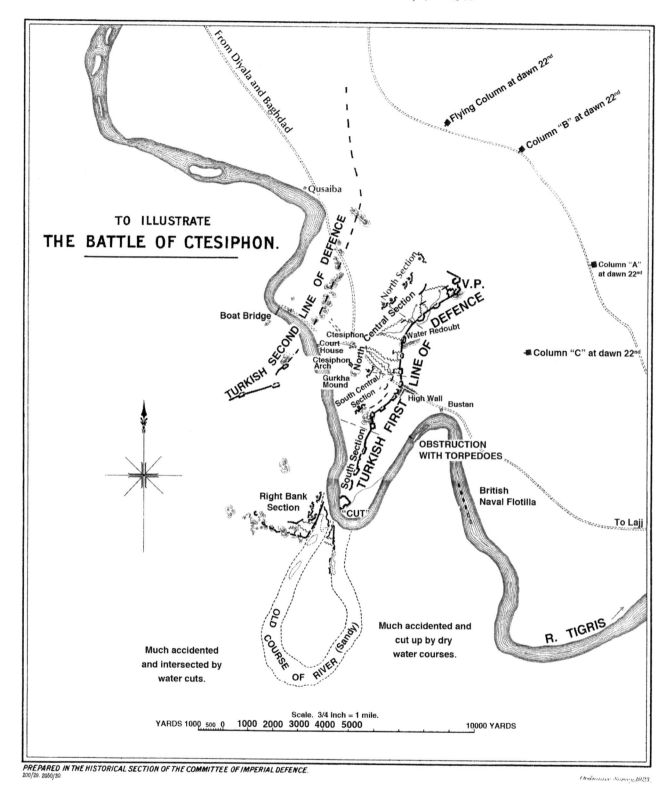

TO ILLUSTRATE
THE BATTLE OF CTESIPHON.

Battle of Ctesiphon, 21 to 24 November 1915

To assault these defenders, Townshend had at his disposal 13,700 infantry, five batteries of artillery and 11 squadrons of cavalry.[24] When you consider that the modern British Army prefers to attack with a 3:1 advantage, even with the most optimistic figures available to Townshend he only possessed a slight advantage, and the situation was not favorable. He would need to achieve another Kut, and without the hiccups, to defeat the enemy without the massive losses he feared from a frontal attack. This is what he attempted. If Townshend was to capture Baghdad and remain there, safely, at the end of such a long and vulnerable supply route, he had to destroy the Turkish forces in Mesopotamia. It would not be enough for Townshend to "hold the field."

Townshend's plan to attack the defenses at Ctesiphon — irreverently christened "Pistupon" by the British Tommies — was for three columns and a flying column to act in a similar manner as at Kut. Column C would attack the Turkish trenches to fix them in position. At the center of their objective was a redoubt known as the Water Redoubt. Four thousand yards to their right, Column A under General Delamain would attack the VP (Vital Point) directly. To their right, Column B would sweep around and envelop the Turks from the rear with the Flying Column (cavalry and 76th Punjabis), making an even wider sweep to cut off the Turkish retreat — behind the Turkish defenses was the Diyala River which was crossed by a bridge of boats. If that could be captured or destroyed, the only escape route would be across the Tigris which would be vulnerable to the Royal Navy gunboats. With one eye on Napoleon and another on self-publicity, Townshend explained his intentions with his usual literary flair:

> to make up for want of numbers by exploiting the principle of economy of force ... hoped to paralyse a great part of the forces of the enemy, extended along a large extent of front by the use of an inferior fraction of my troops, acting as a minimum force, disguising its weakness by audacity, or in forcing it to undertake an enterprise which will cost heavily, while I hit the hammer blow on the enemy's flank and rear with my principal mass.[25]

This is, no doubt, what Townshend thought Napoleon would have done. It is what Townshend attempted at Kut and what he wanted to achieve for the breakout from Qurna, but it was impossible to implement: fix the enemy and then get round the flank or rear of them to defeat the enemy through dislocation; that is, by attacking them where they did not expect it, their morale and therefore fighting capability would be degraded, hopefully to the point at which they would surrender. Incidentally, it is also similar to the 1991 liberation of Kuwait, where Iraqi forces were "fixed" on the Kuwait-Saudi border by what Townshend would call "a minimum force" while the "principal mass" crossed the Iraq-Saudi border further to the west and entered Kuwait from the northwest to get behind the Iraqi forces.

Townshend's plan was essentially sound and reflected his knowledge of his profession. The only problem would be whether or not his division had the physical capacity to implement the plan given the terrain — and, of course, the old adage, that no plan survives contact with the enemy.

The columns left Lajj at 1930 hours on the 21st. Delamain's Column A was in position by midnight about 5,000 yards northeast of "VP." Hamilton's Column B carried on a further two miles to its position, and Melliss's Flying Column a further two miles. Hoghton's Column C took a different route and was also in place by midnight. In Column C, Lieutenant

Spackman, posted to the second line of the 48th Pioneers, recorded that they were in position, unobserved, by midnight and then had to wait in the cold for dawn — his medical knapsack lacking even a bottle of "medicinal" brandy! The navy moved up to the village of Bustan. So far, all had gone according to plan, without the "geographical confusions" experienced at Kut. Unfortunately, Turkish headquarters received reports of British movements at about 0500 hours on the 22nd.

Naval gunfire at 0700 hours on the 22nd commenced the Battle of Ctesiphon. Hoghton's Column C moved into extended line and advanced to engage and thereby fix the Turkish forces to their front. No Turkish fire was drawn as the defenders had orders not to fire until the British were 900 yards away. When they were finally engaged, a mirage prevented their supporting artillery from identifying the trenches. Spackman was able to locate the trenches only from the puffs of shrapnel bursts above them. The Turkish response had been initially limited to a few shrapnel shells but increased with long-range rifle fire. The 119th Infantry was also enfiladed from fire from the High Wall.

Hamilton could not hear Hoghton's column being engaged, so he asked Townshend for permission to advance. Townshend agreed, and Hamilton advanced at 0830 hours. As Hamilton's role had been to advance once the battle had commenced, with the Turkish defenders fixed in place, and cut off their retreat, this was a major deviation from Townshend's plan. Melliss' Flying Column advanced in support but was met by the Iraq Cavalry Brigade, and for the remainder of the battle it secured the British right flank but did no more flying. Hamilton's advance was temporarily halted by Turkish troops in hastily prepared positions but was carried by the bayonet.

Delamain's advance against VP commenced at about 0930 hours. Hamilton's men were able to see them advancing away to their left. At 2,000 yards out, the Turks opened fire. The British advanced in 100-yard dashes. The 30th Brigade forced its way through the wire entanglements, where the kukris of the 2/7th Gurkhas made efficient wire cutters, and were in possession of VP by 1000 hours. At this point, part of the 30th Brigade came under fire from another redoubt to their left, reorientated themselves towards the new threat and attacked. They were unable to make much headway, and, more importantly, Colonel Climo, commanding the brigade, arrived in the VP afterwards and was unaware that part of his brigade was engaged elsewhere.

At 1045 hours, Townshend galloped to VP to assess the situation himself. General Nixon would also turn up there. Exactly what Delamain, commanding Column A, thought of having both the divisional and the corps commander on his shoulders while fighting his battle (and he had, after all, achieved his goal) is not recorded. Seeing what appeared to be a general Turkish retreat from the front line, and with no reserves to call upon, Townshend ordered Hoghton to bring his left "shoulder" to VP, and the 17th Brigade was disengaged.

They crossed in front of the Turkish positions at a range of between 1,000 and 1,500 yards, but that was not sufficient to take them out of the range of the Turks, and the brigade suffered casualties just in that move: Spackman with the 48th Pioneers noted how they took casualties during this move.

By 1330 hours, the Turks had abandoned their entire first line, and the 45th Division had been destroyed. Despite their predicament, a counter-attack was launched against VP at about 1400 hours which, although it failed, blunted any further British attacks. In the process, Climo was wounded and evacuated from the battle. Unfortunately for Townshend, he had no reserves to call upon. Attempts were made to collect together whoever could be rounded up, but these were simply not enough to give Townshend a reserve adequate to influence the battle. At 1700 hours, Townshend realized that he could achieve no more that day and ordered the concentration of his division at VP, a process which would not be completed until 2330 hours. Only then did Townshend realize just how few troops he had left at his disposal. A roll call revealed how weak the columns were: A, 1,000; B, 900; C, 700. He had suffered some 4,500 casualties in that day and was clearly in no position to resume the offensive the following day.

Throughout the day, the naval forces had been unable to advance against Turkish guns emplaced on the right bank, most of which were of heavier caliber than the navy's, and they had the range of the bend in the river. Nunn recorded that the river banks were 15 feet high at this point, despite the generally flat terrain, which meant that the gunfire support and counter battery fire he was able to provide was indirect and so less effective than direct fire. The Turkish gunners could spot the ships by their masts and funnels while the high banks blinded the navy. Furthermore, as Townshend had no troops on the right bank, there was nothing to threaten those Turkish guns. Nunn also observed Turkish boats moving troops from the right bank to the left bank. It was clear that the Turks had correctly deduced that was where the attack would be delivered.

With the end of the day's fighting, the casualty evacuation could begin in earnest. It had been proceeding throughout the day, but the attackers had covered a lot of ground in the day, and their casualties were dispersed across the battlefield. Spackman tended to, and recorded, the casualties he came across — a Sikh with his jawbone shot away, wanting a sip of water but unable to swallow; a "quiet temporary officer," "not at all warlike," dead with his sword in hand — it was unusual to take swords into battle but had clearly done so to gain courage in the moment, as his company commander had already been killed; the death of his friends, Major Riddell and Lieutenant Venis, the son of a Burmese planter, who died in his arms. Spackman himself had received a bullet through his ear during the assault but soon found that he and his small team were responsible for 200 casualties until the field ambulance arrived. The Pioneers alone had 60 percent casualties. Of the 10 British

officers, four were killed and four wounded; of the 12 Indian officers, all but one were casualties.[26]

Meanwhile, the process of collecting and treating the wounded continued. Four field ambulances with the division had the capacity of dealing with 400 casualties. They had to deal with eight times that figure. The hospital ships were moored at Lajj, 10 miles south of the battlefield, with accommodation for 500. They were filled with casualties even before the battle had ceased for the day. That night, rain soaked thin summer uniforms and the wind cut through those casualties left exposed to the weather. The infamous "AT carts" (Army Transport) were unsprung, uncushioned and not designed to be ambulances. There were tales of casualties crawling rather than suffering the agony of jolting carts on their broken limbs, or using dead bodies as cushioning. Even when they reached Lajj, the field ambulances were running out of medical supplies and food for the influx. Those who were loaded onto the hospital ships were to face a 13-day journey to the base hospital at Basra. It is clear that the planners assumed that casualties would be evacuated forward to Baghdad, not down the river to Al-Amara or Basra. Most received no further medical treatment once on board, and the ships had to endure sniping from Arabs on the banks as they made their way downriver. This was a medical scandal just waiting to break.[27]

If the 6th Division had been battered to a standstill, the effect on the Turkish defenders was even greater. Fifty days' labor in constructing the front-line trenches had been lost, and the second-line trenches were of a lesser level of preparedness; then the way to Baghdad would be open. The 35th Division had hardly been engaged all day, although it remained weak in numbers and morale. The 38th Division had taken some casualties, but its morale was now at the lowest point. The 45th Division was a mere skeleton. The 51st Division had suffered but was still active.[28]

The Turkish defenders had also suffered significant losses on the 22nd and were also aware that the British attackers had suffered too. Exhausted and disorganized, it would take time for the British to recover from the previous day's attacks. Units were mixed up. The ammunition resupply was at Lajj, 12 miles away. The nearest water was at Bustan. The casualties still had to be evacuated. Townshend revised his plans and decided to concentrate his troops between the river and the Water Redoubt, utilizing the High Wall. The navy was ordered to Bustan to provide gunfire support and so the steamers could resupply the army.

Overnight, the Turks had withdrawn to the Diyala River, but, realizing that the British were in no state to pursue them, they had reoccupied the second-line trenches. Their only reinforcements were the two remaining battalions from the 51st Division, but it was still two more than Townshend received. When a squadron of the 7th Lancers patrolled forward, they were driven back by heavy rifle fire from the second-line trenches. A low mound, christened "Gurkha Mound," a few hundred yards south of the arch was occupied at 1015 hours by the 2/7th Gurkhas and the 24th Punjabis — 400 rifles in total — with a Maxim battery and a section from the 82nd Field Artillery Battery. Shortly afterwards, Turkish artillery some 2,000 yards away commenced a "desultory" fire, but it was sufficient for the cavalry, which was watering its horses, to retire — the horses would not be watered until nightfall. Townshend also realized that he could not bring his ships to Bustan and had to settle for Lajj instead.

A Turkish counter-attack was launched at 1500 hours. The five battalions of the 35th Division (right) and nine battalions of the 38th Division (left) advanced from Ctesiphon village but came under fire from Gurkha Mound and retired in confusion. It would be 1700 hours, before they could be induced to advance again, but again this attack failed by 1900 hours. Gurkha Mound was surrounded and attacked until 0200 hours when these too withdrew. At 1600 hours, the 45th Division (right), and the 51st Division (left), with the Iraq Cavalry Brigade on their left, advanced against VP. Luck was with the defenders. The 51st Division got lost and did not participate in the battle. The 45th Division was cut to pieces during the attack, losing all of its field officers, but continued to attack until 0200 hours. The division ceased to exist as an effective unit. The 51st Division and the survivors of the 45th were withdrawn to the second-line trenches.[29]

The British casualties were finally evacuated in the afternoon of the 24th, two and a half days after the battle had commenced.[30]

Ctesiphon was a British victory; it was a Pyrrhic victory in the purest sense — the British could not take advantage of their victory; they could not even hold their ground; and they had insufficient strength to safeguard their lines of communications. Townshend was in no doubt about his predicament, yet he drew some strength from what had been undertaken:

> From a strategic and tactical point of view, the situation was as bad as could possibly be imagined — that was evident. Never in the history of civilised warfare have we seen small unsupported bodies successfully opposed to large ones, except in savage warfare, or war in India and on its North-West frontier, and in Afghanistan, where the fundamental principles of war may sometimes be violated with impunity.[31]

Yet in a telegram to Nixon on the 24th, Townshend could justifiably declare with pride, "The effort of driving four divisions out of a fortified position has exhausted my division — the officers and men have done splendidly."[32]

In the morning of 24 November, Nixon retired to Lajj where his vessel, *Malamir*, was moored and was never seen by the 6th Division again. Townshend, still in VP, assessed his situation. One option was to retire to Lajj. Initially, he decided to make a stand where he was. He arranged with Nunn to have the ships brought up to support the trenches. Townshend confirmed his intention to Nixon by wireless: "This I have arranged with the SNO [Nunn]. Thus I get rid of any retire-

ment whatever — I remain on here on the field of battle.... It will have a much better political effect not to retire, both here, Indian and at home."[33]

Nixon agreed. Nunn was unable to bring his ship far enough upriver. Townshend was unable to advance without significant reinforcements, which were not available. This left retreat as the only option open to Townshend. Thus, he was faced with his nightmare scenario — withdrawal in the face of a revitalized enemy and surrounded by rapacious Arab tribes, significant casualties and exhausted fighting troops.

Nixon, himself, retiring down the Tigris to arrange reinforcements, did not approve of Townshend's decision to retire:

> I do not like your proposed retirement on Lajj for military reasons.... You should of course prepare a fortified position at Lajj on which to retire in case of necessity and to cover your advanced base but for military reasons I do not consider retirement desirable at present.... Remember the moral is to the physical as five to one.[34]

Townshend had been comprehensively told off by his superior. In response, Townshend reminded Nixon of his 4,300 casualties which had reduced his brigades to little more than a battalion each. Air reconnaissance had observed two Turkish columns of 5,000 each. To remain at Ctesiphon, he told Nixon, would be madness and nothing else. Nixon conceded to Townshend's assessment.

Townshend ordered the retreat to Lajj on 25 November. It was one month and one day since Delhi had authorized Nixon's advance on Baghdad. Now it had all gone horribly wrong, and worse was to come.

On the same day, Khalil Bey arrived at the front. He would be the senior Turkish commander on the front for the next phase of the campaign. It is not know how Nur-ud-Din took Khalil's arrival. Nur-ud-Din had, after all, successfully, for now at least, halted the British advance and sent them back down the river.

Retirement

The 6th Division commenced its retreat to Lajj at 1930 hours on 25 November. The movement was completed five hours later, but aerial and cavalry reconnaissance reported the approach of some 12,000 Turkish troops. Townshend ordered another withdrawal, to Aziziya, 22 miles to the south. The navy's guns brought up the rear. At Aziziya, the division halted for two days to complete the evacuation of casualties and stores. The Arab tribes, however, were now becoming a nuisance. When *Shaitan* went aground and was being unloaded, she and other ships were fired upon from both banks by Arabs. Townshend sent out a section of field artillery with the cavalry brigade to drive off the Arabs, who left about 100 dead behind them.[35]

As if Townshend did not have enough to contend with, Nixon, en route to Basra, signaled that he, on board *Malamir*, and escorted by one of the new Fly Class gunboats, *Butterfly*, had been attacked. The 30th Brigade was dispatched to reopen the lines of communication.[36]

The next leg was to Umm-at-Tubul, which the division entered on 30 November. That night, Townshend was woken to be told that the Turks had caught up with them. The Turkish cavalry, it would seem, who were fulfilling their scouting and reconnaissance role, had entered Aziziya and discovered the supplies abandoned by the British. After a drunken night, the cavalry had set off late and found itself behind the main body, who had then blundered into the British. The British column was ordered to commence its journey before dawn, but with dawn came the view of the Turkish camp, full of white tents, just 2,000 yards away. This was too good an opportunity to miss, and the British artillery opened up, cutting through tents and scattering columns of infantry. The Turkish advance was totally disrupted, and, in Nunn's words, "the effect on the Turkish troops and camp was paralysing as we now know. Their whole XIIIth Army Corps fled in panic." The cavalry brigade (reinforced at Umm-at-Tubul by the 14th Hussars) also rode out to keep the Turkish infantry at bay. Nunn quotes from an unnamed Turkish historian that, except for the actions of the 7th Regiment, the British cavalry would have ridden down and captured all three Turkish divisions. As it was, Townshend observed the confusion and decided to break off the action, allowing the transport column to make its way southwards.[37]

In Spackman's account is a reference to an unusual addition to the column not mentioned elsewhere — the 1,500 Turkish prisoners from the battle which were escorted. He also records his fear of the "predatory" Sheikh Ghadban with 5,000 horsemen who hovered on their flanks. Why didn't they attack the retreating column? Those "unfortunates" who fell into the hands of Arabs suffered a "fate worse than death" or equally painful mutilation.[38] Perhaps Sheikh Ghadban was aware that the 6th Division was still able to inflict tactical defeats, just like they had done that morning, and so were not quite ripe for attacking just yet.

From Nunn's account, it appears that Nur-ud-Din, seeing the 30th Brigade's departure, assumed that was the main body and thought that he was facing only the British rearguard which was expected to retire in the night. He halted for the night and then sent the Turkish 44th Regiment to occupy the (presumed) empty British camp. Fortunately for the 44th Regiment, they got lost, missed the camp, and halted to the southwest of the camp when they reached the river.[39]

Worse was to come when the 44th Regiment and its accompanying two mountain guns attempted to block the river. *Firefly* received a direct hit to the boiler. *Comet*, being an old design of paddle steamer, but without independent paddles, was finding maneuvering in the river extremely difficult. She tried to tow *Firefly*, but that just made *Comet* completely un-

manageable. *Firefly* had to be abandoned. *Comet* was also soon on fire from repeated hits. *Shaitan* would also be lost during the retreat.

Firefly would later be refloated by the Turks and used to shell Kut, only to be recaptured and returned to the Royal Navy when the British pushed on to Baghdad for a second time. She was the first of a new class of "small China gunboats," the Fly Class, which were sent out from England in "kit form" and assembled at Abadan. The Fly Class gunboats were equipped with a four-inch and a six-pounder gun, Maxims, and wireless radios. As they drew only 2 feet 9 inches of water, they were extremely useful in the shallow rivers where the maximum draft was 3 feet 10 inches. All of the class were named after various types of fly — rather appropriate in Iraq — and *Butterfly* has already been mentioned in passing, above. Spackman commented on *Firefly*'s arrival, describing her as a "new and competent river monitor" "of shallow draft, good speed and firepower." Her first period of service under the White Ensign lasted just 10 days.[40]

A 26-mile, 10½-hour night march brought the division into Qala Shadi. When they arrived at "Monkey Village," there was no accommodation, so the soldiers bedded down as best they could. The place was hardly restful due to Arab sniping and a single, narrow stone bridge over a deep *nullah* which caused traffic chaos, exasperated by overturned vehicles and thrashing animals. Once across, the engineers blew the bridge.

With the decreasing depth of the river, more vessels were going aground and had to be abandoned, including a barge of sick and wounded. A few days later, these were delivered to the British camp; the Turks said that they had enough of their own to care for.

Spackman tells a different story of a grounded barge full of wounded. This one was pillaged and looted, and the passengers abused by the Bedouin Arabs, except for a "portly and sedentary Colonel of the Supply Department" who escaped by plunging through the mud to the bank and sprinting across country to the column. These prisoners, mostly sick and wounded, were sent into captivity, ultimately to Anatolia, as those who made it to Kut would follow them in the months to come. It may be that the able were sent to prisoner-of-war camps and the sick and wounded were returned to the British, although it is strange that Spackman did not mention this repatriation.[41]

At dawn, the retreat resumed. There were 21 miles to Kut, but after 18 the division made camp for the night. Bread was sent out from Kut, but it was another bitterly cold night and no lights could be shown or fires lit for fear of attracting fire from the Arabs. The following day, the 6th Division entered Kut. From there, Townshend telegraphed Nixon: "I mean to defend Kut as I did Chitral."

Townshend's basic plan at Ctesiphon was largely that which he implemented at Kut, and which had nearly succeeded for him there: to fix, encircle, trap and destroy the only enemy field force in Mesopotamia, thus opening the road to Baghdad without the fear of a retreating enemy force being able to reform and threaten him at some point in the future. Could it have succeeded on the second attempt?

There were several problems with Ctesiphon which meant that Townshend was unlikely to succeed from the outset. Firstly, the 6th Division was weaker — numerically and physically — at Ctesiphon than it had been at Kut. It simply did not have the strength to achieve Townshend's objectives in the terrain experienced in Mesopotamia. The division had been well rested after a summer of inactivity at Al-Amara. The deterioration in the physical and numerical strength then impacted on the moral strength. For the first time, we see Indian troops starting to waver, with the 110th Mahratta Light Infantry causing concern on two occasions. Townshend's command was unlikely to be able to achieve more than they had at Kut.

Secondly, Townshend's plan for Ctesiphon omitted one essential factor from that for Kut: the Turkish right wing. At Kut, Delamain's column had successfully deceived the Turkish defenders that at least part of the attack would fall on their right flank on the right bank, thus occupying defenders who could otherwise have been deployed on the left bank where Townshend's attack would fall. At Ctesiphon, there was no deployment on the right bank, and, in part from Major Reilly's crash and map, the Turkish commanders were better informed of the British plan. Nunn blamed the Turkish guns on the right bank for preventing his gunboats from advancing and commented that throughout the battle, neither his ships nor the artillery were able to move forward. This, he said, was due to the lack of a threat to the Turkish right flank.

Townshend was obsessed, although not without good reason, it should be said, with Napoleonic strategy, of which he prided himself on being an avid student. The right-flanking move to cut off and capture the enemy was perfectly sound, but it failed for him twice successively. Why? Firstly, the range of weaponry had increased exponentially in the century since Napoleon last took to the field, and, in simple terms, this dictated the radius within which the attacking troops were vulnerable to the fire of the defenders. The greater the radius, the greater the circumference to be followed on the advance. At Kut, this distance proved to be too great, although in Townshend's defense, the extra distance was due to error by the com-

mander on the ground, not his plan. At Ctesiphon, the route cut inside this radius and the attacking troops suffered casualties accordingly. Add to this the nature of the terrain and we are drawn to the conclusion that the plan was beyond the capability of Townshend's troops to perform.

There was a final weakness with both plans — although at Kut this did not prove fatal — which was the lack of a reserve. At Ctesiphon, Townshend thought that another brigade would have brought victory. Another brigade at Kut may well have captured more retreating Turks and prevented them from opposing him at Ctesiphon. However, he simply did not have the manpower to form a reserve. It was, as he realized, an all-or-nothing gamble — Baghdad or bust.

Add to all of this more, and more resilient, Turkish defenders, and Ctesiphon was fraught with difficulties which had not been seen in Mesopotamia to date.

The question has been asked whether or not Townshend could have refused to advance and dug in, waiting for reinforcements before advancing on Baghdad. Ultimately, the fate of the division was Townshend's responsibility — that is what he was there to do. The same could be said of Nixon. There were also military and political reasons why Townshend could not refuse to advance. In the first place, the refusal to carry out Nixon's orders would have resulted in Townshend's removal with potentially serious military repercussions, and would be almost certainly career ending, and Townshend was not going to follow a career-ending option if he could at all help it. Secondly, for the only successful general of 1915 to refuse to advance would almost certainly bring the whole weight of the British and Indian political establishments on him.

Townshend was also faced with intelligence of significant numbers of Turkish reinforcements reaching the theater. Such numbers were sufficient to overwhelm his small, tired force at the end of the long and vulnerable supply lines. Could he sit and wait and hope that more British reinforcements would join him first? Given the Indian government's inability (or unwillingness) to provide more divisions, and the distinctly peripheral nature of the Mesopotamian theater to the British government's war aims, this was an extremely unlikely scenario. Attack may well have been the best, if not the only, form of defense open to Townshend.

6

The Siege of Kut, December 1915–April 1916

The Siege of Kut began on 7 December 1915 and would last for 145 days. It was, and remains, the longest siege in British military history. In 1915, memory of the siege of Ladysmith during the Boer War was still fresh in the military mentality. Ladysmith lasted 118 days between 30 October 1899 and 28 February 1900.

Kut would also be the greatest British surrender since Yorktown, Virginia, in 1781, and would retain the dubious honor until the surrender of Singapore over just seven days in 1942. Eighty thousand British, Australian and Indian soldiers would surrender that day.

Of the three great disasters, Yorktown and Singapore are at least remembered in the different spheres of the Anglo-Saxon and Commonwealth worlds. Today all of the suffering of the "Kuttites" (and the relief columns) is forgotten. Kut did not even fall within the British sector of Iraq following 2003, unlike Basra and Al-Amara. Kut and Singapore were recovered which allowed the vanquished to restore their honor. Cornwallis' surrender at Yorktown, Virginia, would give birth to a new nation, the United States of America, just a few miles from where that nation was conceived, at Jamestown, Virginia. Yorktown is barely known of today in the United Kingdom.

There were, in the end, two factors which went in Britain's favor and which prevented the impact of the surrender being as bad as it might have been. Firstly, although Turkey captured a British division, it took them five months. Enver Pasha boasted of this achievement to a British officer and asked what the officer thought of that. In reply, the officer asked Enver Pasha whether, had the tables been turned, it would have taken five months for the British Army to capture a Turkish division?[1] Secondly, it was well known that the British had driven the Turks out of Kut in 1915, but that the British had been starved into submission, not driven out by the Turks, in 1916. Turkish prestige was not restored by the nature of their return to Kut.

The most controversial factor about Kut was Townshend's decision to stand there. It has been questioned whether it was the most appropriate location to make a stand, and even if a stand had to be made at all.

When the 6th Division reached Kut on 3 December, it was in an exhausted state. Having fought at Ctesiphon, the division had then marched 44 miles in 36 hours. The division needed a rest, which Kut afforded. Despite the mauling as it advanced and retired along the Tigris, the division was still a formidable force with "1,305 sabres, 39 guns and 7,411 bayonets,"[2] which had kept the Turkish vanguard at bay during the retreat from Ctesiphon. Whatever logistical problems the 6th Division was encountering, the Turkish soldiers were almost certainly suffering far worse. Had Townshend been able to keep his division together and retired in good order, forming when required for rearguard actions to repulse the Turkish pursuers, then there was no reason why he could not have continued his retreat to a location of his choosing. Of course, the further south he retired, the shorter became the British lines of communication while those of the Turks lengthened. It may even have been possible to disengage from the Turkish army entirely. This would have meant surrendering the terrain which had been captured during the summer with so much sweat, blood and nerve. Galling as that may have been, the sacrifice of land for a more defensible position deserved serious consideration, but the question remained, "How much land"? Townshend had already traded terrain to reach the illusory safety of Kut.

There was a further factor which had to be included in any withdrawal — the Arabs. They had already shown their willingness to turn on the defeated party, or even those wounded or isolated from the protection of a large body. They would turn on their former allies if the allies were the defeated party. Even while advancing from victory to victory, on the Tigris and the Euphrates, the Arabs had shown no reluctance when it came to conducting small-scale attacks and raids on the British Army. What would be their reaction when it was clear that the division was in full-scale retreat? Authors like Spackman had already expressed their concerns during the limited withdrawal to Kut. Had the division withdrawn further, becoming increasingly fatigued in the process, the task of keeping the division as a coherent and defensible whole would have become more and more difficult. That is where the Arabs would have attacked. The experience of modern, Western armies in Afghanistan and Iraq since 2001 give a feel for what that experience would have been like in December 1915. Townshend was also a student of military history. His battle plans were Napoleonic in concept, and perhaps he feared a similar retirement as that from Moscow, when the adverse weather and vengeful indigenous populations combined to destroy his army. The 1915 generals had been subalterns and junior officers in the aftermath of significant defeats of modern armies by "native" armies: Little Big Horn (1876), Isandlwana (1879), and Adwa (1896). Surprisingly, though, the Arab factor only appears to have had a minor role in the justifications for standing at Kut.

To a large extent, the decision was already being made by the time Townshend arrived. On 1 December, Brigadier General Rimmington made it clear that he favored a further withdrawal to the Es-Sinn positions. He felt that Kut was unsuitable for an entrenched "defensive position covering [the town] which could not be turned. Enemy will certainly surround us in a very confined camp and will hold us with a small force while he will occupy Es-Sinn position against our reinforcements."[3] Unfortunately, that is what did happen, as Rimmington elaborated, admittedly with the benefit of hindsight, in *The Army Quarterly* after the war: "In the result, the view given in my telegram was amply justified, as the enemy closed the neck of the peninsula with a semicircle of trenches, held by a small portion of his Army, and from that time Townshend was sealed up as surely as the Genie in the jar of the Arabian Nights tales."[4] Sir Percy Cox was of a similar opinion, even taking into account, as he must, the political dimension:

> We arrived at the unanimous opinion that, although from a political point of view the further ahead that our front was, the better for stability among the tribes behind it, yet from the purely military point of view Kut bend was a death-trap.[5]

Not all agreed. In 1972, General Rich (formerly a subaltern in the 120th Rajputana Rifles) sent questionnaires to the survivors to see whether or not they thought that they would have been able to carry on. Some thought that after a day's rest and a good meal they could have, but many more considered that they needed a week's rest—they were simply exhausted after everything they had been though.[6]

On the day his division arrived in Kut, Townshend made his decision to stand there, writing in his diary, "I mean to defend Kut as I did Chitral."[7] One is reminded of the glory in which Townshend basked following the earlier siege, and, given his desire for promotion (which, as we will see, reached ludicrous levels even when besieged), it is difficult not to imagine that another glorious siege would seal his career. This course of action would appeal to Townshend despite the exertions and sacrifices which would be made trying to relieve him.

On this occasion, Townshend was able to communicate his intentions to Nixon, who gave his wholehearted approval:

> The army commander is glad to hear of your decision, and is convinced that your troops will continue to show the same spirit in the defence as they have shown throughout your operations. Reinforcements will be pushed up to you with every possible speed.[8]

With Townshend's decision officially sanctioned, he informed the division of his intention:

> I intend to defend Kut-al-Amara and not to retire any further. Reinforcements are being sent at once from Basra to relieve us. The honour of our mother country and the Empire demands that we all work heart and soul in the defence of this place. We must dig in deep and dig in quickly, and then the enemy's shells will do little damage. We have ample food and ammunition, but commanding officers must husband the ammunition and not throw it away uselessly. The way you have managed to retire some 80 or 90 miles under the very noses of the Turks is nothing short of splendid, and speaks eloquently for the courage and discipline of this force.[9]

Despite this apparent certainty, Townshend was a doubter and a worrier, as he had worried before he had launched his regatta against Qurna. It is only natural for someone burdened with the responsibility of Townshend to worry: it would have been concerning if he had not contemplated his predicament. On 6 December, Townshend put to Nixon the proposal of withdrawing to Ali-al-Gharbi. This would have closed the gap between him and the 28th Brigade, the next nearest British formation. Now that the division had had the opportunity to rest, it was feasible for the retirement to resume. Townshend had now been in Kut for three days, and perhaps he had had the opportunity to examine the position in greater detail, which would have highlighted the problems which Rimmington had raised a week earlier.

Nixon was not convinced. His reply gave seven grounds why Townshend should stay put in Kut:

1. Relief could be expected within two months.
2. The 28th Brigade should be in the Ali-al-Ghabi/Sheikh Sa'ad area with supplies coming up to Kut within a week.
3. Further retirement would open the Shatt-al-Hai to the Turks.
4. Turkish overall strength needed aerial confirmation.
5. Any retirement from Kut should only be undertaken as a matter of last resort; pressure on Kut would be relieved by Russian pressure on the Turks.
6. Reinforcements were arriving while the 6th Division was fixing superior numbers.
7. There will be concentrations at Sheikh Sa'ad and Ali-al-Gharbi.

Nixon concluded, "Taking all of these pointes into consideration, the Army Commander does not approve of your proposal to fall back on Ali-al-Gharbi." Townshend wrote, with hindsight, in his autobiography: "Thus it was finally settled that I was to stand at Kut."[10]

He had, however, made it clear three days earlier that the decision had already been made. What is clarified from the 6 December exchange of telegraphs was that Townshend was having second thoughts about the wisdom of staying in Kut. This Townshend/Rimmington train of thought would prove to be correct, although it has to be noted that, as we shall see, Townshend greatly hampered the relief efforts by failing to accurately estimate and communicate food stocks.

There was another advantage in staying put in Kut. It was a major depot. He would not find the same stockpiled supplies at any of the towns he could expect to reach by marching downriver.[11]

It is also clear from Nixon's and Townshend's responses, above, that they were at best overly optimistic, and at worst negligently interpreting the situation. On the first point, reinforcements were on their way from France in the form of the 3rd and 7th Divisions, but given the chronic shortages of shipping, not to mention the submarine threats in the Mediterranean, it would take time to transport the divisions from France to Basra; they could hardly just up sticks and abandon miles of Western Front trenches. Once in Basra, Nixon must, or should, have been well aware of the logistical problems faced in Mesopotamia. How were two whole divisions going to be transported to Ali-al-Gharbi and maintained there? Nixon's sole maneuver unit was now the 28th Brigade. Everything else was "fixed" in Persia, around Basra/Qurna/Shaiba, on the Euphrates or in Kut.

On the second point, Nixon also miscalculated the impact of the closure of the Tigris, either at Kut by the British or at some other place chosen by the Turks. If the Turks chose to close the Tigris, as they could and indeed did, then the supplies promised to Townshend within the week would simply not get through. Conversely, Townshend could potentially close the Tigris to Turkish shipping, but the number of Turkish river craft had been severely curtailed by Nunn's flotilla throughout 1915 and, in any case, with the exception of the *Marmaris*, had shown little offensive capability. The Turks did not and had not relied on the Tigris to the same extent as the British for either supplies or fire support. They could simply bypass Kut. Indeed, the very fact that Kut sat within a peninsula effectively prevented the garrison from impeding the southwards progression of the Turkish army. The latter merely cut across the base of the peninsula and continued on their way south, as indeed they would have done even without the presence of Townshend. Had the division occupied a position like Sannaiyat, for example, which lay between the Tigris and the Suwaikiya Marshes, then they would have been able to block any further southwards movement of the Turkish army. As the crow flies, Sannaiyat was 13 miles south, perhaps twice as far as Es Sinn, but only halfway to Shaikh Saad.

Thirdly, that the Turkish strength required confirmation was a serious admission of failure to accurately assess the enemy threat and consequently to plan an adequate response.

Fourthly, any assistance from the Russians was illusory. Although a party of Cossacks had visited the British lines, communications between the two armies had to pass through London and St. Petersburg. Although the presence of large numbers of Russians east of Baghdad on the Turko-Persian border did tie down some Turkish troops, it would have required an offensive towards Baghdad to relieve any pressure on Kut. This did not happen.[12]

On 6 December, Townshend's cavalry brigade, "S" Battery Royal Horse Artillery, together with aircraft, spare transport and the gunboats other than *Sumana* left Kut.[13] They made their way to the 28th Brigade, where they would strengthen the relief force while reducing the number of mouths to be fed in the besieged town. Had Townshend been able to retire the rest of the division, he may well have extricated himself from the trap which Kut would become and made his way to the 28th Brigade. There, the remnants of the 6th Division, with the attached 30th Brigade also besieged in Kut, could have joined the 28th Brigade, occupied entrenched positions and rebuilt their strength over the winter in preparation for a renewed advance on Baghdad in 1916. As it was, the moment was lost when Nixon forbade any further retreat.

Where did responsibility lie for the siege and ultimate surrender of the 6th Division at Kut? Townshend was the divisional commander, and responsibility lies with him. On the 3rd, it is clear that he intended to stand at Kut and obtained Nixon's permission for this. Three days later, he had reconsidered his position. The division clearly needed to rest on the 3rd but could have resumed the march by the 6th, as was shown by the withdrawal of several assets on that day. Townshend wanted to break out to a more secure position, closer to supplies and reinforcements.

Although there was the matter of maintaining "face" amongst the tribes of Mesopotamia as well as the allied sheikhs of the Gulf, any withdrawal which included the loss of Kut was by no means fatal to the British war aims. Kut was beyond the border of the Basra *vilayet*. A withdrawal to the Es-Sinn, as Rimmington proposed, would only take them to the northernmost defensible position inside the Basra *vilayet* on the Tigris. If that position could then be held, then the original objectives laid down to Delamain and IEF "D" just over a year before would have been fully achieved. A "gamble" on taking Baghdad had been taken and had failed, but to no loss, as the original objectives had already been achieved and preserved. Nixon would have had his laurels for achieving those objectives and Townshend would have the glory of leading his division on an outstanding campaign: the skill of amphibious operations at Qurna, the great bluff at Al-Amara, the ambitiously planned battles defeated by the extremes of the operating environment, fighting to a standstill at Ctesiphon but not being defeated, and the skillful extraction of his division back to the safety of Basra.

However, Townshend's intentions to withdraw south of Kut were categorically blocked by Nixon. Furthermore, Nixon's assessment of the situation was deeply flawed, as was shown in his reply. The authority to request a withdrawal was in Townshend's hands; the authority to grant that request or to refuse it and oblige Townshend to endure the coming siege lay with Nixon. Although Townshend's mistakes during the siege contributed to its ultimate failure, the ultimate responsibility must lie with Nixon.

On 7 December 1915, the Turkish army reached and encircled Kut. There was now nothing to do but wait to be relieved.

The Town of Kut

Kut sits in a horseshoe bend in the Tigris about two miles deep and one mile wide, running northwest-southeast, with the Shatt-al-Hai joining the Tigris opposite the southernmost point of the town. At this time, there were some 600 houses in the town. Aerial photographs show a well-apportioned town surrounded by the river, open ground and date palms. The buildings facing the river, at least, were well-built and pleasing to the eye. The *Official History* also paints a pretty picture, describing a small town "flanked on either side by palm groves, fruit orchards and the remains of former extensive vegetable gardens." The *Official History* continues with a less picturesque description: "the whole place was indescribably filthy, owing to the insanitary habits of the inhabitants and to the accumulation of refuse and filth on the thoroughfares, the riverbanks and the immediate confines of the town." Colonel P. Hehir, the 6th Division's senior medical officer whose duties included the sanitation of the town and its inhabitants, both civil and military, considered Kut to be "the most insanitary place we occupied in Mesopotamia."[14] These were not good omens.

The town consisted of some 7,000 inhabitants. The main employment was the grain trade, as two caravan routes passed through the town. These were supported by a *serai*, a hostel for pilgrims or other travelers. The presence of the grain trade in Kut would be fortuitous for Townshend's ability to feed his division. There were also a Turkish administrative building, a couple of bazaars, a turquoise-roofed mosque and some wool presses. It was not a substantial town. Across the river, in a peninsula between the Tigris and the Shatt, lay the village of Yakasub or Elhan, know to the defenders as "Woolpress Village." Actually a liquorice factory, this would be defended as part of the town.

Outside of the town, due north, but within what would become besieged area, was an old fort, sitting at a point where the Tigris turned sharply east. As the only defensive feature in the town, Townshend decided to incorporate it into his defenses even if it meant making the defensive area larger than he would have liked. Known to the Turks as Kudeyra Kale, the fort could not have been surrendered to the Turks. It became the right anchor of the front line of trenches, which would stretch southwest to the Tigris. Beyond this line, into the desert, were a line of sand hills which overlooked much of the British entrenchments. Ideally, these sand hills would also have been occupied, but there were simply not enough men to dig and occupy a trench system that long.[15]

Within this perimeter, the first dilemma was what to do with the local population. Seven hundred "visitors" were expelled to reduce the demand on food, just as those units which would be of no value in the forthcoming siege had been sent south. But what about the remainder of the population?

There was a three-way debate between Nixon, Cox and Townshend about which course of action to adopt. Townshend, on grounds of military expedience and relying on his experiences of Chitral, wanted to expel all of the inhabitants. Cox, on the grounds of political expedience, thought otherwise: "We had to remember that winter conditions prevailed and the nights were bitterly cold and it was a serious step to turn our four or five thousand people into the blue." In any case, Townshend was informed that there were supplies in the town for three months and the relief was expected in two. So the population remained, and later Townshend would blame Cox for this decision. Having decided to keep the population within the town, Captain Arnold Wilson thought that Townshend's decision to send away Captain Gerald Lechman (the only other officer with experience in Arab affairs) was a mistake. It left Townshend without anyone who could liaise with the civilian population. Given the Arabs' reputation for theft, the certainty that at least some of them would be in communication with the Turkish besiegers, and the additional stresses and strains imposed on the civilian population during the siege, it is understandable that Wilson would consider not sending them away to be an unwise move.[16]

Where Townshend did make a major error of judgment was in not making a thorough survey of all the food stocks in town. Having done that, he would have had a clear and accurate account of how long the besieged town could hold out. He would have brought the townspeople onto the official ration strength too, but at least it would have prevented the townspeople from making their own arrangements and eating their own supplies.

The Defenses

As previously mentioned, the only defensive structure within the perimeter was the fort. Ultimately, there would be three parallel trenches with interconnecting communication trenches reaching back to the town. The First Line ran from the fort to the Tigris opposite and incorporated four blockhouses, A to D. Behind lay the Middle Line and Second Line. In total, some 30 miles of trenches would be dug. Although they

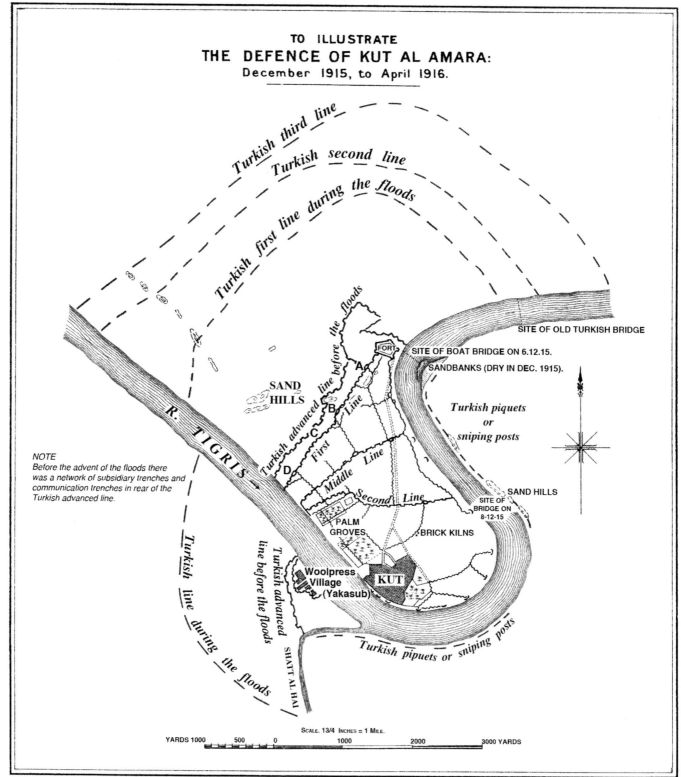

TO ILLUSTRATE
THE DEFENCE OF KUT AL AMARA:
December 1915, to April 1916.

Defense of Kut al Amara, December 1915 to April 1916

would be commenced before the Turks arrived, the First Line would not be completed until 15 December. The Second Line would be finished sooner, on the 12th, but it would be Christmas 1915 before the Middle Line was finished.[17]

Townshend divided the area into three sectors with a general reserve, each being the responsibility of one of his brigade commanders.

Northeast Sector: Hoghton's 17th Brigade was responsible for the fort and the eastern parts of the First and Second line, and the riverbank. The fort was clearly going to be the main objective of any Turkish attack. Responsibility for its defense was given to Lieutenant-Colonel Walter Brown, 103rd Mahrattas, with

- 103rd Mahrattas
- 119th Indian Infantry
- Fifty "bombers," Ox and Bucks LI
- Two 15-pounders, Volunteer Artillery Battery
- Maxim Battery, six guns under Captain C. Stockley
- Sirmur Company of Sappers and Miners

Northwest Sector: Delamain's 16th Brigade, opposite 17th Brigade.

Southern Sector: Hamilton's 18th Brigade was responsible for the Second Line southwards, including the Woolpress Village. This defense was manned by the 110th Mahrattas and the 120th Indian Infantry under the command of Major Pocock.

General Reserve: Melliss' 30th Brigade lived in the town but was stationed north of the town during the day.

Divisional Assets: Now that the majority of the cavalry, aviation and navy had departed, the main divisional asset was the artillery. The only cavalry remaining was a squadron each of the Indian 7th Lancers and 33rd Cavalry, but they would play no mounted role. There were two artillery parks. One was located 500 yards north of the town, the second located in the palm groves. The former was the larger and contained

- Six 18-pounders of 63rd Field Battery
- Two five-inch of 86th Heavy Battery
- Four howitzers of 1st/5th Hampshire Battery

There were also four 4.7-inch guns on two horse boats with *Sumana* plus her own 12- and 3-pounder guns moored on the Tigris. The transport lines, not that they would be transporting a great deal during the siege, were located in palm groves to the south of the town. Other assets like the headquarters, hospitals stores and signals were located within the town.

One of the most important engineering features to be improvised was a water supply. The *bhisties*, the Indian water carriers whose sterling performance at great risk and loss kept the fighting troops hydrated in the most appalling conditions imaginable, would be placed at great risk by extracting drinking water from the Tigris. The water was unlikely to do the drinkers any favors either.

The garrison and civilian population at the beginning of the siege were composed of:

Effectives:

British officers	206
British rank and file	2,276
Indian officers	153
Indian rank and file	6,941
Followers (approximate)	3,500
	13,076

Sick and wounded:

British officers	12
British rank and file	258
Indian officers	22
Indian rank and file	1,176
Followers	42
	1510
Ration strength	14,586

Civilians:

Men	1,538
Women and children	3,803
From Woolpress Village	504
Mahiellah (boat) men	316
Coolies	64
	6,225[18]

December 1915

On 7 December, 1,500 Turkish soldiers arrived outside Kut and began constructing the trench system which would cut off the peninsula and then form a base from which to sap forward in preparation for attacks on the British front line. The first Turkish troops to arrive were from the 35th Division, soon to be joined by the 38th, 45th and 51st. The 26th and 52nd Divisions would arrive later. This amounted to some 40,000 men, not the 12,000 previously expected. At the end of December, the 2nd Division, battle hardened from Gallipoli, was dispatched. When it arrived, the 6th Army would consist of two corps each of three divisions.

The same day, the Turkish commander, Nur-ud-Din, sent a demand for Townshend to surrender the town. In typical Townshend style, he recorded his response in his memoirs:

> I sent a reply that I had no answer to give to such an absurd demand as the laying down of my arms. But I thanked him for his courtesy in conforming to the usual custom in war in summoning the commandant or governor of a town to surrender before starting bombardment of it.[19]

Following the rejection of Nur-ud-Din's offer, there were thirty British casualties that day from shelling and sniping. The trenches were not yet complete, and the deadly effect of shelling and sniping had evidently not yet made sufficient impact on the besieged that they were as wary as they might have been. Major Barber, Indian Medical Service, described how a few near misses changed their attitude:

Those of us who had never been under shell fire before were inclined to take it very coolly at first. But after being nearly hit once or twice, we developed a healthy respect for an approaching shell, and ceased to take unnecessary risks.[20]

Adequate food supplies were essential for the garrison to hold out until relieved. In the fortnight either side of the Turkish investment of the town, there were three estimates of food supplies:

- 3 December — one month for the British soldiers, two months for the Indian soldiers, estimated to the beginning of January 1916, subsequently extended to mid–January.
- 7 December — 60 days for both British and India (until 5 February).
- 11 December — 59 days for all ranks other than meat (until 8 February).[21]

On the 8th there was the first major artillery barrage of the siege which inflicted significant damage on the fort. The following day at 1500 hours, the 35th Division made the first attack on the First Line. The attack was held, but the Turks were able to dig trenches some 600 yards from the First Line, closing in on the British even more.

That evening it was decided that the bridge of boats across the Tigris had to be destroyed in case it fell into Turkish hands and then offered them a route into town. Turkish soldiers had occupied trenches previously occupied by the 67th Punjabis and from there were able to bring down fire onto the bridge. As a result, it was not possible to dismantle the bridge, so orders were given to blow the far end, which would allow the remainder of the bridge to swing on the river back against Kut. Lieutenants Alec Matthews, RE, and Roy Sweet, 2nd/7th Gurkhas, led a party of volunteers from the Gurkhas, 48th Pioneers, and Sappers and Miners across the bridge, where they successfully detonated their charges. Throughout this the Gurkhas provided covering fire, but this should not detract from the bravery of the whole party on an exposed bridge across such a wide river as the Tigris at Kut. For their bravery, Townshend recommended the officers for the Victoria Cross and was disappointed when they were awarded the Distinguished Service Order (DSO):

> They volunteered for what appeared certain death, for the enemy as this bridge at the mercy of their rifles at 300 to 400 yards range and were firing down on to it. They waited all day to carry out the operation under cover of darkness — a very different proceeding from doing it on an impulse.

Spackman knew Matthews and recounted how he dined with the Pioneers before the attack and appeared "outwardly calm."[22]

Throughout the siege, Townshend would recommend a large number of his men for gallantry awards. Although awards would be made, lesser awards such as the DSOs awarded above were usually substituted. No Victoria Crosses were awarded,

in contrast with those of the relief force. Perhaps "the powers that be" decided that having got themselves into this mess, it would be inappropriate to grant the Kut garrison the highest awards.

There were 199 British casualties recorded on that day.[23]

On 10 December, the new commander of the Mesopotamia Corps and the relief effort was appointed, Lieutenant General Sir Fenton Aylmer, VC. Commissioned into the Royal Engineers and having served with the Bengal Sappers and Miners, he was a man of acknowledged bravery — he was awarded his VC in 1891 — but lacking in charisma which is generally considered to be a necessary attribute for the successful commander. He had already relieved Townshend from one siege, Chitral.

The Turks did not let up the pressure on Kut. Heavy bombardments and attacks by the 38th, 45th and 51st divisions on the 10th and 11th failed to gain any ground or breach the First Line, but they did inflict about 150 British casualties per day. Turkish casualties were even higher as they attempted to cross open ground. One of the sand hills was named "Corps Hill" for the obvious reason. Another four Turkish battalions attempted to break into Woolpress Village but were driven off.

In response to these repeated Turkish attacks, Townshend telegraphed Aylmer. There would be a constant stream of telegraphed advice, no doubt well meaning, to Aylmer throughout the siege. How well it was received was not recorded. On this occasion, Aylmer was informed that:

- There was a casualty rate of 150 to 200 per day.
- A strong division was required for the relief.
- There was a danger from a determined Turkish assault.
- There was a shortage of British officers for Indian regiments.
- Morale was dropping.[24]

It should be noted that Townshend's assertion that morale was dropping at this stage was probably more indicative of his melodrama than based on the actual feelings of the troops; see for example the words of Sergeant Munn and Major Sandes, quoted later in this chapter, which indicated that although things were getting more difficult by the end of the year, there was no significant drop in morale. The garrison had been told that there was food for three months and that the relief column would be there in two. Furthermore, with all of the reinforcements arriving from Europe, no one expected an attempt at relief until the new year. Daily casualty figures would fall, probably in response to a combination of improved entrenchments; fewer risk-takings (as Major Barber commented, above); and a pause in determined Turkish assaults. During pauses in the Turkish attacks, it was possible for the British to sally out, driving the Turks from their trenches and scoring minor victories.

The 103rd Mahratta's history recorded these raids and their limited military impact, although, from the morale-raising perspective, being able to "give it back" to the enemy (despite the personal risks involved) was far preferable to hiding at the bottom of a trench waiting for the next attack:

> On the 17th [December] two raids, carried out simultane-ously by parties of this battalion and the 119th, captured sev-eral enemy trenches and prisoners and, to some extent, re-lieved the fort of the fear of mines; but in no way arrested or intimidated the Turkish sappers. Every night brought their sap heads closer to the short listening trenches we had pushed out under the fort walls, and our barbed wire entanglements, never very strong, were shattered nightly by the cannon bombs which the Turks rolled into them. It was easy to see where the next attack might be expected.[25]

From this short passage, a vivid picture of the terrain in front of the fort (where both the 103rd and 119th were based) can be built up. The Turks held the high ground (although not necessarily higher than the fort's walls) from which they could roll explosives into the inadequate barbed-wire defenses. Mines were a real fear. Listening trenches in front of the walls must have been nerve-wracking posts during the long nights, espe-cially as it was well understood that the Fort was the main Turkish objective. Those listening trenches would have been very exposed and vulnerable places.

The author of the 103rd's history, although writing with the benefit of hindsight, was correct in identifying the target of the Turkish attack. The 52nd Division began probing on the night of 23 December by cutting the wire. Heavy artillery fire battered holes in the walls of the fort, and a mine was exploded under the wire at 0700 hours. Shells also fell on the First Line and in the town itself. Across the river, Woolpress Village was subjected to intense rifle fire from 0515 to 0830 hours.

The majority of the Turkish fire was aimed at the fort. The walls were breached and the fort was isolated from the remain-der of the garrison. Both 15-pounder guns were disabled. The defenders were forced in from their forward positions. One single shell killed the acting commander of the Royal Artillery, a staff officer and an ordnance officer. Observers from outside the fort assumed that everyone inside the fort was dead due to the lack of outgoing fire.

They were not. At about 1100 hours, the shelling ceased, and the 52nd Division commanded by Kaimakam Bekir Sami assaulted the fort. Their forward trenches were only 100 yards from the breached walls. The sepoys of the 103rd and 119th, supported by thirty Ox and Bucks Light Infantry and the crews of the disabled guns put up a stiff resistance. Four Maxims cut down the assaulting Turks, but they still entered the fort and established a lodgment. The Turks held on for some thirty minutes, supported by waves of reinforcements, but were even-tually driven out by bayonets and hand grenades. The remain-ing 200 men from the Ox and Bucks were able to enter the fort and reinforce their beleaguered colleagues.

The fort was saved, for now. There were a hundred Turkish bodies within the walls. Given the perilous state of the defenses

and the effort already devoted to breaching the British defenses, further attacks were expected, so the afternoon was spent shor-ing up the defenses. Command was given to Lieutenant Col-onel Lethbridge, commanding officer of the Ox and Bucks Light Infantry, with what remained of his battalion. This bat-talion was split in half, with one portion in a stockade with the artillerymen below the eastern wall, and the remainder on the eastern wall. In front of them were the 103rd, with orders to retire left and right into the side galleries, thus clearing the field of fire for the stockade. The Rajput Company of the 119th occupied the eastern corner. This would subject any attackers to cross fire from three directions at once.

The second attack came at 2000 hours with supporting ma-chine-gun and rifle fire. British howitzers fired immediately in front of the fort to catch the Turks in the open as they left their trenches—"danger close," to use the modern military ter-minology where supporting fire is delivered within safety dis-tances. It was now dark with a rising moon. Nighttime and shadows added to the confusion of the assault and fire. Star shells cast their eerie light, which further added to the mayhem. As the lights hung in the night sky, rocking, the light thrown out cast constantly oscillating shadows which added to the un-worldliness. The 103rd withdrew into the galleries, but it was not without problems:

> A party of "D" Company of this battalion, under Subedar Ramchander Roa Mohite, in the gallery to the right of the stockade, was destroyed man by man; but not before it had achieved its purpose and saved the stockade and the fort and possibly the whole front line from capture.[26]

With the loss of D Company, the regiment effectively ceased to exist.

One hour into the confused fighting, the machine gun in the stockade jammed. The Turks were able to take advantage of this, resulting in almost all of the defenders being killed or wounded. At about 2230 hours, the 48th Pioneers entered the fort, stabilizing the situation, and around about midnight the Turks finally withdrew again.[27]

A third assault by the Turks was launched about 0230 hours on Christmas Day, but without the determination of the first two assaults. The Norfolks joined into the fray, and the Turks withdrew at about 0300 hours.[28]

With first light, the full extent of the previous day's fighting became apparent. Estimates of Turkish losses vary between 1,000 and 2,000. Without a truce in the fighting, there was no opportunity to offer comfort to those caught between the lines. Lieutenant Heawood of the Ox and Bucks described the scene:

> Turkish dead and seriously wounded lay thick right up to our trenches. We made an attempt to bring them in; but the Turks from their trenches barely a hundred yards away, opened a heavy rifle fire on us until we desisted. Our men succeeded in passing out water and food to them. For some

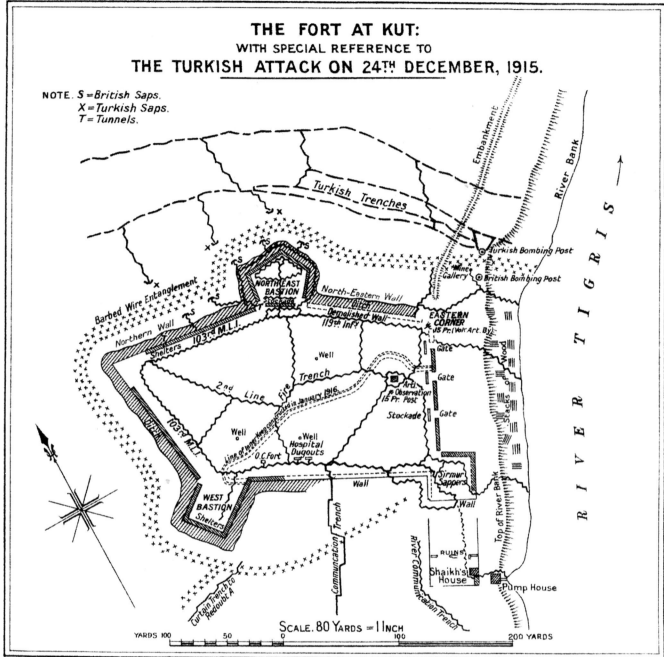

The Fort at Kut: the Turkish attack on 24 December 1915

reason the Turks themselves would not succour their wounded, as we saw some of them crawl back and get right onto their parapet, only to remain there for want of a helping hand from their friends. Presumably, they were afraid that we would fire on them if they showed themselves, though of course, we had no such intention.[29]

The stench of those unremoved, decomposing bodies remained throughout the length of the siege.

British casualties amounted to 315 in the fort and a further 67 elsewhere in Kut.[30]

The main impact of the failed attacks on the fort was that it brought an end to major Turkish attacks on Kut. Field Marshal von der Goltz's plan had been to isolate Kut on the peninsula and also to deploy troops further south to block against any relief efforts. Nur-ed-Din launched the attacks on Kut when Gotz was absent and in contradiction to his plan. Such costly attacks were not repeated. Despite the reinforcement of the Mesopotamia front, the 6th Army remained a low priority. Replacement soldiers were unlikely to come through. Time was on the side of the Turks, and they could afford to allow the British to struggle through the mud of the Tigris until Townshend's food or ammunition ran out.

Christmas Day might have been a muted affair. In the aftermath of the attacks on the fort, there was clearly a lot of clearing away and rebuilding to be undertaken in case the most recent attack was not the last. Within the fort, the remnants of those regiments which had stood at the center of the storm would naturally have been shell-shocked by what they had been through. Tired, shocked and contemplating lost friends or lucky escapes, they were unlikely to have been full of the festive cheer. And, of course, a great many of the survivors were not adherents of the Christian faith. For those who were, it is clear that there were imaginative efforts to celebrate Christmas. There were homemade Christmas cards and decorations, and improvised altars for padres to lead hymns. Rations were prepared into imaginatively and topically titled dishes. The limited stocks of alcohol were imbibed. Anecdotal evidence suggests that the officers fared better than the other ranks. Their greater buying power and smaller numbers no doubt assisted, especially while the *souks* were still open. However the overall effort to make the day special with whatever means were available will be recognized by all soldiers throughout the ages who have served away from home over the Christmas period.

The Christmas Eve assault on the fort did indeed mark the end of major Turkish attacks, but that did not mean that the garrison was left in peace. Sniping and shelling continued. Work continued, which will be familiar to students of the Western Front: wire was repaired, trenches were dug deeper or extended, rainwater was emptied. The weather took a turn for the worse, becoming cooler and wetter, which made living conditions even more uncomfortable. Pneumonia was starting to afflict the troops.

Townshend was not complacent throughout this period. In the event that the First Line was lost, the Middle Line was intended to become an alternative front line from which to maintain the defense of the town. He also telegraphed Aylmer with another of his running commentaries. He asked about the progress of the relief column and hoped that they would come before 10 January. He also commented on Turkish troops in Baghdad and the activities of the Russians. On 28 December, he announced that the relief column would set out from Ali-al-Gharbi on 3 January 1916. They would have to cover just 56 miles to Kut.

Sergeant Munn, Ox and Bucks Light Infantry, described life:

> At this time the weather was bitterly cold, the nights especially. We used to dress to go to bed. I used to put on a pair of long trousers over my puttees and shorts, a British warm coat round my body, a balaclava cap and scarf round my head, mitts and woollen gloves on my hands, all this besides two blankets. For a long time no man was allowed to take his boots off. I had mine on continuously from 24 December till

23 January. We lived in the trenches: some never left them until we surrendered. About this time foodstuff was getting a bit short, but as we expected to be relieved any day, nobody troubled much.[31]

And from Major Sandes, as 1915 came to an end,

> In the last days of the year 1915 the 6th Division and 30th Brigade were holding their own against the enemy, and were in fairly good health and good spirits. All were looking forward with confidence to a speedy relief. The defences around Kut were more or less complete; there was an abundance of food for a considerable time; ammunition was sufficient for probable requirements; the weather was fine and cold, and the river line fairly low. Optimism prevailed.[32]

Munn and Sandes' optimism, despite the hardships now being faced, was not unfounded. They could also look back on 1915 with a great deal of pride. They had broken out of Qurna and chased the Turk almost to the very gates of Baghdad. Townshend had done them proud. They had achieved far more than any other division in that year, far more than those whose misadventure in Gallipoli was just now coming to an end, or those on the Western Front who had failed to break through the German trenches, or those in Egypt still sheltering behind the Suez. They had been promised relief in the beginning of 1916. What could possibly go wrong?

January 1916

The year 1916 did not get off to a good start, with a number of setbacks in the first week alone. On New Year's Day, a sepoy of the 103rd while on sentry duty deserted his post, shot at an officer and attempted to desert to the enemy. He was captured, court-martialed and shot at dusk.[33] On the 3rd, the first rain came. This was a taste of things to come, and when combined with shortages of firewood, it made life even more uncomfortable. It would only be possible to provide one hot meal a day after breakfast, and the theft of firewood would become a capital offense. Fortunately a lighter of Persian crude oil had been left behind at Kut and the garrison learned how to utilize that for cooking. Nevertheless, unnecessary buildings were dismantled. Two days later, some 8,000 Turks were observed marching past Kut southwards. The following day, Townshend telegraphed more advice to Aylmer, and on the 6th the Battle of Sheikh Sa'ad was fought. News of this costly victory by Younghusband's 7th Division reached Kut on the 8th.

The Battle of the Wadi would be fought on 13 January, and the artillery barrage could be heard from Kut. This second failure to break through seems to have worried Townshend, and now we see some attempts to ration the garrison effectively for the first time. On the 15th, Townshend announced that had he realized that he would not be relieved by that date, he would not have halted at Kut. Aylmer almost certainly did not need this additional pressure from Townshend, as it was his men who had struggled and died in the mud of the Tigris over the previous week to reach Townshend. More critical though was Townshend's fourth food estimate of 21 days' rations for British soldiers and 18 for the Indians. This was a longer date than had been previously announced. Had Aylmer known that prior to launching his first two battles, he might well have delayed those battles until his reserves of men and ammunition were greater, which might have resulted in a less costly battle and reserves that could have pushed through the Turkish positions. The operative word here is *might*. We cannot know what Aylmer and Younghusband would have done. They did, however, deserve access to the most accurate information possible so as to make the best-informed decision. Even with that information, there was no guarantee that the opening battles would have been any more successful, but it was Townshend's responsibility to assist the relief force. In this respect, Townshend had let down those who were trying to relieve him.

It was at this time that Aylmer made his assessment that he could not break through to Kut with the forces available in the face of the Turkish opposition which they had experienced and in those weather conditions without the loss of half of his force. He suggested on the 16th that if Townshend could cross the Tigris and attempt a break-out to Sheikh Sa'ad, he would send a division to meet them. This would be a shorter distance than following the Tigris and possibly less well defended too. Nixon did not believe that the relief force was already capable of completing the task. He telegraphed Aylmer to refuse to sanction this course of action, calling it disastrous to 6th Division, Mesopotamia operations and the empire. Townshend's response was that he was unable to cross the river in significant numbers.

Nixon was by now a sick man and was struggling to manage the deteriorating situation. He asked to be replaced, and Sir Percy Lake was appointed on 19 January. Lake had previously served as chief of the general staff in India (previously he had served in the Sudan and Afghanistan and commanded a division in India) and so was fully conversant with the deteriorating situation on the Tigris. He was an infantryman, unlike Nixon who was a cavalryman and noted for his "ginger," that is, his aggressive, thrusting approach which had driven Townshend onwards. Whatever Lake's credentials, he was taking command at a critical time when most of the important decisions had already been made. Once these were in motion, there was only so much that any commander could do, even if he was a lieutenant general.

Coincidentally, at the same time, Nur-ed-Din was replaced as the Turkish commander by Colonel Khalil Bey. As with Lake's appointment, many of the key decisions for this stage of the campaign had already been made, although they were at least going in Khalil Bey's favor. He reaffirmed the Kut policy of blockade and starvation.

On 21 January, the Battle of the Hanna Defile was fought. The relief force was still 25 miles from Kut. The following day

Townshend's fourth food estimate was now transmitted. There were 21 half-days' rations left, but more food in the town. Three days later a sixth and final food estimate was made. Following searches of the town, there were now 84 days' half rations available, plus 3,000 horses and mules which could also be eaten. The garrison could hold out until 17 April 1916.[34]

Unusually for the time, Townshend issued several communiqués throughout the course of the siege to keep the soldiers abreast of events. Townshend had a theatrical flair, as we have seen, and these communiqués were probably part of his mentality. He also liked to think that he was well liked by his men (which is supported by their own accounts), but throughout the siege he was not a visible commander. His link to his men was via these communiqués, as he was not a visible general — for example, he is not known to have visited the hospitals during the siege.

COMMUNIQUE NUMBER ONE
26 JANUARY 1916

The Relief Force under General Aylmer has been unsuccessful in its efforts to dislodge the Turks entrenched on the left bank of the river, some 14 miles below the position of Es Sinn, where we defeated the Turks in September last, when their strength was greater than it is now. Our relieving force suffered severe loss and had very bad weather to contend against. They are entrenched close to the Turkish position. More reinforcements are on their way up the river, and I confidently expect to be relieved during the first half of the month of February.

I desire all ranks to know why I decided to make a stand at Kut during our retirement from Ctesiphon. It was because, so long as we hold Kut, the Turks cannot get their ships, barges, stores and munitions past this place, and so cannot move down to attack Amarah. Thus we are holding up the whole of the Turkish advance. It also gives time for our reinforcements to come up river from Basra and so restore success to our arms; It gives time to our allies, the Russians, who are now overrunning Persia, to move towards Baghdad. I had a personal message from General Baratoff, commanding the Russian Expeditionary Force in Persia, the other day, telling me of his admiration of what you men of the 6th Division and troops attached have done in the past two months, and telling me of his own progress on the road from Kirmanshah, to Baghdad.

By standing at Kut I maintain the territory we have won in the past year at the expense of much blood, commencing with your glorious victory at Shaiba, and thus we maintain the campaign as a glorious one instead of letting disaster pursue its course down to Amarah and perhaps beyond.

I have ample food for 84 days, and that is not counting the 3,000 animals which can be eaten. When I defended Chitral some 20 years ago, we lived well on atta and horseflesh, but, I repeat, I expect confidently to be relieved in the first half of the month of February.

Our duty stands out plain and simple. It is our duty to our Empire, to our beloved King and Country, to stand here and hold up the Turkish advance as we are doing now, and with the help of all, heart and soul with me together, we will make this defence to be remembered in history as a glorious one. All in England and India are watching us now and are proud of the splendid courage and devotion you have shown. Let all remember the glorious defence of Plevna, for that is what is in my mind.

I am absolutely calm and confident as to the result. The Turk, though good behind a trench, is of little value in the attack. They have tried it once, and their losses in one night in their attempt on the Fort were 2,000 alone. They have also had very heavy losses from General Aylmer's musketry and guns, and I have no doubt that they have had enough.

I want to tell you now, that when I was ordered to advance on Ctesiphon, I officially demanded an army corps, or at least two divisions, to perform the task successfully. Having pointed out the grave danger of doing this with one division only, I had done my duty. You know the result, and whether I was right or not; and your name will go down to history as the heroes of Ctesiphon, for heroes you proved yourselves in that battle. Perhaps by right I should not have told you of the above, but I feel I owe it to all of you to speak straightly and openly and to take you into my confidence. God know I felt our heavy losses, and the sufferings of my poor brave wounded, and I will remember it as long as I live. I may truly say that no general I know of has been more loyally obeyed and served than I have been in command of the 6th Division. These words are long, I am afraid, but I speak straight from the heart, and you see I have thrown all officialdom overboard. We will succeed; mark my words. *Save your ammunition as if it is gold.*

Kut-al-Amarah
26th Jan, 1916

Charles Townshend
Major-General
Commanding 6th Division[35]

This document is quite truly an amazing piece. It is very "Townshend" in its content. Before it is analyzed, it should be remembered that the aim was to inform the garrison of the state of affairs, a very important and commendable purpose, and also to maintain and if possible raise morale. The evidence at the time would tend to support that.

What is most surprising is the underhand attack at Aylmer's failure to break through the Turkish positions despite the 6th Division's success there against greater numbers in the summer. Whether or not Townshend faced greater numbers is a moot point; it is likely that Aylmer faced more, better prepared, better motivated and with much higher morale. In January 1916, it was the Turks, not the British, who were on the winning run.

The mention of "very bad weather" is a massive understatement of the atrocious conditions which Aylmer encountered, although they are almost inconceivable to imagine unless one had been there. Taken together, these two statements are grossly unfair to Aylmer who was, once again, digging Townshend out of a mess.

Townshend gives two grounds for standing at Kut. The first was to prevent the surrender of ground gained at great expense

by the division during the summer. This was a perfectly valid point aimed at the target audience. There were, of course, good strategic grounds for halting the Turkish advance somewhere— it would have to happen somewhere—but as has been discussed above, there were more suitable locations further down the river which could have been reached once the division had rested for a few days at Kut. The second reason, to deny the Turks the use of the Tigris, did not carry much weight as this impediment clearly did not hamper the Turks' efforts to blockade either Kut or Aylmer's advance.

Plevna is an unusual choice of siege to use as an example to inspire the troops, assuming that they had even heard of it. Today it is Pleven in Bulgaria, but between July and December 1877, it was the scene of a Russo-Romanian siege of a Turkish garrison. Townshend was alluding to the effects of Plevna in halting the Russian advance which allowed international support to be galvanized in Turkey's favor during the peace negotiations. Likewise, Kut was serving to halt the Turkish advance until reinforcements could be brought into the theater to reverse the current territorial losses.

Unfortunately, there were other parallels which Townshend probably did not intend but which would plague the British. At Plevna, there were a series of four bloody battles. The Turkish garrison was eventually forced to surrender. The Turkish commander, Osman Nuri Pasha, was well treated but his men died in their thousands during marches in the snow. There were more parallels to Kut than Townshend anticipated.

In Townshend's last paragraph he commits a major breach of military etiquette, which he attempts to cover up by telling his men that he owed it to them to speak "straightly and openly" for their sufferings. However justifiable Townshend's comments are, it is not appropriate to reveal such high-level debates amongst the rank and file today, and certainly was not in an era when rank, deference and class made such comments unheard off, no matter how much Townshend might consider that his soldiers loved him.

The final comment is most telling, "save your ammunition." There would be plenty of ammunition left when the food ran out. The Turks did not give the defenders the opportunity to use it all. As Townshend wrote, the Turk is good behind a trench but of little use in the attack, but at Kut the Turk did not need to be any good in the attack. After the Christmas attacks, there were no large attacks. He simply had to be good in the trenches (either at Kut or lower down on the Tigris) and wait for the food to run out.

February

Patrick Crowley describes February as a quiet month. After the flurry of activity preparing for the commencement of the siege, the Christmas attacks on the fort, and the relief battles in January, this is an accurate description.

On the Tigris, Aylmer still hoped to break through to Kut before the food ran out. He used the month to make more thorough preparations for future attacks than he had been able to achieve in January.

The main military change was when command of the Mesopotamia theater was transferred from Delhi to the War Office in London. This allowed it to be more efficiently managed by the appropriate departments who possessed the manpower and material to conduct a campaign which had already grown out off all proportion to the original instructions given to Delamain, which were to protect the oil and to occupy Basra if war broke out with Turkey.

In Kut, there were no large-scale attacks, but the sniping, shelling and occasional trench raids continued. At the beginning of the month, the weather improved and the ground began to harden. This was a prerequisite for Aylmer's advance, and so this was seen as a good omen for imminent relief.

Food was becoming scarcer, in particular certain types which would have added flavor to an otherwise monotonous diet. The loss of these foodstuffs seems to be more keenly felt than a general reduction in the quantity of food. For Lieutenant Spackman, RMO with the 48th Pioneers and still running their mess:

> Food is now getting an acute problem, I killed our last-but-one chicken yesterday to prevent its being stolen. A great find among my precious tinned stores (I run the messing) was two tins of snails, "escargots," and jolly good too! Sugar is now one teaspoonful each per day. Luckily, I have a lot of jam and tinned meat saved up (and butter) so am not entirely dependent on our ration. Bread is only 12 ounces each, which is a blow, with meat at eight ounces only.'[36]

Exactly how Spackman managed to acquire two tins of snails in Mesopotamia is not made clear. At the beginning of the siege, he had acquired a case of tinned butter which, having been carted around Mesopotamia for the summer, was considered so rancid that no one would eat it. By the end of the siege it was consumed, even though is appearance, taste and smell was of sump oil.[37] The officers' messes had the opportunity to stockpile extra rations before the siege through their extra purchasing power and access to mess transport. If the officers' mess was suffering from food shortages, then the sergeants and soldiers who relied more on the rations were going to be suffering even more. For Sergeant Munn:

> About half-way through February the rations were sadly diminishing. Tobacco was first out, and we were smoking anything that would smoke, and green leaves (dried over a fire), tea leaves and sawdust mixed, ginger cut up into small lumps. Tea ran out, and we had ginger water instead (ginger crushed and steeped in boiling water). Milk and sugar had given out long ago, likewise beef and mutton, and all the bully was gone with the exception of two day's emergency rations which were kept back until the very last.[38]

Eggs and tinned milk were reserved for those in hospital. As the Indian troops would not eat horseflesh on religious grounds, the last three camels were slaughtered to feed them. The remaining horses went hungry and ate blankets and even their own hair. Dysentery and scurvy became rife, and the hospitals filled up with these cases.[39]

Then, to add to their tribulations, a new weapon appeared — aerial bombing. The first appearance was on 13 February, and in this quiet phase of the siege the novelty created a diversion from mundane life. There was relatively little damage, but a series of anti-aircraft precautions were implemented. Six machine guns and one 13-pounder gun received improvised emplacements so that they could fire skywards. The infantry had to be controlled to prevent their enthusiastic firing at the airplane.

In the middle of the month, the Turks were heard to give three cheers for the German victories at Verdun. The besieged were able to respond in kind when news came of the great and unexpected Russian capture of the supposedly impregnable fortress city of Erzerum. There was even speculation that the Russians might capture Baghdad and relieve Kut before the British. There was a very real risk of a general Turkish collapse in Anatolia, which would have threatened Constantinople. Troops who could otherwise have been sent from the former Gallipoli front to Mesopotamia had to be redeployed to stabilize the Erzerum front instead. Indeed, it is possible to speculate that had Erzerum held against the Russians (in John Buchan's novel *Greenmantle*, the supposedly impregnable city falls to espionage, not direct military action), and with the British stationary behind the Suez, a far greater force could have been unleashed along the Tigris. In this scenario, there would have been the prospect of greater Turkish resources on the Tigris so that the blockade against the relief force could have been turned into offensive action.[40]

A warm, dry spell brought a new form of misery to the besieged — lice — which was both irritating and potentially dangerous as a known spreader of typhus. Without the ability to change clothes, let alone wash, there was no chance of avoiding this plague. The only option was to pick them from your clothes and blankets. Then the weather changed again, for the wetter, and the building of bunds took priority.

The quiet period came to an end in the fourth week of February. On the 22nd, friendly guns were heard as Aylmer battered the Hanna Gap position. The garrison stood ready to sally forth in a supporting action to link up with the relief column, which never materialized. Townshend wrote that "Apparently much confusion was caused in the enemy's main camp behind the Hanna position; but they did not retreat."[41]

At the same time, Townshend became concerned about the morale of his Indian troops. A sepoy of the 119th Infantry was shot for killing his adjutant, while desertions were reported amongst the 66th and 76th Punjabis and the 120th Infantry. There were also reported incidents of Indian self-mutilation.[42]

A great boost to morale occurred on the 26th when four British aircraft flew overhead on their way to bomb the German airfield at Shumran, from where the garrison's own tormentors originated. Two days later, on the penultimate day of the month, a dinner was held for the 16th anniversary of the Relief of Ladysmith. Optimism remained that Kut would also be delivered.

March

The new month commenced with probably the largest artillery bombardment of the siege, which was coordinated with a bombing raid by three German aircraft. The perception was that casualties were disproportionately felt by civilian women and children and in the hospitals. Townshend recorded the growing anger felt towards the pilots:

> If any of the German pilots had fallen into the hands of my troops he would have been torn to pieces. It was not fear of their bombs, for everyone treated the aeroplanes as a joke, running to cover at the last moment with shouts of laughter. But the victims were often women and children and our poor wounded in the hospital.[43]

In conjunction with the small-scale terror bombing campaign, mysterious metal cylinders were seen to be unloaded from a barge. It was assumed that these contained poison gas which was being used at that time on the Western Front. Gas masks were issued. Townshend was scathing at the prospect of chemical weapons, considering it "a cowardly barbarism worthy of Chinese pirates."[44] It is not known whether or not Townshend had dealings with Chinese pirates.

In and amongst all of the trials and tribulations of managing a besieged division with shortages of food, mounting casualties, the declining health of his men, the prospect of the horrors of chemical warfare and the disappointing progress of the relief column, Townshend was able to revert to type and pursue his main goal in life — self-promotion. He petitioned Lake for recognition of his successes the previous year and complained that his pre-war fellow major generals had been promoted over him. Once again, he did not seem to realize the impact of his petitioning for promotion. Unlike his previous campaigns, Townshend was now lacking powerful friends who were willing to support (or at least humor) his wishes. Furthermore, Townshend had got his command into a situation which was not conducive to promotion. Was he beginning to realize that even if he was successfully relieved, he would struggle to capitalize on Kut in the way he had been fêted after Chitral? If his future career and promotion were based on his last action, then the achievements of 1915 would be overshadowed by the ignominy of Kut.[45]

Meanwhile, outside Kut, both the Russian general Baratoff and Aylmer were on the move. The Russians attacked from Persia towards Baghdad with 15,000 men and 46 guns, but their progress was slow and the Russians failed to draw off significant numbers of Turks from their positions opposing the British. The next British advance finally commenced on 8 March after being delayed twice by yet more bad weather. Townshend shows more sympathy for the adversities facing Aylmer in his memoirs than he had done in Communiqué Number One:

> Throughout the siege the weather conditions were entirely in favour of the Turks. Never had a commander worse luck than General Aylmer in this respect; he had only to project an attack for driving rain and a regular gale to arise, wash away his bridge, and make the ground like a pudding, rendering it impossible for his troops to march or move the guns.[46]

Aylmer's objective this time was the Dujailah Redoubt on the right bank of the Tigris and some eight miles due east of Kut. In preparation, the garrison stood to in order to break out and support the relief column when it broke through. Four groupings were arranged under Major Generals Delamain, Hoghton and Melliss, and Colonel Evans. The guns were repositioned so as to give the best assistance. At 0710 hours on the 8th, an artillery barrage was heard from the east until 0830 hours. There was then silence until rifle fire was heard between 1400 and 1600 hours, followed by another artillery barrage. Then silence. The silence was ominous. It did not bode well for Aylmer's much-hoped-for-breakthrough and, indeed, was the sound of defeat.[47]

Two days after the battle, Townshend issued another communiqué to the garrison to inform them of the latest defeat:

COMMUNIQUE NUMBER TWO
10 MARCH 1916

> As on a former occasion, I take the troops of all ranks into my confidence again, and repeat the two following telegrams from General Aylmer, from which they will see that our Relieving Force has again failed to relieve us.
>
> **First Telegram, March 8th 1916:**— Today's operation terminated in gallant but unsuccessful attempts to storm Dujaila Redoubt. Troops pushed home the attack and carried out the operation with great gallantry, but the enemy was able to mass reinforcements, which arrived from the left bank at Magasis and from Shumran, and we were unable to break through. Unless the enemy retires from his present position form the right bank, which does not seem probable, we shall be unable to maintain ourselves in present positions, owing to lack of water; and unless the enemy evacuate the Es-Sinn position tonight, we shall be obliged to withdraw to our previous positions at Wadi. The Relief Force under General Aylmer has been unsuccessful in its efforts to dislodge the Turks entrenched on the left bank of the river, some 14 miles below the position of Es Sinn.
>
> **Second Telegram, March 8th 1916:**— We have been unable to break through to relieve you today, and may have to withdraw to Wadi tomorrow, but hope to make another attack before long and relieve you at an early date. Please wire movements of enemy, who in any case suffered most severely as their reported counter-attacks have been repulsed with heavy losses.

I know that you will be deeply disappointed to hear this news. We have now stood a three month's siege in a manner which has called upon you the praise of our beloved King and our fellow-countrymen in England, Scotland, Ireland and India, and all this after your brilliant battles of Kut-el-Amarah and Ctesiphon and your retirement to Kut, all of which feats of arms are now famous. Since the 5th of December you have spent 3 months in cruel uncertainty and to all men and to all people uncertainty is intolerable; as I say, on the top of all this comes the second failure to relieve us. And I ask you to give a little sympathy to me also, who have commanded you in three battles referred to, and who having come to you as a stranger now love my command with a depth of feelings I have never known in my life before. When I mention myself I would couple the names of the Generals under me, whose names are distinguished in the Army as leaders of men.

I am speaking to you as I did before, straight from the heart, and, as I say, ask your sympathy for my feelings, having promised you relief on certain dates on the promise of those ordered to relieve us. Not their fault, no doubt, and do not think that I blame them. They are giving their lives freely, and deserve our gratitude and admiration.

I want you to help me again, as before. I have asked General Aylmer, for the next attempt, which must be made before the end of this month, to bring such numbers as will break down all resistance and leave no doubt of the issue. Large reinforcements are reaching him, including an English Division of 17,000 men, the leading brigade of which much have reached Wadi by now, that is to say General Aylmer's headquarters.

In order to hold out I am killing a large number of horses, so as to reduce the quantity of grain eaten every day, and I have had to reduce your ration. It is necessary to do this in order to keep our flag flying. I am determined to hold out, and I know you are with me in this, heart and soul.

	Charles Townshend
Kut-al-Amarah	Major-General
10th Mar, 1916	Commanding 6th Division[48]

In comparison with Communiqué Number One, this document is far less controversial and is much more balanced. It commences by empathizing with the soldiers in their mutual predicament and reminds them of their former glories, implying that there will be more to gain in the future. Townshend is also grateful for the efforts and sacrifices of the relief force in trying to reach Kut.

Yet Townshend is unable to stop himself from having a "dig" at Aylmer. Townshend has asked him to attack with a larger force next time. This despite the fact that the first attempts were launched prematurely to meet Townshend's time estimates, and in explaining the problems faced by the most recent failure, Aylmer makes clear the difficulties of maintaining his current force, let alone a larger one, in those positions. Aylmer would have been justifiably angered had he been made aware of Townshend's lecturing him in front of the very troops whom he was attempting to rescue. Also, knowing that any telegrams

to Townshend may now also be published to the rank and file, Aylmer would be understandably cautious of what he wrote in future to Townshend. This could then impact on the free and frank passage of information between the commanders, which would have been essential for mutual cooperation.

Finally, Townshend showed a lack of "cultural awareness" by his apparent delight at the imminent arrival of an "English division," the 13th. To date, all of the divisions involved in Mesopotamia, the 3rd, 6th, 7th and 12th, had all been Indian. The 3rd and 7th Divisions had failed to relieve the 6th. Was an "English division" able to do any better? Townshend seemed to think so. This does not indicate a great deal of faith in the performance of the Indian divisions so far.

On the same day, Townshend received a second offer to surrender from Khalil Pasha Bey. The timing of this offer was no doubt due to the failed attacks on the 8th and the Turkish assessment that, after so many attempts, Kut was unlikely to be relieved in time.

> Your Excellency,
> The English forces that came to relieve you were compelled to retreat after giving battle at Felahieh and suffering 7000 casualties.
> After this retreat, General Aylmer, who was a month and a half in making his preparations, yesterday, when he thought he was strong enough, resumed the offensive with the 5th, 6th, 8th and 12th Brigades of infantry and one cavalry brigade on the right bank of the Tigris, as you saw. But he was again compelled to retreat, with 4,000 casualties, and I am left with adequate forces.
> For your part, you have heroically fulfilled your military duty.
> From henceforth I see no likelihood that you will be relieved. According to your deserters I believe that you are free without food and that diseases are prevalent among your troops.
> You are free to continue your resistance at Kut, or to surrender to my forces, which are grown larger and larger.
> Receive, General, the assurance of our highest consideration.
> Halil Commanding Turkish Forces in Iraq, Governor of Baghdad

True to form, Townshend declined with his usual flourish:

> I thanked him for his courtesy and said I was glad to find again as I had found in my operations at Kut-al-Amarah and Ctesiphon, that the Turk was a good soldier and a gentleman.[49]

Townshend did communicate the offer to Lake and suggested that a negotiated surrender had its merits. History was full of besieged garrisons which had been able to negotiate an honorable withdrawal. Now that the Turkish advance down the Tigris had been halted long enough for British troops to arrive and stabilize the front, one of the key reasons for holding Kut had gone. Thus Townshend could negotiate from a position of strength. When negotiations did commence, in April, both

Khalil Pasha and Townshend knew that the Kut garrison was on the verge of starvation and so had nothing to negotiate with.[50]

Khalil's assessment of both the besieged and relievers was succinct, to the point, and very accurate. When compared with Townshend's communiqués, there was no need for any flourish or attempts to inspire. Khalil knew the facts. So did Townshend. Now Townshend knew that Khalil knew that Kut's end was in sight. The Turks would not allow such a prize to slip through their fingers at the 11th hour. By this message, Kut's fate was sealed. Yet Townshend had to reject the offer. There was still the chance, however slight, of relief. There was also "face." The British could not be seen to be capitulating to the Turk without a loss of face amongst the Arab tribes, which would have disastrous diplomatic and political consequences. The agony for all parties must continue.

The consequences of failure to capture the Turkish positions at the Dujaila Redoubt was twofold. Firstly, there was a noticeable decline in morale for the first time, and secondly, rations were reduced still further. It was the lack of food which drove home their predicament: see the quote from Captain Spackman, below. On 15 March, the ration was reduced to 10 ounces of barley bread and 1½ ounces of horse flesh for the British soldiers, and for the Indians eight ounces of barley meal and four ounces of parched barley. Further reductions occurred on the 18th, 20th and 29th. Tea and tobacco ran out. Starlings were shot, and there were unsuccessful attempts to use explosives to stun fish in the Tigris.[51] Townshend's assessment of the garrison painted an uncharacteristically bleak picture:

> The effect of the repulse was soon apparent among my troops. There was a general feeling of gloom and depression, and desertion amongst the Indian troops increased; the Arabs of the town now looked upon our course as lost. If I had not been lucky enough to find the hidden grain at Kut we should have fallen by the first week in March.[52]

There was one glimmer of hope with the news that Aylmer was replaced by Gorringe on 11 March 1916. Captain Spackman was not alone in seeing hope in the new appointment, especially after Gorringe's successes on the Euphrates. Whether Melliss, who had fought under Gorringe on the Euphrates and who was now besieged at Kut, thought the same is not known. It should also be remembered that Gorringe had been less successful on the Karun:

> We had a great disappointment on the 8th and 9th when a great attack was made on the right bank. We could see the shells bursting clearly and the Turkish reserves moving about; but old Aylmer muffed it again, and now like Nixon and others is away on account of "ill health." So we are condemned to hang on interminably, but are still fairly confident of being relieved at last "next month," (always "next month") especially as it is now Gorringe who is directing attack at Qadi River, 20 miles downstream, Gorringe who we know as the successful general at Nasiriaya last July.[53]

Gorringe decided that he would wait for the arrival of 13th Division before he could resume the offensive. This would be on 1 April. For the rest of the month, the besieged settled down to garrison routine and awaited the next relief attempt. There were a series of heavy bombardments, both artillery and from the air, which continued to produce a steady stream of casualties (one shell went through the roof of the hospital and exploded), as well as a lot of lucky escapes, as many of the shells were "duds."

A far more debilitating foe was about to inflict the garrison: floodwaters. This was the result of melt water from Anatolia and rain. In the middle of the month, the Tigris rose two feet eight inches. The following week Redoubt B was in danger of flooding, and it became a constant task to keep it dry. By the end of the month, the First Line had to be abandoned and the Middle Line became the front line. The Turks suffered in a similar way and had to abandon some of their trenches. There was one benefit: sniping was reduced.

After the 26th, the worst of the flooding subsided, and the weather became warmer but was replaced by swarms of flies, billions of them, which added further misery to the damp trenches. Then there were hordes of frogs. Steps were cut so that the frogs, heavy from eating the flies, could hop out of dugouts, often tumbling back to the bottom.[54] Rain continued, often in violent thunderstorms. It was as if every torment imaginable was inflicted on Kut.

On 25 March, the 13th Division reached Sheikh Sa'ad. Townshend informed Gorringe that his food would run out on 15 April. This would be his final assessment. The Turks also received additional reinforcement.

April

At the beginning of April, Field Marshal General Frieherr von der Goltz lay dying of spotted typhus in Baghdad. He was the architect of the Turkish policy at Kut which, with the exception of Khalil Pasha's costly failed Christmas attacks, had been conducted at relatively little cost. Goltz died on the 6th and so missed the final victory at Kut.[55]

Gorringe's attack was launched on 5 April. Townshend was aware of it in advance, and the garrison was able to watch the flashes in the sky at night or climb onto rooftops with binoculars to look for any sign of movement. There was none. Townshend became impatient with suspense and lack of news. The following day he telegraphed headquarters:

> Can you give me any news of Gorringe? I have not heard from him since 8.30 yesterday morning, when he wired he had carried the first lines of the Hanna position. I wired this morning asking for news. It is now 4.30pm and I have heard nothing. No news I suppose is good news but it makes my people uneasy. I do not want to bother Gorringe in the midst of work, but he should not keep one like this without news.[56]

The replies contained no news of Gorringe's progress. No news was not good news. While Townshend fretted, the Tigris rose over three feet in 24 hours, which kept his garrison fully engaged in maintaining their own defenses.

Despite the hopes of Spackman and others, and the faith placed by Townshend in the arrival of the "English division," Gorringe's attacks in early April failed, just as those before him. On 10 April, Townshend was informed that he could not be relieved by the 15th. Townshend's response was to cut the ration still further and give a new date of the 29th, if certain foodstuffs could be air-dropped. Kut would be the first example of an attempt to sustain a besieged garrison by air. Townshend immediately informed the garrison of the situation:

COMMUNIQUE NUMBER THREE
10 APRIL 1916
The result of the attack of the Relief Force on the Turks entrenched in the Sannaiyat Position, is that the Relief Force has not as yet won its way through, but is entrenched close up to the Turks in places some 200 to 300 yards distant. General Gorringe wired me last night that he was consolidating his position as close to the enemy's trenches as he can get, with the intention of attacking again. He had had some difficulty with the flood, which he had remedied. I have no other details. However, you will see that I must not run any risk over the date calculated to which our rations would last, namely 15th April, as you all understand that digging means delay, though General Gorringe does not say so.

I am compelled, therefore, to appeal to you all to make a determined effort to eke out our scanty means so that I can hold out for certain till our comrades arrive, and I know I shall not appeal to you in vain.

I have then to reduce the rations to five ounces of meal for all ranks, British and Indian.

In this way I can hold out till April 21st if it becomes necessary. I do not think it will become necessary, but it is my duty to take all precautions in my power.

I am very sorry I can no longer favour the Indian soldiers in the matter of meal, but there is no possibility of doing so now. It must be remembered that there is plenty of horseflesh, which they have been authorised by their religious leaders to eat, and I have to recall with sorrow, that by not having taken the advantage of this wise dispensation they have weakened my power of resistance by one month.

In my communiqué to you on January 26th I told you that your duty stood out plain and simple; it was to stand here and hold up the Turkish Advance on the Tigris, working hand in hand together, and I expressed the hope that you would make this defence to be remembered in history as a glorious one. I asked you in this communiqué to remember the defence of Plevna, which was longer than that of even Ladysmith.

Well, you have nobly carried out your mission, you have nobly answered the trust and appeal I put to you — the whole British Empire, let me tell you, is ringing with our defence of Kut. You will all be proud to say one day, "I was one of the Garrison of Kut." As for Plevna and Ladysmith, we have outlasted them also. Whatever happens now, we have all done our

duty; as I said in my report of the defence of this place, which has not been telegraphed to Headquarters, I said that it was not possible in despatches to mention everyone, but I could safely say that every individual of this Force has done his duty to his King and Country. I was absolutely calm and confident as I told you on 26th January and I am confident now. I ask you all, comrades of all ranks, British and Indian, to help now in this food question in the manner I have mentioned.

Kut-al-Amarah | Charles Townshend
11th Apr, 1916 | Major-General
Commanding 6th Division[57]

Townshend's appeal to duty and his frank and open assessment of both the Relief Force's predicament and his own food supply is commendable. There cannot have been an individual in the garrison who was not fully briefed with the situation. But he seems unable to resist a dig at somebody. In the last communiqué, it was the prospect of relief by the "English division," which subsequently failed. Now the siege was curtailed by a month because the Indians refused to overcome their religious and cultural scruples by eating horse. It ignores his and his staff's mismanagement of the garrison's food stocks from the beginning.

COMMUNIQUE NUMBER FOUR
11 APRIL 1916
General Sir Percy Lake, the Army Commander, wired to me yesterday evening to say: "There can be no doubt that Gorringe can in time force his way through to Kut; in consequence of yesterday's failure, however, it is certainly doubtful if he can reach you by April 15th."

This is in answer to a telegram from me yesterday morning to say that, as it appeared doubtful that General Gorringe would be here by the 15th April I had reluctantly still further reduced the rations so as to hold out till 21st April. I hope that the Indian officers will help me now in my great need in using common-sense, talk the Indian soldiers [into eating] horseflesh, as the Arabs in the town are now doing.

Kut-al-Amarah | Charles Townshend
11th Apr, 1916 | Major-General
Commanding 6th Division[58]

The question of making Indian soldiers eat horse flesh was a contentious one. We have already seen that Townshend did not think highly of his sepoys, and he wrote that without his British troops, Kut would have fallen at the end of March. His brigade commanders thought more highly of them, but then they were old India hands who also saw their sepoys on a daily basis. There were also established concerns about whether Indian Muslims would fight fellow Muslims and in Muslim holy places. On the whole, though, they had fought, and with great distinction. In the end, Indian officers sat down to eat horse in front of their men, which seems to have worked. There is evidence that Indian soldiers suffered more than their British counterparts by failing to eat horse flesh. There were 30 deaths from diseases amongst the approximately 1,250 British soldiers, whereas there were some 300 deaths from diseases out of the

4,000 Indian soldiers. At the end of March, there were over 500 scurvy cases, and under these conditions wounds took longer to heal. British soldiers managed better, as they did not have the same religious or cultural qualms about eating all types of meat, but they were still wasting away. Spackman's daily walk to the hospital tired him out so that he had to rest halfway there.[59]

Airdrops of food and other supplies commenced on 16 April but were not a great success. There were limited available aircraft for all duties. They could only fly at dawn and dusk due to the heat during the rest of the day. They had limited lift capacity and the "drops" had to use improvised delivery systems which were not ideal, and it was difficult to predict the release point to hit the town from 6,000 feet. Many loads were dropped either in the Tigris or on the Turks. Second Lieutenant Davidson was wounded in the shoulder by an enemy aircraft, and thereafter escorts had to be provided, which further reduced the number of airplanes available to drop supplies. Townshend's staff estimated that 5,000 pounds of grain were required per day. The most that was delivered was 2,450 pounds, and the average just 1,600 pounds. These drops did not prevent the ration from being cut still further. It has to be considered that had these drops commenced earlier, then they may have had some effect on the outcome of the siege, especially if the drops were of critical foodstuffs to maintain the health of the garrison. Scurvy has already been mentioned, which is easily preventable through fresh vegetables or fruit juice. The complexities of the Indian dietary requirements are another issue which could have been alleviated, if not prevented, by airdrops of specific foodstuffs. The airdrops were too little, too late.[60]

On the day the airdrops commenced, Townshend proposed a breakout on the *Sumana* with some 600 to 700 men. At least some of the garrison would be saved, assuming that the vessel made it through the 20 or so miles of the meandering Tigris in full knowledge that the banks would be lined with Turks shooting at it. The plan was not rejected by Army headquarters, but they made one alteration: Townshend should stay with his garrison to the end. It was, of course, the right thing to do, for a commander to remain with his troops. One might even read that Townshend had no place in the new Mesopotamia Corps. The siege had, after all, created a great deal of difficulty, loss of life and cost several generals their careers. The writing was on the wall for Townshend, even if he was relieved. Perhaps unsurprisingly, he did not mention the plan again.[61]

On 12 April, Brigadier General Hoghton died and was replaced by Colonel W. Evans as commanding the 17th Brigade.

The final two attempts to relieve Kut took place on 17 and 22 April. Both failed to achieve the desired breakthrough. It was now becoming clear to observers that Kut was doomed. In April, Gertrude Bell in Basra wrote, "Nothing happens and nothing seems likely to happen at Kut — it's a desperate business. Heaven knows how it will end."[62]

The relief force remained 15 miles away from Kut on the left bank, 12 miles on the right bank along which a more direct route could have been taken. Townshend, and indeed the whole garrison, now knew that the end was in sight and that negotiations for surrender would have to commence soon unless something unexpected or spectacular happened.

There would be an attempt at each.

The first was an attempt to break the blockade by the *Julnar* carrying 250 tons of food on 24 April. The attempt failed, and at dawn the following day the stranded vessel could be seen from Kut. Of the all-volunteer crew, the captain, Lieutenant Firman, was killed along with a seaman. Lieutenant Commander Cowley and five seamen were injured. The two officers were awarded the Victoria Cross for their roles. Cowley was a long-term resident of Mesopotamia and was looked on as a traitor by the Turks for his assistance to the Royal Navy. It is understood that he was captured, wounded, and died shortly afterwards. The circumstances were never fully explained. The Turkish authorities claimed he was shot while attempting to escape, but investigations at the time and after the war suggest that he was murdered after being separated from the rest of the survivors.[63]

The final attempt was controversial from the outset — to pay for garrison to be released. Although Lord Kitchener, as secretary of state for war, approved the scheme, neither of the two most prominent political officers in Mesopotamia, Sir Percy Cox and Captain Wilson, wanted anything to do with it. Negotiations took place on 29 April led by Colonel Beach, Townshend's chief of intelligence; Captain Herbert, MP, with connections amongst the Turkish ruling elite; and Captain T.E. Lawrence (more famous as Lawrence of Arabia, although that was in the future), Cairo Intelligence Staff. These negotiations failed, and, in any case, the decision to surrender had already been made. Nothing was achieved except to hand the Constantinople press a propaganda coup. Lawrence was appalled at the reception he received:

> The local British had the strongest objections to my coming; and two Generals of them were good enough to explain to me that my mission (which they did not really know) was dishonourable to a soldier (which I was not).

He and Herbert were at least entertained by Gertrude Bell in Basra.[64]

Townshend attempted to negotiate with Khalil Bey on the 26th, but Khalil was well aware of conditions inside Kut and demanded nothing short of an unconditional surrender. Townshend had nothing to negotiate with. Hostilities ceased the following day. The garrison emerged from their subterranean existence to walk around ruined buildings in safety for the first time in months.

COMMUNIQUE NUMBER FIVE
28 APRIL 1916

It became clear, after General Gorringe's second repulse on 22nd April at Sannaiyat, of which I was informed by the

Army Commander by wire, that the Relief Force could not win its way through in anything like the time to relieve us, our limit of resistance as regards food being 29th April. It is hard to believe that the large forces composing the Relief Force now could not fight their way to Kut, but there is the fact staring us in the face.

I was then ordered to open negotiations for the surrender of Kut, in the words of the Army Commander, "The onus not lying on yourself. You are in the position of having conducted a gallant and successful defence, and you will be in a position to get better terms than any emissary of ours. The Admiral[65] who has been in consultation with the Army Commander considers that you, with your prestige, are likely to get the best terms — we can of course supply food as you may arrange."

These considerations alone, namely, that I can help my comrades of all ranks to the end, have decided me to overcome my bodily illnesses and the anguish of the mind which I am suffering from now, and I have interviewed the Turkish General-in-Chief yesterday, which is full of admiration at an "heroic defence of five months" as he put it.

Negotiations are still in progress, but I hope to be able to announce your departure for India on parole not to serve against the Turks, since the Turkish Commander-in-Chief says he thinks it will be allowed, and has wired to Constantinople to ask for this, and that the *Julnar*, which is lying with food for us at Magasis, now may be permitted to come to us.

Whatever has happened, my comrades, you can only be proud of yourselves. We have done our duty for King and Empire; the whole world knows we have done our duty.

I ask you to stand by me with your ready and splendid discipline, shown throughout, in the next few days, for the expedition of all service I demand from you. We may possibly go into camp, I hope, between the Fort and the town, along the shore, whence we can easily embark.

Kut-al-Amarah   Charles Townshend
28th Apr, 1916   Major-General
                        Commanding 6th Division[66]

This communiqué would prove to be massively optimistic.

The destruction of all military stores commenced. Captain Spackman "fired my revolver into the prism of my beautiful binoculars and then smashed my revolver with a sledge hammer and then burned my saddler."[67] Larger items, like artillery pieces, were blown up, with pieces flying off in all sorts of dangerous directions.

COMMUNIQUE NUMBER SIX
29 APRIL 1916
The GOC has sent the following letter to the Turkish Commander-in-Chief:

Your Excellency,

Hunger forces me to lay down our arms, and I am ready to surrender to you my brave soldiers, who have done their duty, as you affirmed when you said: "Your gallant troops will be the most sincere and precious guests."

Be generous then: they have done their duty. You have seen them in the Battle of Ctesiphon; you have seen them during the retirement; and you have seen them during the siege of Kut for the last five months, in which I have played the strategic role of blocking your counter-offensive and allowed time for our reinforcements to arrive in Iraq.

You have seen how they have done their duty, and I will be certain that the Military History of this war will affirm this in a decisive manner.

I send two of my officers, Captain Morland and Major Gilchrist, to arrange details.

I am ready to put Kut into your hands at once, and go into your camp as soon as you can arrange details, but I pray to you to expedite the arrival of food.

I propose that your chief medical officer should visit my hospitals with my Primary Medical Officer. He will be able to see for himself the state of some of my troops — there are some without arms and legs, some with scurvy. I do not suppose you wish to take these into captivity, and in fact the better course would be to let the wounded and sick go back to India.

The Chief of the Imperial Staff, London, wires me that the exchange of prisoners of war is permitted. An equal number of Turks in Egypt and India would be liberated for the same number of combatants.

Accept my high regards.

                        Charles Townshend
                        Major-General
                        Commanding 6th Division
                        and Forces at Kut.

I would add to the above that there are strong grounds for hoping that the Turks will eventually agree to all being exchanged. I have received notification from the Turkish Commander-in-Chief, to say I can start for Constantinople soon. Having arrived there, I shall petition to be allowed to go to London on parole and see the Secretary of State for War and get you exchanged at once. In this way I hope to be of great assistance to you all.

I thank you from the bottom of my heart for you devotion to duty and your discipline and bravery, and may we meet soon in better times.

Kut-al-Amarah   Charles Townshend
29th Apr, 1916   Major-General
                        Commanding 6th Division[68]

The garrison surrendered on 29 April 1916, after a siege of 147 days.

The Turkish authorities executed a number of inhabitants for collaboration and made it known that this was the fate of all collaborators. Sir Percy Cox's insistence that the Turk must not be allowed to return to Basra if the inhabitants were going to be persuaded to support the British was proved correct at Kut. Although Kut was the only Mesopotamian town to be recovered by the Turks, in Palestine when As-Salt on the Jordan River was evacuated, collaborators were also executed.[69]

7

The Relief of Kut, December 1915–April 1916

When Kut was invested, the 6th Division and the 30th Brigade from the 12th Division were effectively removed from operations along the Tigris. Even Townshend's claim that, by holding Kut, he could prevent the Turkish army from advancing further down the Tigris, proved to be unfounded.

General Nixon, now commander of the Tigris Corps, was initially left with just the remnants of the 12th Division plus the cavalry brigade, which left Kut shortly before it was invested.

12th Division: GOC Lieutenant General Gorringe

- 6th Cavalry Brigade
  - ○ 14th Hussars
  - ○ 4th Cavalry
  - ○ 7th Lancers (less one squadron in Kut)
  - ○ 33rd Cavalry (less one squadron in Kut)
  - ○ "S" Battery Royal Horse Artillery (four guns)
  - ○ Brigade Ammunition Column
  - ○ Brigade Signal Troop
- 12th Infantry Brigade
  - ○ 4th Rajputs
  - ○ 44th Merwara Infantry
  - ○ 90th Punjabis
- 33rd Infantry Brigade
  - ○ 1/4th Hampshires (less one company with 30 Brigade in Kut)
  - ○ 11th Rajputs
  - ○ 66th Punjabis
  - ○ 67th Punjabis (less half battalion with 30 Bde in Kut)
- Divisional Troops:
  - ○ 2 Squadrons, 33rd Cavalry
  - ○ 56th Heavy Battery RGA (four guns)
  - ○ 104th Heavy Battery RGA (four guns)
  - ○ 1/5th Hampshire Howitzer Battery (four howitzers)
  - ○ 12th Field Company (Sappers and Miners)
  - ○ Sirmur Imperial Service Company (Sappers and Miners)
  - ○ 12th Divisional Signals Company

Nixon also had the resources of the naval flotilla less those vessels sunk or abandoned during the retreat to Kut, and *Sumara* which was left behind in Kut. The above list shows just how few troops had been available to Nixon until the two reinforcing divisions arrived. As Nixon's forces were spread out along the Shatt-al-Arab, the Euphrates and Tigris, it would have been difficult to concentrate these units into a coherent force to withstand any concerted Turkish attack. Fortunately, the Turks were not in a position to attack, but the prospect must have been a great worry to the staff officers and generals in Basra.

Whatever the merits or otherwise of Townshend's decision to halt and make a stand at Kut, the situation now stood that Townshend had to be relieved. The year 1915 had not gone well on the Western Front, and the decision to evacuate Gallipoli was taken that December. Townshend had to be relieved to prevent yet another disaster. It was fortunate for Nixon that the Turkish forces halted to besiege and storm Kut. With the forces available to him to hold the lower portion of the Tigris, plus the Euphrates, the base area around Basra-Qurna-Shaiba, not to mention the oil facilities in Persia (the original reason for arriving in Mesopotamia), Nixon would have found it difficult to withstand this new, reinvigorated Turkish army.

Halting at Kut, investing Townshend and attempting to storm the town was the sensible option for the Turkish forces now. The 6th Division was a potent beast. Even during the retreat from Ctesiphon, the division had proved its mettle; it had not been panicked into a rabble and had turned to give the pursuers a bloody nose as and when required. Rested and refreshed, the old 6th Division which had chased the Turks up the Tigris that spring was not a formation which any commander wanted in their rear. While XVIII Corps, of the 45th and 51st Divisions, besieged Kut, XIII Corps, with the 35th and 52nd Divisions, moved 18 miles downriver to block the relieving force.

Lieutenant General Fenton Aylmer, VC, arrived in Basra from India to command the relief of Kut. Aylmer was commissioned into the Royal Corps of Engineers and had won his Victoria Cross in the Hunza-Nagar Expedition of 1891–1892 for blowing the gate to Nilt Fort despite being seriously wounded. He would have known Townshend and he also participated in the Relief of Chitral. It would be interesting to know Aylmer's response when he heard that Townshend was besieged, again, and Aylmer had to help him out (again). However, at least in public, Aylmer's response was upbeat, and he telegraphed Townshend accordingly: "Have utmost confidence in defender of Chitral and his gallant troops to keep flag flying till we can relieve them. Heartiest congratulations on brilliant deeds of yourself and your command."[1] Unfortunately, Townshend's mess would be career ending for Aylmer too.

Townshend's initial assessment of his supplies was that he had enough for one month for the British troops and two months for the Indian troops. Aylmer concentrated his force at Ali-al-Gharbi and estimated that he needed to commence his advance on 3 January 1916 to meet Townshend's deadline. By that date, he would command the 7th (Meerut) Division, the 6th Cavalry Brigade and one additional infantry brigade, the 21st:

Tigris Corps: Lieutenant General Sir Fenton Aylmer

7th (Meerut) Division: GOC Major General Younghusband[2]

- 6th Cavalry Brigade
  - "S" Battery, RHA (four guns)
  - 14th Hussars
  - 4th Cavalry
  - 7th Lancers (less one squadron)
  - 33rd Cavalry (less one squadron)
  - Brigade Ammunition Column
  - Brigade Signal Troop
- 19th Infantry Brigade
  - 1st Battalion, the Seaforth Highlanders
  - 28th Punjabis
  - 92nd Punjabis
  - 125th Rifles
- 28th Infantry Brigade:
  - 2nd Battalion, the Leicestershire Regiment
  - 51st Sikhs
  - 53rd Sikhs
  - 56th Rifles
- 35th Infantry Brigade:[3]
  - 5th Battalion, the East Kent Regiment (the Buffs)
  - 37th Dogras
  - 97th Infantry
  - 102nd Grenadiers
- Divisional Troops
  - 13th Company, Sappers and Miners, and Bridging Train
  - 128th Pioneers

- No. 20 Combined Field Ambulance
- No. 3 Combined Field Ambulance (half)
- Royal Artillery
  - 9th Brigade, RFA ⎫
  - 20th Brigade, RFA ⎬ eighteen 18-pound guns
  - 28th Battery, RFA ⎭
  - 1/1st Sussex Battery, RFA four 15-pound guns
  - Heavy Artillery Brigade
    - 72nd Heavy Battery ⎫ four 5-inch howitzers each
    - 77th Heavy Battery ⎭
    - 104th Heavy Battery (one section) two 4-inch guns
- Other troops in theater
  - 16th Cavalry (less one squadron)
  - 107th Pioneers
  - 1/4th Battalion, the Hampshires Regiment (less one company)
  - 67th Punjabis (one company)
  - 1st Provisional Battalions (composed of drafts for units in the Kut garrison)
  - 23rd Mountain Battery (less one section) four guns
  - Volunteer Artillery Battery one gun
- Signals Units
  - Four wireless stations
- Medical Units
  - No. 18 Cavalry Field Ambulance (one British, one Indian section)
  - No. 131 Indian Cavalry Field Ambulance (three Indian sections)
  - No. 1 Field Ambulance (two sections)
  - No. 5 and 6 Field Ambulances (improvised, of two sections each)
- Royal Flying Corps
  - 2 aircraft

Meanwhile, forming up behind the 7th Division at Basra was:

3rd (Lahore) Division: GOC Major General Henry D'Urban Keary[4]

- 7th Brigade
  - 1st Battalion, the Connaught Rangers
  - 27th Punjabis
  - 89th Punjabis
  - 128th Pioneers
- 8th Brigade
  - 1st Battalion, the Manchester Regiment
  - 2nd Rajputs
  - 47th Sikhs
  - 59th Rifles
- 9th Brigade
  - 1st Battalion, the Highland Light Infantry
  - 1/1st Gurkhas

- o 1/9th Gurkhas
- o 93rd Infantry
- • Divisional Troops
  - o 4th Brigade, RFA
  - o 20th Field Company, Sappers and Miners
  - o 21st Field Company, Sappers and Miners
  - o 34th Sikh Pioneers
  - o 16th Cavalry (one squadron)
  - o No. 3 Divisional Signals Company
  - o Mobile Veterinary Section

If supply and supporting equipment had been in short supply for Townshend, Aylmer found his position no better. At least Townshend had the advantage of commanding a division which had served together previously — Aylmer's force was a mix of established and new brigades, but the division itself was an agglomeration. Aylmer's one strength was the arrival of four more of the Fly Class river gunboats. Nunn took *Gadfly* as his flagship.[5]

As we have seen, the army operated best when supported by the navy, and the arrival of these riverine gunboats can only have provided more support. These vessels had originally, and optimistically, been designed to operate on the Danube, but fate would prevent that theater of operations from opening up to the Allies, and that twist would be all the more fortuitous as the Fly-boats would prove sterling and invaluable service

in the difficult years ahead. Furthermore, with winter approaching, the depth of the Tigris would increase, helping with the transport situation which had plagued Nunn between Al-Amara and Ctesiphon. The winter rains would be double edged for the infantry.

The logistical effort of moving the Tigris Corps to Ali-Al-Gharbi was to be even more challenging than moving and supplying the 6th Division. Townshend's advance had been one division and one cavalry brigade; Tigris Corps would be two divisions with one cavalry brigade, and several steamers had been lost following Ctesiphon or were besieged in Kut so there was even less shipping capacity. Even for those troops on board steamers, life was hardly restful, as Father S. Peal, padre of the Connaught Rangers, recalled:

> The steamer had the ordinary canvas awning, but this was quite insufficient as we were crowded on deck. Those on the barges were worse off. A few loose mats tied to poles were the only protection. When a barge is crowded and men move about on an iron floor with hob-nailed boots in wet weather it is easy to slip and fall into the river. Many a poor fellow has found his grave in the river while attempting to draw water on deck for making tea. Some corpses of such victims may be seen sticking to the reeds near the bank. Two of our boys in full uniform slipped off one night, but fortunately they escaped drowning as we were anchored at the time.[6]

"P boats" with a pair of barges for extra capacity on the Tigris below Al-Amara, 1916. These were the main form of transport on the twin rivers when a one-way journey could take a week or more. A smaller launch can be seen on the right bank. The flat, low-lying ground relative to the river shows just how easily the land flooded (Imperial War Museum).

The Battle of Sheikh Sa'ad

Aylmer ordered Younghusband's 7th Division to advance from Ali-Al-Gharbi to the Turkish positions at Sheikh Sa'ad to fix them in position until Aylmer could bring up the remainder of the Tigris Corps.

The 7th Division at this point was composed of some 13,330 men with 36 guns. The Turkish defenders were estimated at four battalions and 83 guns at Sheikh Sa'ad and a further 2,500 men and eighteen guns further west at Es-Sinn. On the Shumran Bend nine miles west of Kut were the 12,900 men and 24 guns of the 5th, 31st and 38th divisions.[7]

From Ali-al-Gharbi, which was only about 15 miles from the Persian frontier, Kut lay due west, but the Tigris flowed northwest to the Wadi, and then southwest to Kut with many bends and loops along the way. For this reason, the right bank (looking downstream) of the Tigris is often referred to as the south bank. Most of the fighting would be on the left/north bank.

On 4 January 1916, Younghusband advanced on both banks of the Tigris with the river transport keeping pace and three gunboats leading. On the 5th, the division bivouacked 12 miles south of the town. The following day's advance was delayed due to a dense mist. When they were 800 yards from the Turkish trenches, the 37th Dogra, lead battalion of the smaller force on the right bank, came under rifle and artillery fire. Their view of the Turkish positions was then obscured by a mirage. Their supporting battalion, the 97th Infantry, came up, and both battalions dug in.

On the left bank, the cavalry brigade was being hindered by irrigation ditches. They halted and turned their fire on another impediment on the British right flank, Arab attacks. The infantry was also coming under fire from the Turkish trenches, which extended further than expected. The mirage and the Turkish ability to camouflage their trenches in the flat landscape meant identifying targets was extremely difficult, although that did not seem to prevent Turkish fire in the general direction of the British advance. In places, the attackers had reached as close as 300 yards to the trenches.

Younghusband decided that no further advance could be made that day and ordered his forward troops to dig in and establish outposts. These proved vulnerable to Turkish fire, as was any attempt to resupply the forward troops. Then there was heavy rain to make matters worse. A bridge of boats was built to link up the forces across the river, but with heavy rain and high winds, this was not completed until the afternoon of the following day.

Younghusband issued orders for the attack to resume at 1100 hours on the 7th. On the left bank, a slow, methodical advance lasted all day which brought the British troops to within 300 or 400 yards of the Turkish trenches in the face of constant, sporadic rifle and artillery fire. The mirage and the sun reduced the effectiveness of the British artillery to support their advance. At last light, they dug in while the wind and rain made life uncomfortable.

An anonymous officer of the 2nd Battalion, the Black Watch, left a detailed account of the battalion's tribulations in Mesopotamia. He blamed the difficulties experienced by the Highlanders and the Jats on their orders being changed at the last minute: "No time was given for the issue of orders, no frontage or direction was given, no signal communication was arranged. To all enquiries the one answer was given 'Advance where the bullets are thickest.'" They were tired from their march into the trenches and had no opportunity to practice tactics in this new environment; the Anonymous Officer considered that this plan could only succeed against a weak or fainthearted enemy, and the Turks were neither. The battalion suffered 500 dead and wounded without getting within 200 yards of the trenches, and were forced to withdraw.[8]

On the right bank, the conditions were similar. While the cavalry kept the Arab tribesmen and Turkish cavalry and camalry at bay, the infantry inched their way forward under supporting fire from the 28th Brigade's artillery. Eventually, the Leicesters and 51st Sikhs got up and stormed the Turkish frontline trenches. They were joined by the 53rd and 92nd Infantry. The second-line trenches were soon overrun, but further advances were halted in a maze of irrigation ditches and also because the Turks now turned their guns on their former trenches.

The following day, with his troops exhausted, a pause in the battle was called. On the 9th, reconnaissance patrols reported that the Turks had abandoned their positions and withdrawn to the Wadi. Sheikh Sa'ad was occupied. The rain abated at last. The mud along the rivers of Mesopotamia is "clagging," that is, the sort of mud which clings to your footwear and forms great, heavy lumps. It is glutinous. It prevents effective movement. It would also clog up any weapons dropped in the mud. The terrain is flat. This does not aid drainage. In the scenario of 9 January, it prevented Younghusband, even if he had wanted to, from making an effective advance to rout or capture the retreating Turkish troops.

General Nixon's health now failed him, and he asked to be relieved. This had been a matter of concern for some weeks. Townshend's successes to Ctesiphon had masked the stress of command. Now, with defeat at Ctesiphon, the siege at Kut, and the prospect of Aylmer fighting up the Tigris in winter against more, and more determined, Turkish forces, it was all too much for Nixon. Lord Hardinge, the viceroy, complimented Nixon: "It is by men of his grit and stamp ... that the British Empire has been built up."[9] Nixon had played a pivotal role in the successes of the 6th Division. To the modern audience, though, who largely see the Great War generals in the form of Alan Clark's donkeys, it is difficult to see Nixon as anything other than negligent in the support he supplied to Townshend (be that logistical at Basra, medical to the wounded, or the additional troops needed to safeguard the division as it advanced), which contributed both to the siege of Kut and to the failure of the relief forces. He would also be blamed by the Mesopotamia Commission for the medical scandal which followed. Nixon's military career was now over. He was succeeded by Lieutenant General Sir Percy Lake, former Chief of the General Staff in India.

The Battle of the Wadi

The Turks only withdrew from Sheikh Sa'ad to the Wadi. This was at least good news because Aylmer knew that 3½ miles behind that position was the Suwacha Marsh which created the Hanna Defile between the marsh and the Tigris. This created a narrow gap where Aylmer would have to concentrate his attack which would play to the strengths of the defenders and allow them to secure both flanks on the river and marsh. At the Wadi, although the Turkish right flank would be secured against the Tigris (and where Aylmer at least had naval superiority), the Turkish left flank would be unsecured. If Aylmer could implement one of the right-flanking attacks which Townshend attempted and get behind the Turkish positions, he could capture it en masse, or at least destroy it as a fighting force by harrying it with his cavalry and gunboats through the narrow Hanna Defile. Two battalions were sent five miles up the Wadi to dig in. The Wadi itself was not considered to be a major obstacle.

Aylmer planned to use the 28th Brigade to fix the Turkish defenders in their positions while the 7th Division and Cavalry Brigade crossed the Wadi. The War Diary of the 21st Brigade explains how Aylmer wanted the 7th Division and the cavalry to operate: "The task of the 21st Brigade was to hold the enemy on his left without committing itself too closely, while the 19th Brigade on the immediate right of the 21st Brigade and the 35th Brigade and Cavalry Brigade still further to the right maneuvered him out of his position by action against the rear."[10] The attack commenced on the morning of 13 January once the early morning mist had cleared. Artillery and naval gunfire drove back Turkish forward positions. The 28th Brigade advanced on the Turkish trenches and came under fire at a range of about 500 yards. Despite their best efforts, they were unable to get within 200 to 300 yards of the Wadi.

Meanwhile, the 7th Division and the Cavalry Brigade easily crossed the Wadi, although the steep banks were a major obstacle to the artillery and supply wagons. By midday, the infantry had engaged the Turks who, realizing that they were being outflanked, set up hasty defensive positions in an irrigation channel where they put up an effective defense. During the division's attack, Lieutenant Colonel Thomas, commanding officer of the 9th Bhopals, was wounded in the thigh while moving forward to give orders to his B Company. Seeing his CO wounded and in an exposed position some 200 yards from the Turkish positions, Sepoy Chatta Singh rushed forward and bandaged the wounds. He used his own body to shield his col-

onel from Turkish bullets and then used his entrenching tool to dig a parapet for both of them. Singh remained there for up to 24 hours until Thomas could be evacuated. Thomas later died of shock and exposure in Al-Amara. For his heroism, Singh received the Victoria Cross, to which Indian soldiers had only been eligible since 1911.[11]

With no further prospect of success by either the 7th Division or the 28th Brigade, the attack was halted for another cold and wet night in the open. The following morning, the Turks had retreated into the Hanna Defile in a masterful disengagement which, in the years to come, would be repeated so that final, crushing blow to the Turkish army in Mesopotamia would never be delivered.

An excellent opportunity to destroy the Turkish XIII Corps had been lost at the Wadi which, if it had succeeded, would have opened the way to Kut where the besieging forces would have been trapped between the 6th and 7th Divisions. The attacking forces had been hampered by cold, wet and muddy conditions which were as debilitating as the hot, dry and dusty conditions of the summer. Nevertheless, the failure at the Wadi meant that Aylmer would have to fight the same troops in the Hanna Defile, some 3,000 yards wide, with both flanks secured in the appalling winter conditions. These were conditions which would match the worst of the Western Front.

The Wadi had also cost 2,700 British dead and wounded. The cold and wet conditions added exposure to the wounded soldiers' tribulations. Once again, the medical and evacuation facilities provided were inadequate.

The Battle of Hanna

General Aylmer decided to advance against the new Turkish positions at Hanna on 15 January, but his troops found the conditions so appalling that no forward movement was possible. The rain continued. Not only was the Tigris rising, but the marshes were growing. Townshend's latest assessment of his food supplies suggested that he could hold out until 3 February, but Aylmer thought that with the prevailing conditions, he should push on without delay.

Aylmer planned to attack the Turkish positions on 21 January. Artillery and soldiers would cross to the left bank to provide enfilading fire into the Turkish positions, with naval gunfire support from *Cranefly* and *Dragonfly*. The 19th (on the right) and 35th (left) Brigades would then charge the Turkish trenches.

Once again, the dawn mist delayed the start of the bombardment, but when it lifted to the Turkish second-line trench, the Black Watch and Jats occupied the first-line trenches despite the defensive fire. This was a good start, but it proved impossible to reinforce the occupied trenches. For one and a quarter hours, in the face of fierce counter-attacks, the Black Watch and Jats held the trenches against repeated Turkish

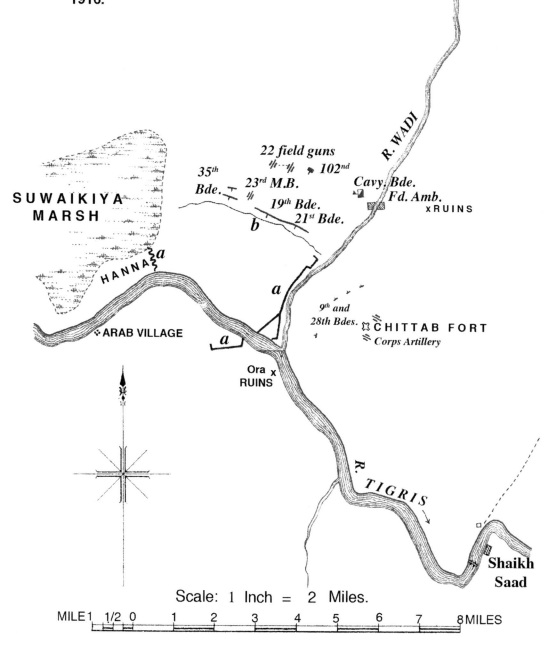

MAP
TO ILLUSTRATE THE ACTION OF THE WADI.

a = TURKISH POSITIONS ACCORDING TO BRITISH INFORMATION AT **10** P.M. **12**TH JANUARY, **1916**.

b = APPROXIMATE LINE OF HASTILY ENTRENCHED WATERCUTS HELD BY TURKS ON **13**TH JANUARY, **1916**,
AGAINST THE ADVANCE OF THE BRITISH **7**TH DIVISION.

APPROXIMATE POSITION OF BRITISH FRONTAL AND FLANKING ATTACKS DURING NIGHT **13**TH/**14**TH JANUARY,
1916.

R. WADI

22 field guns

● 102nd

35th Bde.

23rd M.B.

19th Bde.

21st Bde.

Cavy. Bde.

Fd. Amb.

x RUINS

b

SUWAIKIYA MARSH

HANNA

a

a

a

ARAB VILLAGE

9th and 28th Bdes.

CHITTAB FORT

Corps Artillery

Ora x RUINS

R. TIGRIS

Shaikh Saad

Scale: 1 Inch = 2 Miles.

MILE 1   1/2   0   1   2   3   4   5   6   7   8 MILES

PREPARED IN THE HISTORICAL SECTION OF THE COMMITTEE OF IMPERIAL DEFENCE.
200/29. 2050/30.

Ordnance Survey 1924

The Action of the Wadi, 12 to 14 January 1916

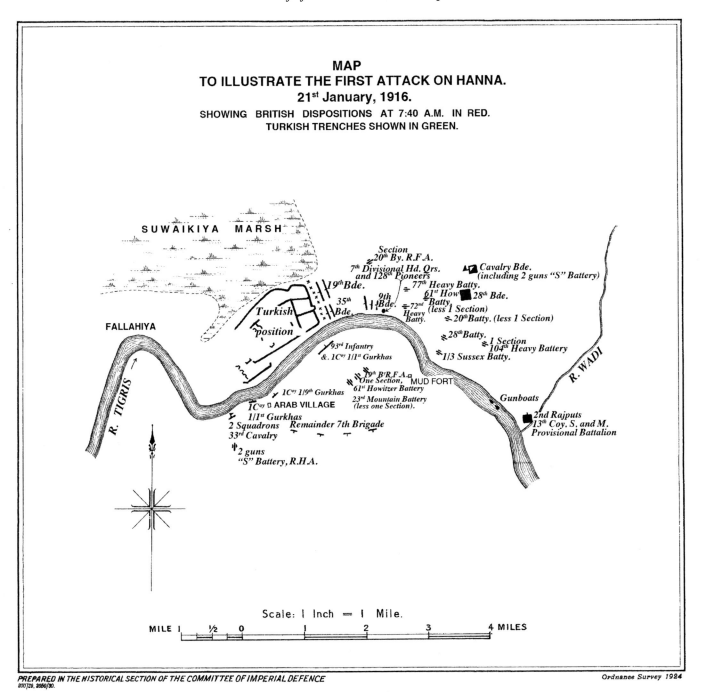

**MAP
TO ILLUSTRATE THE FIRST ATTACK ON HANNA.
21st January, 1916.**
SHOWING BRITISH DISPOSITIONS AT 7:40 A.M. IN RED.
TURKISH TRENCHES SHOWN IN GREEN.

SUWAIKIYA MARSH

FALLAHIYA

R. TIGRIS

Turkish position

19th Bde.

35th Bde.

9th Bde.

Section
20th By. R.F.A.
*7th Divisional Hd. Qrs.
and 128th Pioneers*

*Cavalry Bde.
(including 2 guns "S" Battery)*

77th Heavy Batty.
61st How *28th Bde.*
*2nd Batty.
Heavy (less 1 Section)
Batty.* *20th Batty. (less 1 Section)*

28th Batty.
*1 Section
104th Heavy Battery*
1/3 Sussex Batty.

*93rd Infantry
& 1Coy 1/1st Gurkhas*

R. WADI

*19th Bʳ R.F.A.
One Section, MUD FORT
61st Howitzer Battery*
*23rd Mountain Battery
(less one Section).*

1Coy 1/9th Gurkhas
1Coy ☐ ARAB VILLAGE
1/1st Gurkhas
2 Squadrons Remainder 7th Brigade
33rd Cavalry
*2 guns
"S" Battery, R.H.A.*

Gunboats

*2nd Rajputs
13th Coy. S. and M.
Provisional Battalion*

Scale: 1 Inch = 1 Mile.
MILE 1   ½   0   1   2   3   4 MILES

PREPARED IN THE HISTORICAL SECTION OF THE COMMITTEE OF IMPERIAL DEFENCE
200]29, 2050/30.   Ordnance Survey 1924

The First Battle of Hanna, 21 January 1916

counter-attacks. The Black Watch ran out of grenades, despite capturing and utilizing Turkish supplies. Command of the battalion passed to Second Lieutenant Henderson, who, when it was suggested that the survivors should withdraw, replied, "How can I order the regiment to retire?" They were forced out and back to their start positions. The following day, the Black Watch, in Mesopotamia for just three weeks, had been reduced from 950 to 99.[12]

A renewed attack was planned following an inadequate, 10-minute bombardment. But by now the situation was deterio-

rating. All telephone communications were broken. The attacking infantry was soaked, heading into a gale through standing water, knee deep in places. This attempt also failed.

The above account of the battle, while factually correct, only skims over the horrendous conditions endured that day and night. The infantry had to fight the weather as well as the Turks. The heroism of Sepoy (later Lance-Naik) Lala, 41st Dogras, was recorded in several sources and serves to deepen our understanding of the horrors endured. Lala found a wounded major from his regiment (although another account says it was

Captain Nicholson, adjutant of the 37th Dogras) lying in the open and dragged him into a little shelter where he could dress the wounds. Lala then gathered in four others and treated them. The weather throughout this was described several times as raining hard with an icy wind. Lala then heard, and recognized, the voice of his adjutant, Captain Lindhop, also wounded, exposed and about 100 yards from the Turkish trenches. The major ordered Lala not to go forward to Lindhop, as it was an act of certain death. This was not without some truth. Lindhop later recounted that an officer of the Black Watch and a sepoy had both been shot dead while trying to make their way to help him. Lala was luckier. Lindhop's wounds were dressed, and Lala gave his own coat to protect Lindhop from the elements. For the next five hours in what must have been truly appalling conditions, Lala lay beside Lindhop, protecting and encouraging him, until dusk when Lala went for help. When dusk at last offered some protection, Lala carried the first officer back to the trenches and returned with stretcher bearers for the remaining five. Lindhop dictated his version of events before he died in a field hospital. For his actions that day, Lala was awarded the Victoria Cross.[13]

On the same day, Captain John Sinton, the RMO of the 37th Dogras was also awarded the Victoria Cross. Despite being wounded in both arms and through his side, he refused to go to the hospital but attended the casualties until dusk. After studying medicine in Queen's College, Belfast, Sinton held a post in pathology at the Liverpool School of Tropical Medicine and consequently is honored in a plaque to the Liverpool University VC winners in the mess of Liverpool University Officers' Training Corps, alongside Captain Noel Chevasse, RMO to the Liverpool Scottish, and the first recipient of the VC and Bar. Not only was Sinton an incredibly brave doctor (his citation mentions bravery on three previous actions), but after serving in various military medical posts between 1911 and 1921, he dedicated his life in the Indian Medical Services to malaria. In 1927 he became the first director of the Malarial Survey of India. In no small part due to his efforts, during the Second World War, malarial incidents in the Middle East were minimal. To give an example of just how debilitating malaria was, when General Allenby advanced towards Damascus in 1918, he knew that his men would become exposed to malaria, and from that point he had just the 10- to 14-day incubation period before his men were struck down with high fever, delirium and even death on the march. Four times as many men died in Damascus hospitals from malaria as died in the advance to and capture of the city. This short passage can only touch on Sinton's career and the impact he had on humanity, both on and off the battlefield, but Gerald Gliddon, who has painstakingly studied the Great War recipients of the Victoria Cross, summed up Sinton, simply yet succinctly: surely one of the most talented men to win a Victoria Cross and during his career achieved a very great deal in the service of others.[14]

That night the conditions were appalling as before, and now the marsh froze. The following day a truce was arranged for the collection of casualties. British losses were 2,741. The casualty rates for those battalions which participated in the attack exceeded 50 percent.

Once again, the medical facilities failed the 2,741 British casualties. Two sections from a divisional ambulance train had established a hospital at Orah, but in the steady rain, the tents were pitched on ground already ankle deep in mud. Casualties were crowded onto the hospital ships, and every spare hand was used to bring tea and rum aboard. Those casualties who could stand made

In a scene reminiscent of the Western Front, Captains Rigby and Dawson, 1st Seaforth Highlanders, sit on their trenches at the Hanna Defile facing the Turkish positions, 17 January 1916. The mud and standing water is visible to the rear. It was across this sort of terrain that repeated attempts were made to relieve Kut by incomplete units which had had no time to rehearse and which were lacking their support weapons (Imperial War Museum).

their way to a brazier, the only source of warmth. With their skin covered in mud and blood, teeth chattering, cigarettes hanging from lips, they still managed to joke.[15]

The Battle of Hanna ended the first attempt by the Tigris Corps to break through to Kut. On 5 February 1916, British intelligence estimated the Turkish forces lying between Aylmer and Townshend were:

1. Hanna Defile — 35th, 51st and 52nd divisions: 12,000 men plus 26 guns.
2. Es Sinn (right bank) — 1,500 to 2,000 regular cavalry, two battalions, being reinforced by the 2nd Division.
3. Kut — 45th Division: 4,000 to 5,000 men.

General Lake arrived in Basra and immediately saw the administrative and logistical chaos which lay behind Tigris Corps' predicament. In the middle of the Shatt were a long line of ships waiting to unload. The port facilities had yet to be improved. Stores and supplies occupied every inch of dry land, which was at a premium when the surrounding land was inundated. On shore, there were 10,000 soldiers and 12 guns in Basra which could not be moved up to the front for want of suitable transports. Lack of experienced administrative personnel compounded the chaos.[16]

Taking advantage of Lake's arrival, General Cowper, assistant quartermaster general, drafted a strongly worded complaint to India about the transport situation in Mesopotamia. Paddle steamers, which made up the bulk of the transport capacity, were unwieldy on the Tigris, while an "expert" in London had changed the specifications for barges, provided by the Lynch Brothers, long established in the field of navigation in Mesopotamia, to square-ended barges, which proved to be a failure. Cowper considered that Tigris Corps would have to abandon its attempts to relieve Kut. Lake read the complaint and forwarded it largely intact to India. Duff's response was immediate and biting:

> Please warn General Cowper that if anything of this sort again occurs or if I receive any more querulous or petulant demands for shipping, I shall at once remove him from the force and will refuse him further employment of any kind.[17]

There was also the more immediate fallout from the defeats at Hanna. Both the War Committee in London and Army HQ in India were concerned. The War Committee called for a full assessment of the situation in Mesopotamia and an enquiry into the running of the campaign, which would become the Mesopotamia Commission. In Egypt, the British 13th (Western) Division was warned off for deployment to Mesopotamia. This division of New Army wartime-raised "Service" battalions drawn from Lancashire, Wales, and the English counties bordering Wales had landed at Sulva Bay, Gallipoli, in August 1915 and, following the evacuation of the beachhead in January 1916, was resting and rebuilding in Egypt.

The Imperial General Staff (IGS) in London took respon-

sibility for Mesopotamia on 16 February. Although India would remain the base for the operations and would have a say in matters which affected her internal affairs and regional foreign affairs, the IGS would now coordinate Mesopotamia as part of the overall British war effort. The situation was summed up as follows:

1. that security was to be the main consideration;
2. that the force would not be reinforced, but would be adequately supplied;
3. that no importance was attached to Baghdad or Kut after its relief; and
4. that the force would be ordered to withdraw on Amara or Qurna, but for the fact that such course of action might cause tribal rising and might add to the difficulties in Persia or Afghanistan.

For perhaps the first time since Delamain had on the Al-Fao Peninsula, there was a clearly defined set of objectives, both in terms of geography and manpower, for the operations in Mesopotamia. However, even this relatively straightforward summation offered room for maneuver. The rationale for taking Al-Amara had been to safeguard the oil facilities from a point which was closer to them than Basra was. Cutting Axis access to Persia and Afghanistan was an objective of the Indian government to prevent jihad from pouring across the North West Frontier, and this could be best achieved by closing the Ottoman-Persian border. Finally, the Russians were on the move, and a force left Erzerum for Kermanshah, arriving on 25 February. With Russian successes in Anatolia (the supposedly impregnable fortress city of Erzerum fell to the Russians on 16 February 1916), there was a real possibility of the Russians reaching Baghdad first.

Unfortunately for Lake, he lacked the impartiality to arrive as a "clean pair of hands." It was he who had sent Nixon to replace Barrett and so was considered (and to an extent, this is a fair accusation) to be a part of the problem. However, it was now Lake's job to resolve the predicament. He set off to consult with Aylmer about the situation. At this time, he was informed by Townshend that the Kut garrison could now hold out until the end of March, not 3 February as previously advised. Almost immediately another communication came, saying that following a house-to-house search, more stores had been found and the garrison could now hold out until 17 April 1916. Had Townshend only conducted these searches at the beginning of the siege, Aylmer could have conducted his first two battles in a more leisurely manner, better supported by the men and guns waiting in Basra, instead of being rushed into a premature advance to meet Townshend's 3 February deadline.

Aylmer planned for another attack on the Hanna Defile for mid-February, but the weather remained appalling and the plans were postponed. On 22 February, Gorringe took a force up the right bank of the Tigris and shelled the Turkish camps

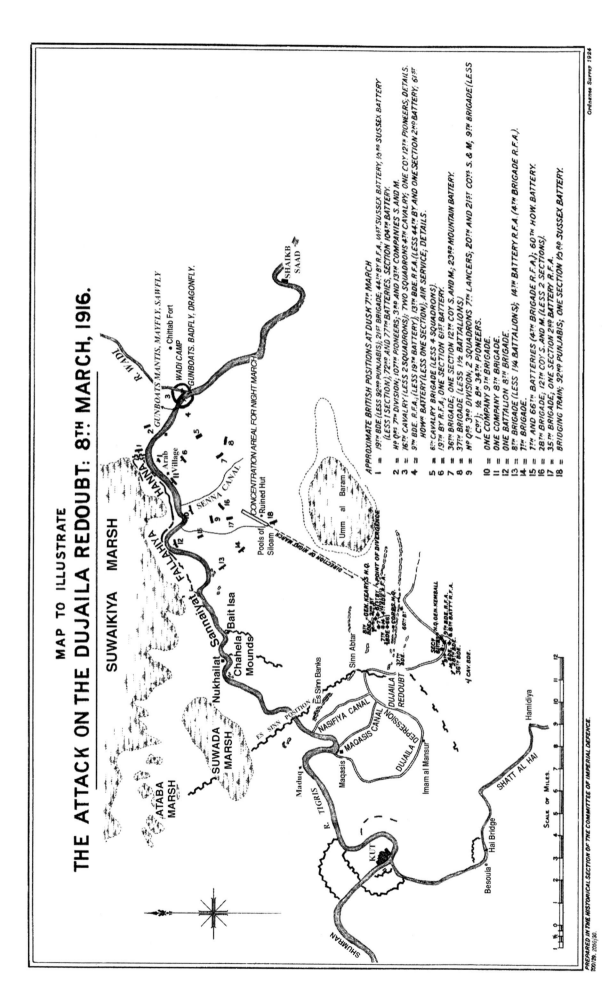

The Attack on the Dujaila Redoubt, 8 March 1916

north of the Fallahiya bend, and part of his force reached San-naiyat. If Gorringe had had access to a pontoon bridge, he would have been able to cross the Tigris and trap the Turkish forces in the Hanna Defile. Despite the rain, the river levels remained low and the flow was slack. As it was, Gorringe did not have a pontoon bridge and so was forced to retire back across the river.

Townshend, 20 miles away to the north, was able to see the gunfire from the roof of his headquarters: "We could clearly see the shells bursting over Hanna and the smoke.... Apparently much confusion was caused in the enemy's camp behind the Hanna position; but they did not retreat. As is the Turkish custom, when defending, they held like grim death, their officers, revolvers in hand, behind them, shooting if any man tried to get up and go."[18]

Dujaila Redoubt

Aylmer began looking around for an alternative to another frontal assault up the Hanna Defile. No routes through the Suwacha Marsh could be found, and it was simply too big for a force, equipped as it was in 1916, to circumvent under the weather conditions. On the right bank, the inundations which had assisted Townshend's advance the previous year had begun, but reconnaissance reports showed that there were still positions from which the British could enfilade the Turkish positions. If a fixing force was left to hold the Turkish defenders in the Hanna Defile positions, then if Aylmer could defeat the Turks on the right bank, he would be able to advance to the Shatt-al-Hai and cross it to the Shumran Bend. Then he could either cross the Tigris to attack the Turks from the rear or, remaining on the right bank, cover the withdrawal of the Kut garrison.

As usual in Mesopotamia, the reality was far more complicated. Twenty-eight infantry battalions supported by 68 guns and the 6th Cavalry Brigade of four regiments would have to cross the Tigris in three forces composed of four columns in a night move to take up their positions. The assaulting columns were commanded by Generals Keary and Kemball, who was another veteran of the Chitral Relif Force.

The Turkish right bank positions extended south from the Tigris for about eight miles and incorporated 20-foot-high mounds into two redoubts, Sinn Abtar and Dujaila, before running back to the Shatt-al-Hai. The terrain in front of the Turkish defenses was what we have come to expect in Mesopotamia—flat, low lying, interspersed with mounds and ancient irrigation ditches which were invisible from any distance. The distances were comparable to those undertaken at Aylmer's previous two battles.

Then Townshend reassessed his food stocks, announced that he had 200 tons of barley less than he thought and could not hold out beyond the end of the month. This forced Aylmer to bring forward his own plans, and, as the difficulties of night navigation in the featureless Mesopotamian terrain were by

now well known, more preparation would have helped with the difficulties faced by the Tigris Corps. At a conference on 7 March, Gorringe explained the plan which aimed to capture the Dujaila Redoubt and break through to the Shatt-al-Hai which reached the Tigris opposite Kut. Aylmer was on hand to reinforce the need for "dash" in securing the redoubt.

On the night of 7 March, the Tigris Corps began to form up for their attack. Colored lights were used to guide soldiers to their correct columns. However, delays soon manifested themselves, including incorporating logistical and artillery wagons into the infantry columns, which slowed down the infantry. The start was 2½ hours late, and it was past dawn before they were in position.

The Turkish soldier in defense was disciplined and did not normally show himself until the attacking British approached. In the featureless terrain, it was often impossible to locate the Turkish trenches, so until the Turks opened fire and gave their positions away, it was impossible for the attacking infantry to be accurately supported by artillery. General Kemball assumed that the lack of Turkish activity was just that — normal Turkish practice. With the delays, his column would no longer be able to advance across the open plain under cover of darkness, and in daylight, the attacking troops would be slaughtered. Kemball telephoned Aylmer to explain his predicament. Aylmer agreed to provide artillery support to the assaulting infantry from the Corps Artillery. But this took time, and it was getting lighter.

Unfortunately, on this occasion, the Turks were not sitting patiently at the bottom of their trenches waiting for the attack. They had evacuated the position. And now that they knew the British had crossed the Tigris, they were hurrying troops back into the trenches. Both of Kemball's brigade commanders could see this happening and requested permission to attack. Kemball was mindful of Aylmer's plan which was now clearly both overly prescriptive and behind schedule. He refused his brigade commanders' request. For want of "dash," a cheap victory which may have been the killer blow to punch through to the Shatt-al-Hai and Kut had been lost. Instead, there would be another bloody battle.

It would be 0935 hours before the attack begun. The Turkish defenders were able to bring rifle, machine-gun and artillery fire on the attacking troops, and the open plain turned into the death trap which had been predicted. The 8th Brigade reached and entered the redoubt after crossing 3,000 yards of open plain. The artillery support, when it finally arrived, focused on the redoubt rather than the trenches. The trenches were occupied and the advance continued into the redoubt where the attackers disappeared into the dust and smoke. Unsupported, and with a major Turkish counter-attack, the British were forced to withdraw.

On the extreme right of the Manchesters, Private George Stringer single-handedly held back the Turkish counter-attack until he ran out of hand grenades. In doing so, he stabilized the flank and aided the battalion's withdrawal. For his efforts, he was awarded the Victoria Cross.[19]

In Kut, Turkish troops could be seen pouring into the support trenches. The attack failed, and with it possibly the best chance of relieving Kut. For the Turkish commanders, the attack was a very serious threat to their rear, which would have relieved Kut and unleashed both a corps and a division (even if weakened from the siege) from which there would have been no retreat for the 6th Army.

By nightfall, it was clear that the attack had failed. With so many men and animals spread out so far, impossible to resupply, the order was given to withdraw to the Wadi.

While the infantry dealt with new floods in their trenches, the recriminations amongst the hierarchy began. The 6th Cavalry Brigade was highly criticized for once again failing to prevent Turkish troop movements, especially when the "cost" in logistical terms of maintaining cavalry was so high. Aylmer was dismissed and replaced by Gorringe for what was to be the third, and final, attempt to relieve Kut. Gorringe now at least had access to Maude's 13th Division, which gave him the opportunity to rest his battered troops — such as it was possible to rest troops in the Mesopotamian winter. Townshend did not sound full of confidence when he realized that the new division was from the "New Army," and he wondered whether this was in addition to, or instead of, the regular reinforcements promised. Wilson considered that the division "fresh from the Dardanelles: it was composed mainly of very young officers and men with limited military training and experience; ... They soon proved their worth."[20]

13th (Western) Division: GOC Major General Sir Stanley Maude[21]

- 38th Brigade
  - 6th Battalion, the King's Own Royal Lancaster Regiment
  - 6th Battalion, the East Lancashire Regiment
  - 6th Battalion, the Prince of Wales Volunteers, South Lancashire Regiment
  - 6th Battalion, the Loyal North Lancashire Regiment
  - 38th Company, Machine Gun Corps
  - 38th Brigade, Supply and Transport Company
- 39th Brigade
  - 9th Battalion, the Warwickshire Regiment
  - 9th Battalion, the Worcestershire Regiment
  - 7th Battalion, the North Staffordshire Regiment
  - 7th Battalion, the Gloucestershire Regiment
  - 39th Company, Machine Gun Corps
  - 39 Brigade, Supply and Transport Company
- 40th Brigade
  - 8th Battalion, the Royal Welch Regiment
  - 8th Battalion, the Cheshire Regiment
  - 4th Battalion, the South Wales Borderers
  - 5th Battalion, the Wiltshire Regiment
  - 40th Company, Machine Gun Corps
  - 40 Brigade, Supply and Transport Company
- Divisional Troops
  - 55 Brigade, RFA ⎱ each of four batteries, each of four
  - 66 Brigade, RFA ⎰ 18-pound guns
  - One howitzer battery, four 4.5-inch howitzers
  - 8th Pioneer Battalion, the Welch Regiment
  - 71, 72 and 88 Companies, Royal Engineers
  - 13th Divisional Cyclist Company
  - 13th Divisional Signals Company
  - 13 Division, Supply and Transport Company
  - Three Field Ambulances
  - Sanitary Section
  - Mobile Veterinary Section

Aylmer was dismissed following his failure at Dujaila Redoubt. There had been missed opportunities at the Wadi too. The conditions faced by his men at the Hanna Defile were arguably as bad as any on the Western Front. Townshend too had missed opportunities or failed to achieve his objectives of trapping and defeating Turkish forces en masse, but Townshend had inspired his men to great things. Aylmer's failure at Dujaila Redoubt, where the pressure on all parties to relieve Kut was so great, made the stakes, and rewards, so much greater and thus the price of failure so much higher. Had Townshend fought the Dujaila Redoubt action while advancing to Baghdad, it could have been written off as the fortunes of war. Aylmer had no such luxury. Aylmer was also no Townshend. Gertrude Bell met him in 1921 and was decidedly unimpressed: "How he got to be a Lt. General is a mystery to me. The more I see of him the more colour-less, indecisive and nervous I think him. The only fixed opinions he holds are violent prejudices, under the fostering influence of which I am rapidly becoming pro–Germans and pro–Bolshevik."[22] Bell's insight would explain Aylmer's overly prescribed plan and the failure to seize the opportunities at the Wadi and the Dujaila Redoubt. But it should not be forgotten that Aylmer's urgency, and arguably premature attacks, were dictated by one factor — the timescales provided by Townshend. These were not only woefully inaccurate but changed regularly, and there was a direct link between the date provided by Townshend and Aylmer's urgency. Thousands of men and scores of guns were available in Basra. With more accurate deadlines from Townshend, Aylmer could have paused, brought up the additional resources and used them to punch through to Townshend. The 8th Brigade did enter the Dujaila Redoubt, unsupported. Another brigade in support may well have secured the redoubt and made the sacrifice worthwhile. High as they were, the 8th Brigade's losses were not excessive for the campaign. In this respect, Townshend held some blame for the losses and suffering of the relief force, and in his own ultimate surrender. In one final respect, both generals were equally cursed: their cavalry brigade had repeatedly failed to achieve its task of indicting enemy troop movements.

"Second Battle of the Hanna Defile": Fallahiyeh, Beit Aieesa

On 18 March, Townshend provided yet another deadline — 15 April. This gave Gorringe a clear deadline. The inundation began in the forward area, and troops were diverted to engineering duties just to keep the waters at bay. Gorringe had several seaplanes which could take off from the river when the wind was in the right direction. Their reconnaissance showed the extent of the inundation. "Land" planes were also expected shortly. Gorringe intended to use these aircraft to photograph the Turkish positions in the Hanna Defile and use them to accurately brief the attacking forces (13th Division) on what they could expect. Wilcox believes this is the first time that the British Army used aerial photography in this manner — yet another first for the British Army in Iraq.[23]

On 4 April, the 13th Division took over the trenches from the 7th Division and prepared to attack the following morning. The division was deployed, from the right, 38th, 39th and 40th Brigades. With artillery and machine-gun support from both sides of the river, the first two Turkish trenches were quickly occupied. When the artillery lifted at 0515 hours, it became clear that the Turks had withdrawn, leaving only a small rearguard. At 0545 hours an attack was launched on the third line which was also quickly occupied.

Information was received that the Turks had withdrawn to positions at Fallaniyah, three miles away. The 4th South Wales Borderers and the 8th Cheshires from the 40th Brigade were ordered forward across the flat, coverless terrain. They came under fire at about 1,200 yards but still advanced another 500 yards before the battalions were forced to dig in, where they remained until 1900 hours when the 38th and 39th Brigades passed through them to capture the Fallahiya position. During the day, Lieutenant Hemingway of the Borderers was wounded 150 yards from cover and lying, as so often in Mesopotamia, in the open. Two men attempted to rescue him, and one of those was also wounded. Lieutenant Buchanan saw this and went out to rescue Hemingway, with the assistance of the unwounded man, and brought him into the protection of the trenches. Buchanan then returned to the wounded man and brought him into the trenches. During this, Buchanan was shot in the arm. For his actions, Buchanan was awarded the Victoria Cross. Already he had been wounded at Suvla Bay and received the Military Cross at Helles. He was Mentioned in Dispatches on four occasions. He would be wounded three more times in Mesopotamia. Following one wound, he was sent to India for several months to recuperate, but on the fourth occasion, on 13 February 1917, Buchanan lost the sight in both his eyes. After resigning his commission due to his injuries, he

learned Braille at St. Dunstan's[24] and then returned to Oxford to read law. Blindness did not hamper his pre-war active lifestyle. He rowed on the college eights, returned to his hometown of Coleford, Gloucestershire, where he qualified as a solicitor and became a partner in a law firm. He was also a noted salmon fisherman, despite his blindness.[25]

As at the Hanna Defile, the Turks were able to delay the British at Fallaniyah long enough to extract the bulk of their force to new defenses at Sannaiyat. In the process, over 1,800 casualties were inflicted on the attackers. From Sannaiyat to Kut was just 16 miles, but if the fighting on 5 April was anything to go by, it would be a bloody and costly process to batter a way through to Kut.

The following dawn, 6 April, the 7th Division assaulted the Sannaiyat positions, into a hail of rifle and machine-gun fire from both banks. There would be three attacks launched by the division that day. The assaulting brigades, 28th and 19th, were cut to pieces — the Ox and Buck lost all of their officers and 220 of 266 other ranks; the 51st Sikhs and the Leicesters lost over half their effective strength. Despite the sacrifice, they could not advance within 500 yards. Following the retreat from one of these attacks, Corporal Ware of the Seaforth Highlanders spent two hours collecting wounded men and bringing them back to the safety of the trenches, a distance of 200 yards. For his heroism in saving those lives, Ware was awarded the Victoria Cross. Four days later, he was wounded and he died on the 16th. He was buried in the Al-Amara Cemetery, unlike two of his brothers who would be killed on the Western Front and whose bodies were never recovered.[26]

The British artillery had been slow in arriving for the Sannaiyat battle due to the Fallahiyeh trenches, but when they did arrive they were able to keep the Turkish heads down while the division dug in. Younghusband planned to resume the assault after dark with his third brigade, the 40th, which moved forward at 2200 hours. The weather then took another turn for the worse. A northwest wind drove the Suwacha Marsh into the British trenches of which some, despite best efforts while under fire, had to be abandoned by 0100 hours on the 7th. The guns only maintained their positions by throwing up encircling embankments. The night attack was canceled.

The relief force was now close enough to Kut for Townshend to be able to attempt to assist them. He ordered his five-inch guns to fire on the Turkish ferry at Maqasis, which they did when the mirage permitted. At Sannaiyat, the British position was consolidated, and the Turks refrained from firing while the wounded were recovered. Motor ambulances made their first appearance in Mesopotamia; the agony of the AT carts was coming to an end.[27]

During the night of 7 April, under a covering artillery barrage from both banks of the river, the 3rd Division moved up the right bank of the Tigris to occupy positions from which they could enfilade the Sannaiyat positions. This was achieved by 2100 hours. That night, the Tigris burst its right bank be-

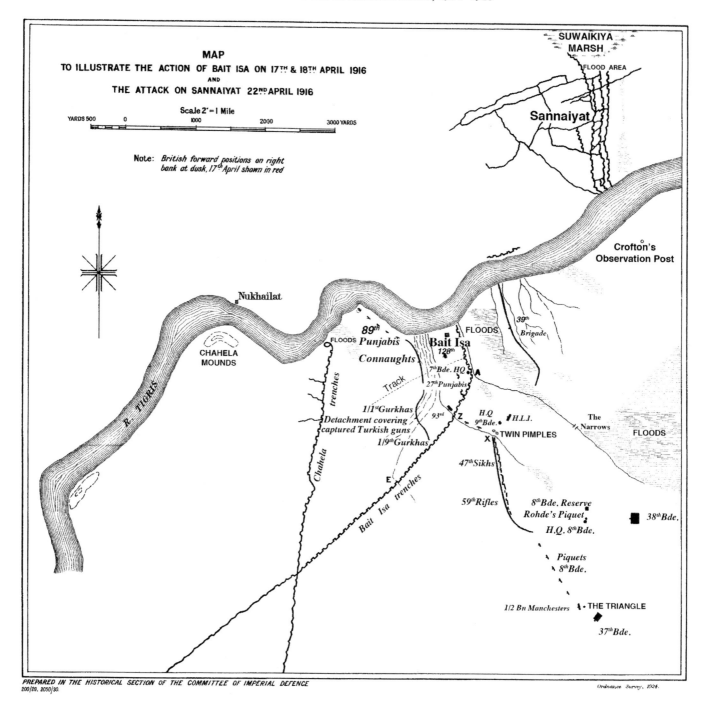

The Battles of Bait Aieesa and Sannaiyat, April 1916

hind and to the south of the 3rd Division, nearly joining up with the existing Umm-al-Baram marsh.

Gorringe needed to occupy the Sannaiyat position by 8 April if he was to relieve Kut in time. On the left bank, the 7th Division was too far from the Turkish positions to attack them, while on the right bank, floods prevented the 3rd Division from moving any more. He ordered the 7th Division to advance as close to the Turkish positions as they could without committing themselves to an engagement, and throughout the following day the lead brigades, 28th and 19th, closed in by

300 yards before they were halted by enemy fire. After dark on the 8th, the British artillery opened fire on the Turkish positions, who responded, allowing the British gunner to accurately position them. When the moon set, the division moved to within 300 yards of the Turkish wire. Patrols identified gaps in the wire. Meanwhile, two officers reconnoitered the Suwacha Marsh and found that it was not as formidable an obstacle as previously believed. Although the water was thigh deep, the bottom was firm enough. This route could have permitted some troops to enfilade the Turkish positions to mirror the

3rd Division's action. Gorringe turned down this option, considering that the bottom would be torn up by heavily laden troops, animals and carriage wheels.

The next assault was carried out by the 13th Division. The 38th and 40th brigades were across a 600-yard-wide front with the 39th Brigade in support. The lead battalions moved into position overnight and lay there, numbed by the cold, until 0300 hours when they moved forward. The first line reached the Turkish trenches, but the second line had been shaken by the Turkish fire and fell back. Unsupported in the trenches, the attackers were eventually forced out and back: they dug in some 400 yards from the Turkish positions, having suffered another 1,807 casualties. The attack had failed, and nature intervened yet another time as the Tigris broke its left bank and reduced the gap between the river and the marsh.

Three more Victoria Crosses were won that day. The first was awarded for recovering and tending to the wounded, this time by a clergyman, the Rev. W.R.F. Addison, the Church of England chaplain to the 6th Loyal North Lancashires, which reported 6 killed, 85 wounded and 160 missing. While the battalion was digging in 400 yards from the Turkish position, Addison tended to the wounded and brought them to shelter in the usual flat and exposed terrain. Born in 1883, he was not ordained until 1913, having first worked in a Canadian lumber camp and studied farming in Devon. Two of his brothers also traveled abroad to make a new life, to Australia, but would die in the war, Lancelot at Gallipoli and Philip in Mesopotamia, both theaters in which Addison served. After the war, he remained in the army and served in the UK and around the world, including Khartoum, Malta and the Shanghai Defence Force, 1927–1929. He retired from the army in 1938 and became rector of Coltishall, Norfolk. He seemed to have been able to switch from the role of the army chaplain to rural rector with ease, where he fished and played cricket. The Reverend Addison was also only the second of three Anglican chaplains to win the Victoria Cross during the Great War.[28]

The second VC went to Private Finn, 4/South Wales Borderers, and the same regiment as Lieutenant Buchanan four days before. Finn was a stretcher bearer who, seeing two wounded soldiers about 300 yards from the Turkish trenches, went to help them. Having dressed their wounds, he brought one into the shelter of the trenches, before returning with an assistant to recover the second casualty. Throughout this, Finn was under heavy fire. Finn survived unscathed but would be mortally wounded during fighting at Marl Plain, north of Baghdad, and he died on 30 March 1917. In a letter to his father, Finn's commanding officer (who had been wounded previously and so was not present) wrote that Finn was buried near to the ambulance with the intention of being recovered later, but the body was never exhumed. Finn's memorial is on the Basra War Memorial.[29]

The third Victoria Cross to be won that day was also for saving lives in the aftermath of that day's fighting. Lieutenant

Myles of the 8/Welsh but attached to the 9/Worcesters went into no-man's-land on a number of occasions to assist the wounded and bring them into the safety of the trenches. During this he was wounded himself. Myles was also awarded the DSO (Distinguished Service Order) in 1917; correspondence suggests that General Maude considered awarding him a Bar to his VC, but he did not want to create such a precedent.[30]

Lake and Gorringe were now concerned about their prospects of reaching Kut by 15 April, when again Townshend announced that he could hold out to the 21 April. Belatedly, Lake attempted to resupply the garrison by airdrops, not entirely successfully given the life capacity of the aircraft available to him — those in Mesopotamia were not even the most modern by 1916 standards — but this was another first for the British Army, aerial resupply of a besieged force. This would be no more successful at Kut than at more famous sieges in the future, like Stalingrad and Dien Bien Phu. Townshend extended his deadline until 29 April, provided that all his feeding requirements could be delivered by the air.

Gorringe's options for another attempt to break through were extremely limited. The inundation severely restricted his options, and the Turks could easily identify those routes open to him. Furthermore, the Turks could to some extent manipulate the floods to their own benefit by breaching the bunds (dykes). Then, regardless of Gorringe's attempts to build around the floods, with a change in the wind direction, the shape of the inundation could change. Meanwhile, the floods were impacting on his ability to resupply the front-line troops.

The weather conditions were simply appalling. On the night of 11 April, there was a thunderstorm, followed by a waterspout, hailstorm and hurricane. The spray behind the bunds was above the height of the tents. Yet on the 12th, an attack was launched by the 7th Division to move the British lines forward, resulting in another 400 casualties.

Across the Tigris, the 3rd Division's next objective was Beit Ayeesa, and an attack was planned for the evening of 12 April by the 8th and 37th brigades. The flooded terrain created inevitable problems and the attack was delayed for a few hours. Before the attack could be launched, the Turks attacked, at about 1930 hours, on the left flank of the 89th Punjabis. The 27th Punjabis move up in support to the left of the 89th, the Connaught Rangers were to the left of the 27th. At about 2100 hours, "A" Company, 89th Punjabis, reported that the 36th Sikhs had retired and that a body of about 100 Turks was patrolling forward to find their right flank. The Turkish advance was halted by Naik Shahamad Khan, 89th Punjabis, who kept up a steady fire with his machine gun while all around him were wounded except for two belt fillers. He held off three counter-attacks from an exposed position with the Turkish positions just 150 yards away. When the machine gun was put out of action, he and the two belt fillers continued with their rifles until about 2330 hours when 100 men from the Con-

BE2c of 30 Squadron RFC being prepared for an aerial resupply sortie during the Siege of Kut, late April 1916. With an engine of around 90 hp and a maximum speed of about 90 mph when they could fly in the extreme climate, it is unsurprising that these machines lacked the lift capacity to maintain the besieged garrison (Imperial War Museum).

naughts arrived to relieve them. Khan and his party withdrew and took with them their machine gun, ammunition and a wounded colleague who could not walk. Khan then returned and removed all of the remaining stores except for two shovels! The preliminary moves had gained another mile, which was all the more important considering that Townshend was less than 20 miles away. For holding off the Turks for three hours and thereby safeguarding that hard-won mile, Naik Khan was awarded the Victoria Cross.[31]

On 17 April, an attack was made on Beit Aieesa, from where the Turks were "controlling" the inundations in their favor and to the discomfort of the British. By occupying Beit Aieesa, it would strengthen the starting point for any future attack on the Dujaila Redoubt. The Beit Aieesa positions were a series of trenches arching backwards from the Tigris and ultimately linking up with the Turkish positions around Kut. The section closest to the Tigris, running due south from the river, was protected by floodwaters to its front, so the attack would be launched against the next section of trenches, where they turned to the southwest. The attackers were assisted, for once, by the disused canals which usually plagued their advance. Two canals, running parallel about 700 yards apart, led into the Turkish trenches, and these would be used to guide the attackers in.

A preliminary attack by the Connaught Rangers and detachments from the 27th Punjabi on a Turkish position on a feature known as the "Twin Pimples" was a complete success:

a night move in pouring rain and an assault which began before dawn.

The attack was timed for dawn on 17 April with a 1,000-yard advance across open ground. An artillery barrage covered their advance from 0645 hours until 0710 hours but in the end the attackers reached the trenches before the barrage ceased. Nine hundred Turks were killed and 180 captured. The 7th Brigade occupied the trenches nearest the river, the 9th Brigade the section of trenches which had been originally assaulted, and the 8th Brigade the "Twin Pimples."

News of an impending counter-attack was received from Townshend, who reported some 1,400 Turks advancing in the direction of Beit Aieesa. The British positions were bombarded before an attack which fell on the Gurkhas before bypassing them to attack the other British positions. The Turkish counter-attack was defeated by 0530 hours, with an estimated 4,000 to 5,000 Turkish dead — the 8th Brigade estimated 1,200 to 1,500 dead in front of the "Twin Pimples": the 7th and 9th Brigade found their trenches blocked with dead. However, the counter-attack had, once again, blunted the British advance, and, once again, the siege of Kut would not be lifted.

Gorringe now planned for the final attack at Sannaiyat to break through to Kut, but the wind turned to the north, flooding the 7th Division's trenches and delaying the attack. While he waited for the waters to subside, 36 machine guns and a battery of 18-pounders were transferred to the right bank for enfilading fire to support the attack. When the water was only ankle deep, Gorringe planned for two brigades to assault, each with a frontage of 300 yards. This was hardly ideal, but the situation at Kut required desperate means. At the last minute, the 21st Brigade decided that the water in front of it was too deep for them, so the 19th Brigade attacked alone at 0700 hours on 22 April.

The 19th Brigade followed closely behind the artillery barrage but soon found itself in places up to its armpits in mud and water. They found the Turkish front-line trench full of water, so they advanced to the second-line trench and found it equally inundated. In between, the ground was pitted with shell holes, filled with mud and water, into which many men drowned or became trapped in the mud. These conditions were those of the Western Front at its worst, not the glamour of Lawrence of Arabia charging across clean deserts.

Khalil saw his front on the verge of another critical collapse and collected every available soldier for a counter-attack. As the 19th Brigade struggled against nature in a deadly morass, Khalil counter-attacked with 10,000 men. The brigade was overwhelmed. The 125th Rifles were all but destroyed in the mud and wire. The counter-attack also fell on the Beit Aieesa position, against the 9th Brigade, who fought off eight attacks,

and the following morning hundreds of dead were lying in front of the trenches. White flags appeared above the Turkish trenches, and the remainder of the day was spent collecting and treating the dead and wounded.

The Battle of Sannaiyat was the last attempt by the Tigris Corps to relieve Kut. On the 24th, the *Julnar* would attempt to break through in yet another heroic failure. When the *Julnar's* fate became clear, Townshend was authorized to treat with the Turks, and on the 26th he wrote to open negotiations.

Negotiations were opened both by Townshend and also by a three-man delegation which arrived from Basra: the Turkish speaking Lieutenant Colonel Aubrey Herbert, MP; Captain T.E. Lawrence from Cairo, later Lawrence of Arabia; and Colonel Beach of the Tigris Corps' Intelligence Branch. The three were taken through the Turkish lines to meet Khalil, whom Herbert had met before the war. They discussed the situation. Khalil was angry that Townshend had destroyed his guns. When Herbert offered £2 million for the release of the garrison, Khalil refused it. It was the Turks, not the British, who held the upper hand and who could dictate terms. The delegation was limited to confirming the details.

It was all over.

8

To Baghdad Again, April 1916–March 1917

The Siege of Kut, with the associated attempts of relief and counter-attack, had exhausted both armies. Both armies needed to rest and rebuild. The summer months were approaching. The daytime temperatures would increase while the river level fell, with the resultant increase in logistical and transport difficulties. Offensive actions would not be undertaken. The higher commands also needed to reassess the strategic situations. Huge numbers of men and material had been concentrated on the narrow front, but they were desperately needed elsewhere.

In London, the War Committee redrafted its policy for Mesopotamia:

1. To uphold British influence in the Basra *vilayet*.
2. To protect the oil wells in Arabistan.
3. To minimize the effect of the fall of Kut by "maintaining a bold front" on the Tigris and "containing" the Turkish Army Corps about Kut and Sannaiyat.
4. To cooperate in the Russian advance in Persia where General Baratoff had 10,000 cavalry, 10,000 infantry and 38 guns.

Furthermore, the position was now to be defensive, and no importance was placed on the capture of Kut or Baghdad.

Beyond that, there was a debate about the positions to be held in Mesopotamia. Some advocated holding a shorter line — Ahwaz-Al-Amara-Nasariya — which required few men and would be easier to supply. However, opposing this view was the potential loss of "face" in Asia, which was to be avoided at all cost. So, while the generals and politicians debated, the Tigris Corps dug into trench warfare where the excavations turned into furnaces as the temperature increased.

The Persian Question would also afflict Khalil Bey's 6th Army. In his memoirs he raged at his superior's instructions that he send troops to Kermanshah where Baratoff's Russians were operating: "At that time we had won a magnificent victory in Iraq. But what we had won was just a battle. The war was still going on.... I said that the British, who didn't forget their defeat at Kut, have now gathered a force of 100,000 rifles only

110 kilometers south of Baghdad. When they were doing this, it would be only an ignorant and bloody adventure if we move our forces from the Tigris to some place in the middle of Persia." He blamed the scheme on German officers in Persia and prevaricated to keep his soldiers on the Tigris.[1] XIII Corps was dispatched to oppose General Baratoff who, it was feared, could capture Baghdad. In June 1916, the Russians were decisively defeated and withdrew, safeguarding Baghdad from the east.

Gorringe was urged to take advantage of the withdrawal of XIII Corps from the Tigris, but he had other matters to contend with. The vessels at his disposal were inadequate to supply the front line with full rations, and it was not even at full strength. In June, 11,000 casualties were evacuated to India while another 16,500 remained in Mesopotamian hospitals. Reinforcements and replacements arriving in the height of summer suffered almost as soon as they landed and many were evacuated straight out again. From his advance base, at Sheikh Sa'ad, the railway was being extended south to Sinn Abtar. Every available vehicle and wagon was being utilized to supply the Tigris Corps with food, water and ammunition. There was no capacity for anything else.

The situation was slowly improving.

Lieutenant Colonel J.E. Tennant arrived in Basra on 30 July 1916 to take over command of the Royal Flying Corps in Mesopotamia. He observed the constant stream of hospital ships to Indian and the queue of shipping waiting to unload — this at a time when shipping was in short supply for the war effort and war material desperately needed at the front was sitting in hulls. There were nine aircraft, crated up, waiting to be unloaded. He thought that Basra was unchanged since Vasco da Gama first arrived, except for six huge high-powered antenna transmitting to Cairo, London and Delhi at 40 words per minute![2]

Tennant found that the RFC contingent had been neglected and consequently was suffering in the extreme climate. The aircraft park at Tanooma near Basra port was incapable of managing the backlog of work which had accumulated. A large proportion of the workforce was sick and in the hospital; those who were left had "little life in them" and could only work between dawn and 0900 hours. Tanooma was not unique. While traveling up to the front, Tennant landed at Al-Amara in a dust storm whipped up by the *shamal* "that burnt the eyes in their sockets." There he found Lieutenant Kelly commanding the RFC's advanced store depot, where the wheels of the carts had all shrunk away from the tires. Tennant then called in at the small treeless RFC base at Ali-Al-Gharbi, where a solitary officer was eventually found wearing pajamas and helmet: "he had been there all summer and had long since lost all interest in life." Sheikh Sa'ad, the main RFC base, was a further 25 miles up the river and little different from Ali Al-Gharbi—in the words on an anonymous British soldier whose sentiments Tennant clearly approved of, "There was miles and miles and miles of sweet damn all."[3]

Tennant's journey up the Tigris was demanding despite traveling without the challenges of fighting. Two batmen who had traveled to Mesopotamia with him "went down," one with heatstroke and the other with dysentery. Their dress for traveling was "topi," shirt sleeves and shorts without shoes or stockings, which must have been all the more unusual for a generation which lacked the modern informal dress codes and propensity for exposing flesh to the sun. In the evenings, passengers were dragged behind the steamer in the river. The water, Tennant observed, was thick and nasty to taste, but at least it was cool.[4] It is no wonder that the batman went down with dysentery, and a miracle that Tennant was not afflicted after tasting the Tigris.

The main RFC aerodrome at the front line was situated at Sheikh Sa'ad (with landing zones at corps and divisional headquarters to aid cooperation). It was not a salubrious location. The camp was situated between two hospitals. The one located downstream was the cholera hospital, and there was a daily procession of funerals, which did little to lift spirits. There was no fresh food. They were all on half rations. Corned beef was liquid and could be poured out of the tin. The only cool water was from a porous earthenware "chatti" hung from the tent overnight where evaporation provided cool water, but only if drunk before the sun rose. Tinned fruit was issued in an attempt to prevent scurvy, but without success, and both scurvy and jaundice were common. In the summer, Sheikh Sa'ad was blessed with flocks of sand grouse. Shooting game occurs in several accounts from Mesopotamia and was an important source of fresh meat. Many officers appear to have taken guns to war with them, but cartridges were in short supply and only entrusted to the experts. The RFC were at least accommodated in "double-skin" tents which provided some protection from the sun. The army was issued single-skin tents which did little to prevent the sun's heat from streaming in.[5]

Tennant found that the RFC was 70 personnel understrength, with most of them sick and unable to leave their tents for days at a time. Given the living conditions described above, this is hardly surprising. Furthermore, the Turks (actually German pilots) from their airbase at Shumran were operating Fokkers and Albatrosses. To oppose them were obsolete BEs, Henry Farmans and Voisins. Sir Percy Lake summed up the situation that summer:

> As regards aviation, the superiority of certain of the enemy planes over any of our machines in the matter of speed, combined with a large reduction in the number of our pilots (due to sickness partly attributable to overwork), enabled the enemy in May and June to establish what was very nearly a mastery of the air.[6]

The future field marshal Earl Wavell, who served in Palestine under Allenby twice and would command British Forces in the Middle East during the Second World War, commented on the "home authorities'" attitude to deploying airplanes for Palestine:

> When a new type was produced they usually insisted on equipping all the squadrons on the Western Front before any of the new machines were sent East. It took many squadrons to produce much effect in France, while a single squadron could change the whole balance of air-power on the Palestine front in a few days.[7]

Exactly the same could be said about Mesopotamia. Tennant set about gaining aerial supremacy, which would mean that, when Maude renewed the offensive in the autumn, he could do so under conditions which denied the enemy the opportunity for aerial reconnaissance, with all of the advantages that delivered. This started with getting more aircraft airworthy and into the air in the early mornings. Within a week a Fokker was brought down. To follow up this success, three planes conducted the first night bombing raid in Mesopotamia. Piloted by Captain de Havilland, Tennant and Captain Herring, the aircraft took off several minutes apart and followed the Tigris, which was illuminated by the moon, before gliding over the aerodrome. De Havilland surprised the defenders, but the last two aircraft were met by a fusillade of rifle and machine-gun fire—worse than anything Tennant had experienced to date. Having bombed the hangers, the pilots made away downwind to the safety of their own lines. All three made it home to a supper of coffee and sardines with others who could not sleep, and no doubt recounting their exploits many times. Night raids were kept up, and Turkish deserters reported that they were amazed to learn that airplanes could fly at night! In response, dugouts were dug for the airplanes and dummies were placed in view. To provide an early warning system, flares were placed at points between the front line and the aerodrome which were lit as the attackers flew overhead. The pilots could see these lighting up behind them and wondered what sort of reception they would receive.[8]

The German aviators did not leave the British raids unavenged and launched what Tennant called a "halfhearted" campaign against the Arab Village aerodrome. Bombs were dropped from a great height, and those which fell in the river provided a supply of fresh fish. Tennant ensured that such raids were equally avenged. Old BEs would try to catch the Germans before they reached Shurman, and there would be a bombing raid by six or seven British machines within a few hours. The anti-aircraft fire was inaccurate, which allowed the British pilots to patiently launch one bomb at a time and correct their bomb sights. The most spectacular result of this patient work was when Captain de Havilland dropped a 20-pound bomb through the fuselage of an Albatross on the ground from 6,000 feet. Such persistence and accuracy would pay dividends when the advance on Baghdad and beyond resumed.[9]

The bombing was not all hostile. One German pilot, known as Shutz, dropped messages on Sheikh Sa'ad asking for gramophone records — they were bored of the tunes which they had captured at Kut — and magazines, although those available on the British side of the lines were months old. In return, fresh vegetables from Baghdad were dropped.[10]

Navigation and target identification remained difficult, even post-war, when the policy of air control to control rebellious (or simply tax-avoiding) tribes was conducted with complete aerial superiority. In theory, the "featureless" desert gave the enemy no place to hide from aviation. In practice, there were plenty of nullahs and wadis to hide in.[11]

An early attempt at psychological operations — psyops — was attempted by dropping leaflets over Turkish positions, as this example reprinted by Tennant shows:

WITHDRAWAL OF THE TURKS FROM EL-ARISH

On the 19th December the Turkish troops occupying El-Arish on the Egyptian Frontier, were driven out of El-Arish by the English, and the 23rd a decisive battle was fought at Magdhaba, which is 35 kilometres S.E. of El-Arish. The Turkish Force was routed and practically destroyed, and 1,350 prisoners, 7 guns, a large number of rifles, 100,000 rounds of gun ammunition, horses, camels and a quantity of telephones and warlike stores were captured.

Further South-West of this defeat British troops moved through the Milta Pass and destroyed Turkish defenses at the Eastern end and burnt their camps at Sudral-Hoitan, about 60 kilometres East of Suez.[12]

Observe how the Germans are powerless to aid their friends. They are asking for peace because they are at the end of their resources; on the other hand, the English strength is now beginning to reach its full development.

To the modern reader, media savvy, constantly assaulted by the marketing man and with access to global, instantaneous communications, this propaganda will seem naive. But it is a product of the time, before "marketing" became mainstream. It would have been virtually impossible for the reader in Baghdad to ascertain whether or not Turkish reversals at El-Arish had happened as reported. It would also have been virtually impossible to confirm reports of German peace offerings, even amongst the Germans serving in Mesopotamia. A modern rule of psyops is never to lie because once a lie is uncovered, it destroys all credibility. The authors in 1916 could perhaps be ex-cused this mistake as the rules had yet to be drawn up and, in the backwaters of 1916 Mesopotamia, the likelihood of the lie being uncovered was limited. What was true, and would have been of direct and real concern to the Turkish soldier, was that the strength opposing them was "beginning to reach its full development," against which there would be little that they could do to stem the flood.

There were increasing numbers of more modern aircraft available, from five to 24 by the end of the year, trained in bombing and aerial photography. The lack of accurate maps had severely hampered commanders for the first 18 months of the war. The Turkish authorities did not have accurate maps either, so those produced from aerial photography were the first accurate maps to be produced in the region. This commenced with 40 square miles around Kut. In September 1916, 51 flights to a maximum distance of 95 miles produced 441 photographs and the following month 63 flights took 344 photographs mostly along the banks of the Tigris. The following month saw the arrival of a specialized William Aero Camera which allowed 807 photographs to be taken. By October 1917, 827 photographs were taken which allowed 327 square miles to be mapped. Simultaneously, dawn patrols were flown along the whole front line and regular reconnaissance flights further afield, some necessitating a 200-mile round trip for ancient BEs across waterless, featureless and hostile deserts.[13]

The featureless deserts could also play into the hands of the aviators: it was virtually impossible for anything to happen unobserved. There were no great woods or urban areas where troops could rest in the daytime, away from the prying eyes of enemy reconnaissance flights, as this example of the daily intelligence telegram to Corps headquarters illustrates:

23/9/16

Reconnaissance 6.30 to 8 am reports: At Shumran aerodrome two machines on the ground. One hanger damaged. Jetties opposite Hai mouth are joined completely into continuous dam from Tigris right bank to sand bank in mid-stream. No sign of work on channel North of sand bank. Suwada camp area unchanged, camps being similar in pitching and number of tents to those prior to yesterday. Shumran camp area left bank unchanged. Kut camp area 40 tents 35B 7/7 reduced to 10 and 50 at 36 C 2/8 reduced to 25. Narwhan area unchanged. Shumran right bank area 30 tents at 35 C 0/4. Hai bridge area camps as follows: 40 tents at 36 B 3/2, 10 at 36 C 2/3, 10 at 35 D 9/1, 40 and transport animals or horses at 46 B 3/5. Total, 100 tents; 50 empty pontoons along right bank at 35 B 42; 6 laden pontoons floating downstream just west of TC 41. Shipping — 3 steamers, 3 barges, 3 mahelas. At Narwhan N.W. gun position is occupied. West position is covered over. East position is empty. New gun position at 16 A 5/6; 2 pits containing tents and 2 empty; 2 or 3 pits occupied B 17. No indication of any considerable withdrawal of troops or alterations in dispositions.[14]

In August 1916, a flight of two Voisins and two Henry Farmans was sent to Arab Village (7th Division's headquarters) where they were fitted with wireless and practiced spotting for the artillery. Given the flat terrain, the distortions of the mirage and the blinding effects of the dust, artillery observers had been repeatedly hampered in their efforts to support the infantry. Now, with aviation, the effectiveness of the artillery could be increased significantly. In and around Sannaiyat, air and artillery cooperated to a high degree of effectiveness which meant that gun positions and ammunition dumps were repeatedly identified and hit more often than the Turks could afford. "Clear line" telephones were installed between the front line and the RFC to warn the aviators of Turkish aircraft entering British airspace.[15]

Flying in Mesopotamia is not without its own special climatic problems, as all arms of service operating in this theater experienced. In mid-summer, the primitive aircraft lacked the power to get airborne later than the early morning until after dark. Cooler air could be reached at about 3,000 feet, but by 5,000 feet there was little difference. Pilots flew in shorts, stockings, shirt sleeves and pith helmets because the sun was as strong at 5,000 feet as on the ground. At night, the cooler air only extended up about 500 feet, then the hot air was encountered again. The hot air, being lighter, rose above the cooler night air. Again, Mesopotamia was a conundrum.

Workshops were contained in 100-foot-long barges which had the advantage of being able to follow the army as it advanced and retreated without placing an extra burden on the already overstretched supply columns. They even contained the darkrooms essential for aerial photography. For land transport, the RFC was even more eccentric. There were three light lorries, one car and 56 Australian mules.[16] In a country without modern roads, the old-fashioned methods of transport were effective nevertheless. When several camels were stolen, two airplanes were dispatched to locate and recover them, which they did and drove off the thieves with machine-gun fire. The camels were returned by a squadron of cavalry. The old and the new were operating together rather than the old being replaced by the new.[17]

The RFC was also employed in pacifying unruly Arab tribes. A rationale for occupying Kut was that it could be reached from Nasariya via the Shatt-al-Hai, and thus the two garrisons were mutually supportive. This proved not to be viable as the Shatt was inadequate for the vessels which were intended to use it. Furthermore, the tribes were notably pro–Turkish and anti–British. Near Sheikh Sa'ad was Gussab's Fort, a "hotbed of these marauders," which was bombed most mornings. It would eventually be captured and destroyed on Christmas Eve, 1916. Tennant also mentions observing an inter-tribal battle from the safety of the air, an event in which neither Briton nor Turk was involved, and which was fought without any reference to the wider war going on around them.

From September 1916, a flight of two airplanes with wireless and photographic equipment operated from Nasariya to support General Brooking's 15th Indian Division. After Sheikh

Sa'ad, Nasariya was like a garden with plentiful supplies of fresh meat, fish, fruit and vegetables. The downside was that the local Arab tribes were particularly hostile, and the town was in a perpetual state of siege with extensive defenses. The only route in and out was by the Euphrates. As in 1915, water levels in the river and in particular Lake Hamar fluctuated seasonally, and a small fleet of steamers, including a Fly-boat, were marooned on the town's side of Hammar Lake until the return of the floods. When Tennant visited to oversee the establishment of the journey, he took the steamer from Qurna to the lake and then was poled and paddled in cramped *bellums* for two or three days across the lake until the deeper water allowed the steamers to tow them into Nasariya. This was the only means of supplying the town with everything it needed. On his return journey, Tennant flew the Tigris leg to Sheikh Sa'ad in an hour and a quarter with the help of a strong southerly wind, proving, for the first time, that airplanes could safely make the journey—previously they had been transported to the front line in crates because of the risk of crashing such a valuable and irreplaceable asset.[18] Flying would also relieve pressure on the hard-pressed river steamers.

Tennant returned to Nasariya in November 1916, where he took the opportunity to visit the ruins of Ur of the Chaldees, a city which was the birthplace of Abraham as well as providing the first examples of writing, written law and the wheel. The author took the same opportunity 91 years later. However, while Tennant was there, a German aircraft appeared over the town for the first time. Tennant took after them, but they gave him the slip. Amongst the papers which were recovered during the subsequent advance were aerial photographs of Nasariya with Tennant's Martinsyde clearly visible and dated to his visit.[19]

The Mesopotamian Railway was extending from Basra. By December 1916, there was a 75-mile railway from Basra to Nasariya along the Euphrates, and along the Tigris from Qurna to Al-Amara, and again from Sheikh Sa'ad to the Es Sinn banks, in all cutting 95 miles from the Tigris journey. Basra to Sheikh Sa'ad was a 240-mile journey which took fourteen days by river; when the railway was completed, it was a nine-day journey. The railway was protected by a chain of blockhouses. Armored trains provided further protection. There were increasing numbers of motor vehicles—petrol, at least, was not in short supply—which were able to complete tasks quicker and cheaper than horses when the ground was hard, as it was in the summer. By the end of the war, there would be hundreds of Ford lorries, Rolls-Royce armored cars, motor ambulances and artillery tractors. Port improvements were starting to take effect under Sir George Buchanan who arrived in late–1915, greatly speeding up the unloading of ships which both delivered their cargoes to the front line quicker and released the ships sooner for further journeys.

Road, port and railway construction required raw materials which were not available in Mesopotamia, as the German railway engineers had found. Britain mobilized its long-cultivated Gulf connections and from across the empire to provide the raw materials needed for victory. Manpower, raw materials and technical specialists arrived at Basra. Twenty miles of embankments were raised around Basra to reclaim 50 square miles of dry land from the marsh. Into this, camps, workshops, store depots, quays, warehouses and railways were constructed.[20]

There were some matters which no amount of infrastructure could overcome. Flies were one of them, and sandflies were a particular annoyance and a spreader of disease. Tennant stated that rubbing the kerosene from lamps over the skin provided some relief until it dried and the torment resumed — men would sell their souls for kerosene because the sandflies were so bad at Sheik Sa'ad. Corporal Lowman agreed with the torment: "These insects and flies in Mesopotamia did not merely tickle and sting, they bit hard. Even sandflies and yet smaller insects, which no mosquito net could keep out, joined the larger beasts in their tormented attacks."[21]

The legendary thievery of the Arabs was another persistent threat and is a reoccurring theme in many accounts. The wire would be strengthened and hand grenades added to deter theft, but to no avail. Weapons, ammunition, and even sleepers' pillows were all at risk. Lives were lost when thieves were disturbed, as they all carried long knives; men slept with loaded revolvers which only added to the hazard of moving about at night. The Arabs were even accused of digging up the dead to steal the blankets which they had been buried in.[22]

Towards the end of the summer, there were a number of senior replacements in preparation for the renewed offensive in the winter. Lake, now over 60, was replaced as GOC Tigris Corps by Maude, then GOC 13th Division. Gorringe was sent to France where he commanded the 47th (London) Division. His chief of staff was Lieutenant Colonel Bernard Montgomery, who recalled that Gorringe adopted the German approach of leaving the majority of the planning to his chief of staff. This suited Montgomery well and provided good training for the man who led several of Britain's precious armies: "I learnt the value of the Chief of Staff system, which I used so successfully in the Second World War."[23] General Sir Charles Munro replaced Duff as commander-in-chief in India. Munro visited Maude in Basra to discuss the situation and future operations.

On 7 November 1916, Tennant observed the first cloud he had seen since he arrived three and a half months before. He took his airplane up just to fly into it. That afternoon there was a rain shower.[24] It is often said that the weather is a favorite topic of conversation amongst the British. The author remembers the same moment at Al-Amara in 2005 when a cloud arrived to break the ceaseless monotony of that bright blue sky. In 1916, this event marked the end of the summer heat. The campaigning season would commence soon.

ORBAT of the Tigris Corps, December 1916

Army Assets

- Royal Naval Air Service
  - No. 14 Kite Balloon Section
- Royal Artillery
  - 134th (Howitzer) Brigade, RFA (two batteries of six 4.5-inch howitzers)
  - 74th Heavy Artillery Group, RGA (three batteries of four 60-pounders)
  - 159th Siege Battery, RGA (four 6-inch howitzers)
  - Anti-Aircraft Battery (four 13-pounders)
  - Anti-Aircraft Section (two 12-pounders)
- Engineers
  - Nos. 1, 2 and 3 Bridging Trains, Bengal Sappers and Miners
  - No. 5 Printing and Lithographic Section
  - No. 6 Printing Section
- Royal Flying Corps
  - No. 30 Squadron
- Supply and Transport
  - Army Troops, Supply and Transport Company
  - Army Supply Column
- Cavalry Division
  - *6th Cavalry Brigade*
    - 14th King's Hussars
    - 21st Cavalry
    - "S" Battery, RHA (six 13-pounders)
    - 6th Squadron Machine Gun Corps
    - 2nd Field Troop, Royal Engineers
    - 131st Cavalry Field Ambulance
    - Mobile Veterinary Section
- 7th Cavalry Brigade
  - 13th Hussars
  - 13th Duke of Cornwall's Own Lancers
  - 14th Murray's Jat Lancers
  - "V" Battery, RHA (6 × 13 lbers)
  - 7th Sqn Machine Gun Corps
  - Field Troop, Royal Engineers
  - 119th Cavalry Field Ambulance
  - Mobile Veterinary Section
- I Indian Army Corps
  - Corps Troops
    - 32nd Lancers (less two squadrons)
    - No. 1 Printing and Lithographic Section
    - No. 1 Corps Signal Company
- 3rd (Lahore) Division
  - 7th Infantry Brigade
    - 1/Connaught Rangers
    - 27th Punjabis
    - 91st Punjabis
    - 2/7th Gurkhas

- 131st Company, Machine Gun Corps
- 7th Brigade Supply and Transport Company
  - ○ 8th Infantry Brigade
    - 1/Manchester Regiment
    - 2/124th Baluchi Infantry
    - 47th Duke of Cornwall's Own Sikhs
    - 59th Royal Scind Rifles
    - 132nd Company, Machine Gun Corps
    - 8th Brigade Supply and Transport Company
  - ○ 9th Infantry Brigade
    - 1/Highland Light Infantry
    - 1/1st Gurkhas
    - 93rd Burma Infantry
    - 105th Mahrattas
    - 133rd Company, Machine Gun Corps
    - 9th Brigade Supply and Transport Company
  - ○ Divisional Troops
    - 4th Brigade RFA (three batteries of three 18-pounders)
    - 125th Brigade RFA (three batteries of four 18-pounders)
    - Two howitzer batteries (of four 4.5-inch howitzers)
    - 34th Sikh Pioneers
    - 3rd Sappers and Miners: 18th, 20th and 21st companies
    - 3rd Divisional Signal Company
    - Five Field Ambulances
    - 3rd Divisional Supply and Transport Company
    - Sanitary Section
    - Mobile Veterinary Section
- 7th (Meerut) Division
  - ○ 19th Infantry Brigade
    - 1/Seaforth Highlanders (the Ross-Shire Buffs)
    - 28th Punjabis
    - 92nd Punjabis
    - 125th Rifles
    - 134th Company, Machine Gun Corps
    - 19th Brigade Supply and Transport Company
  - ○ 21st Infantry Brigade
    - 2/Black Watch
    - 9th Bhopal Regiment
    - 20th Duke of Cornwall's Own Infantry (Brownlow's Punjabis)
    - 1/8th Gurkha Rifles
    - 135th Company, Machine Gun Corps
    - 21st Brigade Supply and Transport Company
  - ○ 28th Infantry Brigade
    - 2/Leicestershire Regiment
    - 31st Sikhs
    - 53rd Sikhs
    - 56th Punjabi Rifles

- 136th Company, Machine Gun Corps
- 28th Brigade Supply and Transport Company
  - ○ Divisional Troops
    - 9th Brigade, RFA (three batteries of six 18-pounders)
    - 56th Brigade, RFA (four batteries of four 18-pounders)
    - 121st Pioneers
    - 1st Sappers and Miners: 1st, 3rd and 4th companies
    - 7th Divisional Signals Company
    - Five Field Ambulances
    - 7th Divisional Supply and Transport Company
    - Sanitary Section
    - Mobile Veterinary Section
- III Indian Army Corps
  - ○ Corps Troops
    - 32nd Lancers, two Squadrons
    - No. 2 Printing and Lithographic Section
    - 3rd Corps Signals Company
    - General HQ
- 13th (Western) Division
  - ○ 38th Brigade (the "Lancashire Brigade")
    - 6/King's Own Royal Lancaster Regiment
    - 6/East Lancashire Regiment
    - 6/Prince of Wales, South Lancashire Regiment
    - 6/Loyal North Lancashire Regiment
    - 38th Company, Machine Gun Corps
    - 38th Brigade Supply and Transport Company
  - ○ 39th Brigade
    - 9/Royal Warwickshire Regiment
    - 9/Worcestershire Regiment
    - 7/North Staffordshire Regiment
    - 7/Gloucestershire Regiment
    - 39th Company, Machine Gun Corps
    - 39th Brigade Supply and Transport Company
  - ○ 40th Brigade
    - 8/Royal Welch Fusiliers
    - 8/Cheshire Regiment
    - 4/South Wales Borderers
    - 5/Wiltshire Regiment
    - 40th Company, Machine Gun Corps
    - 40th Brigade Supply and Transport Company
  - ○ Divisional Troops
    - 55th Brigade, RFA (four batteries of four 18-pounders)
    - 66th Brigade, RFA (four batteries of four 18-pounders)
    - One howitzer battery of four 4.5-inch howitzers
    - 8/Welsh Regiment (pioneer battalion)
    - 71, 72, 88 companies, Royal Engineers
    - 13th Divisional Cyclist Company

- 13th Divisional Signals Company
- 13th Divisional Supply and Transport Company
- Three Field Ambulances
- Sanitary Section
- Mobile Veterinary Section
- 14th Indian Division
  - 35th Infantry Brigade
    - 1/5th East Kent Regiment (the Buffs)
    - 37th Dogras
    - 2/4th Gurkha Rifles
    - 3rd Brahmans (19 December 1916, replaced by the 102nd Grenadiers)
    - 185th Company, Machine Gun Corps
    - 35th Brigade Supply and Transport Company
  - 36th Infantry Brigade
    - 1/4th Hampshire Regiment
    - 28th Punjabis
    - 62nd Punjabis
    - 82nd Punjabis
    - 186th Company, Machine Gun Corps
    - 36th Brigade Supply and Transport Company
  - 37th Infantry Brigade
    - 1/4th Devonshire Regiment
    - 36th Sikhs
    - 45th Sikhs
    - 1/2nd Gurkhas
    - 187th Company, Machine Gun Corps
    - 37th Brigade Supply and Transport Company
  - Divisional Troops
    - 13th Brigade, RFA (three batteries of six 18-pounders)
    - One battery of four 4.5-inch howitzers
    - 128th Pioneers
    - 2nd Sappers and Miners: 12, 13 and 15 companies
    - 14th Divisional Signal Company
    - 14th Divisional Supply and Transport Company
    - Five Field Ambulances
    - Sanitary Section
    - Mobile Veterinary Section

The Tigris Corps provided Maude with 45,000 infantry, 3,500 cavalry and 174 guns. To oppose his advance, Khalil Bey had at his disposal 17,500 infantry and 55 guns on the left bank and 2,500 infantry with 15 guns on the right bank.[25] Maude had a massive advantage in artillery and could achieve a significant localized numerical advantage in infantry if he could fix part of Khalil Bey's force on one side of the river while striking on the other side.

On the afternoon of 12 December the Tigris Corps knew that the offensive would resume. Eight months of inactivity in appalling conditions were over. Despite the full knowledge of the hardships which an offensive would entail, the effect was electric.

III Corps moved to forward positions that evening and the general headquarters left the tented "White City" at Arab Village for Sinn on the right bank. The following day, an artillery barrage broke the peace at Sannaiyat. A solitary Aviatik attempted to cross the British lines to see what was afoot, but the anti-aircraft warning system was now working with pilots waiting in their machines — the German machine was quickly chased back north. The cavalry officers were packing to move out, happy as schoolboys off on holiday. That night, three aircraft bombed and hit, but failed to destroy, a Turkish pontoon bridge which linked the left and right banks and allowed for the rapid movement of troops from one bank to the other. On the night of the 14th/15th, Captain Herring observed Turkish attempts to move a pontoon. They bombed the steamer and forced it to slip the pontoons which it was towing on three occasions (which required him to return to Arab Village to rearm twice), but nothing was achieved by the Turkish engineers that night, and on 15 December the Turkish army was divided by the Tigris.[26]

Maude recognized the difficulties faced by his predecessors through advancing too rapidly and outstripping their line of communications and supply. He planned to defeat the Turks, rather than capture Baghdad, through limited, methodical advances. III Corps occupied the right bank and I Corps on the left. Maude's first offensive was to commence on the night of 12 December 1916 with III Corps making a series of night attacks to surprise the Turkish defenders as far as the Shatt-al-Hai. This would be accomplished by the 18th when III Corps reached the Hai, built six bridges across it and were supported by a railway extension to Atab.

Tennant's contingent of the RFC would provide a service to Maude which Townshend could only have dreamed off. The pilots scoured the planes for artillery opportunities, attacking suitable targets themselves, conducting reconnaissance and maintaining communications with units as they pushed forwards. The flat terrain meant that pilots could usually land next to the infantry or cavalry and discuss the geography or tactical situation ahead. This level of cooperation was vital in terrain lacking significant high ground from which to spy out the land ahead and where maps were still not always reliable. Unfortunately, horses which had already suffered, like their riders, in combat were, on occasion, startled by the arrival of aircraft and could bolt. Messages were flown back to the air commander who spent the days over a map and on the telephone to provide a level of tactical awareness which would have been unheard of the previous year.[27]

As the offensive got under way, Tennant had to manage his resources to provide air cover for an indeterminate period of time. Hundred-hour engine services would take a machine out of action. Replacement machines in Basra were three days away after a pilot had been sent downriver to collect it, three weeks away in Egypt, or eight to ten weeks from the UK. On the Western Front, a new machine and pilots would arrive overnight. The great aerial battles over the trenches in France which could destroy a squadron in a day were inconceivable in Mesopotamia — Tennant could not tell Maude that there was no air cover if his machines were lost through heroics.[28] The weather broke on 26 December. Reed matting had been collected to provide — in vain — a surface over the mud to allow the airplanes to take off and land. Hangars were blown away and bunds were constructed to keep back the floodwaters. The rain allowed the pilots to rest and machines to be overhauled and repaired on "no-fly" days. So bad was the weather on occasions that, on 10 February, only one flight could be made to support the attacks on the Kut Liquorice Factory. When Corps HQ telephoned to inquire if any airplanes would be going up, they were politely told that with the gales, they were struggling to keep the machines on the ground! Aerodromes at Sinn and Arab Village turned into marshes, although flying from flooding was only lost on one day.[29]

The Battle of Mahomed Abdul Hassan

Then, on the 26th, the weather turned wet and it rained constantly until 6 January 1917. The desert turned into a sea of glutinous mud and standing water when the ground became saturated. Maude aimed to attack Turkish defenses at Mahomed Abdu Hassan, which were situated in a bend in the Tigris just below Kut. By occupying the position, Maude would be able to enfilade the base of the peninsula on which Kut was located. The British forces were too far from the Turkish positions to launch an attack. Maude's plan was to send patrols forward at night to establish forward positions while at night a new front line was dug within 200 yards of the Turkish trenches, all done in the constant rain over the "holiday" period.

The battle was launched by the 3rd Division on 9 January 1917 across waterlogged and glutinous mud. After an artillery barrage, the division attacked with the 9th Brigade on the left, beside the river and actually attacking downstream. Next to them were the Manchesters of the 8th Brigade. One of their companies was almost wiped out when their Lewis guns jammed with mud, and only the intervention of the artillery and reinforcements allowed their advance to continue. What followed was a 10-day battle amongst the trenches and canals. Throughout the battle, there was no help from the RFC, as low clouds prevented observation flights. It was a battle of the infantry and bayonets. The Turkish soldiers defended solidly and counter-attacked with aggression until forced back against the river, and they eventually evacuated on the night of 18/19 January.[30]

The 3rd Division suffered 1,639 casualties in the 10-day battle to clear the position. For the Turks, though, it was a serious defeat, despite the dogged resistance. From this point onwards, there would be no more Turkish victories in Mesopotamia, just delaying actions, some being tactical victories, as the Tigris Corps moved steadily and relentlessly northwards. Khalil Bey's protestations against the removal of his troops to fight Baratoff in Persia and his prediction that the British would avenge Kut were coming to fruition. The 3rd Division was opposite Kut already, and this was clearly the next objective. The British were now in greater numbers than Townshend had been when he left Kut in late 1915 for Baghdad, with more resources, and the investment in infrastructure was paying dividends for maintaining the forward area. Khalil Bey had fewer troops than Nur-ud-Din had been able to call upon.

The Second Battle of Kut

Further operations were launched against the liquorice factory (referred to as the Wool Press Village by the defenders of Kut) from 25 January 1917. The factory sat on a salient where the Hai joined the Tigris. Despite operations on both sides of the Hai, the Turkish defense was again vigorous, and it would be 4 February before the liquorice factory was finally evacuated. A total of 8,524 casualties were inflicted on the British attackers. Maude believed that he had inflicted far more on the embattled Turkish defenders.

Two Victoria Crosses were won on the same day, 25 January, when the 39th Brigade attacked on the west bank of the Shatt-al-Hai. The 9th Worcestershires (right) and 7th North Staffords attacked at 0940 hours behind a heavy artillery bombardment which enabled them to get within 50 yards of the Turkish trenches. Despite heavy casualties, the objectives were seized, but then a Turkish counter-attack, well supplied with bombs and trench mortars, forced the North Staffords back onto the Worcesters. To salvage the situation, the 9th Royal Warwickshires were brought forward from the brigade reserve to recapture the lost objectives. Lieutenant Colonel Henderson, commanding the Warwicks, but actually commissioned into the North Staffords, led the Warwicks across 500 yards of open ground through retreating troops. He was wounded before the advance and a second time, but these did not prevent him from leading a bayonet charge which recaptured the lost objectives. While organizing a defense, he was wounded twice more and had to be rescued from the open by his adjutant, Lieutenant Phillips, who was also awarded the VC for that act, and Corporal Scott, who was awarded the DCM (Distinguished Conduct Medal). Henderson died shortly afterwards and today is buried in the War Cemetery in Al-Amara. Lieutenant Phillips gained his VC only in part for rescuing his commanding officer. He also attempted to reestablish communications with a field telephone, which involved running out the telephone cable across open ground while under fire. Another Warwicks subaltern participating in this action was the future field marshal Viscount Slim, who would return to Iraq in 1941 as commander of the 10th Indian Division and later commanded the

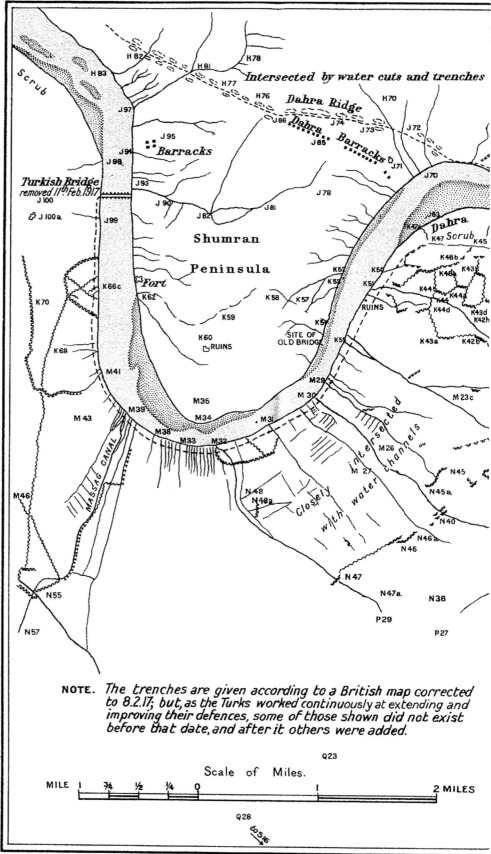

Above and opposite: Operations on the Hai Salient, Dahra Bend and Crossing the Tigris on the Shumran Bend, 11th January to 24th February 1917

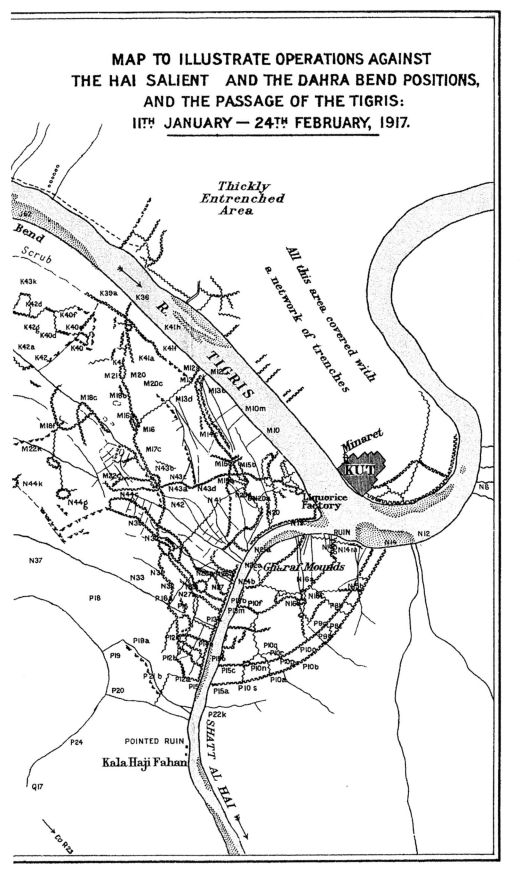

MAP TO ILLUSTRATE OPERATIONS AGAINST
THE HAI SALIENT AND THE DAHRA BEND POSITIONS,
AND THE PASSAGE OF THE TIGRIS:
IITH JANUARY — 24TH FEBRUARY, 1917.

*Thickly
Entrenched
Area*

All this area covered with a network of trenches

Bend

Scrub

R. TIGRIS

Minaret

KUT

Liquorice Factory

RUIN

Gharai Mounds

N6

N12

N14

N37

P18

P19

P20

P24

SHATT AL HAI

POINTED RUIN

Kala Haji Fahan

Q17

to R23

·R19

Ordnance Survey, 1925.

14th Army in Burma. His memoirs, *From Defeat into Victory*, are still recommended reading, as a view into probably the greatest commander of the 20th century. Slim had already been wounded at Gallipoli with his battalion on 8 August 1915 and spent six months convalescing before rejoining the battalion in Mesopotamia in October 1916. He would be wounded a second time, in 1917, for which he was awarded the Military Cross and convalesced in India. Slim's service in Mesopotamia coincided with Maude's rebuilding of the Tigris Corps following the morale-battering battles to relieve Kut and created the efficient military machine which methodically advanced on Baghdad. As a general himself, Slim would oversee rebuilding an army reeling from the repeated blows delivered by the Japanese in an environment no less hostile than the desert — the Burmese jungle. There are parallels between Maude in Mesopotamia and Slim in Burma in how they rebuilt their armies. The future field marshal remembered Phillips' action as "a superb example of leadership."[31]

Despite the heroic action of Henderson, Phillips, and no doubt Slim too, amongst many others which secured the first day's objectives and stabilized the situation by midday, by the end of the day Turkish counter-attacks forced the British back to their starting positions.

The next British objective was against the Dahra Bend where, again as at Mohamed Abdul Hassan and the liquorice factory, Maude was able to trap a Turkish force against natural features and, even if he could not destroy them, force the Turks to fight desperate defensive actions where his local numerical superiority would guarantee success.

Most of the 13th and all of the 14th Divisions attacked the Dahra Bend on 15 February following an artillery barrage, and the positions were taken during that night. Meanwhile, the Cavalry Division with a brigade from the 13th Division swept further west and occupied the Massaq Canal, which entered the Tigris at the Shumran Bend, the next bend up the Tigris. Kut was now surrounded on three sides, although admittedly across the Tigris. Yet, by advancing III Corps beyond Kut before throwing his weight back across the Tigris, III Corps could interdict troop movements in response to any offensive by I Corps on the left bank. At the same time, I Corps was rested while III Corps advanced and now III Corps could rest while I Corps advanced to positions adjacent with or beyond III Corps. Unlike during Townshend's advance, when he lacked sufficient manpower to adequately rest part of his force while maintaining the offensive, Maude had that luxury.

On 17 February, the 21st Brigade launched an attack on the Sannaiyat positions. There was no preliminary bombardment, so the attackers had the element of surprise, although supporting fire was provided by artillery from across the bank. The Turks were known to be withdrawing their troops from the Sannaiyat defenses, probably because Khalil Bey realized that that position was increasingly isolated and, inevitably, would be the object of a British attack. The assaulting battalions were

delayed in the departure by the muddy conditions but reached the front-line trenches without difficulty. While they waited for the 19th Brigade to reinforce them, accurate Turkish artillery fire and an aggressive counter-offensive disrupted the 21st Brigade, who withdrew to the British trenches. Once there, the two brigades became mixed up, and until order was restored, no further attack could be launched.

As part of the 19th Brigade's advance, an Indian regiment to the right of the 1st Seaforth Highlanders were seen to give ground. Sergeant Steele and Private Winder doubled across open ground to take control of a machine gun which the Indians were retiring with, and brought it into action in a gap in the line. This action halted the Turkish advance and allowed the Indians to reform. For their prompt action, Steele was awarded the Victoria Cross, and Winder the Distinguished Conduct Medal and the Medaille Militaire. Despite being of Scottish heritage and serving in a Scottish regiment, Steele was from Saddleworth in West Yorkshire, just east of Manchester. He appears to have found it difficult to gain permanent employment in the post-war world and died in Saddleworth in 1978. Winder rose to become a company sergeant major with the 2nd Seaforth Highlanders. He died on 2 November 1918 in France.[32]

Following the latest failure to break through at Sannaiyat and indeed the difficulties in advancing on the left bank in general compared with the recent successes on the right bank, Maude's attention switched back to the right bank and the Shurman Bend. By advancing further on the right bank, he also forced Khalil Bey to deploy troops along 25 miles of bank of the Tigris against a British crossing, increasing the likelihood that Maude would obtain local numerical superiority in his attacks.

A crossing of the Tigris at the Shurman Bend by III Corps would surround XVIII Corps between them and I Corps at Sannaiyat, and also prevent them from retreating to Baghdad. Khalil Bey had not maintained or manned the various defenses which Nur-ud-Din had constructed during the last Turkish retreat up the Tigris. The only other comparable force available in Mesopotamia which could oppose Maude would then be XIII Corps, which had been dispatched towards Persia to block Baratoff's advance against Baghdad, so there was the prospect of XIII Corps being annihilated between Maude and Baratoff. On 16 February, Khalil Bey realized the threat to Baghdad and ordered XIII Corps back towards Baghdad. True to form, the resources to move a corps across Mesopotamia were unavailable, so units arrived in Baghdad *ad hoc* rather than as a significant force which could threaten Maude.

Maude planned for another attack on the Sannaiyat lines by the 7th Division, but there was constant rain between 17 and 21 February so the attack could not take place until the 22nd, when the division broke through to the second-line trenches and consolidated there for the loss of 1,332 casualties. The second stage was to launch three 1,000-foot-long pontoon bridges at the Shumran Bend, starting at 0530 hours on the 23rd when there was just enough light to work.

The crossing was led by Major Campbell, with D Company, 2nd Battalion, 9th Gurkha Rifles. Each "tow" was of 13 pontoons with 10 men per pontoon. Two pontoons were for the Lewis guns and their crews and two for bombers. There were five rowers per pontoon, many were Southampton waterboatmen from the 1/4 Hampshires. The first tow was led by Major Wheeler, and in his pontoon were three second lieutenants, Russell, Alington and Kerr. They launched at 0530 hours and pushed off 15 minutes later when the light was just good enough to see the far bank. Halfway

2nd Norfolks and 1/4th Hampshires practicing with pontoons on the Shatt-al-Hai prior to the crossing of the Tigris at the Shumran Bend, 23 February 1917. The Shatt-al-Hai is a narrower river than the Tigris yet the pontoons look vulnerable and exposed for their attempt to cross the Tigris and the Diyala in March 1917 (Imperial War Museum).

across, Turkish fire began and increased in intensity. Ten of Wheeler's pontoons reached the far bank; three drifted downriver out of control. Once on the far bank, Major Wheeler ran the 15 yards into Turkish trenches, and, with more bombers arriving, they slowly cleared the trenches. Lieutenant Kerr was wounded in the crossing, and Alington was killed in the trenches.

Lewis guns were sent to the left and right flanks, but when one of the guns jammed, the Turks took the opportunity to counter-attack. Wheeler, Russell and three Gurkhas charged with bayonets and grenades to repulse the counter-attack, during which Wheeler received a six-inch gash to his forehead when a Turkish soldier threw his rifle at Wheeler. He then went on to kill a Turk who was attempting to bayonet Russell. Wheeler and his small team reached trenches 200 yards from the river.

The pontoons returned to the right bank for more men and supplies, but also came under more intense and accurate fire, resulting in more being lost downriver out of control. By midafternoon, the 300-yard bridge of boats was completed, and the 2/9th Gurkhas, 1/2nd Gurkhas and 2nd Norfolks crossed, to be followed by the remainder of the 14th Division.

Major Wheeler was awarded the Victoria Cross, and Lieutenant Russell the DSO for their part in countering the Turkish counter-attack which, according to Wheeler's citation, "undoubtedly saved the situation."[33]

The RFC's instructions were simply to prevent any German

aircraft from leaving the ground. One machine patrolled the Shurman aerodrome constantly, and it was not until 5 P.M. that a German machine got airborne, but by then it was too late. Initially, the Turkish defenders were caught unawares, but they soon recovered and brought two of the pontoon bridges to a halt. The defenders also disrupted the bridge building by launching timber into the river where the strong current after the recent rains caused havoc.[34]

By 1500 hours, the covering force of three battalions had crossed the river and was securing the bridgehead. By midnight, the whole of the 14th Division had crossed. The whole crossing had cost 350 casualties. Meanwhile, the Royal Navy was on the move again, and by the evening of 24 February, three Fly Class gunboats—*Butterfly*, *Gadfly*, and *Snakefly*—accompanied by three larger (drawing five feet of water) Insect Class gunboats which were making their first appearance on the Tigris—*Mantis*, *Tarantula*, and *Moth*—anchored off Kut and raised the union flag again. When Tennant visited, he found the town uncannily silent, empty except for cats feasting on the dead and the stench of death everywhere.[35]

The memoirs of Sergeant Holland, 14th Hussars, starts in the days before the crossing at the Shurman Bend. As well as adding the soldier's-eye view of the subsequent operations, he also gives those details which do not appear in the official accounts. The camp fire made from liquorice roots—grown locally and processed in the factory opposite Kut—and horse dung. There was plenty of water, for once, but it was muddy and colored the tea. Food was stringy corned beef on a Huntley and Palmer's No. 4 biscuit.

Unlike in France, when time out of the front line meant rest, bath and clean clothes, that was not an option in Mesopotamia: "None of the lads here had had a bath since the temperature dropped below 90 in the shade and as for clean underwear, well, just scratch yourself and stir them up a bit." When it rained, the pith helmets were perfectly shaped to channel rain away from their back. A hail storm panicked the horses, which had mostly been injured in the past by bullets and shrapnel. Three horses broke their legs after they pulled out the pickets and tangled their legs. They were put down. In the aftermath, sentries struggled to keep horses secured on the horse lines by hammering pickets into churned-up mud.[36]

The 7th Division relaunched its offensive at Sannaiyat and captured the third and fourth line trenches before the cavalry swept through the Nakhailat and Suwada. On the Shurman Bend, the 13th Division began fighting its way up the left bank and soon ran into opposition on a canal running northwards from the next bend in the river, the Husaini, all day before the Turkish forces withdrew that night. The supporting cavalry again failed to fulfill its purpose by getting tied up in fighting in Imam Mahdi village rather than using its speed and mobility to bypass the village, find a crossing over the canal and then ride down those who had held up the 13th Division. The cavalry then withdrew from the fight to water its horses at the river.

The 38th Brigade advanced to the Husaini Bend, the next upriver from the Shumran Bend and at the foot of the Shumran Peninsula, where they were checked by Turkish artillery. At midday, 700 yards from the Turkish trenches, the brigade began to dig in, "three up," with the South Lancashires as the brigade reserve. The South Lancashires were sent around to the right to try and turn the Turkish flank but found themselves south of the Turkish left flank instead. Their advance was halted by heavy machine-gun fire, rifle grenades and bombs, and by a hill and *nullah* on their left. An attempt to clear the *nullah* by a party led by Second Lieutenant Jackson resulted in the death of Jackson and another second lieutenant, Jefferson, the wounding of two more, plus 21 men killed and another 58 wounded.

It was in this action that Private Readitt took command and held the Turkish counter-attack from a barricade which had been erected by the defenders across the *nullah*. The survivors were forced back slowly, with Readitt holding off the Turks at a forward bend until reinforced. It was not time for the South Lancashires to counter-attack, and they eventually took and held the *nullah*. Readitt was awarded the Victoria Cross for the "action of this gallant soldier [which] saved the left flank and enabled his battalion to maintain its position."[37]

The I Corps offensive up the left bank resumed the following morning with the navy in its familiar position. Indeed the navy soon outpaced the infantry. Nunn commanded the flotilla from *Tarantula*. Above Baghaila, he came under fire for the first time from *Firefly* (renamed *Salman Pak* while in Turkish service) and *Pioneer*, an armed launch. Then, at Nahr-al-Kalak, on a hairpin bend, the flotilla caught up with the Turkish rearguard. Unperturbed, Nunn pushed through even though each of his ships, in line astern in the narrow channel, ran the gauntlet for five miles as they were fired upon from three sides at ranges of 100 to 500 yards. All vessels took hits and casualties. *Moth*, last in the line, was hit eight times, including below the waterline and in the boiler, lost four of five officers and half her complement, yet kept going. Tennant flying over the Tigris noticed the flotilla below, and described them in Nelsonian terms — their decks cleared for action, the White Ensigns spread out by the breeze making a proud and inspiring picture against the last glow of the Arabian sunset. The aviators had been given carte blanche from Maude to harry the Turkish army as it retreated across the flat, open desert.[38]

The flotilla reached the Turkish main body and commenced firing with every weapon available. The armed tug *Sumana* was recaptured. *Firefly*, ablaze, aground and abandoned, was boarded by a prize crew, the fires put out, and the White Ensign was raised again. Nunn's actions turned the Turkish retreat into a route to Baghdad. He pushed on. The steamer *Basra* was captured. It was full of Turkish wounded, all with gangrenous wounds, which could be smelled half a mile away. Nunn anchored a long way ahead of the main army, as he had done with Townshend during the last route up the Tigris.

The RFC had also been let loose on the retreating Turks and showed what their new weapons were capable of by gunning down troops in the open. Tennant recorded the effects of his airmen: "a spectacle amazing and horrible; dead bodies and mules, abandoned guns. Wagons and stores littered the road, many of the wagons had hoisted white flags, men and animals, exhausted and starving, lay prone on the ground. Few of these, if any, survive the attentions of the Arab tribesmen, hanging round like wolves on their trail.... I turned home sickened." Tennant was a relatively new arrival in Mesopotamia. He may have heard of the fear that the Arab tribes instilled in armies in retreat, as the Turks experienced following the Battle of Shaiba, or as Nunn recorded about the Turks who preferred to surrender to a handful of British soldiers and sailors in Al-Amara rather than face the Beni Lam, or Spackman's fears during the retreat from Ctesiphon.

The new technologies were proving themselves in this theater: riverine gunboats, military aviation. Armored cars were starting to appear and would make a significant impact in the fighting beyond Baghdad. These were not limited by the need to drink constantly in the summer temperatures, unlike the infantry and cavalry. Their performances were not limited by the summer heat in the same way.

On 27 February 1917, the British returned to Aziziya, which had been Townshend's furthest success. Maude took the opportunity to halt the Tigris Corps for a couple of weeks. III Corps established itself in the area of Aziziya while I Corps closed up to Qala Shadi. It is testimony to the improvements of the infrastructure that Maude could maintain three infantry and one cavalry division at Aziziya, plus more at Qala Shadi.

The RFC moved its forward aerodrome to Aziziya and based fourteen machines there. All of the heavy equipment was left behind, so pilots slept under the wings of their airplanes and ate the food they carried in their pockets. Fortunately, there was an RFC officer attached to the general headquarters who smuggled out the food of generals to the appreciative airmen and ground crews. They discovered that their old barge, lost with the surrender of Kut, had been recovered and was full of German parts and stores. It was debated whether or not the Germans had any machines left in Mesopotamia until a Lieutenant Lloyd brought down a Fokker while on reconnaissance over Baghdad.[39]

Maude telegraphed London for further instructions. The Imperial General Staff had stated that there was no military benefit to be gained from capturing Baghdad. However, they, like their predecessors when giving direction to Townshend, were bedazzled by the Tigris Corps' successes and the prestige of capturing this worthless city. Maude, just like Townshend, was on a roll. Could he get off? The Imperial General Staff were more cautious this time. Maude could capture Baghdad if he thought it was "useful and feasible" and if he could maintain four divisions there. Both Maude and Townshend were being asked whether they could capture Baghdad rather than being properly directed and resourced by their higher commands. Townshend, in a similar position, had just one division which had fought its way all the way up from Qurna. Both generals considered they could take and hold Baghdad, or at least that is what they told their superiors.

On 5 March 1917, Maude resumed his advance. Turkish troops at Lajj, 20 miles north of Aziziya, held up III Corps for a whole day, retreating in the night, and the advance resumed to the Diyala river. This was the last natural obstacle before Baghdad, which had no modern defenses of its own.

Maude was aware that with I and III Corps pushing from the southeast and southwest, it was only a matter of time before Baghdad itself would be evacuated. Indeed, when the Sannaiyat position had finally fallen, the Germans had started the evacuation. The Berlin-Baghdad Railway had a completed section from Baghdad to Samarra. Two engineering officers were flown in two planes with explosives to blow a section of the track north of Baghdad and limit the Turkish capacity to withdraw. They successfully landed but were immediately met by mounted Arabs who prevented the engineers from reaching the track. They were forced to retire to the airplanes and escaped by flying and firing into the oncoming horsemen. This escapade has all of the hallmarks of Second World War SOE (Special Operations Executive) raids or those of T.E. Lawrence in the Hedjaz the following year, but, as so often is the case,

raids amongst a hostile local populace are inherently difficult and fraught with complications.[40]

Khalil Bey had one last opportunity to halt Maude, on the Diyala. It was a significant river, and if the crossing could be contested, or even repulsed, a significant defeat could be inflicted on the Tigris Corps. It would not be necessary for the defeat to be on the scale of Ctesiphon. The Tigris Corps was too large and well supplied to be defeated indefinitely. Khalil Bey knew that. Summer was fast approaching. The British (and Turks) would not campaign in those temperatures. In 1916, after the surrender of Kut, the pause in major British offensive operations lasted from April until December. Part of that delay was due to the rebuilding undertaken by the Tigris Corps, and part of it was due to the infrastructure developments necessary to support the renewed offensive. Nevertheless, by halting, temporarily, the British on the Diyala, Khalil Bey could safeguard Baghdad until the autumn.

Unfortunately, Khalil Bey seems to have temporarily collapsed under the magnitude of his situation. Shortly after the Shurman Bend crossing was affected, Khalil Bey withdrew his headquarters to Baghdad. From there he instructed Karabekir Bey, commanding XVIII Corps, that he had no intention of making a stand south of Samarra, a town on the Berlin-Baghdad Railway north of Baghdad. The following day, he changed his mind and ordered XVIII Corps to make a stand at Aziziya, but the British were already there. Karabekir Bey, on his own initiative, held the British for a day at Lajj, as we have seen, before withdrawing to the old defenses at Ctesiphon. There XVIII Corps waited for several days before Khalil Bey decided to make a stand below Baghdad and withdrew the corps across the Diyala. Khalil Bey had wasted a fortnight while Maude had rested at Aziziya. Had he been proactive, instead of indecisive, the natural features could have been developed into significant obstacles to the British advance.

The Kharr or Mahsudiay Canal to the west of Baghdad was 25 yards wide, 30 feet deep and with steep sides. It was a formidable obstacle. Its irrigation channels could have been opened to inundate a large area south and southwest of Baghdad. By breaching the bunds during the flood season (which started in March), the area between Baghdad and the Diyala could have been inundated too. About 20 miles up the Diyala there was the option of damming the river to flood the area between the Diyala and the Tigris. Khalil Bey would then have only had to defend two stretches either side of the Tigris: about 14 miles on the Diyala and on the right bank 10 miles from Tel Aswad to the Tigris. Maude would have been faced by the type of narrow assault, hemmed in by inundation, which had plagued Aylmer and Gorringe the previous year. Khalil Bey lost the opportunity. Furthermore, with XIII Corps withdrawing from the east, Baratoff was advancing on Khaniquin on the upper Diyala.

Maude arrived on the Diyala on 7 March. Khalil Bey held the opposite bank with just two battalions from the 44th and

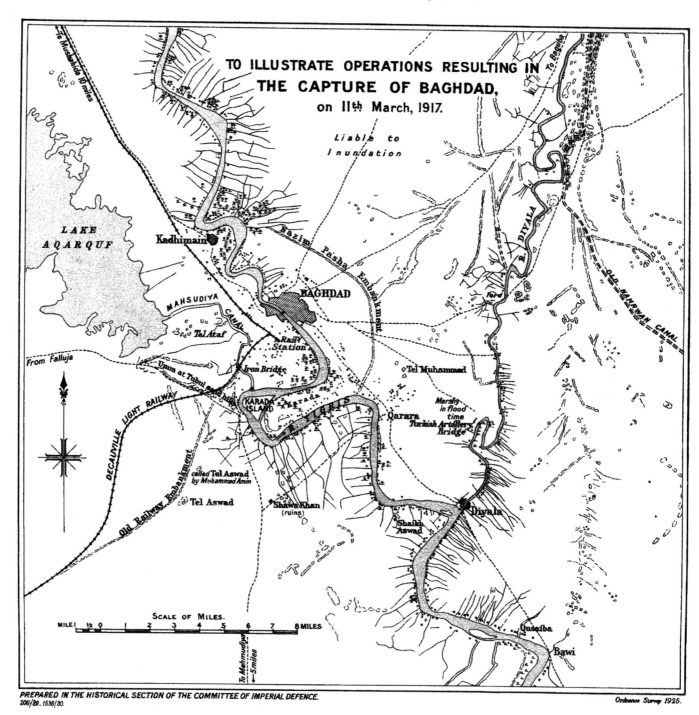

Capture of Baghdad, 11 March 1917

3rd Regiments. The majority of his defenses to the southeast of the city were a second line based at Tel Mahomad. The Turkish resistance on the Diyala was determined.

The responsibility for crossing the Diyala would fall on the 38th Brigade, known as the Lancashire Brigade, part of the 13th Division. The brigade consisted of four New Army "Service" battalions from Lancashire, all 6th battalions: King's Own, East Lancashires, South Lancashires and Loyals.

The Diyala village was cleared on 7 March by the King's

Own. The original crossing point utilized existing bridge ramps, which turned out to be a mistake as the Turks had these prospective crossing points well covered. Four pontoon bridges were brought overland. The Turks were also known to be reinforcing buildings across the river, so planning for the crossing was rushed. The King's Own were to be supported in their crossing by the East Lancashire on their right and the Loyals on their left. The river was some 50 yards wide, and there was a full moon. Unsurprisingly, once the first pontoon entered the water, it attracted fire from across the river. The attempt was abandoned with heavy casualties.

Later that night, a second attempt was made, this time with more artillery covering fire. Even then, one pontoon never made it into the river, and the three which did were swept away by the current, with almost all on board dead or wounded. On board one pontoon was Private White, a signaler and so carrying a drum of telephone cable. He tied one end of the cable to the pontoon and swam ashore, fully clothed, under fire which was so heavy that, when he landed, seven men went forward to help him. Miraculously unscathed, he brought the pontoon ashore and thereby saved the lives of the wounded. For his actions, he was awarded the Victoria Cross, one of only three Jewish recipients of the award during the war, and was subsequently a founding member of the Jewish Ex-Servicemen's Association. A third attempt at a crossing was made that night but was abandoned after another 50 casualties.[41]

On 9 March, a second attempt to force a crossing was attempted further up the river, this time by the Loyals. An artillery barrage was planned to give the impression that the crossing would be at the same point where the King's Own had failed previously. At midnight, four pontoons were launched, named, from the right, A to D. Pontons C and D failed immediately, but A and B succeeded in establishing a bridgehead. After three trips, B also had to be abandoned, but A managed 11 trips to create a 300-yard-wide position. The Turks counterattacked with bombs from woods on the right, slowly squeezing the position to the left. With no more pontoons left, the brigade was ordered to hold the bunds.

Captain Reid's C Column was reduced from 50 to 15 men and so joined B Column. Reid took overall command. During the night, the Turks attempted, but failed, to bomb the Lancashiremen out of their positions. The following day was quieter, with the occasional shelling, but the more pressing matter was ammunition. All attempts at resupply failed. Reid was wounded in the neck during that day but remained at his post. That night, two more attempts to cross the river were to be made. The East Lancashires were to cross to the Loyals while the Hampshires would cross 1,000 yards further upriver. The Loyals were reached at 0400 hrs, just in time—they were almost out of ammunition—but this time the bridgehead was secured and the brigade began to cross in force.

The memory of those who fought to secure the crossing was commemorated when a permanent bridge—Lancashire Bridge—was built. Nearby was a memorial "To the glorious memory of the heroic dead who are buried near this spot who gave their lives to carry out a brilliant feat of arms which resulted in the crossing of the Diyala River on 10th March 1917 in the face of a strongly entrenched enemy. Pro Patria." Captain Reid was awarded the Victoria Cross for maintaining "his position for thirty hours against constant attacks by bombs, machine-gun fire, with the full knowledge that repeated attempts at relief had failed, and that his ammunition was all

but exhausted. It was greatly due to his tenacity that the passage of the river was affected on the following night."

Reid was a South African, born in Johannesburg in 1893, who volunteered as a Second Lieutenant in the 4th Battalion, King's (Liverpool) Regiment, another Lancashire regiment, at the outbreak of war. He served on the Western Front with the 4th and later with the 1st Battalion. He was wounded in the head during the Second Battle of Ypres. Later he served with the 2nd Battalion on the North West Frontier before going to Mesopotamia. He was Mentioned in Dispatches twice while in Mesopotamia. In December 1918, he was posted to Salonika and then at some point in 1919 fought for the White Russians. Demobilized on 6 February 1920, he contracted gastroenteritis which resulted in pneumonia, and he died in October 1920. His military service and the numerous wounds which he sustained undoubtedly contributed to his early demise.[42]

Tennant considered that the crossing of the Diyala should go down in history alongside the Gallipoli landings, where the Lancashire Fusiliers on 25 April 1915 had landed at Cape Helles and famously won six Victoria Crosses before breakfast. Unfortunately, today the crossing of the Diyala is another forgotten battle.[43]

Attempts by the 7th Division to enter Baghdad from the southwest were equally difficult. The Cavalry Division advanced towards the Turkish positions but instead of charging moved around to the flank to outflank the positions, leaving the charge to the 7th Division. With inadequate maps, the cavalry failed in its flanking movement while at the same time losing the element of surprise. The infantry paid for the loss of surprise with 700 casualties for little gain.

Despite these losses, the Tigris Corps was determined to reach Baghdad. They were riding the crest of success, just as Townshend's soldiers had been the previous year. They were infected by the mystique of the City of the Caliphs just like the planners in London and Delhi. Baghdad was also known to be a garden of civilization, and lush and fertile after a summer in the heat of the desert living on liquefied bully beef. The dust storms hampered air cooperation, but that did not hamper the resolve of the infantry.

The quality of maps had again deteriorated, which added to the problems described above—canals and drainage ditches hampered movement and could not be seen in the flat terrain. Aerial photography of the Turkish defenses which were then turned into accurate maps became a priority. The Turks were now assisted by German aviators carrying out the same task, so the Turkish defenders were fully aware of the British movements. This knowledge did little to halt the British advance. On the night of 9/10 March 1917, the 13th Division crossed the Diyala. Despite valiant resistance throughout the 10th, it was now clear to the Turkish commanders that if XVIII Corps attempted to maintain its defensive positions they risked being annihilated as the British squeezed them against the city. Baghdad and its defenses were evacuated on the night of 10/11

March, with the Black Watch famously entering the city just as the last train left the station at 0545 hrs. The 32nd Lancers and Hertfordshire Yeomanry rode into the other side of Baghdad shortly afterwards. In the morning, two machines of the RFC landed at the Baghdad aerodrome, and the Royal Navy proceeded up the Tigris. Lieutenant Eddis, RN, who had lost *Firefly* and was now returned to her command, led the flotilla — he was under orders for the North Sea, but there was time for him to perform this one last act.[44] At last the dust storm had subsided.

General Maude entered Baghdad on 11 March 1917. The first major Axis city had fallen to the western allies. His steamer tied up opposite the former British consulate and he stepped ashore. The building was now a Turkish hospital, and the stench was overpowering.

From the perspective of the Baghdadis, this was the thirteenth time that the city had fallen to a conqueror. It was also the quietest conquest. There was no looting, despoiling, burning, raping or murdering. There was some small-scale souvenir taking. The Baghdad Railway station bell is today in the museum of the Royal Leicestershire Regiment. The Royal Navy steamed into Baghdad in line formation and just tied up. Maude's triumphal entry was notably low key, as was befitting the man's temperament. As with Allenby's entry into Jerusalem on 9 December 1917, Maude was cautious not to be portrayed as an anti–Muslim crusader.[45]

9

Beyond Baghdad, March 1917–October 1918

Baghdad

On the banks of the Tigris I am lying in the shadow of a palm looking down the river on the brick walls and mud roofs, on the mosques and minarets of the city of Baghdad, and as I look I am lost in wonder. For although I am now lying in a grove of date-palms, it is fifteen months since I have seen a tree of any kind; it is fifteen months since I have seen a house or lain under a roof; and this girl coming towards me with hesitating steps, clothed in rags and patches, this little date-seller with her pale face and dark eyes, her empty basket resting on her small, well-shaped head — this is the first woman I have seen or spoken to for more than a year.[1]

Lance Corporal Roe, 6th East Lancashires, bivouacked three miles outside the city in March 1917. Five men per company per day were allowed passes into the city. They had to be armed, carry 150 rounds, and keep together. He was not impressed:

In company with four others I visit the historical and ancient city of Baghdad this afternoon. I entered the city by a hole in the wall dignified by the name of North Gate. Crowds of beggars assail one at every step. Thousands of dogs of the mongrel type wander at will through the streets. The city seems to be in the last stages of decay. The narrow, filthy, evil-smelling streets are blocked in places by tumble-down houses almost meet, thus shutting out the sun.

Words fail me to describe the stench; everything solid and liquid seems to find a resting place in the streets. The Arab quarter of Port Said and the Kaffir kraals in South Africa, in so far as stench is concerned, might be described as mild in comparison to Baghdad.

The mosques are marvels of ancient architecture; their mosaic domes look lovely from a distance (and so does Baghdad). We are surrounded at street corners by bevies of dark-eyed, tarnished and decidedly risky Eastern beauties, with rouged lips and darkened eyelashes that rarely solicit, although their occupation is obvious....

We left the historic and ancient city as the muessins were calling the faithful to prayer from the summits of tall minarets. I was profoundly disgusted and disappointed with

Baghdad and the dreams and romancing of my schoolboy days I left on the heaps of garbage and filth which "decorated" the city's streets.[2]

The next day, Roe bought a bottle of "Black and White" whisky from an Armenian, complete with the silver foil neck covering which he took to be a sign of authenticity. Roe was an Irishman, despite serving in an English county regiment, and with St. Patrick's Day approaching, whiskey was required. When the bottle was opened, it certainly was not whiskey, and St. Patrick went untoasted.[3] Roe was not having a good time in Baghdad. He was not alone. The *History of the War* summed up this general disappointment:

There was no sanitary nor scavenging arrangements, noxious smells abounded and hundreds of diseased and half-starved dogs roamed everywhere. The miserable-looking and rather dilapidated houses of mud-brown brick, and the narrow filthy streets completed the disillusion.[4]

Captain Wilson called the city a "bitter disappointment to the troops." As a political officer, he usually tried to be optimistic about Mesopotamia and the Arabs. Captain Roosevelt considered that the usual view of approach, from the south, was the most unfortunate. The view from the north was much more impressive. Captain K. Roosevelt was the son of the former American president and was attached to the Motor Machine Gun Corps and the 14th LAMB in Mesopotamia, which was commanded by Captain Nigel Somerset, grandson of Lord Raglan of Crimea fame. There were, at that time, only four LAMBs in theater, each of eight cars divided into four sections. These were classed as "Army troops," which allowed their allocation to whichever operation required them. Roosevelt's description of the city did not include any reference to stench, sanitation or ruined buildings:

Coming, as I several times had occasion to, from the north, one first catches sight of great groves of date-palms, with the tall minarets of the Mosque of Kazimain towering above them; then a forest of minarets and blue domes, with here and there some graceful palm rising above the flat roofs of

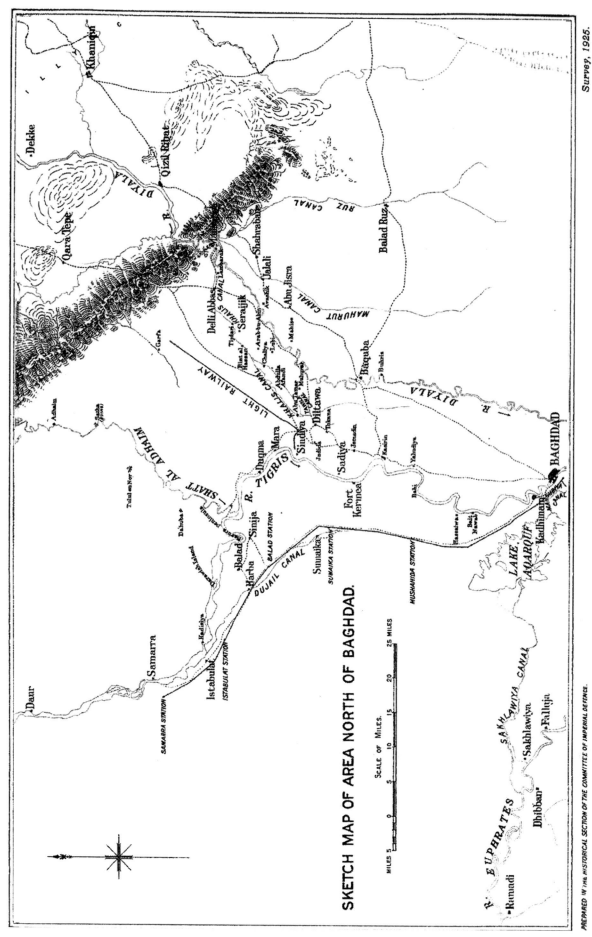

SKETCH MAP OF AREA NORTH OF BAGHDAD.

SCALE OF MILES.

MILES 5   0   5   10   15   20   25 MILES

North of Baghdad

PREPARED IN THE HISTORICAL SECTION OF THE COMMITTEE OF IMPERIAL DEFENCE.

Survey, 1925.

Khaniqin

Dekke

Qara Tepe

Qizil Ribat

DIYALA

R.

Garra

Delli Abbas

Tyidar

KHALIS CANAL

Serajijk

Shahrabad

Talali

Abu Jisra

Arab Abu

Chatya

Lohi

Abdulla Khanit

Mahise

MAHRUT CANAL

Bint al Hassan

Deli Abbas

KHALIS CANAL

Imam Mansur

Dilt awa

Talawa

Baquba

Bahris

RUZ CANAL

Balad Ruz

Daur

Samarra

Adhaim

Tulul en Nor

Istabulat

ISTABULAT STATION

SAMARRA STATION

Daluba

SHATT AL ADHAIM

Kharba

Balad

Sinija

Mediniya

DUJAIL CANAL

BALAD STATION

LIGHT RAILWAY

Dagma

Mara

Sin딕ya

R. TIGRIS

Sadiya

Jadid

Tobena

Jaimadin

Kasrin

Yahudiya

Fort Kerincol

Sunaika

SUNAIKA STATION

MUSHAHIDA STATION

Bahi

Mezairi

Balti Mansaú

DIYALA R.

BAGHDAD

Kadhimain

SUNNI CANAL

LAKE AQARQUF

SAKHLAWIYA CANAL

R. EUPHRATES

Ramadi

Dhibban

Sakhlawiya

Falluja

Baghdad. In the evening when the setting sun strikes the towers and the tiled roofs and the harsh lights are softened, one is again in the land of Haroun–el-Raschid.[5]

Baghdad, the fabled city of the Arabian Nights, which had once been the center of the Caliphate, with an estimated population of 1,200,000 people and a center of learning which linked the Ancient Greeks and Indians — this was the city which had attracted Townshend, Nixon, Lake, Cox, Hardinge and others. This was the city of *One Thousand and One Nights*. That was the dream. That city was long since gone. On 10 February 1258, Baghdad had surrendered to Hulagu Khan, grandson of Ghengiz Khan. On the 13th, the Mongols entered the city and a week of murder, looting and destruction commenced. The Tigris is said to have run black from the ink of the books thrown into it, and red from the blood of scientists and philosophers. The irrigation canals were destroyed, and the depopulated city was unable to restore them. The Caliph, Al-Musta'sim, was also murdered. Baghdad never recovered from 1258. Indeed, it has been argued that Islam never recovered from the loss of its scientific and philosophical heritage. The Sack of Baghdad has been likened to the destruction of Rome or Athens in antiquity. Baghdad was sacked again, in 1401, by Timur — Tamerlane in English — but this time a mere 20,000 were murdered, which shows just how far Baghdad had fallen in a century and a half.

Unfortunately, the city that Maude captured was not that of the Caliphs; it was the city that Roe experienced. And it served no military or political purpose. The closest thing to a justification which anyone could come up with was that the potential consequences of *not* capturing Baghdad were such that it had to be taken. This strategy is reminiscent of 1914-1915 when objectives had to be taken to maintain "face" amongst the Arabs. It may be worthwhile to note that the surrender of Kut did not produce the anti–British backlash which had been feared. On the other hand, continued British successes (which seemed to be unstoppable from the winter of 1916 as they had been up to Ctesiphon) did not cow the Arab tribes from raiding, thieving and murdering the British Army, nor the theocrats who ruled Najaf and Karbala from challenging the British position in 1917.[6]

With the fighting progressing north of Baghdad, there were now plenty of opportunities to visit other towns. Roosevelt visited several other towns. He described Karbala as "a lovely town, with miles of gardens surrounding it and two great mosques." He also saw Hillah, which stands near the ruins of Babylon, and Museyib, which he described as "modern": a compliment. Falluja was a "prosperous agricultural town," although Hit stunk of bitumen which occurred naturally there. Ana was "most attractive, embowered in gardens which skirt the [Euphrates'] edge for a distance of four or five miles."[7]

The capture of Baghdad did not end the fighting. On 25 March, Roe's divisional commander complimented them on their achievements to date but warned them that just because Baghdad was captured, they should not delude themselves that the fighting was over. "The latter part of his address did not go down very well."[8] Maude's victorious army may have achieved the goal which had eluded Townshend and the 6th Division, but that did not mean that the Turkish armies had been defeated. From Baghdad, there were Turkish forces to the west on the Euphrates through Falluja, Ramadi and beyond. To the north Turkish armies were retreating along the Tigris towards Mosul, Kurdistan and their Anatolian homeland. Branching off from the Tigris, but still moving generally northwards, was the Shatt-al-Adhaim towards the Jabal Hamrin and Kirkuk. To the northeast, the Diyala river ran through Baquba and Khaniqin towards the Russians, although there were Turkish forces in between.

There were also serious practical problems in advancing further. The logical direction was further along the Tigris to chase the Turks into Anatolia. East towards Persia would link up with the Russians but was unlikely to deliver a significant blow to defeat the Turks in Mesopotamia. West along the Euphrates would push the Turks back towards Syria. In conjunction with Murray's (later Allenby's) drive from Egypt, this approach may have delivered a major blow to the Turks, but in March 1917 they were still fighting around Gaza. Mosul, however, was 240 miles above Baghdad. The railway only stretched to Samarra, which was also the limit of the navigable waterway. The Basra–Baghdad railway was not yet completed, and stocks of tracks in India were insufficient to extend the railway beyond Samarra. Any advance along the Euphrates would also benefit from a railway. When taken together with all of the other demands on the imperial war effort, Maud was simply not able to demand the resources he wanted to pursue his campaign to its logical conclusions.[9]

Turkish Depositions and Intentions

Karabekir Bey withdrew his troops from Baghdad to Istabulat, from where they could cover the railway terminus at Samarra. He wanted to establish a defensive position which defended territory of some strategic worth where he could reorganize his troops following their battering by Maude. Khalil Bey disagreed. He wanted to make Maude fight for every inch of terrain. With this divergence of strategic opinions, Kaizim was replaced by Shefkat Pasha — "a good soldier but not in the same class as Kaizim" — which resulted in a series of battles which served only to waste Turkish manpower and resources, and delay the seemingly unstoppable British advance.[10]

Khalil Bey's other objective was to reunite his old 6th Army. Ali Ihsan Bey — "one of the ablest of the Turkish generals, a man of great initiative and foresight," or "Old Sandbag" to the Tommies — commanded the corps facing the Russians on the Diyala. His 2nd Division held the ground while his 6th Division crossed back into Mesopotamia from Persia and were in the process of linking up with Shefkat's corps. The process of transferring from one front to another while still in contact with an enemy is extremely complex and fraught with danger. That Ali Ihsan extricated his division is to his credit. Once disengaged, he should have been able to travel via Kifri, Kirkuk and Mosul to concentrate under Khalil on the Tigris. But Maude was not about to allow this maneuver unhampered, and Ali Ihsan ended up fighting two rearguard actions, precisely what he had hoped to avoid.[11]

With the exception of the Euphrates, all of the other fronts involved a change of terrain from desert to mountainous. Many accounts commented on the vast array of wildflowers and grasses through which they would fight, which reminded the British of home. The rolling hills also created tactical problems. The old pre-war Indian Army divisions had perfected fighting in the foothills of the Hindu Kush and the North West Frontier. Those soldiers and officers had long since died, in France, in Basra, at Shaiba and Qurna, on the Euphrates, with Townshend to Ctesiphon and at Kut, and in trying to relieve Kut. The recruits who had joined since 1914 had never fought in the foothills of the North West Frontier. Those tactics had to be learned again.

The Royal Navy Beyond Baghdad

One area where economies were able to be made was with the Royal Naval contingent. With the completion of the last of the sixteen Fly Class "small China gunboats," the work at Abadan ceased. The Navy House in Baghdad was established, which provided better facilities for the crews in the summer heat which made the steel-hulled gunboats unbearable. Nunn returned to the UK in May 1917: his period of service had long since expired. With the future operations still following the rivers Euphrates, Tigris and Diyala, there was still a use for the gunboats, but as the rivers became less easy to navigate in the higher reaches, their function was relegated to line-of-communication duties. Individual gunboats still participated in some of the battles, but as the army received more and heavier artillery, and as the cavalry became better managed and more offensively minded, the role of the gunboats was limited. Army commanders also began to use motor vehicles in greater numbers, which allowed them to leave the rivers for the first time. Indeed, the great service provided to the army by the senior service up to the capture of Baghdad was precisely because the army was short of artillery (both in number and in caliber), lacked effectively managed cavalry for the pursuit, and was unable to operate away from the rivers.[12]

The British Abroad

One of the recurring themes in the primary accounts of the fighting north of Baghdad is the flora and fauna. Keeping up the stereotypes of the British and their gardens, the accounts show a genuine interest in and knowledge of this transitory and irrelevant (to the war) phenomenon:

> The village had palms and rose bushes. A coarse hyacinth, found already at Mashaidiyah, now seeding, grew along the railway and in the wheat. We camped amid green corn; round us were storksbills, very many, and a white *orchis*, slight and easily hidden, the same *orchis*, that I found afterwards in Palestine and in the Hollow Valley of Syria. A small poppy and a bright thistle set their flares of crimson and gold in the green; sowthistle and myosote freaked it with blue; a tall gladiolus, also to be found later by the Aujeh and on Carmel, made pink clusters. Thus did flowers overlay the fretting spikes of our road, and adorn and hide "the coming bulk of Death."[13]

And then on the march to the Battle of Beled:

> As we approached them, the ruffling wind laid its hand on the grasses, and they became emerald waves, a green spray of blades tossing and flashing in the full sunlight.... The poppies were a larger sort than those in the wheat fields, and of a very glorious crimson. In among the grasses were yellow coltsfoot, among the pebbles were sowthistle, mignonette, pink bindweed, and great patches of storksbill.[14]

Before Keary's rebuff at Ruz Canal, Edmund Chandler contrasted the dead plains they had left behind, where death seemed normal, with the verdant uplands where

> None of us could have felt very warlike. A blue sky, willows, a running stream, an English spring, banks bright with charlock; buttercups, clover, veronica, pimpernel; scarlet anemones glowing through the grass. Beyond the stream a plain rolling up to a scalloped ridge of rock.[15]

Prior to the Battle of Mushahidiya Station, the Anonymous Highlander Officer observed the desert:

> But in the dips and hollows below the sandhills the khaki-coloured desert changes into a thick growth of fresh green grass, dotted with countless daisies and dandelions, and a little white flower resembling alyssum giving a sweet smell to all the countryside.[16]

Gertrude Bell who was a keen gardener in her Yorkshire family home transplanted the same interests to her home in Baghdad. She had seeds sent out to recreate the Victorian ideal of the cottage garden and would later boast that she grew the first daffodils in Mesopotamia.[17]

And Captain Roosevelt (although admittedly not a Briton) found an island on the Euphrates near Hit which must have been the sole survivor of the Garden of Eden:

> The entire island was one great palm-grove, with pomegranates, apricots, figs, orange-trees, and grape-vines growing beneath the palms. The grass at the foot of the trees was dotted with blue and pink flowers. Here and there were fields of spring wheat.

And when sent to Ain Leilah in April 1918, he found the changes in just six weeks amazed him:

The desert had blossomed. We ran through miles and miles of clover; the sweet smell seemed so wholesomely American, recalling home and family, and the meadows of Long Island. The brilliant red poppies were more in keeping with the country; and we passed by Indian cavalry reinforcements with the scarlet flowers stuck in their black hair and twined in the head-stalls of the horses.[18]

The author never had the pleasure of visiting those parts of Iraq which inspired the poetry of beauty in and amongst the horrors and hardships of war. Unlike on the Western Front, Mesopotamia was largely a war of movement. This meant that soldiers could literally move to pastures new. These comments also reflect the educational and cultural background of many of the diarists. The officers' diaries are full of cultural references, poetry, Latin and references to the classical works. Roe's diary, as he was not an officer, lacks these flourishes, but that makes his diary all the more important for that. The subject matter of Roe's diary also, incidentally, more closely reflects 21st-century accounts of Afghanistan and Iraq. The officers' diaries reflect the last flourishing of the Victorian and Edwardian world, and are all the more poignant for that.

Trials and Tribulations of Mesopotamia

Despite the pleasure that this change brought, for the ordinary soldier, the problems remained the same. Amongst the flowers there were also "chivvy dusters," the needles of grasses which stuck in feet and stockings with painful effects. Flies remained a constant pest, especially from any failure of hygiene. Black ants were a particular torment. The Reverend Thompson, who ministered to 2/Leicesters, recalls how "at dinner they swarmed over us. Man after man dropped his plate and leapt into a dervish-dance, frenziedly slapping his nose and ears. We tried to eat standing; even so, we were festooned."[19] Snakes and scorpions abounded. Dust storms—"*djinn*," from which the English *genie* comes—whipped away soldiers bivouacs. These poor shelters were made of a blanket supported by a rifle and held down with stones. The result was that your possessions were scattered by the wind while your rifle fell and hit you on the head.[20]

Radiating from Baghdad there were now a number of river systems. This gave much more strategic flexibility compared with simply following the Tigris alone. These rivers were now flowing through upland terrains which posed different tactical problems. Water remained a constant issue. Even when it was available, it was not necessarily potable. Men drank it nonetheless. Sumaikchach was an oasis of eighty wells, but heavily salted, as were most of the wells along the Baghdad–Samarra railway. Thompson called it "bad as water; it was execrable as tea." Everyone who left Sumaikchach left with diarrhea.[21] While serving in Iraq in 2007, the author suffered with a 24-hour diarrhea and vomiting bug. Despite the modern advantages of air-con, plumbing, medication and ample supplies of fresh water, and the ability to rest and take 24 hours' sick leave, it was a thoroughly unpleasant experience. The thought of marching in those temperatures without adequate fresh water or appropriate medication while suffering from diarrhea is not worth contemplating.

Thompson sums up the only respite from this constant toil: "Perhaps nothing will stir the unborn generations to greater pity than this knowledge, that youth in our generation wounds and bodily hurt were a luxury."[22] These wounds allowed the recipient a period in the comfort of the hospitals, and if they were lucky, rehabilitation in India or the UK. Once recovered, Roe of the East Lancashires considered that such men became soft:

> Roused at 6.30 am; move off at 7.30 am. The heat is trying and men are falling out by the dozen. The worst offenders are the men who rejoined us at Baghdad after having a good spell in hospital. I suppose they are hankering after a nice comfortable bed, custards and rice puddings, and a nice and sympathetic sister to take their temperature thrice daily. Once men get a taste of such luxuries it is the very devil to get the men to face an angry Turk.[23]

Who can blame them? At least the prospect of a wound no longer meant the agony of the AT cart to an overwhelmed aid station or field hospital where the wounded lay on the ground, in the rain, unattended, then followed by a weeklong journey down the Tigris on overcrowded vessels to the Basra Base Hospitals, unattended, while wounds festered and basic sanitation was absent. Medical care was now an opportunity to rest, not something to be feared.

And then, of course, there was the army itself, which seemed designed to test the men. Thompson and another dug their trench, a "funk hole" which we would now know as a "shell scrape," "deeply, widely, with much laughter and joyfulness."

> And to us, as the afternoon wore towards evening, came the C.O., and, after watching us for a few minutes, told us we marched in an hour.[24]

Some things never change.

Spring 1917

East to the Russians

Baratoff's Russians on the Persian border had played a peripheral, yet constant, part in the campaign so far. They always seem to have been there, and occasionally groups of Cossacks made the journey to visit British generals, and then disappeared again. Townshend had hoped that Russian offensive action towards Baghdad would have drawn off Turkish divisions to counter that threat and eased the way for the relief force to reach him. He had hoped in vain. Going right back to 1914, one of Delhi's concerns was the effect of a German-inspired Islamic jihad amongst the Muslims of Afghanistan and the

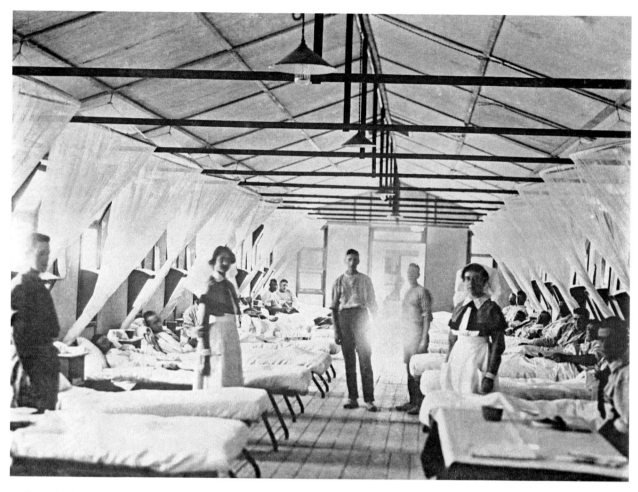

A hutted ward of the Basra Base Hospital with some of the 150 nurses who served there, 1917. By this point in the war sufficient resources had been poured into Mesopotamia to redress the scandalous conditions of 1915–1916, with nurses, linen, mosquito nets and electric lights (Imperial War Museum).

North West Frontier. The Anglo-Russian Persian Cordon had attempted to block the transit of German agents through Persia to Afghanistan. Baratoff's position was approximately due east of Baghdad. By advancing eastwards, Maude could link up with Baratoff and effectively cut off India from German intrigue. In between was Ali Ihsan's XIII Corps. Again, if Baratoff went on the offensive, it should have been possible to cut Ali Ihsan from Khalil Bey and the remainder of the 6th Army and destroy XIII Corps. The prospect of establishing a permanent link with the Russians was attractive to Maude. The Russian Revolution would be later in the year, which would see whole armies melt away back home, freeing up equivalent Turkish armies and threatening to release 200,000 Turkish prisoners of war just as the Turks were being bled dry of manpower. For now, though, the Russian Empire was still a force to be reckoned with, and if Maude could co-opt it towards his aims, so much the better. Unfortunately, the British were once again to be disappointed through Russian inactivity. In his haste and enthusiasm to create this Anglo-Russian link, Maude dispatched a force which was inadequate for the task.[25]

Maude's interpretation of the Russian position was, unfortunately, well wide of the mark. He envisaged a demoralized Turkish force being squeezed between British and Russian armies, with only the weather, terrain, "and perhaps an element of Russian sloth" delaying the coup de grace. So confident was Maude that he asked London to clarify the extent of the Russian sphere of influence so that the two armies could cooperate together. The reality was that the political upheavals which were beginning to sweep Russia were paralyzing the military, and Baratoff lacked everything he needed for offensive action. The Caucasian Corps was nominally 70,000 strong, but in mid–April its commander, Chernozubov, would resign on the grounds that his men did not like him. Baratoff informed Maude that he could do nothing unless Maude provided supplies for 16,000 men. Whitehall informed Maude that Baratoff's strength was likely to be half of that number, but the reality was closer to 3,000 men. Subsequently Baratoff said that he had cleared Persia of Turks and that he would do no more. Moreover, the Turks' withdrawal was so unimpeded by the Russians that there was no detrimental effect on their morale, and they were even able to turn their withdrawal into an offensive. In June 1917, Baratoff withdrew back into Persia, to

Kermanshah, where he argued he would be better able to feed his troops. The Turks were able to take advantage of the vacuum he left.[26]

Both Shefket's XVIII Corps and Ali Ihsan's XIII Corps were converging on a juncture at Baquba. If this was realized, it would be Maude's right flank which would be threatened, not XIII Corps' survival.

General D'Urban Keary took the 7th Cavalry Brigade, the 8th and 9th Brigades of the 3rd Division and five artillery batteries — the "Khanaqin Column" — east to Sharaban. Baquba was occupied on 20 March, and his cavalry advanced a further 15 miles to Abu Jisra. After an initial skirmish, the situation was quiet.

Air reconnaissance estimated there were some 2,000 Turks concentrating and entrenching east of Sharaban, south of the Diyala, at a pass through the Jabal Hamrin — the "red mountains," so named for their red sandstone. They were part of XIII Corps under Ali Ihsan, who was extricating his force across the Diyala. The Turks had dug three parallel lines of trenches along a ridge on the far bank of the Ruz Canal (or Balad Ruz). This was the second of two canals running across Keary's line of advance and was 30 feet wide with deep sides (the first canal, Nahrunia, was not defended by the Turks and was crossed without difficulty). The ridge covered Keary's advance. Meanwhile, British intelligence had failed on this occasion. Keary did not even know how wide the canal was. Even more inexplicably, given the disparity between the forces in the theater, the attacking force was actually smaller than the defending force, giving the defenders all of the advantages.

Keary's plan was to force a passage with a right-flanking night advance on 24 March followed by a dawn attack by the 9th Brigade. Two battalions from the 8th Brigade would attack frontally to fix the Turks in position. The only way to cross the Ruz Canal was to construct a bridge. Aerial reconnaissance on the morning of the 24th showed that the Turks had correctly identified the threat and were moving men and guns to cover the bridge. Keary decided that a change of plan was impracticable at this stage and the attack would proceed as planned. The attack was doomed to failure before it even began.

The attack was delivered with the Dorsets in the center flanked by the 1/1st Gurkha (left) and 1/1st Mahrattas (right). It took all of the 8th Brigade's manpower and considerable difficulty to extricate the attackers. The Turkish fire was so concentrated that over 1,000 casualties were suffered without the brigade being able to close sufficiently to launch their attack. A further 300 were "missing," that is, wounded who had been left behind in the hands of the Turks. It was almost a year since "missing" had been included on a Mesopotamian casualty list. The Turks clearly had the upper hand in this battle and had inflicted a significant, if minor, blow to the revitalized British following their successes under Maude.[27]

A Turkish counter-attack between the Diyala River and the Khalis Canal on 27 March was halted by the cavalry brigade. This was a dismounted action with "S" Battery, RHA (Royal Horse Artillery) in support. The Hussars and two Indian cavalry regiments were handled with great skill.[28]

Further north, at the juncture of the Tigris and the Shatt-al-Adhaim, the Turkish command decided to concentrate XIII and XVIII corps. Keary was ordered to hold his position, while Maude acted to prevent the juncture. This pause, together with a lack of offensive action by Baratoff's Russians, allowed the Ali Ihsan to extricate his troops from a potentially dangerous situation where they would have been trapped between the British and Russian forces. The Battle of Sharaban had served its purpose to halt the British advance temporarily until XIII Corps made its escape. The 8th Brigade resumed its advance and reached Qizil Robat.

On 1 April 1917, a party of Russian Cossacks met the 8th Brigade. Baratoff's 10,000-strong force was now just 3,000. The terrain they had traveled through had been abandoned by villages and any foodstuffs long since exhausted. Seven armies had traversed it in the previous ten months. The Cossacks filled up with British rations and returned to their lines. That was the sole contribution of Baratoff's army to Maude's advance. He refused to enter Mesopotamia. His orders were for Persia alone. With the exception of this meeting, all other communications between Maude and Baratoff were by telegram via London, St. Petersburg through Russia, and into Persia. How long this route took is unknown, but it did not assist attempts to bring the Russians into action against Ali Ihsan, for which Baratoff's price was supplies for 16,000 men. Ali Ihsan had not been hampered in his withdrawal by the Russians. He had been able to conduct such an orderly withdrawal that he had been able to evacuate all of his wounded from Kermanshah in Persia and burn down the British and Russian consulates. The attempt to catch the Turkish XIII Corps had failed, and the allies occupied lands on the verge of famine.[29]

The Tigris to Samarra

Marshall's III Indian Army Corps was allocated the task of defeating the Turkish XVIII Corps along the Tigris. By 5 April, the corps had concentrated around that river: Fane's 7th Division concentrated on the right bank with Cayley's 13th Division on the left bank. Cayley was supported by a weak, composite cavalry brigade composed of two squadrons of the 32nd Lancers, a squadron of the Hertfordshire Yeomanry and a squadron from the 21st Cavalry, an Indian Frontier Force Regiment. This brigade was commanded by Colonel Cassels, later General Sir Robert Cassels, KCB (Knight Commander of the Order of the Bath), Commander-in-Chief, India, 1935–1941. Anglesey called him "undoubtedly one of the most outstanding cavalry leaders to be produced during the campaign," while for Cyril Falls: "His greatest assets were his determination and his *coup d'oeil* on the battlefield. He was prepared to gamble, as he did at Sharqat, and gambling boldly and skillfully is proverbially a necessity for the successful leader, but he did not make a single mistake in the [Mesopotamian] campaign and was never abandoned by fortune. His sense of duty and probity equaled his extreme modesty." Clive Auchinleck, 62nd Punjabis, served under Cassels in Mesopotamia and India and considered that Cassels had certain of Rommel's characteristics. Here was just the sort of cavalry commander which Nixon, Townshend and Maude (before Baghdad) desperately needed. In the Second World War, Auchinleck served as field marshal and succeeded Cassels as commander-in-chief, India. Cassels son, Field Marshal Sir James, was UK chief of the general staff, 1965–1968.[30]

Just two days after the capture of Baghdad, Maude sent Fane's 7th Division to locate the Turks "somewhere near Bait-Nawab," which was one of the potential flood threat locations. Blankets and waterproof sheets were stacked. Officers and men carried their own greatcoats and rations. Water bottles were filled in the afternoon of the 13th. Mules carried enough water to refill the water bottles once the following morning, and then there would be no more water until the 15th. The tribulations of the night march are recorded, and the modern soldier will no doubt recognize the events, except possibly the role of music:

> Night marches, the text-book says, may be made for several reasons, but it does not suggest that one of these ever could be for pleasure. Constant and unexpected checks break the swing that counts so much for comfort on a long march; hurrying on to make up for lost ground, stumbling in rough places, belated units pushing past to the front, whispered but heated arguments with staff officers, all threaten the calm of a peaceful evening and also that of a well-balanced mind. Many a soldier sadly misses his pipe, which, of course, ma not be lit on a night march; but to me a greater loss is the silence of those other pipes, for the sound of the bagpipes will stir up a thousand memories in a Highland regiment, and nothing helps a column of wary foot-soldiers so well as pipe-music backed by the beat of drum. This march was neither better nor worse than its fellows, and we had covered some fourteen miles before we halted at dawn. Then we lay down, gnawed a biscuit, tasted the precious water in our bottles, and waited for what news airmen would bring of the enemy.[31]

The division became lost during the night march. This is unsurprising, given the difficulties associated with night marches and the inaccuracy of maps. Eventually, the division found the Turks dug in four miles south of Mushahidiya Station. The Turks expected the British to follow their usual procedure and keep close to the river, so the Turkish defenses faced in that direction, being placed to the east six miles away. Fane maintained this impression by launching a diversionary, frontal attack from the river by the 28th Brigade with the 19th Brigade in support. Meanwhile, he sent his 21st Brigade round across the railway to attack the Turkish right flank. The diversionary attack suffered heavy casualties: the Black Watch

lost ten officers and 227 men while the 1/8th Gurkhas lost all but one officer. Lewis guns were brought forward to support the attack by suppressing the Turkish troops on "Sugar Load Hill," which was identified as their key point. The extra weight of the Lewis guns and ammunition slowed down their teams, and they suffered heavy casualties accordingly. Through the modern miracle of battlefield telephony, the Black Watch's colonel was able to speak directly to the brigadier who sent up another Highlander half battalion and coordinated a six-minute barrage on the Turkish trenches to the right of Sugar Loaf Hill commencing at 1825 hours. With remarkable accuracy, the barrage began on time, and as it slackened in intensity at 1830 hours, the Highlanders and Indians rose as one, bayonets glinting in the sun, and charged the Turkish trenches. There was little work to be done with the bayonet. Once the 9th Bhopals (nicknamed the 9th Bo-Peeps) successfully captured "Sugar Loaf Hill" just before midnight, the Turks abandoned their remaining positions and made away to the north. After marching 21 miles followed by a bloody engagement carrying only one water bottle, the 7th Division was in no position to pursue the Turks. The Black Watch entered the town just as the last train was departing, which they could do nothing to stop. Yet, despite the losses, one of the flood threats to Baghdad had been secured and the Turks again put to flight. The following day, aerial reconnaissance showed Turkish troops withdrawing 20 miles away to the north.[32]

The anonymous Highland officer states that his brigade moved six miles to Babi Bend on the Tigris, from where they prepared for a Turkish counter-attack which never came. After a week of waiting, they returned to the relative comfort of the palm groves of Baghdad.[33]

The 7th Division's spearhead was now a Mobile Column under Brigadier General Davies — Davies' Column, or the 28th Brigade Mobile Column — consisting of the 28th Infantry Brigade; the 9th Brigade, RFA (Royal Field Artillery) (less one battery); one section of the 524th Battery, RFA; a Light Armored Battery; the 32nd Lancers (less two squadrons); a half company of Sappers and Miners; and an ammunition and ambulance column.[34]

Davies' Column set off at dawn on 4 April, although progress was slow due to the effects of the natural salts in the waters of Sumaikchach. The Battle for Beled Station was fought on 8 April. The 28th Brigade's brigade major informed the brigade that distances were only estimates as their maps were inaccurate and as their intelligence was similarly inaccurate: "The force against us is somewhere between a hundred Turks and two guns, and four thousand Turks and thirty-two guns." And if there were four thousand Turks and thirty-two guns? "Then we shall sit tight, and scream for help," he answered delightedly. About noon, the 53rd and 51st Sikhs were ordered to put in an attack, with the Leicesters in support and the 56th Rifles in reserve. To the left of the Leicesters, across the railway track, were the flank protection force made up of a section from the 32nd Lancers and a section of machine-gunners. This was subsequently reinforced with the Leicesters' "D" Company, plus their bombers and a section of machine guns. The Leicesters reached a ridge and crossed in artillery formation. "D" Company found the going in the hills across the railway track hard, with small positions held by six or seven Turks and snipers. When their commanding officer learned of this, he swung "B" and "C" companies across the railway to advance along a nullah to the hills from where "D" Company was engaged. At this point the brigade attack was diverging into two directions, which is a potentially dangerous development, as it places part of the brigade without support and therefore vulnerable to destruction in detail. The Leicesters' companies advanced up the *nullah* as far as they could and requested further support to continue the advance, but were told

Private E. Sedgebeer from Halton near Lancaster and comrade with a Lewis Gun, 6th Battalion, The King's Own Royal Regiment. Private Roe, 6th Battalion, The East Lancashire Regiment disliked the new weapon: on 6 December 1916 he called it "a toy for young officers to play about with. We have no faith in it. It takes about six men ... to each gun.... Its traversing powers are practically nil and stoppages in the desert-like country are legion. Why not ... dump these toys" (King's Own Royal Regiment Museum, Lancaster).

there was none. They went firm and occupied the Turkish riflemen. The threats did not come from just the Turks. Thompson passed one soldier being treated for heat exhaustion, and he was probably not alone. The Turkish artillery saw the Leicesters' predicament, unsupported by the British artillery, and fired a couple of shrapnel shells. These exploded over the Turkish riflemen, who fled, and the Leicesters were able to take the final ridge from where they were able to overlook the station. To have attacked the Turkish trenches at the station would have meant an attack over open ground. The Lancers also reported hostile Arabs on their left flank. Both of those factors would have resulted in heavy losses for the Leicesters.

Fortunately, it was not necessary for the Leicesters to deliver a charge. Their attack had distracted the Turks' attention, which helped the two Sikh regiments on the right to use the broken terrain skillfully to approach the Turkish guns. This opened a breach in the Turkish line through which the Sikhs poured: the 51st drove the Turks out of their trenches and away while the 53rd made for the station and captured 8 officers, 135 men and two machine guns. The brigade major, McLeod, wanted to transmit a victory message akin to Napier's famous (although almost certainly made up) message following his capture of Sind—*Peccavi*—"I have sinned." The best the Leicesters could come up with for "I have B-led" was *Sanguinevi*. The wells at Beled were sweet, after the salt and ill effects from Sumaikchach.

Although the action was finished, the Turks did not appear

to understand this and continued to shell the environs of Beled Station. This was considered to be part of the usual Turkish rearguard action. Thompson quoted the annoyance in the after-action report:

> During the whole afternoon and til dusk the enemy continued to shell the captured position with surprising intensity, considering what had been heard of his shortage in gun–ammunition.

Most of these shells fell wide and were ignored. When the Turks shortened their range, the first shell skimmed the station roof and exploded at the bottom of an embankment where two Sikhs were cooking. The first one died immediately with the top of his head blown off. The second lost his left leg below the knee, his right heel, and had head and stomach wounds. He died that evening with scarcely a moan.

The shelling continued. Thompson took tea with McLeod, the brigade major, the staff captain and the signaling officer in a tin shed a short distance away from the station. When the latter inquired whether this was a safe location, McLeod replied, "It's quite safe from splinters, and it's no use bothering about a direct hit." The signaling officer's response is not recorded, but Thompson was less confident. Although he was in need of his tea and wanted to drink it quickly, the tea refused to cool down despite the addition of milk. Had it been shaving water, he observed, it would have gone cold immediately. Fortunately, only shrapnel came their way, so there was no need to worry about a direct hit.[35]

Although Beled Station was only a small action, hardly worthy of the title of a battle, it was seen at the time as a model of a small-scale action. The Mobile Column had moved ten miles at night with unreliable maps to attack a prepared defensive position. The attackers had been able to use the ground to the best advantage, which accounted for the slight casualty list, by the standards of the day. There were just over a hundred for the whole action and about half of those were encountered in the station itself rather than on the advance, and Thompson considered that some of those losses were unnecessarily caused by people gathering together around the station. The Leicesters lost about 20, with three killed and others dying later as a result of their wounds. The separate regiments had been able to respond to the threats as they presented themselves and did so with drive and aggression. When opportunities were presented, they were exploited to the full, especially when the Sikhs burst into the station and captured three machine guns that would have done so much damage had a frontal attack been ordered against them. To the Leicesters alone were awarded a Military Cross and four Military Medals in recognition of a job well done.[36]

Although the Turks left the brigade alone that night, the Arabs did not and attempted to raid the camp. In the evening, the aid post was raided and an attendant wounded, who escaped his attackers with difficulty. There were only the dead at the aid post, but the Arabs still stole clothing and cut the finger off one body for a gold ring. That night there were two further raids, both driven off, but taking casualties in the second attempt. The Arabs also desecrated the graves to rob the dead. The dead were reburied. On this occasion, dummy graves were dug and planted with Mills bombs. The 21st Brigade moved up to occupy Beled Station. Sure enough, Arabs came down to dig up the graves and there was the expected explosion. After a short while the Arabs returned to recover two of their number and then continued to dig. At this point, Colonel Leslie, commanding the 21st Brigade, ordered a machine gun to open up on the diggers.[37]

Lance Corporal Roe commented on the same theme:

> The Arabs are notorious robbers and will open up a grave and disinter a dead man for the sake of the socks he was buried with. No cross or mound marks the graves of the British dead on the battlefield, as a cross or mound would indicate to the Arabs that someone was buried there. The graveyards at Baghdad, Kut, Amara and Basrah were wired in and guarded at night by Arab watchmen.[38]

Yet when British officers inquired from Arabs why they dug up the graves, the reply was that the British were wasteful to bury the dead in clothing or their blankets: the dead have no need for clothing but the Arabs did. There is a degree of logic there which it is difficult to argue against. Yet the Muslims were extremely protective of their own graves and were quick to take offence at any action by non–Muslims which threatened their beliefs. Furthermore, in a number of recorded incidents,

soldiers (of all armies) who fell into the hands of the Arabs were stripped before being allowed on their way as well as being murdered. Thompson attributes this to being "strangers in their own land," exploited by the Turks, and reduced from their former glories so that they stole and murdered whenever the opportunity arose, especially amongst those unable to defend themselves. Perhaps naively, Thompson states that it was most surprising just how little retaliation there was by the British on the Arab population. He gives the only two examples which he knew of, one resulting from a misinterpretation of orders and the other being the execution of an Arab caught waiting in a ditch with a knobkerrie for a straggler, although he does not know the individual's fate. He expected that the Arab was shot.[39]

There seems to have been a distinction between punishments for murder, desecration, rebellion, looting, non–payment of taxes on one hand, and committing desecrations and murders. The former were acceptable for the British military. The collective hanging of looters in Basra and Baghdad, for example, was seen as a perfectly acceptable means of restoring order, and the machine-gunning of grave robbers was considered suitable means of deterring desecration. To the modern mind, these punishments may seem harsh and lacking in the "due process of law." There were those at the time, particularly in the political service, who did not believe that such collective punishments served any positive purpose. Until a legal code could be implemented to replace that of the departed Ottoman system, there was no real alternative to such "rough and ready" reprisals.

Accounts are full of tales of thefts by Arabs. The Arabs always escape. What does not appear in the accounts are examples of Arabs who failed to escape. Isolated, caught red-handed and surrounded by war-weary soldiers, the captured thief is unlikely to have received a warm welcome, especially as the soldier who lost a weapon would have been punished for it, and stolen rifles were used against the British soldiers.

The 19th Brigade took the lead and the following day advanced to Harbe Station. There were only a few casualties, and 24 goods wagons were captured. All of this additional rolling stock helped to relieve the logistical burden as the corps pushed its way up the Tigris.

On the Left Bank of the Tigris

General Cayley's 13th Division opened the offensive on the left bank on 29 March with an advance by the 39th and 40th Brigades over 3,000 yards of hard, open ground against positions at Duqma, in what became known as the Battle of the Marl Plain. The terrain was described as being like a concrete floor, "smooth as congealed toffee" and hotter than the "the burning Marl" which received Lucifer and his fallen host. The advance slowed with the heat and mirages. The original plan had been for the 39th Brigade to attack frontally alone with the 40th Brigade sweeping round the flank, but it was not possible to identify the extent of the Turkish defenses, so the brigade was committed frontally.

The 40th Brigade's lead battalion, the 500-strong Wiltshires, suffered 200 casualties before they reached the Turkish positions. Due to their casualties and an inability to clearly identify the Turkish positions, they were ordered to halt while the 39th Brigade's attack developed. This brigade was more successful, and the Turks withdrew towards the Adhaim. For now, though, attempts by the Turkish XIII and XVIII Corps to join up had been halted. The Cavalry Division had advanced to Delli Abbas, northeast of the Marl Plain, which prevented Ali Ihsan from using that route to reach Shefkat and forced him to march on a longer, more northerly route towards Mosul.[40]

Meanwhile, with Turks to the brigade's front, Arabs decided to raid the rear of the brigade headquarters and stole the telephone cables. All of the headquarters staff up to the brigade major took up rifles to drive off the Arabs. The following day, Roe noticed some of the 39th Brigade dead lying about without any attempt to bury them having been made: left for the jackals and vultures.[41]

The weather was getting warmer again, and operating conditions declined in proportion. A plague of locusts cut a swath through the countryside, and the local Arabs had to cut their unripened corn and eat it before the locusts devoured it all. Roe also experienced the locusts. Men were detailed to shovel them out of the trenches day and night. The Tigris was in flood, which normally meant difficult navigation, but on this occasion pilots were aided by snowflies, similar to English mayflies, which congregated in the deepest part of the waterway, so all pilots had to do was navigate through the greatest concentrations of flies![42] Despite the heat and the logistical supply problems, even in the trenches, soldiers had to shave on a daily basis:

> When in the trenches one has to shave every day. The tin case, which at one time enclosed a Williams or any other brand of shaving stick, is used as a receptacle for holding our shaving water. A tobacco or cigarette tin would hold too much water. Shaving is an ordeal never to be forgotten; Quartermaster's "Erasmic soap" and an army razor — a trying combination, and a mild form of Chinese torture. When the ordeal is completed, not without a succession of nicks and gashes, the wet shaving brush rubbed over the face has to suffice for a wash, as we cannot spare water for washing from a quart of drinking and cooking water *per diem*.[43]

Maude decided to put this eastern threat on hold, again, and ordered the 13th Division to resume its advance northwards. The 38th Brigade was tasked to cross the Shatt-al-Adhaim, an 80-yard-wide river sitting in a mile-wide, steep-banked valley. The Turkish positions on the far bank were three and a half miles long and meandered between a few yards to almost a mile from the river.[44]

Before dawn on 18 April, the East Lancashires and South Lancashires crossed the river in an action reminiscent, but more successful than, their crossing of the Diyala. The noise of the wagons drew fire from the far bank, but this does not appear to have continued to prevent the crossing. Roe thought that many had forgotten the lessons from crossing the Diyala. Each man wore a piece of metal on the back of their knapsack, cut from jam tins, to reflect the sunlight so that the artillery could identify their positions. This trick had been learnt in Gallipoli. It permitted accurate supporting artillery fire. The assault companies, one each from the East Lancashires, South Lancashires and the King's Own, launched their pontoons at 0230 hours and crossed unopposed. They formed a line in the brushwood. The attack was such a success that they captured Turkish officers still drinking their morning coffee. The rest of the King's Own followed, and the engineers threw over a bridge across. This construction took longer than expected due to quicksand on the riverbed.[45]

Cassels waited impatiently to get at the fleeing Turks. When it was at last completed, Marshall gave Cassels his instructions: "Now you can go; pursue as far as the outskirts of Samarra and keep between the enemy and the river." The cavalry brigade poured across the bridge to return at dusk with 700 prisoners but frustrated that the Turks had got their guns away. In the crossing, 1,250 Turkish prisoners were taken from an original force of about 2,000, for just 73 British casualties. The Turkish defense of the Adhaim ceased to exist.[46]

On the Right Bank of the Tigris

The next British objective was the railway station town of Istabulat, once the 13th Division had advance level with 7th Division, who was tasked with taking the objective. Advancing from the southeast, the division came across the Median Wall running perpendicular to their axis of advance. This construction was of great antiquity and size (about 30 feet high) which offered the British protection and a vantage point, and the Turks a target. Lieutenant Colonel (later Brigadier General) Wauchope, commanding 2/Black Watch, stood on the wall and mused about all of the armies of all the empires and civilizations which had shed blood there over the millennia, while watching the latest generation march past and on to battle. Only now, following centuries of misrule, there was barely any sign of human habitation, just the ruins of great pasts.[47]

The axis of advance was along the Dujail Canal, actually a river now, but dug and redug so that now it flowed 20 feet below the surrounding ground level. To the left, and running parallel, was the railway and station and to the right, meandering but running largely parallel, flowed the Tigris. The 21st Brigade were to attack north of the canal, the 19th Brigade to the south. Cassels cavalry were further to the south. The plan was to stagger the attacks from north to south with the 21st Brigade's attack starting three hours later. The plan was to offer the Turks an escape route which would take them away

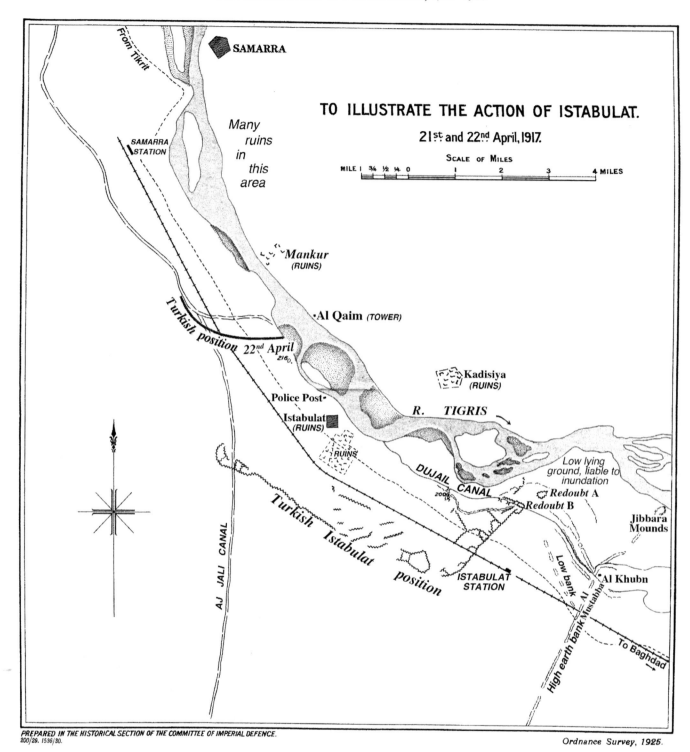

TO ILLUSTRATE THE ACTION OF ISTABULAT.
21st and 22nd April, 1917.

Battles of Istabulat, 21 to 22 April 1917

from the river and onto Cassels cavalry. The Turkish XVIII Corps had dug in, and their defenses ran perpendicular to the British axis of advance. South of the railway, the ground was flat and open. The best prospect of success lay to the north of the Dujail Canal. The 21st Brigade was chosen for the attack, and their initial objective was Turkish redoubts on the Turkish left.[48]

Thompson describes the redoubts as "heights." They were raised up on ancient mounds, well wired and entrenched with 7,400 infantry, 500 cavalry and 32 guns. They had a perfect position, while the British were attacking with two weak brigades. Thompson thought that Maude was playing a magnificent "bluff," hoping that the Turks' morale was so low that they would melt away. Although Maude generally supported his attacks well, there were occasions where he would gamble if the potential prize was sufficient and the morale of the enemy sufficiently weakened. Thompson cites the Jabal Hamrin engagement as an example of this, which had failed. He thought, however, the Istabulat was not one of these gambles, but the Black Watch and 9th Bhophals might have disagreed. Even before Thompson reached the Median Wall, he was told that this was going to be the division's toughest action since Sannaiyat: "This will be a full dress affair, with the Corps artillery." Thompson could not see how they could take the position. Fortunately, the Turks were not of the same caliber as those they had faced at Sannaiyat in 1916, or it would have taken a week of bloody fighting to get past Istubalat, instead of one day. By that calculation, Maude was right. The Turks would fight for a day and then withdraw. When Thompson finally reached the Turkish positions, he found that they had abandoned a great deal of equipment: candles, sugar cones, blankets (the Turks had not been cold like the British), ammunition, clothes, slippers and bivvies. Captain Halstead gave a lecture at Rawalpindi, India, on the battle of Samarra where he established the Turkish intent:

> The Turks intended to spend the summer there; they did not contemplate an attack before the hot weather set in. Three well-concealed lines of trenches had been prepared, on small hills and amongst deep *nullas*, with the water-supply of the Dujail running through the center. Advanced redoubts and strong points made the defences formidable.[49]

So, despite the estimated 1,600 casualties on 21 April, the plan to punch through the main Turkish defenses in one day can be viewed as a success. There was further fighting on the 22nd, but this was as a result of the Turkish withdrawal, which was the normal outcome even when the British attempted to trap the Turks. More importantly, the Turkish plans to hold the British at Istabulat on the Sannaiyat model had totally failed. Furthermore, although the British did not know this at the time, the Turkish forces along the Tigris would not be able to establish another defense position which could halt the British advance until Sharqat, just before Mosul, in late October 1918.

As Thompson's brigade was not involved in the first day's fighting, he was able to observe events from the rear and gives an unusual account of the role of the artillery. The barrage lasted from 0500 to 0700 hours. It was an "artillery battle"; without the artillery, the infantry would have been helpless. The field artillery were well forward of Thompson to start with, with the howitzers behind, but all moved forward until the field artillery were shooting at point-blank range over open sights, literally blasting the Turks from their trenches. Thompson had the unwanted experience of being behind his own artillery.[50]

The Leicesters' "B" Company moved forward on the left with shovels to create as much dust as possible and give the impression of substantial reinforcements advancing to join the battle. This attracted a few shells, but when an enemy aircraft flew low overhead, the ruse was identified. The Turkish artillery moved on to other targets while "Fritz" flew off to machine-gun the attacking troops.[51]

The attack was launched at 0505 hours, and by 0700 hours, the 8th Gurkhas and 2nd Black Watch (in their kilts) had captured the first redoubt. This was a structure several hundred yards long on the front and side faces. The Black Watch attacked on a frontage of just two platoons so as avoid exposing the whole battalion to Turkish fire. The terrain only permitted a frontage of 150 yards. The Turks held the attack and then counter-attacked. Despite British counter-attacks, which included the loss of all four Black Watch company commanders, the Turks regained the redoubts and the British were forced to withdraw to their original positions. Critically, artillery support was unavailable just when it was needed most. Due to the Median Wall, the artillery had originally been placed behind it and fired at extreme range. In order to more fully support the infantry, the guns had to move forward and re-register, and telephone communications had to be reestablished. Possibly as a result of this move, the artillery also suffered, and one of their fatalities was Major the Earl of Suffolk, commanding B/56th Battery and described by Thompson as a "popular, unassuming man." Further disaster struck when the 9th Bhopals crossed in front of a strong machine-gun position, instead of outflanking it, and lost 200 men in three minutes. The battalion never recovered and was sent down the line to be replaced by the 1st Guides.

The 19th Brigade, operating on the left, had occupied their objectives without taking many losses. They did take a battering from artillery fire though.

However, the British withdrawal was not before Private Charles Melvin, of the Black Watch, won a Victoria Cross by charging a Turkish trench armed with just his damaged bayonet in one hand (he was unable to "fix" it to his rifle) and his fists; he floored three Turks, and six more surrendered to him. He also bound the wounds of both British and Turkish casualties, and in his citation Private Melvin "greatly inspired those near him with confidence and courage." Modestly, when interviewed in 1936 about the action, he replied "Well, you don't go out one day with the set intention in your mind to win one, you know."[52]

At midnight, there was a great explosion as Istulbalat Station was blown up. The 28th Brigade was roused at 0300 hours to march on Samarra.

The Battle of Samarra

At first light on the 22nd, the Turks were found to have withdrawn. The 28th Brigade was brought forward and advanced eight miles after the Turks. The brigade passed through the corpses of the previous day's fighting—Gurkhas, Highlanders and Turks. By midday, the brigade had reached the ruins of Old Istabulat, from which they could see the train station and in the distance the Golden Dome of the Mosque of Samarra. The two Shi'a mosques in Samarra hold the mausoleums of the 10th and 11th Imams, and Samarra was the birthplace of the twelfth and final Imam, Muhammed al-Mahdi, the "Hidden Imam." Some Shi'as believe that al-Mahdi did not die but is hidden by God and will return with Isa (Jesus Christ) to bring peace and justice to the world. Many have claimed to be the Mahdi since then as part of Islamic revival movements. It is one of the four holy Shi'a cities, but the city is predominantly Sunni today, which had created tensions. In 2006, a bomb destroyed the Golden Dome, and in 2007, UNESCO named Samarra a World Heritage Site.

"Fritz" flew overhead again and was shot down. No further aerial reconnaissance was conducted, and as a result, the Turkish artillery became less effective than on the previous day so that the attacking British were able to pass under the guns. The lack of aerial reconnaissance seems to have had a detrimental effect on Turkish morale. Following the battle, Thompson talked to a Turkish officer who was convinced that the British had attacked with three divisions and was mortified to find out just how weak the British really were.[53]

At 0900 hours, the double retort of snipers commenced the second day of the battle. The mirage made target identification and ranging impossible. The Turks occupied a position on a ridge, which Thompson calls the Second Median Wall, about 20 feet high; away to their right was a police station. These were the scenes of the current fighting. The Turkish artillery barrage commenced at 1000 hours while the British were in the open, but its effect was minimal. Meanwhile, the British artillery was brought forward, and under the barrage the infantry was able to clear the Turks from the Second Median Wall. From the summit, the Tigris could be seen, which meant drinking and bathing, but it still had to be reached. The Leicesters and 56th Rifles reached the summit of the ruins, rested and reorganized from their previous advance. The two Sikh regiments were about a quarter of a mile to the rear.

Machine-gun sections were brought up to the Second Median Wall to provide covering fire and the 56th Brigade, RFA, were brought forward. At about 1100 hours, the lead companies began their advance towards the Turkish trenches, 450 yards from the wall. In time, all of the Leicester's companies were committed after the assaulting companies suffered excessive casualties — they started the day with 350 bayonets and left with 128. The entire brigade only mustered 1,500 men and went in against 6,000 Turks, admittedly in half-dug trenches.

Thompson describes the nature of an advance advocated in the Leicesters. The theory was that the best way to support a neighboring unit was to advance. The only way was to advance steadily, as this weakened the enemy's morale while making it more difficult for them to select their ranges. Each dash was no more than 20 yards, more usually 10 to 15. The enemy

would focus on one platoon or section, even once they had gone to ground, and as soon as this was seen to be happening, another section or platoon would make its dash. Once they were down, they melted away into the sand, (if they were there for more than five minutes, they dug in with their entrenching tools) and there was nothing to shoot at, especially as the men took full advantage of depressions. Shell bursts were ideal to advance behind too. Most of the enemy's shells tended to explode to the rear. Runners zigzagged to make a more difficult target, and few were lost as a result. Officers and signalers lay flat at their work, and stretcher bearers did not operate in front of the wall. It was the Lewis gun crews who suffered most. They were laden with extra equipment, so their dashes were shorter and slower. When platoons and companies became mixed up, they were easily sorted out, which was put down to the lack of rifle fire from them. By this method it was believed that although the Leicesters were usually at the forefront of battles, they suffered fewer casualties as a result compared with other regiments.[54]

What is most amazing from Thompson's description of the Leicesters' tactics is how modern they seem. The modern British Army teaches "one foot on the ground," whereby one unit is firing, keeping the enemy's heads down while the other moves, and then they swap over. In 1917, the aim was to close in with the bayonet, so although firing back was not encouraged, the idea that the enemy's fire was drawn away before you moved has modern parallels. The use of the ground for cover, officers and signalers operating lying down and runners zigzagging are also modern sounding. Yet Thompson takes some of these details from Hasted's lecture at Rawalpindi. Was this approach to fighting so novel as to warrant a lecture? It would appear so.

Despite this apparently successful use of tactics and the ground, the Leicesters were unable to reach the Turkish trenches and lie in the open within 300 yards between about 1100 hours and 1530 hours. It should also be noted, as above, that the Leicesters suffered over 50 percent casualties that day. The new tactics described by Thompson were not the complete answer.

At 1600 hours, a 20-minute barrage hit the Turkish trenches. When it lifted 100 yards, the Leicesters charged forward, with the 51st Sikhs in support and the 56th providing covering fire. The Turkish defenders were by now demoralized, and 800 surrendered, although many more escaped because the Leicesters, now just 200 strong, were incapable of securing them all.[55]

The Leicesters followed up this success for a further mile when they unexpectedly came across the Turkish artillery, still firing. The Turks were equally surprised when Captain Diggins and three privates appeared. Turkish gunners were not armed with rifles.[56] The battery commander shook the hand of the exhausted company commander and surrendered his battery of seven 14-pounder and two 5.9-inch guns (some damaged), and 50 men. Diggins was awarded the Military Cross for this action. The Turks were able to withdraw more guns to the left and right.

From this position, the Leicesters should have been able to dig in and consolidate their position, but they were not down to their last few rounds—no one had more than five rounds left. The battalion's bombers were sent back to bring up more ammunition. The 51st Sikhs, in support, were nowhere to be seen except for a Subahdar and two sepoys. Shefket was unwilling to accept the loss of the guns and counter-attacked the Leicesters with some 2,000 men. The Leicesters were unable to hold their position, and unable to move the guns, so they had to withdraw. By falling back, the Leicesters now completed the British line. The 51st Sikhs were located where they were occupying depressions in the ground. They passed ammunition to the Leicesters. The artillery opened fire in support but was too late to halt the Turkish advance and missed the target. Thirty out of the Leicesters' 60 bombers became casualties while bringing ammunition forward, but their actions prevented the line from being completely overrun. The Turks were halted about 250 yards from the British position for about 30 minutes, despite the demonstrations of their officers.

At about 1800 hours, the 19th Brigade arrived to reinforce the line. Darkness was falling, but the brigade was well supplied with ammunition. Unfortunately, their arrival was too late to secure the guns. For two hours in the dark the Leicesters had to listen to "their" guns being taken away. Thompson commented on the official explanation of the loss of the guns— that the Leicesters got out of hand and went too far—but considered that "over-confidence somewhere back" was a more accurate reason. Six months later, those guns took a heavy toll on the British at Tikrit. The retirement of the Leicesters did link up the British line, and the front stabilized.[57]

This account focuses on the actions of the Leicesters primarily because of the excellent account provided by the Reverend Thompson. He also took the time to comment on the sacrifice of the Indian regiments that day. The 53rd Sikhs lost their four senior officers, killed, and this was common. Most poignant are the personal connections. Another of the 53rd's officers, Scarth, was brought into the aid station, where he died. He was 19 years old, and his father was a friend of Thompson's.[58]

During this final Turkish counter-attack, the final Victoria Cross of the Mesopotamia front was awarded to Lieutenant (later Captain) John Graham, 136th Company Machine Gun Corps, attached to the 56th Punjabi Rifles, 28th Brigade. With only one working Lewis gun, he disabled it and withdrew, acquired another Lewis gun and then used that until the ammunition was exhausted. Meanwhile, he was wounded four times but continued to control his weapon to hold up a strong Turkish counter-attack which threatened to roll up the brigade's left flank.[59]

About the same time as Graham's action, Cassels' cavalry brigade was maneuvering on the Turkish flanks and reached Samarra Station. On the 21st, the cavalry and the LAMBs (Light Armored Motor Battery) had been skirmishing with enemy patrols and had taken some prisoners, but they had largely been uninvolved in the fighting. On the 22nd, a cavalry charge was launched against the station. Forty men of the 32nd Lancers charged against Turkish troops in trenches, who promptly surrendered. Anglesey gives the reason for this charge as being to assist an unidentified infantry battalion in difficulty. This was an immensely brave charge, as Barker points out that no cavalry charge in the open against riflemen had succeeded since 1870. Unfortunately, the impetus of the Lancers' charge carried them beyond the surrendering Turks onto their reserve trenches, who did not surrender. The "surrendered" Turks then picked up their rifles, and the Lancers were caught between the two trenches and suffered casualties accordingly. The Lancers' colonel (Griffiths) and adjutant (Hunter) were both killed in the charge, and only 15 of the 40 men returned. The charge was reckless and unsupported. The LAMBs were too far away to be of assistance, and the artillery had ceased firing at that point. Had it been supported, then the British might possibly have broken through behind the Turkish positions and cut off their retirement. The *Official History* described the charge as being of "very material assistance" but as another example of the difficulties of launching an attack against unsupported infantry without supporting fire. As it was, the shock was enough for Shefkat to realize the threat to his flank and to consider withdrawing.[60]

The two days of fighting in and around Istabulat are usually divided into two separate battles. On the 21st was the Istabulat or Dujail Canal, and on the 22nd the fighting was at the Istabulat Mounds. The two day of fighting cost some 2,800 British casualties.

The British advanced to Samarra, which Thompson, who would spend the summer of 1917 there, described as a "dirty, sand-coloured town with no touch of brightness but what its famous dome gives it." In and amongst the decay were ruins of former civilizations, like the tomb of the Roman Emperor Julian who died there following a defeat in battle in A.D. 363. When Lance Corporal Roe heard of the capture of Samarra and its association with Julian, he became philosophical. Alexander the Great had died at Babylon. Roe credited the pair with more brains than to die in Mesopotamia. The Greek general Xenophon and his army were lost in the Mesopotamian marshes: "I expect he died too." The soldiers dug up archaeological artifacts as they dug in. The Turks withdrew to Tikrit. In Samarra station, the engines and rolling stock were set alight, but unsuccessfully, and several engines and 60 percent of the rolling stock were saved. These were soon working the line to Baghdad alongside engines in familiar British train company liveries.[61]

The 40th Brigade attacked the Turks at Mara on 5 April. They captured the forward Turkish positions, but as a mirage interfered with the artillery, the advance had to be halted and by the time it was due to resume the following morning, the Turks had left.

XIII Turkish Corps began a westward advance from the Jabal Hamrin. The RFC kept them under constant observation, and the Cavalry Division withdrew in front of them. The Turkish 2nd Division maneuvered to turn the cavalry's flank and get between them and their lines of communication to III Corps. Marshall put aside his plans to cross the Adhaim and sent the 39th and 40th Brigades on a 20-mile forced night march to assist the cavalry. Neither the two brigades nor the Turkish division were aware of each other's presence until they clashed. The Cheshires and Royal Welsh Fusiliers ran to occupy a ridge from where they were able to pour fire onto the advancing Turkish troops. They were joined by 55th Brigade, RFA, which galloped its 18-pounders to the crest and opened fire. The Turks withdrew into the mountains, where Marshall was not prepared to follow them. Leaving the cavalry division and two infantry brigades to protect his right flank, Marshall was able to look to the north again.[62]

Maude was now able to focus on the Turkish XIII Corps, which was advancing southwards down the Shatt-al-Adhaim. The 14th Division halted near Dahuba for the Turkish 2nd Division to catch up. Marshall was ordered to attack and destroy the Turkish column. Unfortunately, with most of his troops fighting around Istabulat, all that Marshall had at his disposal was the 38th Brigade, some 1,200 strong, and 350 cavalry. The 14th Division was ordered to dispatch the 40th

Brigade and as much artillery as it could spare to join Marshall, who marched with the 38th Brigade. Marshall set off at 0130 hours on 23 April and halted at dawn. The Turks were expected to be miles away. In the night, lights had been seen on the right, and Roe thought that the figures moving there were West Kents until they opened fire — the two forces had marched into each other. Battle was joined. The North Lancashires and South Lancashires deployed to attack in two lines with the King's Own in support and the East Lancashires in reserve. The cavalry moved round to the left flank while the machine-gunners and artillery prepared to give covering fire as the infantry prepared to advance over 2,000 yards of billiard-table-flat terrain. Roe reported that the North and South Lancashires moved in sectional rushes as if for a visiting general with the benefit of accurate covering fire, until the final bayonet charge, at which point the Turks ran. Fortunately the dust from the feet of the 40th Brigade could be seen. The Turks also saw the dust of the second column and began to withdraw across the Adhaim. Marshall rested his infantry, while the cavalry harried the Turks. Marshall found the Turkish positions on either side of the Adhaim around a position known as the Band-i-Adhaim — the Gate of the Adhaim, known as the "Boot."[63]

After dark on 29 April, Marshall moved to the northeast and was in position at 0300 hours. The artillery commenced a barrage at 0500 hours, and the infantry moved behind it. Three East Lancashires were killed and another two were wounded when British shells dropped short. In the 38th Bri-

A field battery, Royal Artillery, coming into action south of Samarra Station, April 1917. The flat terrain made spotting the fall of shot and providing accurate infantry support extremely difficult and impossible when mirages were present. In this terrain, aerial observation was essential. Here the battery commander uses a limber pole for observation, protected by an iron plate. Beside him is a heliograph (Imperial War Museum).

gade, the East Lancashires captured an enemy position known as the Mound, with the King's Own on their right and the South Lancashires on their left, and the North Lancashires in reserve. To the left of the 38th Brigade, the Cheshires and South Wales Borders of the 40th Brigade commenced their advance at 0500 hours. Their objective was either side of an abandoned village. The Turks were driven out at bayonet point by the Cheshires, but others surrendered en masse to the Borderers. The battalions then took the Turkish second-line positions where they were then supposed to halt and consolidate. However, elated by success, with the Turks on the run, the sight of two artillery batteries was too tempting for the Cheshires, and they pushed on to take the guns on top of 300 prisoners. Seeing the Cheshires, the Borderers ran to catch them up. Then things went wrong. A dust storm obscured the whole battlefield, and Ali Ihsan counter-attacked to recover his guns. Passing in front of the 38th Brigade in the dust with all of his reserves, he hit the two British battalions. They had commenced the battle 330 and 340 men strong respectively. Now they were outnumbered six to one. Disorganized from the attack and the dust, Ali Ihsan hit them, recovering seven of his eight guns, most of the Turkish prisoners and taking 150 British prisoners. When the brigade commander, Lewin, realized what had happened, he pushed his two reserve battalions, Wiltshires and Royal Welsh Fusiliers, forward in support, but with orders not to advance beyond the village. The survivors of the Cheshires and Borderers were pushed back beyond the village. The storm abated at about 1600 hours. Lance Corporal Roe with the 38th Brigade to the right wrote, "All is quiet on our left. What has happened to 40 Brigade?" Although the remainder of the 40th Brigade gave chase, Turkish XIII Corps withdrew with its prisoners into the *jebel* and towards Tikrit.[64]

A.J. Barker considered that the Battle of the "Boot" was the bloodiest in terms of numbers involved. It was also the last of a series of battles which had begun around Kut the previous December. On 2/3 June, Lance Corporal Roe wrote in his diary, "Nothing doing. Fighting is over until September when the cold season starts."[65]

West on the Euphrates

West of Baghdad, there were a number of significant towns which were not occupied by British troops yet. The 7th Brigade reached Falluja on 19 March. Their departure had been delayed by transport shortages. The Turks did not make a stand but withdrew 25 miles to Ramadi although the local Arabs put up some resistance. The town was occupied with minimal casualties. Like Mushahidiya Station, this action was to secure Baghdad from flooding. Unlike Mushahidiya Station, this operation failed, as the Turks breached the Sakhlawiya Canal as they left.

There was now an urgent need to repair the Sakhlawiya Dam in the dry season before the rainy-season floods threatened the Samarra Railway and Baghdad. The Euphrates flood level at this point was 14 feet higher than the surrounding countryside as in Baghdad. Fortunately, the pre-flood water levels were unusually low at the time, which limited the damage. A new bund had to be constructed to protect the Decauville railway and road, without which communications along the Euphrates could not be maintained. A simpler option would have been to create breaches in the bunds at right angles to the flow of water and divert the floods into Lake Habbaniya, but this would have flooded the lands of the Dulain Arabs, and Maude had no desire to create additional problems with them. They were already anti–British and were only brought to terms with the British when it became apparent that they would receive no more assistance from the Turks.

Bunds to the east of Baghdad held back more floodwaters. If those bunds were breached at the same time as the Sakhlawiya Dam, Baghdad would become an island in a six-mile-wide sea. In this scenario, Maude would be largely trapped in Baghdad with his troop movements severely curtailed while the Turks would gain the freedom to move beyond the floods. British troops occupied Dhibban to protect the work parties on the dam. The Turks were still in occupation in Ramadi, with a thousand troops and six guns.[66]

Najaf and Karbala

These two Shi'a holy cities stood on the Euphrates and had maintained a degree of independence from the Sunni Ottoman sultan by constant rebellion. Their position regarding the arrival of Christians, with their Hindus and Sikhs, remained to be seen. They telegrammed their congratulations to the king-emperor, who replied, which Cox saw as an attempt to assert their independence. When the Shi'a leaders visited Baghdad, they paid their compliments to Cox, who interpreted their actions as acts of submission. In return, Cox provided them with subsidies and a mandate to maintain order. Cox only intended this to be a temporary measure while the greater Ottoman threat was dealt with.[67]

Summer 1917 to Spring 1918

Ramadi

From Dhibban, Maude launched an attack against Ramadi on 11 July, at the height of summer, and the summer of 1917 was the hottest in living memory: Baghdad reached 123F, Samarra a slightly cooler 110F, but inside the tents where most soldiers lived, the temperature could be 10F higher.[68] Colonel Tennant, RFC, described that summer:

> By 11 A.M. on the 9th the thermometer stood at 122 deg. Fahr. in the shade. A strong wind had sprung up which dried the moisture out of the eyes until they became so bloodshot it was difficult to see. I lunched with Buxton, of the "Mantis,"

under double awnings and behind a screen on deck. Baghdad was enveloped in a haze of sand and a scorching gale. The glasses we drank out of were too hot to hold, and had to be cooled with the ration of ice, which the Supply and Transport Corps now manufactured in the town. The plates, knives, and forks, everything was burning. Men were dropping like flies with heat-stroke; the hospitals could take no more, they were lying in rows between the beds. This is no time to waste in heat-stroke; a man fit and well will be suddenly seized, and if he is not better is dead within two or three hours.[69]

Unfortunately, medical professionals did not yet understand the importance of salt in combating heat illnesses.

To support the attack by the 7th Infantry Brigade, 127 Ford vans and lorries were collected to transport 600 men at a time at night. Tents for shelter and ice for heat exhaustion were also carried. These were needed. The official thermometer showed 160F in the sun on the day of the attack. It was hoped that when the Turks realized that an attack was imminent, they would abandoned Ramadi. They did not. A combination of bad going, the canal and Turkish artillery fire halted the advance. A dust storm hampered the forward movement of reserves and the artillery from registering its targets. Aerial observation to support the artillery was maintained until 1000 hours, but three airplanes which left Baghdad at 0430 hours on a bombing mission were forced down, the heat boiling away radiator water and striking the pilots even at that hour. The attack was a failure. Of 566 casualties, 321 were heat related. As the British withdrew to Dhibban, 1,500 Arabs harassed them all the way. The attack achieved nothing and showed that even with the most modern equipment, operations in the Mesopotamian summer were to be avoided if at all possible.[70]

Summer Camps

The East Lancashires took up summer quarters at Sindiya, which Row described as an oasis in the desert with date palms and plentiful, cheap fruit, provided it was dipped in chlorinated water first. There were defensive works to be constructed in preparation for an expected Turkish counter-attack from Mosul in the winter. The weather did not help make the rest camp restful:

> At 2.30 pm the sandstorm was upon us. The sun became obscured and a blanket of darkness descended on the camp. We were engulfed in an avalanche of sand backed up by a 40 miles an hour wind. We rolled blankets around our heads to keep the sand from blinding us. Tents went down like skittles. Blankets, shirts and suits of khaki drill were whirled away and never seen again. At 3.0 pm daylight reappeared, and with it plenty of work; the tent floors were inches deep in sand, sand everywhere.[71]

The Cavalry Division's summer camp was at Chaldari, eight miles north of Baghdad, on the edge of a palm grove which reduced the temperature by 10F compared with the city:

> The moment of waking on a hot-weather morning is one of the least pleasant of the day. The air seems charged with apprehension. Before midday most things are too hot to touch. The rim of a tumbler or the metal-work of a saddle burn the hand.... From 9 A.M. until late afternoon there is nothing for it but to lie in a tent in a state of nature except for a wet towel round the head and gasp through the long weary hours of dust and sweat. An early morning and a late evening bathe [in the Tigris] are the only moments worth living for in the hours of daylight, and the nights, though bearable, seem only a rather boring interval in the long-drawn-out agony of unrest.[72]

The Regimental History of the 10th Lancers gives a description of the heat which the reader may think excessive, but nothing in Mesopotamia should be a surprise now. By the end of the summer, 20,000 men were sent out of the theater to recuperate:

> The heat of the sandy ground was so great that it blistered the feet through the soles of thick boots.[73]

Those encamped near Baghdad, one assumes, if they had the income and the inclination to do so, could have a more comfortable life than the above quotes suggest. There was an ice barge, a cinema and an ice-cream shop with many colored drinks. Everyone dressed as they pleased. The larger officer's tents could be kept cooler if they were sunk down two or three feet, with rushes on top and on the windward side, a framework of wet camel thorn. Other tents had mud walls constructed around them. Concerts were provided. There were race meetings and regattas — Captain Roosevelt commented on the colored silks worn by the Jewesses when he attended a race. The sports club at Baghdad was created with golf, tennis, cricket, racing, polo and boating. There was also shooting, although there was limited scope around the city. Several Bombay merchants set up shop, which supplied a range of unwarlike products, including "dainty silk lingerie" (this was by 1917 standards) which the officers bought for the nurses.[74]

India Leave

In June, Roe was one of a party of 30 given a month's leave in India. With a new uniform and money in his pocket, he appears to have spent most of his leave drinking: at a dinner hosted by the Southern Mahratta Railway Rifles, there was one bottle of "Johnnie Walker" between two, and tankards of Tennant's beer were lined up shoulder to shoulder. Lessons on the use of cutlery and china were also required. In an attempt to instill some moderation, the Ladies of the Scottish Kirk organized a religion-free and alcohol-free "bun fight." Roe reported sick, and was upbraided by the medical officer:

> You leave men from Mesopotamia come here with pocketfuls of money. You get another pocketful to go on leave with, you indulge in all kinds of excesses, particularly drink. You have

no regular meals, if you have any at all. You behave as men who had only one month to live, spend all the money you've got recklessly in gratifying your passions and come back physical wrecks. If you are not in possession of a packet of VD you've got gastritis or some other ailment brought on by your excesses, and we have got to make you whole and well again.

Roe was not entirely impressed with what he found in India. Thousands of apparently fit men stationed there for months instead of relieving battalions which had been fighting through Mesopotamia since March 1916. Thousands more were infected with venereal diseases. There was no medical supervision of brothels, unlike when Kitchener ran the Indian Army.

On his return to Basra, Roe commented on the changes since he passed through last:

> YMCA's and soda fountains have sprung up since I left Basrah last. These YMCA's and kindred Institutes are run by well mentally equipped and stalwart young Yanks, who instead of hymn singing and tea walloping could be better employed on the battlefields of France, helping President Wilson to make Europe safe for Democracy.[75]

Manpower Predicament

Throughout 1917, Lloyd George's government saw nothing but stalemate in France but saw the war of movement against Turkey as one front where gains could be made. Despite India's pleas that it was being bled dry of men and material for its own defense, London saw success in Mesopotamia as a method to secure India's security, although in practice this had been secured by the South Persia Rifles. Consequently, Maude was granted two more Indian cavalry regiments, a British cavalry regiment and a horse battery from France, another RFC squadron (63rd), Ford vans to replace the mules due to the availability of fuel from Abadan, more artillery, the 18th Indian Division, more light armored motor batteries and more machine-gun companies. 63 Squadron RFC arrived in August equipped with RE 8 and Spads, but it immediately had to deal with the local climactic conditions. In the heat, the wooden frames shrunk. Planes had to be rebuilt, but for several months there were a number of flying accidents from planes disintegrating in flight. In an era when crews did not wear parachutes, these incidents were invariably fatal. In January 1918, a DH4 flown by 30 Squadron was destroyed by a direct hit from an anti-aircraft shell. The squadron was sent to Samarra, where it produced maps for the forthcoming campaign. Colonel Tennant commanding the RFC observed that the Axis aviators were on "interior lines" and so could introduce a new aircraft into Mesopotamia a fortnight before the British. The expected arrival of current Halberdstadts prompted the dispatch of the Spads. A third squadron, the 72nd, would arrive in March 1918.[76]

Light armored motor batteries were equipped with armor-plated Rolls-Royce cars weighing three and three quarters to four tons each. The armor was protection against small arms fire, but nothing more. Their armament was limited to a machine gun. When the circumstances permitted, it was possible for most of the crew to ride outside, either behind the turret while hanging on to leather straps riveted inside for that purpose, or sitting on the toolboxes outside the body. When engaged, all retired inside and closed the steel plating until the largest aperture was the tube around the machine gun. Bullet splinters constantly entered. It was extremely unlikely that a bullet would enter; Roosevelt mentioned one driver who was shot through the head near Ramadi. Underneath was unarmored, and bullets did ricochet through the wooden floor. Heat inside the armor plating and the vulnerability of the fuel tanks were the greatest problems. They were used in the reconnaissance role where their ability to operate away from the river (unlike horses) was a great advantage. Their maneuverability allowed them to deliver their machine gun to best effect,

Indian soldiers of the 7th (Meerut) Divisions in the trenches, 1917, before the division was sent to Palestine. Mesopotamian accounts do not refer to steel helmets but, if their usage was the same as in Palestine, the extreme summer heat rendered them impractical (National Army Museum).

especially when operating in cooperation with the cavalry. Their disadvantage was in their weight, especially in wet and muddy weather, and, of course, mechanical failures.[77]

The British commitment to Mesopotamia outnumbered the Ottoman commitment three to one in manpower and artillery.[78]

The extra cavalry formed the 11th Cavalry Brigade:

- 7th Hussars
- Queen Victoria's Own Corps of Guides (Frontier Force) (Lumsden's) or Guides Cavalry for short
- 23rd Cavalry
- W Battery, Royal Horse Artillery
- 25th Machine Gun Squadron[79]

The 18th (Indian) Division was dispatched to Mesopotamia over the winter of 1917–1918. Regiments like the 1/5th West Kents were pre-war Territorial Force units which had been sent out to India to relieve regular units for combat duties. The commanding officer, Lieutenant Colonel Frazer took only five other pre-war officers with him, and the battalion was brought up to strength with drafts from the 4th Royal East Kent Regiment (the Buffs) and the 1st/1st Kent Cyclist Battalion, Army Cyclist Corps. The percentage of men from the battalion mobilized in 1914 who would go to Mesopotamia with Frazer would have been fairly small.[80] The first units were in place for Christmas 1917, but it would be mid–March 1918 before the whole division was concentrated. While the concentration proceeded, the in-country units conducted military training and worked on embankments for the new railways around Baghdad. The original composition was as follows:

53rd Infantry Brigade
- 1/9th Duke of Cambridge's Own (Middlesex) Regiment
- 1/3rd Queen Alexandra's Own Gurkha Rifles
- 1/7th Gurkha Rifles
- 1/89th Punjabis
- 207 Machine Gun Company

54th Infantry Brigade
- 1/5th Queen's Own (Royal West Kent) Regiment
- 52nd Sikhs Frontier Force
- 1/25th Punjabis
- 1/39th Garhwal Rifles
- 238 Machine Gun Company

55th Infantry Brigade
- 1/5th East Surrey Regiment
- 1/116th Mahrattas
- 1/10th Jats
- 1/94th Russell's Infantry
- 239 Machine Gun Company

Artillery
- 336th Brigade, RFA
- 337th Brigade, RFA

Engineers
- Nos. 2, 5, 8 field companies, 1st King George's Own Sappers and Miners
- 18th Divisional Signal Company

Pioneers
- 106th Hazara Pioneers

Ambulances
- Nos. 37, 38, 39 and 40 combined field ambulances
- No. 22 Sanitary Section, No. 12 Mobile Veterinary Section

Divisional Machine Gun Company
- 249 Machine Gun Company

In addition there were "B" and "D" Squadron, 10th Lancers, and a section from the 14th LAM Battery which were already in Mesopotamia.[81]

Yilderim Group

The Wagnerian-sounding *Yilderim* (Thunderbolt) Group was the German advisors' answer to British advances in the Middle East. It was composed of two Turkish infantry divisions and three German Asiatic Corps infantry battalions plus supporting arms. The German contingent was small, but it was intended that they would provide the backbone of the force. Command was given to the German General von Falkenhayn with more Germans occupying most of the other key positions. This situation would inevitably cause friction with the Turkish officers who made up the majority of the group.

In June 1917, von Falkenhayn reported that an attempt to recapture Baghdad was possible by the group. It would concentrate at Hit and then march down the Euphrates. Success required adequate communications, and the necessary railways would not be completed until December of that year. The prospect of the *Yilderim* Group being launched down the Euphrates was one which had to be taken seriously, especially as any British reversals, actual or predicted, would inevitably be accompanied by Arab harassing actions.

The *Yilderim* threat never materialized in Mesopotamia. The necessary railways were not completed on time, which arose from a great number of difficulties, not least of which were the engineering challenges posed by the Taurus and Amanus mountains. More important was the change of the strategic picture in Palestine. In November 1917, the Gaza-Beersheba line was finally broken. The *Yilderim* Group was redirected to stem Allenby's advance to Damascus.[82]

Development of Mesopotamia

One often unreported aspect of the campaign was attempts at economic development. The roads, railways and port facilities have already been mentioned. Communications were extended northwards. The issue of stone for laying down the railway tracks remained. Thompson noted in his diary that they were camped on what looked like an old pebble beach somewhere between Beled and Istabulat in late April 1917. These were the first stones he had seen.

The cost of the campaign, in particular in shipping and other transport costs, was one aspect which could be reduced "in country." With unrestricted submarine warfare threatening to starve Britain out of the war, any attempt to reduce the demand on shipping was examined. The Anglo-Persian oil was used to fuel lorries, which reduced the need for draught animals and fodder. Wilson estimated that petrol was 20 times better than fodder in terms of "ton miles," and was available in unlimited quantities from Abadan, instead of being imported by sea. Attempts were made to convert the river steamers to oil as coal exports from the UK became restricted. Colonel Tennant reports that attempts to refine aviation fuel were unsuccessful and caused the engines to seize up. Had they been successful, it would not have been necessary to import 10,000 gallons per month. Experiments in oil for cooking were also made to reduce the import of wood for cooking from India, which in time ceased.

Previously barren land was irrigated and cultivated. The Hindiya Barrage was a pre-war project designed by Sir William Wilcox and built by the British engineering firm of Sir Jon Jackson with the aim of irrigating land for agriculture. The barrage had been completed, but the irrigation projects had never been started. At Hindiya, the Euphrates forked into the Shatt-al-Hilla and the Shatt-al-Hindiya, which rejoined near Samawa. The majority of the water used the Hindiya, but by redirecting some of the water down the Hilla (which was the original channel before the course of the river changed), some 300,000 acres of unproductive desert could be cultivated. Barker called the 1918 harvest the greatest in that part of the world since Nebuchadnezzar: the 1918 spring crop fed the population and produced a surplus of 55,000 tons for the army.

Administration of the newly conquered lands had to be created from nothing, together with the "rule of law." Edgar Bonham-Carter arrived from the Sudanese legal department and, after eight weeks of studying the Turkish legal code, announced that it did not work at any level. His first change was to make Arabic the language of the courts. The Auqaf (or Waqf), or Department of Pious Bequests, turned out to be the largest landowner in Mesopotamia, and the revenues were intended to maintain religious institutions and mosques but had been stripped bare by the Turkish authorities. Under the Judicial Department, all such properties were listed and inspected, and then the bequests were used for their original purposes, although, despite this, the Shi'a religious cities of Karbala and Najaf were centers of unrest. The British authorities offered an almost insatiable demand for labor and produce, and paid

for it, so that the areas behind the fighting experienced prosperity unknown under the Ottomans.

The white-tabbed political officers spread out to establish influence, control and order. A railway was laid to the coal mines at Kifiri. Kut was rebuilt with a new arcaded *souq*, the "crowning glory of Kut." Bodies were properly buried and munitions disposed of. Grants were given to the families of those killed in the siege, and 2,000 people had returned by May 1918, although it remained a dirty and evil-smelling town for the British. When Captain Roosevelt passed, he said that "in spite of appearances it is an important and thriving little town, and daily becoming of more consequence." The Reverend Thompson passed going upriver and noted the townspeople growing lettuce on the sandbanks. The local Arabs were impressed that here was a government willing and able to undertake such a task. During the 1920 uprising, there was no outbreak of violence around Kut. Sanitation was introduced in Baghdad — when plague broke out in 1918, 80,000 people were inoculated, and the plague was halted. It was into this world

Captain Kermit Roosevelt, son of former American president Theodore Roosevelt, crossing the Aq-Su River by the Khasradral Ford, 29 April 1918 while serving with the 14th LAMB (Imperial War Museum).

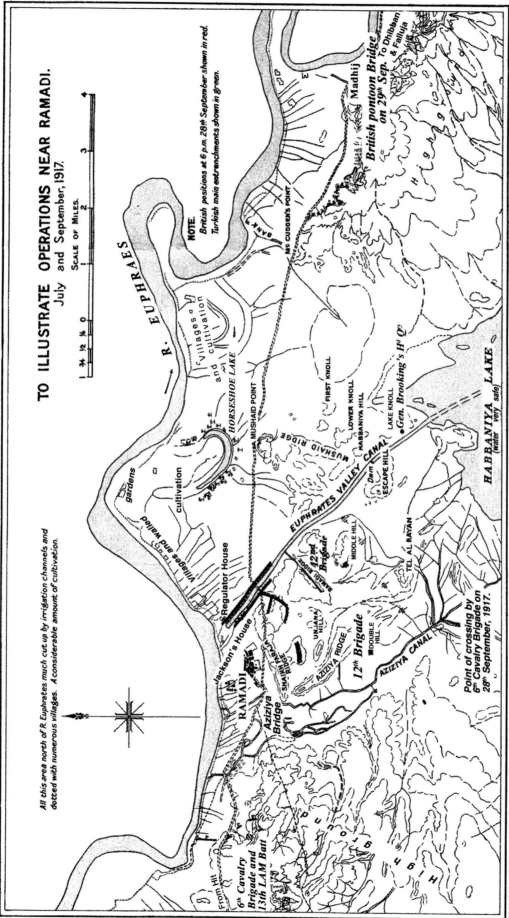

Operations near Ramadi, July and September 1917

that Gertrude Bell would pour her energy until her death in 1926. Perhaps her most lasting legacy would be the foundation of the Baghdad Archaeological Museum, now known as the National Museum of Iraq, which was looted in 2003 while the soldiers of that conquest watched on.

On the negative side, by March 1918, 45,000 men had been enrolled (some said conscripted) into the Arab Labour Corps to work on the infrastructure projects which threatened to depopulate agricultural areas and create unrest.[83]

Captain Roosevelt appreciated the extent that Britain and India had invested in Mesopotamia. The role of the Anglo-Persian Oil Company was not to be underestimated, and Roosevelt estimated that there were over 5,000 Ford trucks in Mesopotamia: motor transport was nowhere else a great necessity. He beheld with incongruity "a great bearded Sikh with his turbaned head bent over the steering-wheel of a Ford." The railways were built by ripping up double lines in India and created despite the lack of grading stone in Mesopotamia. Agriculture was developed to sustain the army, and the port of Basra was now developed with roads and wharfs, much of which had, out of necessity, a look of permanence:

> Indeed, one of the most striking features of the improvements made by the British. In order to conquer the country it was necessary to develop it, — build railways and bridges and roads and telegraph systems, — and it has all been done in a substantial manner. It is impossible to contemplate with equanimity the possibility of the country reverting to a rule where all this progress would soon disappear and the former stagnancy and injustice again hold sway.[84]

The infrastructure investments also had to be guarded. With his LAMB, Roosevelt traveled 30 miles by train to Baghdad to refit the cars. The railway snaked through the desert with water tanks guarded by a company of infantry scattered along the way. At one desolate spot, they were met by the British officer, 20 years of age, lonely and homesick, with just his Sikh company, who invited them to tea. His tent was already set out for receiving guests as he met the two trains which passed his post daily. Many young officers who were wounded in France were sent to India to recuperate and to train up new drafts. This particular officer had been in theater just a month and for the last 10 days had been guarding this water tower in the desert.[85]

If only he had been able to see the state of Mesopotamia at the beginning of the 21st century.

1917–1918 Campaigning Season

West on the Euphrates

In September 1917, the weather cooled and the British offensive against Ramadi resumed. Major General Brooking's 15th Division took the lead. This division was formed from units that had previously been garrisoning Nasariya. Dummy roads and a bridge were constructed to fool the Turks into believing that he would attack along the Euphrates. The RFC moved its photography section to Falluja so that prints could be available at the front line as quickly as possible. They also underestimated the ability of Ford trucks to supply water to troops away from the rivers (14,000 gallons on the 28th alone), which gave Brooking a degree of tactical flexibility which had not been available to commanders in the past. Instead, on the night of 27/28 September, Holland-Pryor's 6th Cavalry Brigade made a flanking march south of the town to occupy the Aleppo road to the west. The horses' hooves kicked up dust so that the cavalry wore handkerchiefs over their mouths. Sergeant Holland, "C" Squadron, 14th Hussars, was with the brigade headquarters and RHA battery almost south of the town with the brigade extending to the west then turning north with the remainder of the 14th Hussars blocking the road — they were only 120 rifles strong. From a ridge, he could clearly make out the Turkish guns.[86]

Concurrently, Brooking's 12th (right) and 42nd (left) brigades occupied the Mushaid Ridge. Ramadi lay between two canals, the Habbaniya and Aziziya, which linked the Euphrates and Habbaniya Lake (incidentally, in 1941, Habbaniya was the site of a Royal Air Force (RAF) base which stood against the anti-monarchist and pro–Nazi Iraqi military coup of that year). The following night, the Turkish defenders attempted to break through the cavalry brigade, but failed. Sergeant Holland on the right of the cavalry brigade heard firing to his left and joined in: his rifle became so hot that oil seeped through joints in the woodwork. Meanwhile the infantry brigades crossed the Habbaniya Canal at the dam, which was the only crossing point. The dam had been secured at 0330 hours, although the previous evening there had been a rare engagement — cavalry versus cavalry. Both commanders maneuvered skillfully, a Turkish squadron against a troop of the 22nd Cavalry, before the latter successfully extracted under fire.[87]

The infantry then attacked the town. With the road cut, the only route out of the town was a bridge about 1,000 yards forward of a position held by the 39th Garwhalis from the 12th Brigade. They charged in the face of three Turkish guns firing at them over open sights. They seized the town end of the bridge but were now only 100 strong. The Turkish commander, Ahmed Bey, who had been fighting the British since Shaiba, still had 2,000 men who could have counter-attacked this little band but misinterpreted the action — surely this charge could not have been made in isolation? It had to be the lead of something bigger. Ahmed Bey decided to surrender. The haul included 3,500 men and 13 guns, virtually the entire garrison. Maude called the action "an instance of as clean and business-like a military operation as one could wish to see." The following day, a German pilot attempted to land in the town before realizing it had fallen and making his escape.[88]

Maude was justifiably pleased with the cavalry's performance, which he made clear to both Whitehall:

> A salient factor of [the battle of Ramadi] was the part played by the cavalry. First by their rapid movement round the enemy's rear and subsequently by the tactical disposition of their machine guns they prevented the enemy's columns from breaking out and so drove them back into the arms of the infantry.

and to the brigade:

> Amongst all the troops who fought so well [at Ramadi] none did better than the cavalry. They had long distances to cover, they were long hours in the saddle, they were many hours without water.... It was you who threw [the enemy] back into the arms of the infantry, thus sealing their doom.[89]

"Sealing their doom" was the very action which commanders had required of the cavalry going right back to the Battle of Shaiba. Finally it had happened.

It is perhaps worthwhile comparing the role of the cavalry in Mesopotamia and that in Palestine, which was the only other comparable British theater of operations. In Mesopotamia, successive commanders going back to Townshend's battles as he advanced from Al-Amara had attempted to use the cavalry to get behind the Turks, cut off their retreat, destroy the enemy and prevent them from retiring to depth positions, and thereby open the way to the British objective, such as Baghdad. It had taken time to perfect this tactic and the implementation of modern technology to support the horses. With a few exceptions, like at Lajj before the crossing of the Diyala, the cavalry in Mesopotamia did not charge home with the sword but were used as mounted rifles, in that they dismounted to engage the enemy and used the horse for mobility.

In Palestine there were far more cavalry available and the famous mounted rifle and light horse regiments from Australia and New Zealand. They were not intended to fight on horseback like cavalry but to dismount to fight the enemy. There were also conventional cavalry regiments trained to fight with sword and lance. Yet in Palestine there was a greater use of the cavalry charge including, most famously, the 4th Australian Light Horse Brigade at Beersheba in October 1917 when they charged with their bayonets drawn like swords. Allenby's plan for Beersheba was a breakthrough followed by a "pursuit," in other words, chasing the retiring enemy. Following Beersheba, two Australian Light Horse brigades were equipped with, trained with, and used the sword. In August 1916 at Romani (the last Turkish attempt to cross the Sinai), General Chauvel has been criticized for pursuing the enemy too directly rather than working his way around the enemy's flanks. Faulty aerial intelligence resulted in a charge by a brigade at Magdhaba in December 1916 being aborted when the true weight of rifle and machine-gun fire was felt, but only after commencing the charge. The brigade was only saved by diverting it into a wadi.

Other repulsed charges were launched at Irbid, near Deera, Syria, in September 1918 and at Haritan, near Aleppo, Syria, in October 1918.[90]

In Mesopotamia there was a move away from the traditional cavalry charge, whatever the instincts and urges of cavalry commanders. Those charges which did take place were generally unsuccessful, and the merits of them were criticized at the time. The "mounted rifles" doctrine was adopted. In Palestine, by comparison, despite the deployment of mounted rifles alongside the cavalry, there seems to have been a greater desire to charge home and use the sword. While in Palestine, the more traditional weapons and tactics were evidently in favor (even amongst the Australians who were supposed to have a healthy disregard for all things British); it was in Mesopotamia that the cavalry tried and adopted newer tactics.

North on the Tigris to Tikrit

Mandali, east of Baghdad on the Persian border, was occupied, which secured the British eastern flank. In mid–October, the Turks advanced eight miles from Tikrit and dug in. Cobbe, commanding the Tigris front, was uncertain of their intention and ordered aerial reconnaissance. They reported that islands in the middle of the Tigris were packed with Turks. A plan was put into motion for a frontal attack at dawn on 24 October following a night march. At about midnight a Turkish cadet was captured while talking to Indian mule drivers. He was found to be armed with a penknife and a pair of gloves. But the operation was going to get even more surreal. At 0700 hours, the Leicesters broke cover, expecting to come under fire, but there was none. They dug in, in a semi-circle around their objective. Patrols were sent forward, expecting that they were being drawn into a trap. The patrols found only 5,000 sheep and a couple of shepherds! The battle of Juber Island, or Huweslet, was called off, and a sheep's head was voted as a gift from the Leicesters officers' mess for the RFC officers' mess.[91]

Cobbe's 7th Division and the Cavalry Division were tasked with clearing the Tigris northwards towards Anatolia. The river by now was inadequate to supply the advances it had further south, so there was a greater reliance on Ford trucks. Although there were a great number of these in the theater, they were insufficient to permit fighting on three fronts concurrently. Ramadi was fought in September, Tikrit in November and Kifri in October. Even then, during the advance on Tikrit, the demands of ammunition and rations meant that blankets and greatcoats were left behind.

The divisions advanced from the forward base at Samarra towards Turkish forces at Huwaislat, who promptly withdrew to Daur. During his advance toward Daur, Captain Roosevelt was introduced to "shorts," and he had to explain their construction and the methods of wearing them (with "wrap puttees, or leather leggings, or golf stockings") to his American readers. He explained their advantages during the daytime, but unfortunately he found them uncomfortably cold around the knees at night while sleeping without a blanket. The following March, Roosevelt also explained the lamb kebab, where "the meat is cut in pellets, spitted on rods six or eight inches long, and lain over the glowing charcoal embers," and then placed in a big flap of bread.[92] Today, both shorts and kebabs are commonplace in Western society. The fact that Roosevelt though it sufficiently important not only to mention them but to have to describe them shows what novelties these were a century ago.

The 7th Division advanced on the right bank of the Tigris towards Daur with the 28th Brigade taking the lead and the 9th and 18th brigades following. The 21st Brigade was on the left bank of the Tigris and, according to Thompson, played no part in the following actions. The division set off for a 17-mile night march on 1 November. Dawn was colder than at Juber Island—the season was getting later and the terrain higher. At 0600 hours on the 2nd, the Turkish pickets were driven in as the British advanced in artillery formation. Fifteen minutes later, the British artillery bombardment commenced, and aircraft flew overhead with klaxons sounding—the whole effect must have been similar to the sirens of the Second World War *stuka* dive-bombers. The 56th Rifles led the brigade's attack, "as if on parade," and rising high in the Leicesters' estimation, who followed behind. The 51st and 53rd Sikhs brought up the rear.

The advance was rapid, and whenever the RMO stopped to treat a casualty, he then had to run to rejoin the main body. The Turkish positions were taken by 0900 hours, by which time it was starting to get warm. Although the Turks shelled their former positions, there were surprisingly few casualties in this attack. The Turks, again, withdrew, this time to Tikrit.[93]

The Cavalry Division had been tasked with cutting off the Turkish retreat, but, during a night march, the 6th Cavalry Brigade turned too soon and at dawn was facing the Turkish defenses, not behind them. By the time the mistake was realized and corrected, the Turks

were already fleeing their trenches. The 7th Cavalry Brigade also became lost, but when they arrived on the battlefield, for some inexplicable reason, neither they nor the LAMBs pursued the fleeing Turks until 1100 hours. Several reasons have been given for the inactivity, including lack of maneuvering space between the Turkish positions at Daur and Tikrit. Anglesey considered that the most likely reason was that the cavalry were worn out by the night march.[94]

The Reverend Thompson with the Leicesters remembered sleeping out that night: "The night was maddening with cold, and the rum ration came as a sheer necessity. All through the brief Tikrit campaign the British troops were without coats or blankets.... The night was one of insane wretchedness."[95]

On 3 November, the 19th Brigade took the next line of Turkish positions, at Aujeh, which opened the way to Tikrit. The cavalry attempted to force the passage and reach Tikrit, but without success. The Turks had not defended their positions, and slipped away as the British advanced, but their artillery was registered on the trenches, and it was their shelling which inflicted casualties. Certainly, Roosevelt with the LAMBs was of the opinion that the Turks could have given the British attackers a much stiffer fight as they were in a well-prepared defensive position.[96]

III Corps moved on Tikrit by a night march which commenced on 4 November. They "rested" between 0230 and 0430, but nobody lay down. In Baghdad there was frost. They

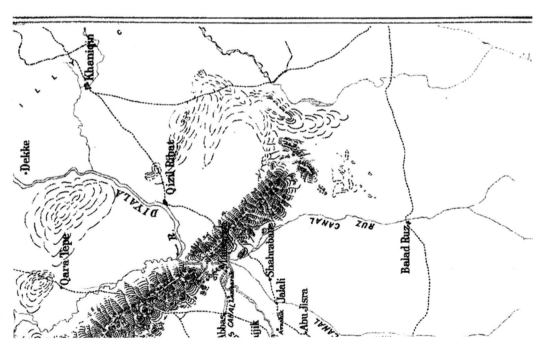

45th Rattray's Sikhs marching with Guru Granth Sahib to attend a Diwan service, 1918. Throughout the campaign, the multi-national and multi-ethnic makeup of the British Army did create operational difficulties (as Townshend found during the Siege of Kut with the eating of horse meat) but the religious differences were respected. The presence of large numbers of non–Christian officers and men helped to defuse religious tensions, for example with Muslim soldiers standing guard at mosques (Imperial War Museum).

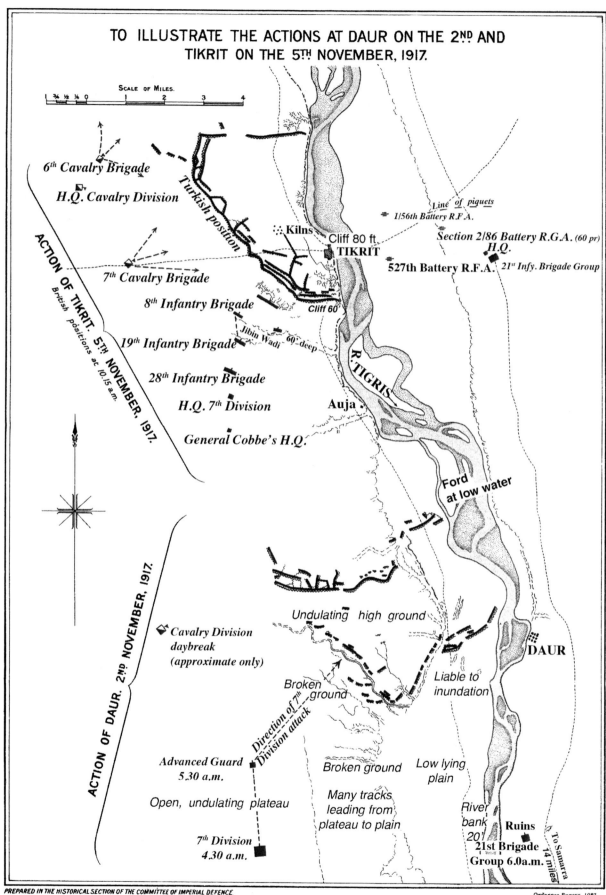

TO ILLUSTRATE THE ACTIONS AT DAUR ON THE 2ND AND TIKRIT ON THE 5TH NOVEMBER, 1917.

SCALE OF MILES.

6th Cavalry Brigade

H.Q. Cavalry Division

ACTION OF TIKRIT. 5TH NOVEMBER, 1917.
British positions at 10.15 a.m.

Turkish position

7th Cavalry Brigade

8th Infantry Brigade

19th Infantry Brigade

28th Infantry Brigade

H.Q. 7th Division

General Cobbe's H.Q.

Kilns

Cliff 80 ft

TIKRIT

Cliff 60'

Jibin Wadi 60' deep

Line of piquets

1/56th Battery R.F.A.

Section 2/86 Battery R.G.A. (60 pr)
H.Q.

527th Battery R.F.A. 21st Infy. Brigade Group

R. TIGRIS

Auja

Ford at low water

ACTION OF DAUR. 2ND NOVEMBER, 1917.

Cavalry Division daybreak (approximate only)

Undulating high ground

Broken ground

Direction of 7th Division attack

Advanced Guard 5.30 a.m.

Open, undulating plateau

7th Division 4.30 a.m.

Broken ground

Many tracks leading from plateau to plain

Low lying plain

DAUR

Liable to inundation

River bank 20'

Ruins

21st Brigade Group 6.0 a.m.

To Samarra 14 miles

PREPARED IN THE HISTORICAL SECTION OF THE COMMITTEE OF IMPERIAL DEFENCE.

Ordnance Survey, 1927.

Action at Daur, 2 November 1917, and Tikrit, 5 November 1917 were now far north of Baghdad and in the uplands swept by what Thompson called "arctic" winds. Nobody stopped moving during their "rest," and all were pleased when the advance resumed![97] Tikrit was defended by seven miles of extensive trenches with both ends secured by the river. The town itself stood on a 150-foot cliff above the river. Captain Roosevelt observed British heavy artillery lumbering forward towed by caterpillar tractors, at about three miles per hour. On 5 November, the 8th Brigade ("the Fighting, Starving Eighth"[98]) attacked from the south (Turkish left) where the trenches butted onto the river, with the 59th Rifles right and the 47th Sikhs left, and the 124th Baluchis in support. They crossed 1,000 yards and captured the Turkish first-line trenches. The Manchesters joined the battle. For three hours there was confused fighting in the trenches. The Seaforth Highlanders and the 125th Napier's Rifles were then added to the fray, but the sight of the "Abu Reish"— the Father of the Feather — the Arab name for the Highland regiments, was enough and the Turks began to surrender.

The fighting continued, and the Seaforths and Napier's Rifles pushed forward to attack the second-line trenches. They attracted fire from their left from where the cavalry was fixing the Turkish right. Seeing a rare opportunity to charge, two squadrons of the 13th Hussars and one of the 13th Bengal Lancers mounted, drew swords and charged, jumping over trenches and scattering the Turks fleeing from the Seaforths and Napier's Rifles. The charge advanced 1,000 yards beyond the Turkish front-line trenches until they were halted by wire entanglements, dismounted and covered their own retreat. The wisdom of Norton, the cavalry brigade commander, in charging entrenched infantry, as at Istabulat Station and Lajj, can be questioned. The cavalry may have been smarting from comments on their inactivity at Daur and stung into action to prove their worth. If so, it was a dangerous policy to follow. On this occasion,

the risk paid off. The infantry was already demoralized by the infantry attack, and smoke could be seen from the town as military stores were destroyed. The Reverend Thompson with the Leicesters, who were not committed that day, considered the cavalry charge to have been a mistake and held that, had the infantry been sent in instead, the Turks would have been trapped in the town against the river. As it was, the charge was "gallant but useless." When the British entered Tikrit, they only captured 320 Turks. Once again the chance of bagging the whole force had slipped through their fingers. They did, however, recover the *Julnar*, aground in the river, which was the scene of the last, unsuccessful attempt to relieve Kut.[99]

The following day, Tikrit was evacuated, and the houses were festooned with white flags to proffer their friendship to their new masters. The bazaar was quickly reopened to show their faith in British commerce. On the second day, British troops pushed through to clear the Turks from the north of the town, only to find empty shell cases and abandoned material.[100]

Tikrit was not a particularly successful British battle. The Turks had held up the advance, inflicted casualties, but once

1/8th Gurkha Rifles occupying Turkish trenches at Tikrit, 7 November 1917. The narrow trenches in the flat terrain without a parados or parapet were invisible to the attacking infantry and are commented on in a number of battles. Note also the absence of barbed wire which meant that there was nothing to protect the Turkish infantry from an infantry or cavalry charge. The Gurkhas are wearing the pith helmet rather than the more familiar and traditional slouch hat (Imperial War Museum).

again withdrawn men, artillery pieces and machine guns. Thompson noted the piles of spent cartridges where the machine guns had been placed, and withdrawn. Similarly, dumps of field artillery shells were captured, but no artillery pieces. Thompson blamed this on the cavalry for charging at the trenches, which the uncommitted 28th Brigade should have done, instead of blocking the escape route.[101]

Tikrit ended the British advance on the Tigris for the time being as the Ford trucks were needed elsewhere. There was insufficient logistical capacity to support such a large formation so far up the Tigris, and most of the corps withdrew to Samarra. The RFC continued to take the fight to the Turks in their new camp at Jabal Hamrin. Amongst the supplies captured were two aircraft, one of which was a recovered British machine. Bombs were also captured, which the RFC delighted in returning to their former owners.[102]

East Along the Diyala

Marshall's III Corps was tasked with clearing the Turks from the Jabal Hamrin and the town of Mendali, 30 miles southeast of the Balad Ruz on the Persian border. The town also lay to the south of the Jabal Hamrin range. Sharaban had already been captured without much opposition. On the night of 18 October, Brigadier General Norton's 7th Cavalry Brigade set out from Balad Ruz to Mendali where they captured the small Turkish garrison. They then turned north following a road along the far side of the Jabal Hamrin towards Qizal Robart.

Meanwhile, Egerton left the 35th Brigade at Sharaban and marched the 36th and 37th Brigades on the direct road to Qizal Robart through the Jabal Hamrin. The 35th Brigade now moved to the Balad Ruz to face Ali Ihsan's troops. The 35th Brigade bridged the Balad Ruz at three points and waited for the other two columns to get into position. An elaborate trap had been set based on the assumption that, faced by a frontal attack, the Turks would retire to Qizal Robart where they would be caught by two infantry and one cavalry brigades. Cayley's 13th Division was also operating on the right bank of the Diyala, away to the Turkish right. When the 35th Brigade launched its attack on dawn of the 20th, they found that their prey had already slipped the net, as they were apt to do, but not towards Qizal Robart as expected. They slipped across the Diyala River, which was very low at that time of the year, and away into the mountains beyond.[103]

The whole operation was a disappointing failure. A huge number of men had been used to trap an enemy well versed in slipping out of such traps. On the plus side, the Turks were now removed from the south of the Diyala. The men were now able to enjoy a few weeks of relative rest in and amongst the mountains which contrasted with the deserts behind them. There were game to shoot, rivers to fish and pigs to stick for the cavalry. For those without fishing rods, hand grenades pro-

duced the same result. The countryside reminded many of their homes, wherever that was around the empire.[104]

The Death of Maude

On 18 November 1917, General Maude died in Baghdad of cholera. Rumors exist about possible poisoning. The most likely explanation is that he contracted cholera from untreated milk in his coffee during a performance of *Hamlet* in Arabic by the Alliance Israelite of Baghdad. Mrs. Eleanor Egan, an American reporter visiting Baghdad, noted that Maude added cold, raw milk to his coffee while she took hers black. Captain Wilson took his coffee in the same manner as Maude, without any ill effects. The performance was attended by the full range of ethnic groups represented in Baghdad, so there was never any suggestion of a Jewish plot. However, the slur had been made, which Captain Wilson regretted because their "attitude and behavior had at all times been exemplary." Threats against members of the British military were commonplace against Maude and the military governor of Baghdad, Brigadier General Hawker. Ten days previously, one of Hawker's staff officers had deputized for him at a function. The catering contractor at this event was the same one for the performance of *Hamlet*, and the staff officer died of cholera a few days later. After a three-month investigation, nothing was proven, but the contractor who supplied the milk was deported as an undesirable — according to Wilson, this decision did the British position no favors.[105]

In 18 months, Maude had rebuilt the Tigris Corps, revenged Kut and restored British prestige. In Barker's words: like Alexander the Great and the Emperor Julian before him, he was a victim of Mesopotamia. Maude was replaced by General Sir William Marshall. Maude's last instructions to his staff were to "carry on," but in truth, if there was a policy, Maude took it to his grave. More likely, Maude was reacting, skillfully, to situations as they presented themselves. Marshall abolished the Cavalry Division, reroled the 13-pounder of the Royal Horse Artillery to line-of-communications duties and replaced them with 18-lbers. He considered that the 13-pounder was "a very moderate weapon" and that the cavalry should be supported by a "long-range gun." His place as commander of III Corps was taken by General Egerton, who resumed Marshall's task of clearing the Turks in the northeast, beyond the Jabal Hamrin to Qara Tepe, on a tributary of the Diyala.[106]

By the end of 1917, the object of British imperial policy shifted from Mesopotamia and the defense of India to the collapse of Tsarist Russia and a Turko-German threat to the Caucasus. This also raised the prospect of a return of the Great Game which Britain thought had ended in 1907, but now that Tsarist Russia was no more, what would the new Russia, in whatever form it emerged, do? This is the story of Dunsterforce, but the fighting in Mesopotamia was not over just yet.

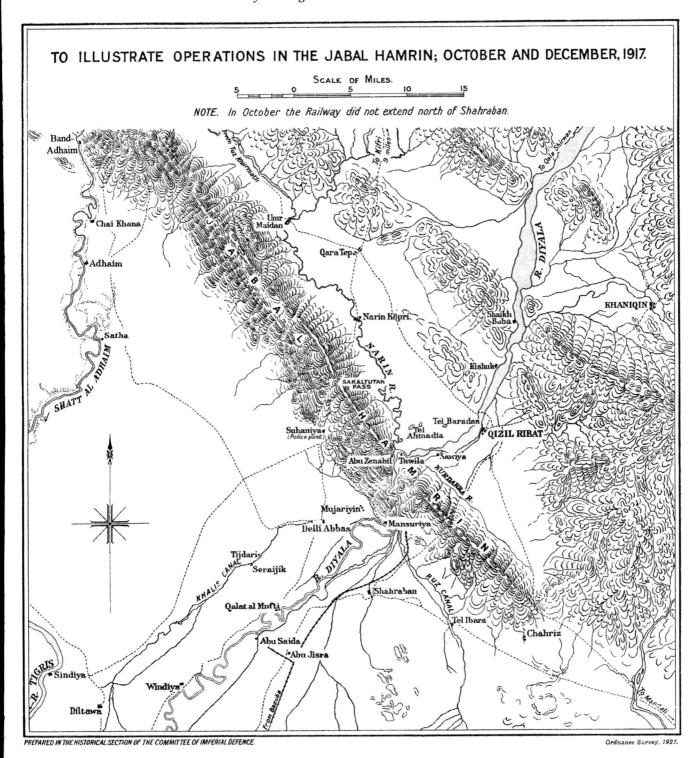

Operations in the Jebel Hamrin, October and December 1917

Field Marshall Sir William Robertson, Chief of the Imperial General Staff, took the opportunity of Marshall's appointment to reestablish London's control over the campaign. The objectives were reiterated:

• Safeguard the oil supplies.
• Maintain British influence in Baghdad.

• Encourage Arab cooperation.
• Enlist Baratoff's cooperation.
• No rash offensives.

But at the same time, Robertson was looking at ways of reducing the manpower burden in Mesopotamia. There were the

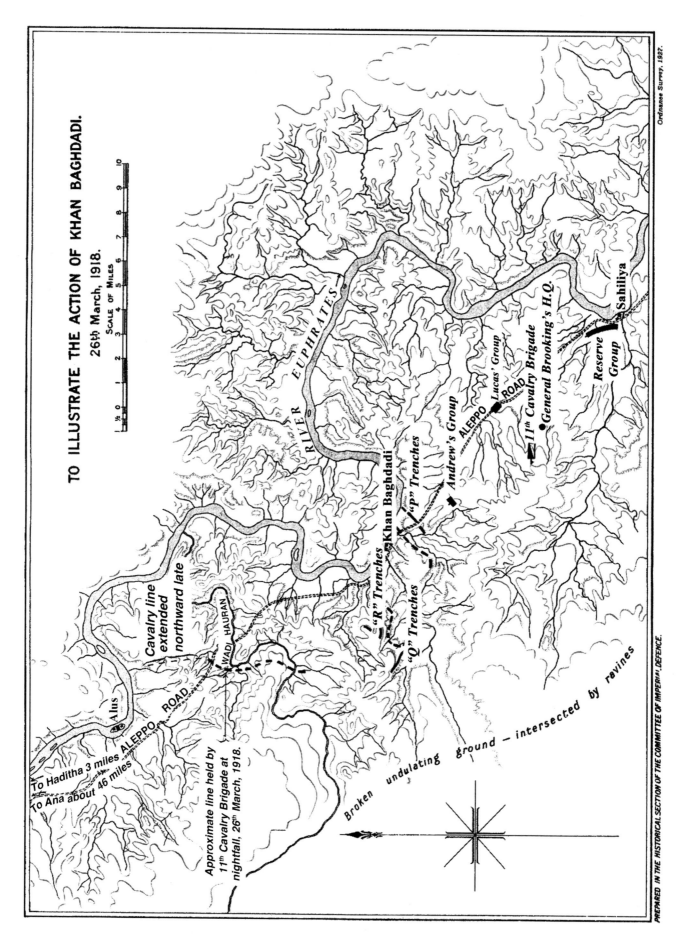

TO ILLUSTRATE THE ACTION OF KHAN BAGHDADI.

26th March, 1918.

SCALE OF MILES

RIVER EUPHRATES

Sahiliya

Reserve
Group

General Brooking's H.Q.

11th Cavalry Brigade

Lucas' Group

ALEPPO ROAD

Andrew's Group

"P" Trenches

Khan Baghdadi

"R" Trenches

"Q" Trenches

Cavalry line extended
northward late

WADI HAURAN

Alus

ALEPPO   ROAD

To Hadritha 3 miles
To Ana about 46 miles

Approximate line held by
11th Cavalry Brigade at
nightfall, 26th March, 1918.

Broken   undulating   ground — intersected   by   ravines

PREPARED IN THE HISTORICAL SECTION OF THE COMMITTEE OF IMPERIAL DEFENCE.

Ordnance Survey, 1927.

Battle of Khan Baghdadi, 26 March 1918

- I Corps a long way up the Tigris,
- III Corps on the Diyala near the Jabal Hamrin, and
- the 15th Division on the Euphrates

These were deployed against Turkish forces which were not posing any major threat to the Allied war aims. At a time when the objectives of the old IEF "D" had been long completed (protect the oil supply and occupy Basra if war broke out with Turkey), the burdens on the British war effort were immense: there was the slaughter of the Third Battle of Ypres, the Russian Revolution, French Army mutinies and the Italian disaster at Caporetto. There were real and persuasive arguments for a reduction in the forces deployed in Mesopotamia and their redeployment to other theaters where the demand and the potential rewards were greater.

West on the Euphrates

Brooking's 15th Division continued the advance along the Euphrates to counter an advance by the Turkish 50th Division from Hit. An attempted raid on Hit by a motorized force of Dorsetshire Yeomanry and Royal Engineers failed to reach its objective by dawn. With surprise lost, the force withdrew. The planning considerations for these new tools were not fully understood, and the planners were experimenting. In a terrain which was so different from anything previously experienced and with all of the new weapons of war, the staff planners were on a constant learning curve.[107]

A renewed attack on Hit was launched in March 1918. When the Turks learned of the British advance, they withdrew to Khan Baghdadi. Their commander, Subri Bey, was dismissed for not attempting to resist Brooking, so his successor, Nazim Bey, could be expected to make a stand at Khan Baghdadi. To capitalize on the increased mobility available to the British, and their improving skill in using it, Brooking broke his command into four columns:

- Andrews' 50th Brigade advancing on the Aleppo road
- Lucas' 42nd Brigade following on the Aleppo road
- Cassels' 11th Cavalry Brigade with most of the LAMBs under Hogg sweeping round the Turkish right flank
- Brooking's column consisting of:
  - 2 Companies, 1/5th Queen's Own Royal West Kents
  - 2 Companies, 2/39th Garhwalis
  - Engineer detachment
  - 2 machine-gun sections
  - 8th LAMB
  - 1 battery, RFA with double-horsed teams for greater mobility
  - 300 Ford vans

Orders were given to move at night and hide during the day. The RFC was ordered to keep away from the area to avoid arousing suspicion.[108]

On 26 March, the 50th Brigade charged and captured the Turkish first-line trenches and waited while the 42nd Brigade came up before assaulting the Turkish second-line trenches. Turkish resistance held up their attack until 1300 hours. Meanwhile, the 11th Cavalry Brigade made a flanking movement, getting behind the Turkish positions and cutting off their retreat. To facilitate the cavalry's move, they traveled with the minimum equipment per horse: arms, a tin of bully beef, a few biscuits, a bandolier, the canvas water bag and one blanket. Everything else was left behind. At 1105 hours, Brooking informed Cassels, by wireless, that the Turks showed no inclination to retire. The motorized troops were offered, but Cassels declined them, as the off-road terrain was barely passable for wheeled vehicles.[109]

The first retreating troops which fell to the cavalry were seen just before last light. They were described as "artillery" but turned out to be field kitchens with the smokestacks "at the trail." The prisoners indicated that the remainder of the Turkish 50th Division were now withdrawing. In the dark, the division withdrew into the rifles of the waiting cavalry. The survivors of the initial fusillade tried to bypass the cavalry only to run into the waiting LAMB:

> Shooting died away, lamps were lit and waved; shouts of surrender went up; here and there a camp fire began to twinkle and the Turkish 50th Division as a fighting formation ceased to be.[110]

As at Ramadi, a British general in Mesopotamia had a cavalry force which could perform its expected role. Townshend and Maude had been repeatedly frustrated by the failure of their cavalry to perform its expected role, and as a consequence the Turks had been able to withdraw time and time again instead of being cut off and defeated. Brooking's cavalry had cut off the Turks at Ramadi and now Khan Baghdadi. Anglesey, the historian of the British Cavalry, went even further in his admiration for the actions at those two battles, and Tikrit. They were, for him,

> among the most perfectly conceived and conducted minor battles of the whole war. They have very special importance in the history of military mobility, for they took place during that brief period which saw the joint employment of infantry and mounted troops with primitive armoured vehicles, motor transport and aircraft. That the successes of this combination were not achieved against a totally demoralised enemy is shown by the tenacity of the Turks in their entrenched positions on all three occasions. Further, to a certain extent the mounted arm, under special circumstances, had at last justified its presence in Mesopotamia.[111]

To which this author would add, that those battles were fought in climatic conditions which were demanding in the extreme.

One thousand Turks were captured by the infantry and a further thousand surrendered when they ran into the British cavalry. LAMBs continued along the Aleppo road, and a further 2,000 surrendered to them the following dawn. Haditha, 35 miles beyond Khan Baghdadi, was captured. From positions overlooking the town, the garrison could be seen in full retreat. Caves had been used for storage, and these had been set alight. Attempts were made to rescue munitions, medical supplies and papers from the blaze. Ammunition which had been captured at Gallipoli was recovered and returned to its rightful owner, but more important were any papers which identified which of the local Arabs were trustworthy and which had been betraying the British. Incriminating papers were found later in Ana, which linked a German agent with instigating the murder of the British political officer in Najaf. There were also letters of thanks from various sheikhs to the kaiser for the Iron Crosses which they had been awarded. The irony of Muslim sheikhs receiving the insignia of the Holy Roman Emperor was not lost at the time. The LAMBs continued the pursuit another 35 miles until they captured the Turkish commander, Nazim Bey, and large numbers of German officers in the town of Ana. The RFC added to the route while the local Arabs hovered on the flanks until night, when they could start to loot.[112]

LAMBs pushed on a further 32 miles beyond Ana to rescue Lieutenant Colonel Tennant and his passenger, Major Percy Hobart, RE, who was the brigade major of the 8th (Indian) Brigade. Flying low due to clouds, their plane had been holed in the fuel tank and the pair captured:[113]

> But there, a hundred yards along the road, as large as life, was an armoured car with others behind. I howled it to Hobart, and we went with heads down as if all the devils of hell were behind us. The Turks scattered behind the rocks under the machine-gun fire; we never looked round. The officer commanding the cars, Captain Tod, leapt out and dragged us into the turret, the men yelling with excitement. It was beyond our wildest dreams. We lay and panted and talked till the open plain was reached, where sniping would be impossible; whiskey and bully-beef were produced — the most wonderful meal of one's life.[114]

Lieutenant C.R.A. Hammond, ASC (Army Service Corps), who provided the armored car for the rescue, wrote in his diary his own account of the affair, which has a different slant on the incident:

> From here [Auah] an Armoured car went on to Alona about 70 miles to see if they could re-capture Colonel Tennant, a cousin of Asquith [Prime Minister of Great Britain, 1909–1916], who is chief of the flying Corps in Mesopotamia & had we were told written instructions not to fly over the Turkish lines, which however he not only ignored but took with him a Brigade Major from the Tigris front & flew over the Turkish lines at under 1000 feet & got a rifle bullet in his radiator & were forced to come down in their lines & were captured, & serve them jolly well right. Lieut. Todd was in charge of this Armoured car which went to rescue them & took enough petrol for 100 miles out & 50 back & a reserve was sent after him 50 miles. However when about 70 miles up they came

round a bend on a hilly & rocky road & saw Tennant & Major Hobart & a Tarter guard about 50 yards off. They opened fire on both sides at the guard who were so surprised they fled. The car then drove alongside the trotting camels & Tennant & Hobart slipped off into the turret of the Armoured car which at once turned round for home before the surprised guard had sufficiently recovered to resist or to realise what had happened. They met their reserve of petrol all right & got back to Khan Baghdadi without any mishap.

> I am glad to say Todd got the DSO for this. Tennant who should have got the sack & would have if he had not been related to Asquith, was sent to India to a bigger job & married the governor's of some state, or G.O.C. or some other big wig's daughter. A scandalous affair & we all wished our little general had not taken the trouble to get him back.[115]

The pair were taken to Baghdad under arrest until a court of inquiry exonerated them: "capture was due to the chances of war."[116] As Hammond wrote, Tennant went to India. Hobart rejoined his brigade which was by then in Palestine.

Major Percy Hobart is one of those "Mespot" veterans whose post-war career was of such importance that had he been killed in that 1918 plane crash, the Second World War would have been significantly changed. In the aftermath of the failed British and Canadian raid on Dieppe in 1942, a requirement for a specialist armored division to deal with amphibious landing was identified. This task was given to the 79th Division with Hobart as its commander. His "Funnies" were critical to the success of D-Day, and by the end of the war the division contained some 7,000 specialist vehicles which were assigned to support other units, including mine flails, fascine carriers and flame-throwing armored vehicles. Of these vehicles, only the Duplex-Drive amphibious Sherman tank was adopted by the U.S. Army.

The Turkish defeat at Khan Baghdadi, with the loss of 5,000 men and material which had been carefully built up over the summer months, ended Turkish options along the Euphrates. It also potentially opened the road to Syria, which was Allenby's objective, although the strategists considered that Allenby's operations through Palestine were preferable for the capture of Aleppo, and Damascus, than Marshall's Mesopotamian army. Brooking's division had performed outstanding feats. They marched two days and two nights with little or no sleep; they fought all day and part of two nights; the cavalry covered about 90 miles in two days, and the armored cars advanced 170 miles. Marshall's west flank was now secured.[117]

One of the innovations which came out of Brooking's offensive was the creation, probably for the first time in the British Army, of truly motorized infantry. These were "Lewis gun detachments" each of 150 men, 30 Lewis guns and 50 Ford vans. These were expected to be hard-hitting, mobile units but to fight dismounted, unlike the LAMBs. The experiences of the three previous raids using motorized infantry showed that engineers or pioneers were necessary, but oddly, these were not included in these units.[118]

East to the Persian Border

Marshall's next objective was to remove the Turkish threat from beyond the Jabal Hamrin, where the Turkish 6th Division was in the Mosul-Kirkuk area and the 2nd Division between Kirkuk and Qara Tepe. The defeat of the Turks in this area would also strengthen the position of Dunsterforce in Persia.

Egerton planned to concentrate his forces at Qara Tepe expecting that the Turks would conform to their usual tactic and withdraw. On this occasion, though, Egerton's objective was Kifri, 20 miles to the north, through which the Turks would withdraw, and so cut off their escape route. Qara Tepe is located near where the Diyala crosses the Jabal Hamrin. The 13th Division, with most of the cavalry, reached it with little opposition. Their movement was assisted by a fleet of 1,300 MT (Motor Transport) vans which were increasingly common in Mesopotamia. The 14th (Muray's Jats) Lancers from the 7th Cavalry Brigade made for Abu Gharaib through another pass in the Jabal Hamrin along the River Adhaim, which was renamed the Aq-Su beyond the mountains. The advance was conducted on the night of 26/27 April.

As expected, the Turks slipped away from Qara Tepe and Abu Gharaib. Mechanized troops of the 37th Brigade occupied Kifri without opposition. The Turks made for Tuz-Khurmatli pursued by the British cavalry and the 40th Brigade, who caught them just short of Tuz-Khurmatli at Kulawand. First contact was at 0815 hours. The plan was for the cavalry to hold the Turks while lorried infantry and LAMBs moved in a right-flanking attack. The ground was found to be impassable for the wheeled vehicles, so the roles were reversed at the last moment, and in contact with the enemy, which is never a desirable situation for a commander to be in. Holland-Pryor's 6th Cavalry Brigade achieved this so that by 1130 the cavalry were probing the extent of the Turkish right flank. The trenches had been dug out of an existing ravine by German engineers the previous year and were now entirely overgrown with grass, making it impossible for aerial reconnaissance to determine whether the trenches were occupied or not.

An hour later the cavalry brigade moved forward at a trot in a scythe-like formation, with the 22nd, 21st and 13th from the right. The two Indian regiments advanced in an extended line while the 13th Hussars advanced in a column of wings — two squadrons in the front line and one and a half in a second line 200 yards to the rear. The horse artillery provided a creeping barrage, and the cavalry's own Hotchkiss guns fired the charge home. Lance Corporal Bowie, 13th Hussars, takes up the narrative:

> We drew our swords ... as we rode on at [a slow trot] parties of the Turks started running down the road, while other groups took up positions in the rough ground and water-cuts, or kneeling in the high corn opened fire on us. Here the Turks showed some of their old spirit in the stand they made, but the sudden flash of our swords in the sun which made a wide arc of light seemed to take the heart out of them, and their fire was wild and high and our casualties few.... Our line maintained this pace until within some 500 yards of the enemy, when we lowered our swords and charged into them. Our aeroplanes which took part in the action flew very low and increased the enemy's confusion with bombs and machine-gun fire.

On flat desert battlefield, the cavalry charged with supporting fire from artillery and Lewis machine-guns to capture over 500 Turks and putting the rest to rout. The cavalry was able to use its sabers to good effect. The cavalry pursued the fleeing Turks to Tuz-Khurmatli, but it was too late for a follow-up attack that evening.

This action was a daring decision by Holland-Pryor. His brigade could so easily have lost its momentum in and amongst the trenches and watercourses to become easy prey for Turkish infantry. The gamble paid off. The cavalry were launched on the sort of action which they excelled at. The Turks were routed. British losses were just 14 men and 36 horses — smaller casualties from a larger force than the cavalry actions at Samarra Station and Tikrit. And the cavalry had proved it could operate in terrain where the wheeled vehicles could not.

The following day, the Turks had melted away, again. Two squadrons of the 13th found the seven-mile road from Tuz to Yanija Buyak to be one long, intermittently held, Turkish position. A ford over the Aq-Su was located three miles west of the town which, after work to improve it for wheeled vehicles, allowed the cavalry and motorized vehicles to cross and occupy a hill one mile north of the town. That night, the infantry crossed the Aq-Su and captured Yanija Buyuk. Although Turkish opposition was melting away, artillery and machine-gun fire still held up the advances: the 21st Cavalry lost their commanding officer to shell fire. When the cavalry captured Kuchuk Buyuk a few miles further along the Kirkuk road, Turkish resistance in the area turned into a general surrender. An Indian cavalry officer, K.D. Abdulla Khan, with eight men, was tasked to watch a body of Turkish cavalry. He drove them off and pursued them eight miles along the road, capturing a further 128 men in the process. Tuz-Khurmatli was entered at 0930 hours on the 29th, and an hour and a half later, all resistance ceased. The following day, LAMBs entered the next town, Tauq, to find it empty of Turkish forces.[119]

The capture of the Tuz-Kurmatli area and the surrender of the remaining Turkish troops in the area brought to an end the 1917-1918 campaigning season.

Summer 1918

Mesopotamia was afflicted by the Spanish Flu which was sweeping the war-weakened world in a global pandemic and which carried off more victims than the war had. The British Army and Arab tribes alike were victims. Two-thirds of the

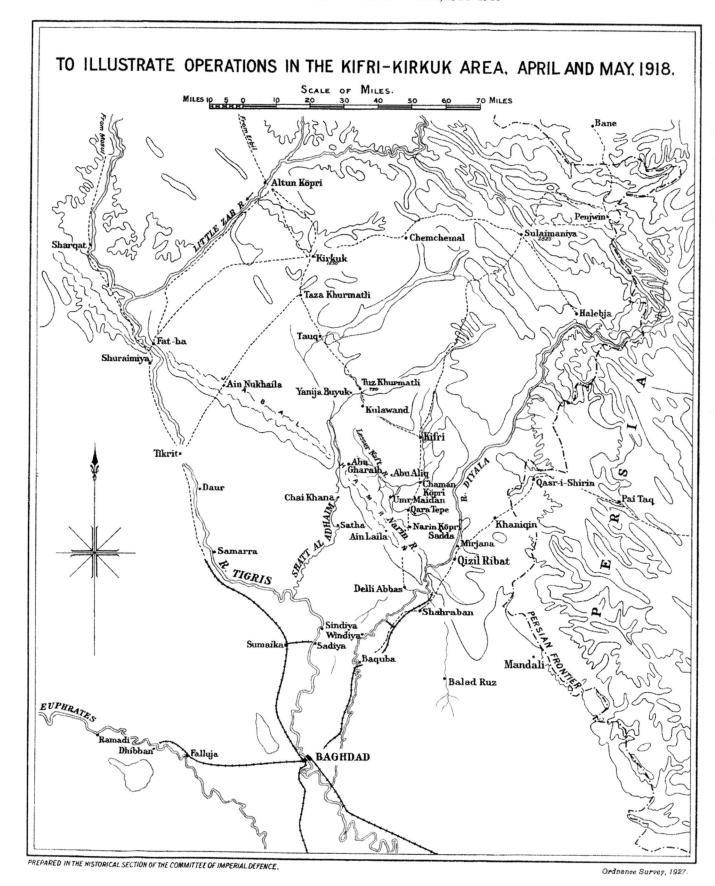

Operations in the Kifri-Kirkuk Area, April and May 1918

6th East Lancashires suffered, although Lance Corporal Roe reported no fatalities, which he put down to the warm weather. Had it been the rainy season, the fatalities would have been much worse.[120] The 11th Cavalry Brigade developed a fishing craze during the summer months. The cavalry received bayonet training, which they did not like, as the sword bayonets were another article to hang and impede the horse.[121]

1918-1919 Campaigning Season

In September 1918, Bulgaria sued for peace, and following Allenby's successes in Syria, it was hoped that the Turks would soon follow suit. Indeed, it was believed that Turkey's influence in Mesopotamia and Syria/Palestine was about to crumble, which the British could then exploit. Planning for the next campaign went on regardless, and London proposed a cavalry advance along the Euphrates into Syria to draw Turkish resources away from Allenby, and concurrently along the Tigris to Mosul, where there were expected to be economically attractive oil reserves. With the end of the war in sight, attention was being given to securing economic resources which would repay the wartime outlay. It should be noted that under the 1915 Sykes-Picot Agreement, Mosul fell within the French sphere of influence. Clearly this was no longer a consideration to the British planners, not least that there were only minimal French forces in the whole of the Middle East. Marshall objected to the dual strategy, stating that as so much of his logistical support had been diverted to support Dunsterforce, he was only able to conduct one operation. Mosul was chosen.[122]

The Turkish 6th Army was now commanded by Ali Ihsan. The Tigris towards Mosul passed through the Jebel Hamrin, which was now becoming familiar to the British soldiers, but was renamed the Jabal Makhul around the Tigris. There were two natural features in which the Turks had had eighteen months to prepare the defenses. Fat-Ha (or Al-Fatha) village was located 35 miles north of the railhead at Tikrit and within a 20-mile-long gorge. The next major obstacle was the Little Zab River which flowed in from the east joining the Tigris at Humr, 20 miles north of Fat-Ha. There were an estimated 2,600 rifles and 28 guns at Fat-Ha, and at Humr 5,500 rifles with 42 guns. Near Kirkuk to the east were 1,700 rifles and 26 guns which could move down the Little Zab to reinforce Humr. The 6th Army remained a formidable force. Morale was high under the circumstances. They lacked many systems which the British were now taking for granted, like armored cars and wireless communications, and there were almost no mounted troops. The German advisors (never popular) had withdrawn to Aleppo with most of the aviation, heavy artillery and transport. The Turks were now alone to stem the British advance. If they were abandoned by allies to their fate, it did not prevent them from soldiering on and gaining the admiration of their foe.[123]

In May 1918, the 7th Brigade in Ford trucks and the 32nd Lancers with LAMBs reconnoitered both banks of the Tigris as far as Fat-Ha. Their reports were the basis for the final Mesopotamian campaign.[124]

Lieutenant General Cobbe's I Corps resumed its advance up the Tigris. With some 3,000 sabres, 15,400 rifles and 136 guns, Cobbe had almost a three-to-one advantage which was approaching the ideal ratio for an attacking force. However, this was almost an entirely new corps from that which had fought to, through and beyond Baghdad. The 17th Indian Division on the right bank of the Tigris and the 18th Indian Division on the left bank were new formations, inexperienced, under-strength with incomplete staffs which were not used to working together. The two cavalry brigades, 7th and 11th, would also operate on the left bank. Most of his transport had been withdrawn for Dunsterforce, so Cobbe had to borrow III Corps' transport which took time to arrange and redeploy. Spanish Flu afflicted the corps, although the symptoms disappeared once the fighting started. LAMBs would operate on the right bank.[125]

The terrain also became much more restrictive and in many ways reminiscent of the fighting south of Baghdad, which had been restricted to a single river. There was no water away from the Tigris, as south of Baghdad, although now Cobbe had LAMBs which could operate wide-flanking moves. The Jebel also hemmed in Cobbe's freedom. These restrictions raised the pre–Baghdad problem of restricting the commander's courses of action to attacking on either the left or right bank (or sometimes not even that option).

Cobbe established a supply dump 10 miles south of Fat-Ha. From this position he could still strike east or west. This dump was completed on 18 October. On the same day, two passes over the Jabal Makhul were found to be clear, at Darb-al-Khalil and Ain Nukhaila. The roads were improved over the next five days. There were limited water supplies at either pass, so that Ford trucks had to bring it from the Tigris, 15 and 27 miles away respectively. A depot was established at Ain Nukaila sufficient to provide both cavalry brigades with two days' rations. To easet their passage, the cavalry left Tikrit over 21 to 23 October and traveled as lightly as possible, with extra transport carrying that day's rations and the emergency rations.[126]

Once again, though, all of this careful preparation and planning would be for naught. On arriving at Fat-Ha on 24 October, both of Cobbe's infantry divisions found that the Turks had once again decamped for their next line of defenses. The 7th Cavalry Brigade was also at the Fat-Ha position, having traveled via the Darb-el-Khalil Pass. It was too late for the cavalry on the left bank to pursue the Turks while the infantry on the right bank found that the retreating Turks had so damaged the road that pack animals could not use it, let alone wheeled vehicles. While the 17th Division rebuilt the roads, the 7th Brigade advanced to the Little Zab before withdrawing due to heavy shell fire.[127]

Cobbe now launched a wide, right-flanking move by the 11th Cavalry Brigade and the LAMBs. His aim was for them to cross the Little Zab 25 miles above its confluence with the Tigris, and to reach the Tigris above Sarqat, 35 miles above Fat-Ha. Cassels led his brigade in person, leaving the Jabal Hamrin at the Ain Nukhaila Pass at 0200 on 24 October and reaching the Little Zab at 1500 hours. This march was after covering 27 miles in the previous 39 hours. The Little Zab was found to be held in force by some 800 Turks with four guns from Kirkuk. The 7th Hussars crossed the river by a lower ford and turned the Turk's position with support from the horse artillery and a spotter plane. With the Turks driven off, the brigade made camp on the south bank of the river and commenced to cross the next morning. It was established that there were no more Turkish forces on the east bank of the Tigris.[128]

The Turks were found in positions along Humr-Mushak-Ain Dibs. The 17th Division attacked, without success, on 25 October, and again on the 26th. Uncharacteristically, the Turks did not attempt to slip away in the night. In an attempt to break the deadlock, the 7th Brigade advanced 12 miles up the east bank of the Tigris. When it was mistakenly reported that the brigade had exhausted all of its rations (the poor state of the roads delayed the supply convoys, although they did arrive that evening), the brigade was ordered back to recross the

Tigris at Fat-Ha to become the divisional reserve. For their 20-mile march, the brigade brought in just 100 prisoners.[129]

Concurrently, the LAMBs (8th LAMB less two sections; 14th LAMB, three motorized Lewis gun detachment and the 13th Motor W/T Station) drove to Hadr, 35 miles west of Sahrqat in the desert. They reached Hadr without encountering any Turks. They then turned towards Sahrqat but were driven off by howitzer fire. When they cut the telegraph cable with Mosul, they cut off the Turkish army from the outside world.[130]

The Turks were now suspected of holding their Humr-Mushak-Ain Dibs line while withdrawing their heavier equipment. To cut off the Turks for a (hopefully) final time, Cassels was ordered to cross the Tigris 13 miles north of Sharqat, where he would link up with the LAMBs. He set off on the 26th at maximum speed and reached the Tigris at 1300 hours. While a search for a ford was undertaken, a party of the Guides Cavalry swam the Tigris and cut the telegraph cable, again. When a ford was found, opposite Hadraniya, the water came up to the breasts of the mounted men, and several Indian cavalrymen were swept away and drowned. A Turkish doctor said that the watching Arabs had been very impressed with what they had seen — they had never known the river to be forded there before. That evening, Cassels and the Guides moved south through Huwaish to Wadi Muabba where, on the north bank, the found a strong, south-facing positions. A ferry, Cassels' Ferry, would be established two miles above Huwaish. The following day, the 27th, the entire brigade was across the Tigris, after covering 83 miles in two days. The action had gone undetected by the Turkish Army, but not by the LAMBs. The rest of the brigade moved down to join Cassels and the Guides, and that evening the transport column joined them. Further south, infantry patrols discovered that the Turks had abandoned their positions.[131]

Cassels sent a squadron of the 23rd Cavalry on a reconnaissance. Two and a half miles south, they encountered a force of some 900 Turks with artillery and machines guns. These opened up on the 23rd,

Rolls-Royce armored car of 14th LAMB with Turkish shells bursting in the distance during the Battle of Sharqat, 28–30 October 1918. Armored cars were first used operationally by Townshend at the Battle of Kut in 1915, and their ability to operate away from water provided a major asset to British commanders (Imperial War Museum).

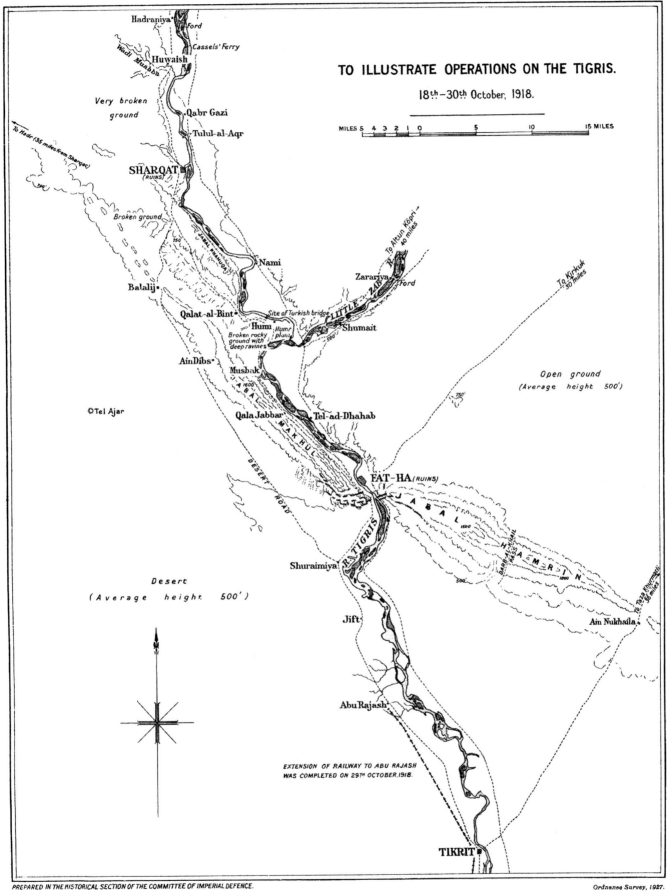

TO ILLUSTRATE OPERATIONS ON THE TIGRIS.

18th–30th October, 1918.

MILES 5 4 3 2 1 0   5   10   15 MILES

Hadraniya
Ford
Wadi Muabba
Cassels' Ferry
Huwaish

Very broken
ground

To Hadr (35 miles from Sharqat)

Qabr Gazi

Tulul-al-Aqr

SHARQAT
(RUINS)

750

Broken ground

JABAL HAMRIN

Nami

To Altun Köpri
40 miles

Balalij

LITTLE ZAB

Zarariya
Ford

To Kirkuk
30 miles

Qalat-al-Bint

Site of Turkish bridge

Humr

Humr
plain

Broken rocky
ground with
deep ravines

500

Shumait

AinDibs

Open ground
(Average height 500')

Musbak

JABAL MAKHUL

1600

Tel Ajar

Qala Jabbar

Tel-ad-Dhahab

750

DESERT ROAD

FAT-HA (RUINS)

JABAL HAMRIN

1500

Shuraimiya

TIGRIS

500

DARB-AL-KHAIL PASS

1000

To Taza Khurmatli
56 miles

Desert
(Average height 500')

Jift

Ain Nukhaila

Abu Rajash

EXTENSION OF RAILWAY TO ABU RAJASH
WAS COMPLETED ON 29TH OCTOBER.1918.

TIKRIT

PREPARED IN THE HISTORICAL SECTION OF THE COMMITTEE OF IMPERIAL DEFENCE.

Ordnance Survey, 1927.

Operations on the Tigris, 18 to 30 October 1918

and on the LAMBs which were operating away to the west. Cassels also identified a force of some 400 Turks to his north advancing southwards. Cassels sent "C" Squadron, 7th Hussars, and two armored cars to deal with the northern threat. He requested additional ammunition for his 18-pounders and prepared for a spoiling attack to the south.

Cobbe realized just how isolated and vulnerable Cassels was, with just 1,000 rifles and six 18-pounders but with 60 machine guns.

The 53rd Brigade with their guns were dispatched as reinforcements, together with two troops of the 32nd Lancer and six pontoons, commanded by Brigadier General Sanders. They made their way up the left bank with orders to assist Cassels however they could. Norton's 7th Cavalry Brigade was brought out of reserve and ordered to reach Hadrianiya by 1100 hours on the 28th. The 63rd Squadron, RAF, was tasked with providing aerial support. The Turks probed the British defenses, but as more reinforcements crossed the Tigris, the British positions strengthened and the noose was tightened. Despite this, they were dangerously isolated until the 17th Division arrived, and the Turks were not inactive. About midday on the 27th, the 900-strong body of Turks attacked Cassels' position in an action which lasted until nightfall. The 23rd Cavalry were sent to the west in order to harass the Turkish left flank, which they did to such effect that they were about to capture the Turkish guns. Reinforcements saved the guns, and the 23rd were obliged to retire. They suffered 49 casualties, including five British officers, but they achieved their aim. That night there was just the normal sporadic sniping.[132]

The following morning, Sanders' advanced patrols of the 28th made contact with those from Cassels. The 53rd Brigade had marched 33 miles in 21 hours. Using the pontoons, first the 800 rounds of 18-pounder ammunition and then the infantry crossed the Tigris to secure the positions. Meanwhile, to the north, two squadrons of the 7th Hussar's were using their Hotchkiss machine guns to good effect in slowing down the advancing Turks. They opened fire at 500 yard, and then retired in bounds three or four times, with one squadron firing while the other moved. The Hussars retired on their own gun positions which fired in support. They lost only a few men. They did lose their pack ponies, which had carried their entrenching tools, so when the cavalry reached their guns, they were exposed to the Turkish guns. They also almost lost their RMO, who stayed too long tending to the wounded when Turkish cavalry charged at him, firing their rifles.[133]

Observers at Cassels' camp noted Turks to the south retreating northwards at about 0700 hours, across a 700-yard front with their right on the Tigris advancing steadily. Twenty minutes later, the Turkish artillery opened fire. Cassels' artillery, "W" Battery, replied. Across the Tigris, Sanders' artillery could only respond by identifying the location of "W" Battery's bursts. By 0800 hours, aircraft spotted the Turkish gun positions for Sanders and their fire became more accurate.[134]

To counter the Turkish southern attack, Cassels sent the same two squadrons of the 7th Hussars along a wadi to attack the Turkish left. They started their attack at 600 yards, taking the Turks by surprise. When the Turkish front appeared to be collapsing, the Hussars remounted and closed to within 250 yards of the Turkish guns. Reinforcements saved the guns and obliged the Hussars to retire, but their route included climbing a steep escarpment. The men dismounted to lead their horses up in full view of the Turks. Although the disengagement cost only three horses, reaching cover behind the escarpment cost 30 officers and men.

Around midday, Cassels used the two Hussar squadrons and then the 23rd Cavalry to extend his line to about five miles in an attempt to prevent the Turks from outflanking his. Further west, the LAMBs also acted to delay the flanking movement. It was not until 1400 hours that the first of 53rd Brigade'scompanies arrived. This Gurkha company took over from two squadrons of Guides, who then moved to assist the 7th Hussars, now astride the Mosul road. Despite the reinforcements, by 1700 hours, the Turks had pushed the cavalry back almost to the Hadraniya *wadi*. As more Gurkhas arrived, more Guides were relieved to form a reserve.[135]

The 7th Cavalry Brigade traveled nearly 50 miles from 0100 hours and began to cross the Tigris at about 1615 hours. This crossing proved to be very dangerous: 21 men were drowned, including 12 from the 14th Lancers and three from the 13th Hussars. Numerous horses were lost too. "V" Battery, RHA, and a squadron from the 13th Hussars remained on the left bank of the Tigris overnight to cross the following day. Aircraft bombed the Turks until dusk—these were now pilots of the Royal Air Force which was created from the Royal Flying Corps on 1 April 1918. The fighting continued until after dusk, by which time Cassels' brigade had been fighting 72 hours. On top of Norton's brigade's march, these were exhausted troops.[136]

At first light on the 29th, soldiers were seen away to the south, but it was unclear whether they were Turks or the 17th Division. A squadron from the 13th Lancers reconnoitered to the north and found that three battalions of Turkish infantry, machine guns and two nine-pound camel guns had occupied a bluff—known afterwards as Richardson's Bluff. "V" Battery was in the process of crossing the Tigris and was shelled, so chose to remain on the left bank and brought its guns into action against the camel guns, forcing them to retire. After a reconnaissance in person, Norton determined that the bluff must be captured. If the Turks could be fixed in their positions, there would be ample dead ground at the base of the bluff to protect an attacking force. The 14th Jat Lancers were selected to support the attack, together with Vickers machine guns and "V" Battery.

The first attack failed when Captain Evans, commanding the lead squadron, was wounded and fell from his horse. The troop leaders changed direction and took their commands into the shelter of Cemetery Hill, which proved to be a fortuitous,

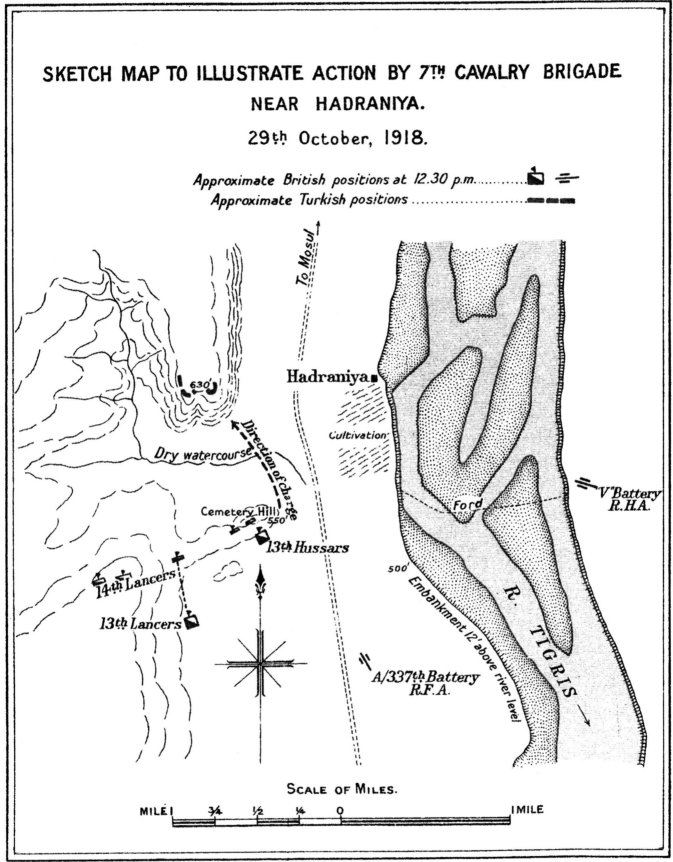

SKETCH MAP TO ILLUSTRATE ACTION BY 7TH CAVALRY BRIGADE
NEAR HADRANIYA.

29th October, 1918.

Approximate British positions at 12.30 p.m..........
Approximate Turkish positions ....

To Mosul

Hadraniya

Cultivation

630'

Direction of charge

Dry watercourse

Cemetery Hill
550'

13th Hussars

14th Lancers

13th Lancers

Ford

V" Battery
R.H.A.

500'

Embankment 12' above river level

R. TIGRIS

A/337th Battery
R.F.A.

SCALE OF MILES.

MILE 1   ¾   ½   ¼   O   1 MILE

PREPARED IN THE HISTORICAL SECTION OF THE COMMITTEE OF IMPERIAL DEFENCE.   Ordnance Survey, 1927.

7th Cavalry Brigade's Action near Hadraniya, 29 October 1918 if unplanned, event. The Turkish positions were more formidable than expected. A second attack was launched at 1330 hours following a second, greater barrage. Lieutenant Colonel Richardson, commanding officer of the 13th Hussars, wrote to the regimental colonel, Sir Robert Baden-Powell, who is more famous as the founder of the Scout movement:

> [Richardson] led the regiment from the cover of Cemetery Hill in two waves, "A" and "D" Squadrons in the first and "C" and "D" in the second under Captain Godfree.
>
> The first wave reached the foot of the bluff with only one casualty, a man whose horse fell in jumping a deepish nullah which lay across part of our course — dismounted to climb the almost precipitous cliff-side, the footing on which was made the worse by the loose rolling gravel surface; how the men scaled that cliff carrying their Hotchkiss guns and ammunition-bags will always remain a marvel to me.
>
> Meantime the second wave had reached the hill, also without casualties, and taken position on the right of the first. As we appeared on the crest fire broke out on us from all sides, but the *moral* of the Turks had been so severely shaken by the artillery that our casualties were very slight, and by bringing our right forward we were soon able to bring enfilade fire on the trenches in front.

The 13th Hussars galloped to the foot of the bluff, dismounted and climbed to the Turkish positions where 730 Turks were captured and the fleeing remainder were captured by a squadron from the 14th Lancers.[137]

With his northern flank secured, Cassels was able to turn his attention to the south. He dispatched the 13th and 14th Lancers northwards, who rounded up some 1,200 men, a paddle steamer and other war material.[138]

The 17th Division's advance was delayed by "poor communications and inept staff work"[139] over the supply of ammunition to the artillery: it was unclear whether or not it had been expended. The Royal West Kents had broken through the Turkish positions three and a half miles south of Sharqat, which had finally sent them northwards towards Cassels. It was not until the 30th that Cobbe was satisfied and the advance resumed. An attack on the 29th failed to dislodge the Turks. The following dawn, when they closed in on the Sharqat positions, a huge explosion was heard and white flags were seen. At 0730 hours, Ismail Hakki surrendered. Half an hour later, Cassels was informed of the development. He ordered the LAMBs and 7th Cavalry Brigade southwards to round up the Turks.

The Battle of Megiddo on 20 September 1918 in Palestine has been called the last great cavalry victory. There the Desert Mounted Corps of Allenby's Egyptian Expeditionary Force broke through and destroyed three Turkish armies, opening up the open plains of northern Palestine into Syria. Syria was far more important to the maintenance of the Turkish war effort than Mesopotamia. This was known to the British planners which is why the two divisions in Mesopotamia were sent

to Palestine. Both Megiddo and Sharqat were dominated by the cavalry, but they were actually all-arms battles where cavalry, aviation, infantry, artillery and armored cars cooperated.[140] This approach is usually, and anachronistically, termed blitzkrieg. These all-arms tactics had been experimented with since the 16th Brigade landed on the Shatt-al-Arab and received naval gunfire support, and had been used successfully at Ramadi in September 1917, the month before Allenby finally broke through at Bersheeba to open the road to Jerusalem. Where the two British armies differed was in their strategic approach. In Palestine, the breakthrough was the aim — through the mud and blood to the green fields beyond, to use the Western Front description. This was an appropriate use of the four-division-strong Desert Mounted Corps. Mesopotamia was never so well provided with cavalry, which was only ever one division strong at best. The Mesopotamian tactic was to use the cavalry in a flanking move, to get behind the enemy and trap him there. This had been tried at Kut, perfected at Ramadi and used to great effect at Sharqat. It is also a use of the maneuver assets which the modern army commander would recognize: the enemy is dislocated by appearance of unexpected forces in his rear areas which degrades the will to fight and hastens the enemy's surrender. When the Turkish forces surrendered at Sharqat, the last field army in Mesopotamia was destroyed and with it the means for Turkey to wage war there.[141]

The Turks had fought with their usual tenacity and conducted a number of their skilled withdrawals, but being hemmed to the north for six days while waiting for the 17th Division to arrive from the south had broken their will to fight. The Turkish 2nd and 5th Divisions surrendered 11,322 men. This action also secured for Britain the Mosul oil fields, although it should be remembered that *Mesopotamian* oil was never a war aim. In fact, the Cabinet did not discuss the matter until late July 1918 when Admiral Sir Edmond Slade (a major APOC [Anglo-Persion Oil Company] shareholder) sponsored a paper entitled "The Petroleum Situation in the British Empire" which advocated that Mesopotamian oil should become a "first class war aim." In any case, Baku held London's attention for oil.[142]

The 18th Division was sent towards Mosul, about 50 miles to the north, in pursuit of any escaping Turks. At 0845 hours on 1 November 1918, when the division was 12 miles south of Mosul, news came of the armistice and the end of the war. The 18th (Indian) Division, 7th and 11th Cavalry Brigades and a LAMB were the northernmost British formations in Mesopotamia at that point and the only ones actively pursuing objectives against the Turks. The Turkish commander, Ali Ihsan, requested that Fane withdraw his division to the point it had occupied when the armistice was signed: midday on 31 October 1918. Fane refused and his division bivouacked outside the town.[143]

Lance Corporal Roe's armistice celebrations consisted of a firework display — Very lights and rockets — and a beer issue.[144]

Marshall and Captain Wilson traveled to Mosul for a conference with Ali Ihsan. The armistice terms were not well defined, and although Ali Ihsan did his utmost to uphold his position, Marshall made it clear that he would occupy the Mosul *vilayet*. In the end, Ali Ihsan had no option but to sign Marshall's terms although their informal resistance and defiance continued for several days. In the end, the Turks had to acknowledge the de facto ruler of Mosul as the nation with the greatest might. Constantinople ordered the withdrawal of Turkish forces from Mosul town on the 15th and the *vilayet* by the 30th. The British occupied Mosul on 10 November.[145]

The Great War in Mesopotamia was finally over.

But the soldiers were still there. On 27 December, the 6th East Lancashires were informed of the demobilization plan, which would be based on occupation — farmers and miners first. The first party left two days later. Roe said that this scheme did not work smoothly and those who had done least were clamoring to get away first. The adjutant asked Roe to extend to complete his 21 years (with promotion to sergeant), but he had had enough and wanted to go home. He made his way to the Makina demobilization camp at Basra on 27 February 1919 and embarked for India on 6 March and, having changed there onto a troopship, disembarked in Marseilles on 24 April and made England on 3 May, but, as there was an infectious disease on board, the ship was quarantined. From there, he took a train to Prees Heath, where he was demobilized on 6 May. That night he took a train to Holyhead and then a steamer to Ireland, where he saw troops in Dublin in battle order and tin hats. Then there was a further three-hour train journey, in which he began to wonder if he should have accepted the adjutant's offer. At his hometown, he went to the pub for a bottle of Bass ale. "If it's Bass, porter or whiskey you want, you will have to go back to Dublin as the strongest drink I have in the house is ginger wine," came the reply.

"Hells Bells!" he ejaculated, "so this is the land Lloyd George made fit for heroes to live in?"[146]

10

The Fates of the Kuttites,
April 1916–November 1918

When the 6th (Poona) Division and its various attached units surrendered, 13,309 marched, or staggered, into captivity. Of these, 3,248 were Indian non-combatants. From the 10,061 combatants, there were:

British officers	277
Indian officers	204
British other ranks	2,592
Indian other ranks	6,988

Of which:

Sick	1,456

Repatriated from:

Kut	1,136
Baghdad	345

After two and a half years of imprisonment:

British exchanged	209
British dead or missing	1,700
Indians exchanged or escaped	1,100–1,200
Indians dead	1,300
Died in captivity:	
British	755
Indian	3,063[1]

The experiences of the officers and men varied greatly. Some, like Major General Townshend, were treated as "honored guests" and lived out the rest of the war in luxury. Captain Spackman, the 48th Pioneer's RMO enjoyed relatively comfortable captivity by virtue of his profession. Lieutenant E.H. Jones of the Volunteer Artillery Battery was able to manipulate his Turkish jailers to his own advantage. Sergeant Long tells the story of the "other ranks." He was fortunate to know Arabic and became an interpreter. He also knew joinery. Both skills enabled him to survive.

For those men without a skill, or without the means to purchase additional food (which affected the other ranks more than the officers), life was much more difficult. Many did not leave the prison camps on the banks of the Tigris.

The treatment of the Kuttites was similar to those of the Allied prisoners of war taken by the Japanese, which is of course a far more familiar story to a modern audience. Whether or not there was a deliberate state policy to murder the Kuttites through overwork, underfeeding, or both, or whether murder was a by-product of negligence, neglect and official incompetence is a moot point. It made little difference to the Kuttites. Their captivity took place against the backdrop of the Armenian massacres, which are still denied by the modern Turkish state. Again, whether or not the death of thousands of Armenians was the result of a state policy, or whether it was the by-product of negligence, neglect and official incompetence is a moot point. It made little difference to the Armenians.

Major General C.V.F. Townshend, KCB, DSO

Of all of the survivors of Kut, the captivity of Townshend was the most comfortable and the most controversial. He believed that he would travel to Constantinople, then to London, on parole, where he could arrange for the freedom of his division. Whatever was promised, the Turkish authorities had other plans. What they wanted was a fit division to parade in front of the cameras. What they got was a ragged body of men incapable of marching far and certainly not looking like a conquered valiant foe. They did, however, have Townshend as a figurehead to show off the achievements of Turkish arms.

Townshend would spend the rest of the war in luxurious captivity while his men suffered unaided. How much Townshend (or the other officers) knew of their men's suffering is unclear. After the war, he would be vilified for failing to do more for his men, although this did not prevent him from becoming a member of Parliament before his death in 1924.

In the House of Lords, on 4 May 1916, Lord Kitchener, secretary of state for war, made a statement on the fall of Kut:

> General Townshend and his troops in their honourable captivity will have the satisfaction of knowing that in the opinion

of their comrades, which I think I may say that this House and this country fully share, they did all that was humanly possible to resist to the last. And their surrender reflects no discredit on themselves or on the records of the British and Indian Armies.[2]

Personally, Kitchener had been a supporter of Townshend's promotion from lieutenant colonel to major general, so to see one of his protégés fail so spectacularly must have come as a blow. Politically, coming so close after the defeat at Gallipoli in January 1916, the government had to make some mileage out of the latest fiasco. Only Townshend would enjoy "honorable captivity," but it brought him post-war dishonor.

Townshend's initial actions following his surrender did him little credit. He does not appear to have done anything to protect the townspeople of Kut from revenge. While it was normal practice for officers to be separated from their men in captivity, the speed at which the officers, led by Townshend, left the remainder of the division was almost indecent in its haste. With the officers removed, the men were more vulnerable in their weakened state, with even less access to money, so less able to resist the brutalities ahead of them. Townshend certainly had no intention of joining them on their march to Anatolia and, to be fair, as a general, nor should it have been expected of him. But his mind-set at this time is shown by the pathetic final telegram sent by him from Kut to his wife, Alice:

Write Alice tell her the hole I am in here through the fault of others. When I think, tell her thou all conduct of operations was put on to me & not one word of praise & no thanks for all I have done throughout the campaign. I have only one desire that to leave the Army as soon as peace comes. I am ill and weak but a little better today. Tell her I have some six or seven hundred pounds pay at ? Which I will instruct them to send her. *If I have to go into captivity, It will kill me.* [Author's italics]

Charles Townshend Apl 27[3]

While this was a personal telegram (although sent at public expense) and the contents were intended for his wife, the self-pitying whining is clear. There is not a single word for the fate of 13,000 men, nor for the similar number killed and wounded in attempting to relieve him. Townshend is justified in feeling let down after all the promises from Army HQ, but to suggest that they alone bore the responsibility for his fate is disingenuous. His determination to resign his commission smacks of a petulant child throwing a toy into the corner.

And yet, when his launch with his entourage[4] steamed past his captured division at Shumran, they rushed to the banks, ignoring the whips of their Turkish guards and cheering him. Townshend stood at the rails and took the salute, with tears rolling down his cheeks. The emotion of the moment must have been indescribable. In the future, none of the Kuttites would blame Townshend for their fate, which does at least substantiate part of his telegram, above. And then there was

silence as the launch steamed onwards. The Turkish guards whipped their charges back into order.[5]

In Baghdad, Townshend was accommodated in the former Italian consulate for a week where he was well treated. Von der Goltz, the architect of his downfall, had recently died, but Khalil Pasha entertained Townshend and discussed strategy. One can imagine Townshend in his element in luxurious surroundings, discussing his favorite topic, being feted over by the Turkish military and free from the cares of command. When news of a dinner party leaked out, it was the beginning of a public relations disaster for Townshend. He had never been able to see the effects of how his actions were seen by others.

Townshend was invited to Constantinople, which he readily accepted, and his account of the journey in *My Campaign in Mesopotamia* (which did not include walking) reads, in the words of his biographer, Nash, as "a travelogue" with "a succession of interesting sights, comfortable beds with clean sheets and agreeable meals with fawning Turks."[6] Townshend traveled first class, whereas von der Goltz's coffin traveled with the baggage.

Although he was now away from Kut, Townshend could not entirely escape the fate of his men. On the journey, he met 40 of the survivors of the *Julnar* commanded by Sub-Lieutenant Reid. Reid made the conditions that he and his men were enduring perfectly clear. Townshend gave them some money and words of comfort and lectured the Turkish commander before departing, apparently considering his duty done. Melliss, in comparison, is reported to have been a much more forceful advocate of the Kuttites and their fate, earning the title Melliss Pasha, but there was little in practice even he could do to improve the day-to-day conditions of so many men in such harsh conditions.[7]

On arrival at Constantinople, Townshend was met by Enver Pasha and relaxed in the war minister's private train where he made another public relations gaffe by saying that he would be "the honored guest of [Enver Pasha's] nation." In Townshend's defense, he did then raise the question of the conditions of the prisoners of war, but all his approaches were brushed away. By now Enver Pasha was well aware of the conditions being endured as he had seen the prisoners in Baghdad.[8]

Townshend's treatment in Constantinople was closer to that of a returning victorious general than as a defeated prisoner. He was saluted and photographed, and allocated an additional ADC, a Turkish naval officer named Tewfik Bey. All of this played to the ego of a man like Townshend, who undoubtedly played the part, much to the delight of the Turkish authorities who had a very useful, high-profile and, on balance, successful British general in their hands. The party was accommodated in a large house on the fashionable island of Halki, in the middle of the Sea of Marma. Life was pleasant on the island amongst the great and good of Constantinople, where he was free to walk, swam every day and was waited on hand and foot. There was regular mail from England and he even tried to get his wife sent out to him. The Turkish authorities agreed and suggested that they live in the former British embassy at Pera, but it was a step too far for the British authorities and the prime minister wrote to inform Alice Townshend that it was inappropriate to turn an embassy into a place of internment. Townshend was moved for the winter to a larger, but more sheltered island, Prinkipo, and the summer house of the British consul.

On a personal level, Townshend received both a knock and a boost, although the latter was not received with the best grace. After 11 years of childless marriage, the Marchioness of Townshend gave birth to a baby boy who would succeed the title instead of the general. This ended one of his long-cherished dreams. He was, however, awarded a knighthood as a Companion of the Order of the Bath, but he grumbled that it was not before time, after 35 years of service, nine campaigns and nine Mentioned in Dispatches.[9]

Tewfik Bey was summarily dismissed for passing fraudulent receipts for pay drawn by Townshend and Morland and was replaced by one Hussein Bey, an altogether less pliant ADC. Townshend repeatedly complained to London about lack of pay and the cost of maintaining his household. As can be imagined, the replies were less than accommodating.

The months of inactivity while great things were happening around him must surely have played on Townshend's mind. Maude captured Baghdad with seven divisions, far more men and far better supported than the single division with which Townshend had been sent to capture Bagdad, and came close to succeeding. It is understandable that Townshend felt aggrieved. Townshend had failed to secure either the exchange of his men or his own parole to England. Despite the distractions, luncheons and luxury, captivity chafes on a man of action. Townshend did attempt to ingratiate himself into the Turkish hierarchy, perhaps in an attempt to play a pivotal role in the peace settlement which, as 1917 progressed (capture of Baghdad, the Arab Revolt, Allenby's offensive in Palestine, the entry of the United States of America into the war), was increasingly likely to go against Turkey. It is alleged that he even wrote to Melliss defending Enver Pasha and complaining about the mistreatment of Turkish prisoners of war in Egypt.[10] If Townshend was set on leaving the army, and as he was no longer going to inherit the Townshend estates, he would need a new career, and he was well placed at the heart of Turkey to advise on future relations.

In October 1918, with Germany on the brink of collapse, Townshend took the opportunity to step in as an intermediary in the peace process. Field Marshall Izzet Pasha was appointed Grand Vizier and Minister of War on 12 October. This was a man with whom Townshend had got on well, and so with whom he presumed that he could negotiate. On the 17th, a letter was taken to Izzet Pasha offering his services, which went on to lay down terms for a peace settlement, entirely off his own initiative, with no authority from or consultation with

anyone in the Allied governments. Izzet Pasha had Townshend released, and he became a diplomat, traveling first to Smyrna (now Ismir) where he took a yacht to the British-held port of Mitylene on Lesbos, arriving on 20 October. He was under the union flag and free at last. Whatever expectation he might have had for his future use and employment, he was sorely disappointed. He sent his peace terms to the Foreign Office and received a reply from the chief of the imperial general staff to stay where he was until he received further orders. When the commander-in-chief Mediterranean, the Honourable Sir Arthur Calthorp, arrived, Townshend was made welcome, but when the Turkish delegation arrived on the 26th, Townshend was sidelined as negotiations proceeded without him on HMS *Agamemnon*.[11]

Townshend had secured his own release and had done so ahead of the end of hostilities, which on the face of it is the duty of every officer. However, Townshend's war was over. His actions had won him no friends in the dark days of the war, but he had pursued his life and career in his pre–1914 fashion. Even his journey to London was leisurely, as usual, and he stopped off in Rome and Paris to meet his wife and the French premier, Clemenceau. In Paris he gave an interview to the *Times*, so that when he finally arrived in London, he was not met with open arms.

Captain W.C. Spackman, Indian Medical Service, Regimental Medical Officer, 48th Pioneers[12]

On 29 April 1916, although the siege ended, Spackman's work did not. The hospitals were full, and disease was taking away 20 patients per day. The field treasure chest was opened and distributed to the whole garrison according to rank. Those who were careful with their money could use it to survive, but Spackman saw one British soldier hand over a gold sovereign for a hunk of bread and a bunch of dates. When the Turks entered the Kut, they were well disciplined in ragged, war-torn uniforms, and there was none of the thievery which would follow. The Arab inhabitants were the first object of Turkish revenge. The sheikh of Kut, a wealthy Jewish banker named Sassoon, and several others including some interpreters, were immediately hanged.

The following day, the survivors began the march from Kut to the Turkish headquarters at Shumran. They should have been moved by steamer, but the Turks claimed there was a lack of coal, and many had to march nine miles. Many died on that first march. In Shumran camp the prisoners received Turkish Army biscuits which were hard and dry, likened to dog biscuits, and had to be smashed to break into pieces, or heated so that they would become chewable. The only water was from the Tigris. There was no administrative system in place to deliver the supplies which had been sent upriver from the Relief Column, so they were dumped on the river bank. Conditions at Shumran sound worse than at Kut. Three hundred men died that first week.

On 4 May, Spackman and 100 other officers were moved by steamer to Baghdad, arriving on 9 May. The rest, coupled with access to food (and the means to purchase it), greatly strengthened these officers for the marches ahead. They were accommodated in the cavalry barracks where a contractor fed them for four shillings a day ("a high price") and sold vegetables and cigarettes on top. They also received an advance of pay from the Turks and a visit from the American consul, who took their names, promising to inform their families, and handed out a pound or two in Turkish gold.

Spackman left Baghdad on 9 May to take the train to Samarra, part of the Berlin-Baghdad Railway, where they then waited for two or three days while transport was arranged for the 150 miles to Mosul. The time was spent bartering anything which was no longer necessary for food. When transport arrived, it was one donkey per officer but nothing for their orderlies, who would have to walk. The donkeys varied in age and strength.

The marches started off at night, which was preferable to the midday sun and fine so long as there was a full moon and the way was smooth. There would be a halt every hour for the stragglers to catch up. From the outset it was essential to protect and bring along the weaker members of the party. Anyone left behind would be stripped by the Arabs and left for dead. One night, an Indian officer collapsed and so was placed on the back of Spackman's donkey, with a second officer to hold him in place. He kept slipping off the donkey and so was placed face down over the donkey's back. When there was a halt, they found he had died, although neither knew when he had died. There was just enough time to bury him in a shallow grave before they were off again.

The first stage ended at Tikrit, which Spackman notes as being notorious as the birthplace of Saladin, who captured Jerusalem in 1187. A modern reader would know the town as the birthplace of Saddam Hussein. They were crowded into a dirty, smelly, hot and airless cow shed with the doors guarded. Spackman arranged for half the party to lie outside in the shade for fear that they would have died of heatstroke had they remained in the cow shed, while Arabs brought them water — for a price. He was not upset when he heard that Tikrit was destroyed by Maude's army in 1917.

Spackman considers that first leg to be the worst he undertook, but he was also well aware that the relatively young and fit officers with money to help them had a far easier journey than the soldiers who followed. They reached Mosul on 25 May after a march of 170 miles and only lost one man.

Although they had only lost one man, it was clear that others would not survive the next leg. It was also clear that other parties would pass this way in similar or worse conditions. Spack-

man remained in Mosul with two officers and six other ranks, who were too ill to proceed to Ras-el-Ain.

The Turkish officer commanding the Mosul barracks, Bimbashi Umar Bey, was notable for his dilatory nature and absence, during which nothing was done. At this point Spackman knew no Turkish but managed with a little French, the lingua franca of the Middle East. He was also fortunate to meet Enver Pasha, the Turkish war minister, and was able to play on this "friendship" in the future to obtain concessions from Umar Bey. Almost 100 British soldiers died in a few weeks that summer. A small International Red Cross fund allowed the purchase of cooking pots, food, shoes and sandals.

Spackman also observed the difference between the Indian and British regiments as they came through. Several of the Indian regiments arrived under the command of their Havildars marching as formed units. Some of the British arrived half naked with puttees on their feet, having sold or lost their boots. Discipline broke down in some units, and one "bad hat" was bastinadoed for stealing a colleague's boot, which was tantamount to murder.[13]

Mosul possessed a single European restaurant, the Stamboul Locanta, run by an Italian, Enrico, with a French wife where the Turkish elite plus any transiting German officers ate, including Spackman. This at least gave him a touch of Europe in his captivity.

In May, Spackman also met with one Akbar, a Muslim soldier from the 48th Pioneers dressed in the uniform of a German follower. He asked why, and although Akbar professed his hatred of the Germans, he said,

> The desert is a bad place, many are dead, more dying from lack of food and care. A man must get back to the English before winter or die in misery over there. My Germans are going to fight the Russians at Ravandooz. It is better to ride back with them and wait one's chance than run away as a poor starving hajji to be robbed and beaten by Arabs or perhaps caught and hanged by the Turks. The Germans know that an Indian is the best cook between Stamboul and Singapore, so I have charge of their kitchen. Allah, in is mercy, has given me a poor understanding and, ... they sleep in the afternoons.[14]

Finally, in November 1916, the last two soldier patients left Mosul for Ras-al-Ain. Their physical condition was as well as could be expected, and Spackman arranged a lift on an Austrian lorry. The journey had killed hundreds of others, so this little act of Austrian kindness saved that pair of lives. Spackman was sent back to Baghdad on a *kelek*, a raft of poles on goat skins, the type that were mentioned in the days of Cyrus and by Xenophon.[15]

In Baghdad, Spackman was placed in the prisoner-of-war depot commanded by one Cassim Bey, an Arab "with a reputation for homosexuality and other venal vices but not hostile to the British."[16] One of his fellow prisoners was a Lawrence Eyres, an Oxford don serving as a private in the Dorsets retained for clerical duties, who was planning to escape. Spackman's repatriation papers were signed just before Christmas, but when Maude launched his offensive, that route out was effectively blocked. Eyres' escape plan now looked attractive.

By February it was clear that Maude's offensive was making headway, and on the 28th, the Tigris was suddenly full of local craft evacuating the German administrative staff ahead of the British arrival. Spackman and Eyres decided this was the night to make their bid for freedom, but the Turks moved them to a more fortified location with increased guards. Soon Spackman found himself back on the Mosul road again, this time without the train journey to Samarra. Feigning illness, he managed to get himself sent back to Baghdad where he failed to convince the doctors of any ailment. He was evacuated from Baghdad a third time, this time by train, on 3 March, a week before the British arrived.

Having marched from Samarra to Tikrit, a steamer was provided to Kalat Shergat, which was the navigable height of the Tigris. During the journey, Arabs would shoot at the steamer, without causing damage, but evidence that the local Arabs were as opposed to the Turk as to the Briton. For the next stage of the journey, Spackman and his guards were attached to a brigade of Turkish heavy artillery, which was en route to join von Falkenhayn's Yilderim Division on the Syrian front. The battery officers were Turks but the brigade staff were Germans and there was no love between the two. Spackman preferred the company of the Turkish officers who at least spoke French so there was a common language, unlike the Germans who spoke only German. The Turks lamented being placed under the command of Germans, while Spackman played on the common heritage between Britain and Turkey, especially their navies.

Once in Mosul they received news that Baghdad had fallen, and everyone seemed depressed. Many of Spackman's friends were absent, but Enrico cashed a check for him with which he was able to purchase supplies for the next leg to Ras-al-Ain. Fortunately a convoy of Austrian lorries was about to make that journey, which reduced a week's hard marching into one day. Sitting behind the driver's cab was not all that pleasurable, as he was suffocated by the swirling dust, and the skin was rubbed raw from him by the jolting. They passed through deserted Armenian villages with signs of recent cultivation where bodies had been thrown down wells to prevent reoccupation, and they heard other tales of massacres.

On the second day the convoy reached Ras-al-Ain, the terminus of the Berlin-Baghdad railway up to this point. It was no great railway terminus. The great long dusty camp was fly infested. The tracks ran a short way into the desert and then halted, as if too tired to proceed. Locomotives stood idly, and it appeared that their only purpose was to provide hot water for tea or coffee. There were dumps of stores everywhere. And sepoys. These were the survivors after a year of captivity. There were also gangs of Russian prisoners. Spackman stayed there

just long enough for news of his arrival to spread through the camp, and, as he was sitting in a carriage ready to depart for Aleppo, the 48th Pioneer's Quartermaster Havildar appeared at the window and threw in a blanket containing shirt, shorts, socks and a cooking pot. This was all followed by a large, raw fish!

Spackman was sent at first to Kutahieh camp, only to find out that it was a mistake as this was a Russian-only camp. He was made to feel welcome, unwisely played chess with them and comments that he does not remember being aware of the great revolution which was shaking Russia at that time. After three days he went on to Kedos camp by cart over the mountains.

Spackman arrived at Kedos on 27 April 1917, two days short of a year since Kut had fallen. The journey from Baghdad had taken eight weeks. There were no other prisoners, despite the camp having been completed for three months. The commandant was one Habib Nuri Bey, a lieutenant colonel of Albanian birth but ridiculous appearance:

> Below his military cap and shabby tunic, unbuttoned at the throat, he wore a pair of uniform trousers made for a much taller man, so that they fell like a concertina round his slippers. The sling of his sword was also too long so that the weapon's tip trailed on the ground and occasionally tripped him up! Often he would appear without his cap, his scrubby white hair testifying to its lack of recent acquaintance with a brush and comb. The town barber came to shave him twice a week. Later, when more officers arrived at the camp and his character was more closely observed, he was given the nickname "Dippy Dick" or more simply "Dippy."[17]

More officers arrived, some from the Baghdad fighting, others from Gaza. A check service was arranged through the American Express Company in Constantinople, and the townspeople provided various services.

The main battle was with Dippy and his subordinate, Ali. When an inspector, Colonel Yusuf Zia Bey, arrived to find the prisoners without furniture, he had planks and nails sent up from the town. Ali was sacked on the spot and Dippy was replaced by Edhem Bey, a considerable improvement.

The Turkish doctor in Kedos was old and useless, so Spackman performed minor surgery but without adequate instruments, drugs or dressings. There was no dentist. The nearest was at Ouchak, a day away, where it was also discovered that a number of French ladies were interred. There was a steady flow of dental conditions inspired by the prospect of some female company, until the dentist decided to visit Kedos once a week.

By Christmas there were about 100 officers at Kedos. Some of the transferees (including some Kuttites) were as a result of several successful escapes from Kastamuni including one by E.H. Keeling, who sailed across the Black Sea to Russia in the middle of the Revolution.[18] Spackman comments on the common theme of the slight chance of success being offset against the collective punishment which those who remained received. Paroles were given to the Turks in exchange for a promise not to escape from the town, which in turn allowed the prisoners a greater degree of freedom to develop a more comfortable existence. Musicians and actors (distinctly amateurish) and craftsmen flourished. There were educational and news-related lectures. Some of the more distinguished prisoners were Godfrey Elton, later Lord Elton and a noted historian; Leonard Woolley (later Sir) the famous archaeologist who excavated Ur; and John Alcock (later Sir), a Handley Page bomber pilot shot down over Turkey but who would, in 1919, be the first to fly the Atlantic with Whitten Brown.

A field club allowed members to roam the countryside and study the flora and fauna while others became beaters for the local elite when they hunted wild boar.

Then, unexpectedly, Spackman's exchange certificate, which he had received in Baghdad, was honored and he was sent to Smyrna to accompany other invalids. There, in the port, waiting for a steamer, he met Jones and Hill, fellow Kuttites, and sailed for Alexandria on 18 November 1918.

Lieutenant Henry Rich, 120th Rajputana Rifles (later Major General, CB)[19]

Rich spent the siege in Woolpress Village, the outpost of Kut across the Tigris. When Townshend surrendered at Kut, Rich just went and sat beside the river. A well-disciplined Turkish regiment with a French-speaking major took them into captivity. The last tin of biscuits was opened and some offered to him; in return he offered his prisoners coffee. The Rifles were moved to Shurman camp and issued Turkish army biscuits, six inches in diameter, two inches thick, which had to be smashed between stones, mixed with water and eaten as porridge.

Supplies were received from the British lines. It was the Christmas order, too much for the five surviving officers, who ate what they wanted and left the rest to the others.

The officers were separated from the men and moved by steamer to the cavalry barracks in Baghdad where they were paid, and then moved by train to Samarra. From Samarra, they marched to Mosul, where Rich remembers dining at a Greek restaurant, although it may have been the Stamboul Loccarno mentioned by Spackman, who spent several months there. Beyond Mosul was a further 200-mile march. There was one donkey between two officers and one orderly. Although the orderlies were later removed, one can speculate that these orderlies had a better journey than those who traveled without officers. Oddly, Rich says that he got fitter throughout the 200-mile march, which shows what could be achieved with the correct treatment and access to food.

From the railhead (Ras-al-Ain) they traveled by train, eventually reaching Kastamuni, where he was billeted in a house from which an Armenian family had been evicted.

As Rich knew some Turkish, he produced a "pass" for the Keeling escape, but as a result of the escape they incurred a "spite" (collective punishment) and were moved to another camp (possibly Kedos). The same issues of parole existed. Here, a British colonel collected paroles from the prisoners of war and threatened to name those who did not give their paroles to the Turks!

To obtain money, a Greek merchant agreed to accept checks until the end of the war. This seems to have been commonplace throughout the war, requiring a degree of trust as the checks would be in the name of British officers who would leave the country as soon as (if not before) the war was over. However, it may also have been a shrewd business move for turning Turkish pounds into pounds Sterling. Rich met the Greek merchant after the war and found that he had bought up some £8,000 worth of officers' checks, which could be redeemed for hard currency in the chaos of post-war Turkey. It also meant that the officers gained access to cash to buy necessities.

Rich made one attempt to escape, despite the disapproval of fellow officers. His group planned to go east, where they knew that Dunsterforce was operating in the Caspian region. They were free for eight days until being picked up in a Turkish village at night. They tried to bluff their way out by claiming to be Germans, but their guard had worked with Germans and knew the differences in the languages.

Rich was returned to Kastamuni to find that the entire escape group had been rounded up. From there, they were moved to the officers' prison in Constantinople, where he developed Spanish flu and was hospitalized.

When the armistice was announced, Rich and a group of freed officers took themselves to the train station and simply asked for a train to Smyrna.

Lieutenant E.H. Jones, Volunteer Artillery Battery, and Lieutenant C.W. Hill, RFC

Probably the most unusual escape attempt of any prisoner of war was that of Jones and Hill. Jones was a Kuttite whose account, *The Road to En-Dor*, commences in late February 1917 at Yozgad camp with the arrival of a postcard from "a dear aunt," which mentioned spiritualism. Over the next 18 months Jones and his accomplice Hill (an Australian pilot shot down over Syria) developed an entirely fraudulent "spiritualist" routine with Ouija boards and séances in a bid to escape. They did leave Turkey early: they were repatriated a fortnight before their colleagues. They also managed to control a prisoner-of-war camp to the benefit of the interred and thereby extract revenge.

Yozgad is described as a camp where the inmates had everything they wanted, except their freedom. There was an orchestra; a Christmas pantomime, *The Fair Maid of Yozgad*, which was preformed after the guards had gone to bed; a ski club in winter and a hunt club in the summer; and evening lectures provided on a diverse range of subjects including languages, sciences, how to operate a submarine, command an artillery battery, fruit farming in Kent, tea planting in Ceylon, campaigning on the North West Frontier, and the Jamerson Raid and capturing Pekin (Beijing). Jones recounts the sight of a raggedly dressed officer in a corner translating *Decline and Fall of the Roman Empire* into Urdu.

Yozgad was also the punishment camp to which failed escapers were sent. The "gamekeepers" were mostly old men with equally old weapons. They did not need any more. There were 350 miles of mountains, rocks and deserts surrounding it. These were the real guards. The only party to escape reached Cyprus in September 1918, and that was only by 9 of the original 27 escapees. The other guards were self-imposed. Following any escape, those who remained suffered a "strafe," a loss of privileges. The first escape of note was by Cochrane, Price and Stoker from Afion Kara Hissar camp in 1916. They were recaptured and sent to Yozgad. The remaining inmates at Afion Kara Hissar were confined to a church for six weeks without exercise as collective punishment. This process turned prisoners on each other. Hill was prevented from escaping in June 1917 by his fellow officers. Jones explains the mentality:

> The belief acted in two ways in preventing escapes. Some men who would otherwise have made the attempt decided it was not fair to their comrades in distress to do so. Others considered themselves justified, in the interest of the camp as a whole, in stopping any man who wanted to try. And the majority — a large majority — of the camp held they were right. The general view was that as success for the escaper was most improbable, the trouble for the rest of us most certain, nobody ought to make the attempt. For we know what "trouble" meant in Turkey. Most of the prisoners in Yozgad were from Kut-el-Amara. We had starved there, before our surrender: we had struggled, still starving, across the 500 miles of desert to railhead. We had seen men die from neglect and want. Many of us had been perilously near such a death ourselves. We had felt the grip of the Turk and knew what he could do. Misery, neglect, starvation and imprisonment had combined to foster in us a very close regard for our own interests. We were individualists, almost to a man. So we clung, as a drowning man clings to an oar, to the few alleviations that made existence in Yozgad possible, and we resented anything which might endanger those privileges.[20]

When Jones' attempts at spiritualism failed, he improvised. What started out as a bit of entertainment soon grew out of all proportion. He took known facts about the "sitter": prewar career, wartime posting, some fact from a half-forgotten conversation. Then the sitter was allowed to give himself away and the "conversation" developed. One strict rule was always obeyed; there could be no "conversations" with close family members.

In time, news of Jones' abilities came to the attention of the camp commandant, Bimbashi Kaizim Bey, who wanted to dis-cover hidden treasure from an Armenian who used to live in the town. Communications were always between Jones and the camp interpreter, known as the Pimple, who was universally disliked for pilfering the prisoners' parcels. A fellow prisoner informed the Pimple that Townshend had used Jones' skills at Kut, which explained why none of the Turkish attacks succeeded.

Jones and Hill were first tested to find something that had been lost. They directed Pimple to a pistol, which had been pre-buried for the purpose. When Jones and Hill were taken away, apparently in a state of exhaustion, Pimple and the commandant's cook continued to dig in the hope of greater treasures. When this was discovered, the "spook" was angry that his instructions had been disobeyed. Pimple and Cook were fearful of incurring the spirit's displeasure and begged for forgiveness. In this way, the prisoners began to control the prison.

Jones was invited to an interview with the commandant, an unheard-of occurrence. Jones was able to establish his control over the commandant by revealing what help was required: "You are going to ask me to find for you treasure, buried by a murdered Armenian of Yozgad. You want me to do so by the aid of Spirits. And you are prepared to offer me a reward." When the commandant revealed that this had to be conducted without the Turkish War Office knowing then the scene was set for blackmail in the event of an escape attempt, which would protect those who remained from a "strafe."[21]

The first stage was for Jones and Hill to concoct a trail with the commandant's full knowledge so that the commandant could place the pair in solitary confinement. The charge was communicating with the enemy through spiritualism. This was achieved despite the well-intentioned intervention of their fellow prisoners. Solitary confinement for the pair was in a house adjacent to the main prison accommodation. In doing so, the pair gained a house to themselves for the next stage in their plans and freed up space in the main prison. All of this was willingly provided by the commandant. When the pair were alone with the spook, the spook was able to manipulate the Turks into providing better food, firewood, lamp oil, servants, and even alcohol. These were all in short supply as the war progressed, or normally available to the prisoners at inflated prices.

The spook's achievements were not all selfish. When the commandant realized that his authorization for a hunt club broke the regulations, he sought the spook's advice on how to proceed. The spook convinced the commandant that if the prisoners were happy they would not try to escape, but if the promised hunt club was withdrawn they would become angry and attempt to escape. Therefore the hunt club should be allowed to continue, provided that the officers gave a parole not to escape while out with the hunt club. Furthermore, the more "privileges" which were granted to the prisoners which they could participate in "on parole," there would be fewer days when they were "off parole" and therefore they were less likely to escape. Not only did the spook save the hunt club, but he also laid the groundwork for more privileges. Johnston and Yearsley's *450 Miles to Freedom* called the hunt club "most useful" and "Some of the happiest recollections of our captivity are those glorious early morning in the country, far away from the ugly town which was our prison."[22]

The location of the buried Armenian treasure had been entrusted to three men, two of whom were also dead, but the spook could obtain directions. Two clues were revealed (both pre-buried while on ski club activities), and in the process photographic evidence of collusion between the camp staff and the prisoners was obtained. The holder of the third clue resided in Constantinople, but his business took him to Adalia, Tarsus, Alexandretta and Damascus, that is, on a route close to the Mediterranean Coast. The presence of the mountains blocked the thought waves to Constantinople, so the psychics and the camp officials would have to move. Constantinople was out of the question in case the War Office got wind, but a short holiday on the Mediterranean coast would provide the perfect excuse to visit a location from where they would be able to access the thoughts of the third man. From there, it would be a simple matter of drugging the camp staff, bundling them onto a boat and sailing for Cyprus.

At the last minute, the commandant got cold feet and abandoned the plan to find the treasure. Evidently, his current post was far too comfortable to risk losing for any amount of treasure.

Jones and Hill then implemented Plan B, which was to be certified insane and sent to a military hospital in Constantinople. Again this was undertaken with the full cooperation of the commandant. The British camp doctor (who was in on the ruse) refused to sign the pair as insane, but the local Turkish doctors were more than happy to, as it showed their superior knowledge in these matters over the British-trained doctor. All of this just added more weight to Jones and Hill's plan. The escape equipment that they left behind was used to good effect by the Cochrane group, who eventually reached Cyprus.

The two "lunatics," whose experiments with the occult had clearly taken their toll, set off for Constantinople accompanied by Pimple in April 1918. To keep up the ruse, a double suicide attempt was conducted, in which the Pimple's intervention was not as quick as they would have liked. In Constantinople, the pair had to maintain their "illnesses" for months without any mutual support under constant supervision (both overt and covert) from the Turkish military medical authorities and even the well-meaning wife of a Dutch embassy official. They were not even able to support one another without giving away their "game," even when Hill was genuinely ill with a severe bout of dysentery which was deliberately left unattended to see if it would break him out of his lunatic state. This very nearly killed him.

They did at least have their revenge on both the commandant and Pimple. The latter was persuaded to enlist, much to the delight of the Turkish War Ministry that they received a volunteer so late in the war. He was commissioned and survived the war. The location of the third "clue" was also revealed. Investigation in Yozgad revealed that it had already been found by "accident" by one of the prisoners who had kept a gold coin but discarded the "clue," which he could not read. Three months after Jones and Hill left Yozgad, on 7 August, the Cochrane group made their escape attempt. Verbal instructions had been left with the incriminating evidence of the camp staff's complicity with Jones and Hill. The instructions were misinterpreted to be applicable for any escape attempt, not just an attempt by Jones and Hill. The evidence was released prematurely. This increased the suspicions of the Constantinople medical military community into the "lunacy" of Jones and Hill, but the pair failed to break. It did result in the removal and court-martial of the commandant.

Hill was removed to the Haidar Pasha camp where he suffered further abuses to try and break him out of his lunacy, without success. He left there on October 10 for Smyrna where he took ship to Alexandria, Egypt. Jones' departure was delayed due to his pathological hatred of all things English (one of his symptoms), and it was feared he would commit suicide. He was able to take the following ship and rejoined Hill in Alexandria, free, a fortnight ahead of the "healthy" prisoners.

In Alexandria they met their fellow prisoners from Yozgad. Twelve fellow prisoners had died since they had left, including several good friends. The pair also had to explain the real aims behind their erratic behavior over the previous 18 months, including the senior British officers whom they had had to dupe. There were also "true believers" in spiritualism, converts of their duplicity, who simply would not or could not believe that it had all been a giant hoax.

Sergeant P.W. Long, Royal Artillery (Later Flight Sergeant, RAF, MM)

Long's account of his captivity is titled *Other Ranks of Kut* and is especially important, as it is the most detailed account of captivity from one of the other ranks. Although the officers' accounts do make mention of the other ranks, their removal in the first days following the surrender of Kut means that they did not experience and endure the hardships of the other ranks. Many of the officers did attempt to relieve these hardships, like Captain Spackman, above, but did not have to live through them. Spackman's account, for example, records only one death on the first leg of his journey from Samarra. In comparison with Long's journey, Spackman's was benign.

When the garrison at Kut surrendered, Long was in the hospital. News was brought to him by a friend, Joe Creswell, who would later die in a labor camp in the Amanus Mountains. He was placed aboard the "shot-riddled" *Julnar* to Baghdad, which at least saved him the horrors of Shumran camp, yet the *Julnar* stopped each day to bury the dead. At one stop, north of Az-izieh, Long went ashore with a party of officers as an interpreter while they bought fruit and fish, for which Long received some fruit, as he had no money of his own. He then sold his "British warm" jacket which, as it was May and getting warmer, he decided that he would not need, and received 3 shillings 8 pence, with which he was then able to buy a large portion of cooked fish from the crew. His ability to make himself useful and to sell his assets to purchase food is a key theme in Long's ability to survive the years ahead.

He described the remainder of the division, marching along the river bank, catching up with the *Julnar* at this point:

> No words can adequately describe the appalling misery of that scene. Here were men who had suffered and fought through the long months of the siege, although they were gradually starved, and were not fit to do a day's march, yet they were being driven across the pitiless wastes under a scorching sun, herded along by a brutal and callous escort of Arab conscripts. Limping and staggering along they all finally arrived, some of them being assisted along by comrades, who themselves were in dire need of assistance.[23]

Medical Officers went ashore to select a limited few who could join the *Julnar* and take the places of the dead. As the *Julnar* departed, there were pitiful, dejected faces on the banks of those who were too ill to continue, yet there was simply no more space to take them. The fortunate few told of the march:

> Some of the party had collapsed early in the march, suffering from dysentery and kindred complaints, and these had been tied by the wrists or ankles to the pommels of the escorts' saddles and literally dragged to death. Others had been clubbed or beaten as they stopped by the wayside to answer Nature's urgent call. Many were the horrible tales we listened to that day, and we began to wonder what fate awaited us on our arrival at Baghdad.[24]

Baghdad did bring one pleasant surprise, unveiled women leaning out of the balconies, smiling and waving, shouting *Bonjour* and "Good morning." Once off the *Julnar* and marching through the streets of Baghdad, the welcome was not so warm. Women, veiled or unveiled and tattooed, shrieked and spat at them. That night, they were woken by screams and found two of their colleagues, naked, beaten and bleeding. They had gone to the latrines (not unreasonable as they all had some ailment) when four Arabs had jumped them, robbed and beaten them. Their guards simply said not to go to the latrines at night and went back to sleep. Thereafter they went to the latrine naked so as not to invite robbery. The second night passed successfully, but on the third night the Arabs, realizing they needed a new tactic, stripped naked to enter the sleeping area and stole from the sleepers. Long took the decision to sell everything, including his blanket and boots, to raise money and at least get something for them before they were stolen. Others carried their kit, only to have it stolen or die before they could benefit from it.

Long observed Indian Muslim deserters. They were dressed in baggy black uniforms with a green Astrakhan fez and yellow braided badges of rank.[25]

After receiving a five-piaster note, worth 10 pence, his sole pay from the Turkish state during his captivity, Long joined a party which was crammed into goods wagons and traveled by rail to Samarra where they waited for some time.

The party made of 150 British, Indians and Russians left Samarra at dusk with an escort of one *onbashi* (corporal) and five private soldiers. Long was appointed *terjiman* (interpreter) and noticed that while there were five Turks at the head of the column there was only one at the rear. This last *askari* was armed with a whip with which to beat those who fell out to answer the call of nature or the stragglers, of which there were many, as none of the prisoners were fully fit at the beginning of the journey. Long had acquired a cudgel in imitation of the walking sticks adopted by the Indians. This particular *askari* quickly overstepped his mark, and when he approached Long, who was kneeling, Long knocked him off his horse and killed him with several more blows. Long informed the *onbashi* that the *askari* had been kicked by his horse and was lying unconscious, and without questioning or investigating, the surviving Turks simply rifled the saddlebags and proceeded without their fallen colleague.[26]

That night they rested at the village of Duer, but in the morning the prisoners reported that their kit bags had been cut open in the night and their belongings stolen. A guard was called, but he simply threatened to whip those who complained. There was no food in the village except what could be begged for, and there were already prisoners who were suffering. The *onbashi* offered Long a cigarette, and they discussed the British Army. Long was able to establish that the next leg to Tikrit was 25 miles. There were one or two British and four or five Indians who, it was clear, would not be able to make the next leg. Rather than take them on the journey and risk leaving them on the roadside, they were left in the care of the villagers of Duer. Their fate is unknown.

At Tikrit, the party was given flour and salt which had to be divided into national piles based on the group size, and the piles confirmed by national representatives (the Indians had a Muslim and Hindu representative) before being mixed with water and cooked over bracken, straw or dung fires into chapatis. Eight further sick were left at Tikrit. Again their fate is unknown.

The next stage was 25 miles to Kirkuk, but as the *obashi* did not know the way, they had to march by day. Not all of prisoners had water bottles, and even those who did had no means of refilling them. Nor did they see man or beast. After a few miles a Hindu soldier collapsed. A *naik* from his regiment asked to stay with him and catch them up later, but the *onbashi* would not allow it, and the soldier was left to die, alone, on the roadside.

At the village of Bisereria on the Lesser Zab, the Muslim

Indian soldiers began to alienate themselves from the other prisoners by begging and declaring themselves as "Islami, Islami," while the Gurkhas and Sikhs were ridiculed for their own religious beliefs which included wisps of hair or knots of hair respectively. While the British (and probably also the Russians) were prisoners who could be abused, they did at least belong to nations which were to be respected for their global prowess. The "native" troops were both prisoners and from nations subjugated by the British, which may have made it easier to abuse them with apparent immunity. An old Arab with whom Long talked taught him how to soft-boil eggs by placing them in the embers and waiting for them to "pop."

When the party reached Kirkuk there were only 100 prisoners left. They were told it was another two days to Mosul, which turned out to be a lie, but when at last they crested the ridge they found a verdant oasis before them after the dun dryness of the desert. They were not the only impoverished in Mosul. A group of Armenian women begged the commandant for daily sustenance and in return were given the menial jobs in the barracks.

After five days, a group of prisoners from the hospital joined the party. They recounted the horror of the Mosul hospital where scores of men had died from neglect as much as disease. As well as Kuttites, some of the men were from the Relief Force. The Muslim Indians had been separated from the others for preferential treatment and the Sikhs and Gurkhas had, again, been separated out for ridicule.[27] The prisoners did receive gifts of slippers and bags of raisins from "an English lady" in Mosul. Captain Spackman also mentioned gifts of slippers and raisins from an English lady in Mosul.

From Mosul, the prisoners climbed steadily. The weather became cooler as they climbed, and the appearance of the locals changed as they entered Kurdish villages. Long found that many of the Kurds understood Arabic, and there were common words with Hindi, which he also spoke. They also seemed much more easygoing than the Arabs, and it was clear that the women enjoyed equality with the men. The Kurds had no liking for the Turks and sympathized with the British, being friendly to them. Long had heard of the evil reputation of the Kurds but saw none of it.[28]

At Nisbin, the last town before the railhead at Ras-el-Ain, Long was taking the sick party to the hospital when he was surprised to meet a "huge negro, resplendent in the uniform of a German Sergeant-Major" who informed him that a party of Germans picnicking under a mulberry tree wished Long's group to join them. They were given bread rings, fruit, eggs and lemonade. In the hospital, Long noticed a group of bodies laid out, apparently dead, but he thought he recognized the tattoos on one of them. On closer investigation the "corpse" turned out to be alive. An orderly was called who brought a water bottle, innocent enough, but then the water was poured into the man's mouth until he choked to death. "Now he's dead, go, go" said the orderly.[29]

There was a final five days' marching to Ras-el-Ain, which at least saw the end of most of the marching, but the beginning of laboring on the railways. Fortunately, Long was not to stay there, which is just as well from his description:

> Nearly all of [the prisoners of war] were of the Kut garrison, and all were Indians of various races and religions other than Mohammedans. Their condition was truly pitiful they resembled animated skeletons hung about with filthy rags. No tents or other shelter had been provided, and they were living in holes in the ground, like pariah dogs. To the fanatical Moslem Turk anything was too good for *giours* (infidels), and those unfortunate Indians were being treated far worse than even the Arab treats his animals. Scores of them were too sick to move from their holes, and I saw men who were obviously dying, yet I was told that they received no medical attention whatever. I chatted to a few of those men, and as we talked the tears streamed down their faces. These were loyal soldiers of the British Empire, and it was awful to think that this was the end of their service of devotion. They told me that if anyone was too sick to draw his rations himself he had to go without, and the normal ration was so small that it scarce sufficed to keep alive those that were working, so that they had none to spare for the sick. Despite that they did share their rations, with the result that they all suffered together.[30]

Long moved on by rail and walking:

> So we arrived at Mamourie; ten Englishmen out of a party of one hundred and fifty Britishers, Russians, and Indians, to leave Samarah. Some had died by the wayside, other had been killed on the road, some have been taken away from us, and many too ill to continue.[31]

From there he and a "Sgt R," whom he had befriended since Samarra, were informed that they were to be sent to Bagtchi camp. Rather than endure more captivity, they decided to make a bid for freedom and make for Adana, the nearest town two days to the west. Totally unprepared and still tired from the march from Samarra, with Sgt R suffering from reoccurring bouts of malaria, the attempt was doomed from the beginning. They were fortunate to be taken in by a Kurdish family after a few days who cared for them while Sgt R recovered from a malarial episode, but a few days after setting off again they were captured by gendarmes who threw them into Adana civil prison.

After a few days in prison, they noticed a man in European dress accompanying a gendarme. Long assumed it was an American and shouted, "For God's sake get us out of here, we are Englishmen." When asked who they were, Long explained that they were escaped prisoners of war from Kut, but the reply came back, "Mein Gott." Long expected no help from a German, but he spoke with the gendarme and the pair were moved to a room holding three Turkish policemen in detention. Not only was it a conventional room compared with an Oriental prison, but that evening they were fed and received money from the Germans with which they could buy necessaries.[32]

Three days later an official arrived to take their details, and they were sent to the local doctor who sent Sgt R to the local hospital where there were, apparently, a lot of other British patients. Long was not ill enough to accompany the sergeant. Instead, he was taken to the main prison and placed in a hut of civilian prisoners, which included three Australians, more would-be escapees. These had already established a routine and soon arranged for a haircut and shave — using real soap — from the local barber.

Being a civil prison, the routine was different. Bread was provided, but all other foods were brought in by family members. The barber came daily, and a general shop was attached to the prison. Around the edge of the hut was a raised platform for sleeping on. Very few people knew what they were in prison for or the length of their sentence. At one end was a pair of Beys; one of them was serving a portion of a hundred-year sentence passed down to his father, which would probably be completed by his son. It was possible for the prisoners of war to get money through the American consul's agent.[33]

The Australians were returned to their camp, which left Long alone as the only English speaker, but otherwise life was comfortable until, after 16 days, one of the *chaoush* inquired after his health. Not suspecting anything, Long said he was well, thank you. He was invited into the middle of the hut and told to lie on his back. The hut went quiet as Long's feet were raised and a rifle sling twisted around them into a vicelike grip. He was bastinadoed — whipped on the soles of his bare feet — which was a painful punishment for a Turk used to walking barefoot, but unbearable for a European used to wearing footwear. He passed out, only to be woken by the *chaoush* with a cigarette, apologizing for what had happened, but he had been forced to do it.[34]

It would be weeks (Long is unsure of the length of time) until another English speaker entered the prison, another escapee, Corporal Dade of the Royal West Kents, by which time Long was so used to speaking Arabic or Turkish that he found it difficult to speak English without interjecting non–English words. About that time, bugs began to afflict Long and nothing he could do prevented bites. He asked to see the doctor, who diagnosed a contagious disease from several yards away and sent him to the Adana hospital.

The hospital was run by an American Doctor Haas, a Welsh Matron Miss Davies, and English-speaking untrained Armenian nurses. Long was scrubbed and shaved, and his clothes were burned before he was allowed into the crisp linen of the hospital ward where Sgt R was still a patient. Unfortunately, Sgt R died a few days after Long rejoined him. Most of the patients were from Kut, working on the railway at Bagtchi camp where the conditions were so bad that even the Turkish authorities became alarmed. Despite this, there were very few medicines and consequently little that the hospital could offer most of the patients apart from making their last days comfortable. A Turkish medical officer visited the hospital and se-

lected those who were fit enough for Afion Kara Hissar camp. Most did not make it. After a second party was dispatched, the remaining patients were moved to the American Mission to free up beds for Turkish patients. There they found members of the first party who had not made it very far before collapsing. Long spent Christmas 1916 in Adana, but he was eventually sent to Afion Kara Hissar.[35]

In the camp, Long and five others were allocated to a house where they were confined for the first five days. On the sixth day they were allowed an hour's exercise on the road outside before being confined in the house for a further four days. On the second day, they received a strange visit from a Cypriot *terjiman* to the commandant, Musloum Bey, who took each to the window, inspected them and then announced to the guard, "No one." The answer to this strange behavior was revealed later when it was explained that Musloum Bey had a reputation for committing "unnatural practices" on younger members of the Kut garrison.[36]

After the enforced isolation, the six were allowed to meet the other other-rank prisoners, who were billeted in an Armenian church. For a short while, Long was a batman in an officer's house. He was able to see how well the officers lived in comparison with the other ranks. The officers clearly had the means to make their lives more comfortable so that no matter how difficult their existence was, it was not as bad as what the other ranks experienced. Long was keen to make the point that his observations were not churlish but an assessment of the realities of life.[37]

Long was selected to move through several work camps with Corporal Dade from Adana until Injilli, from where the pair decided to make a bid for freedom. On this occasion, they were able to stockpile two weeks' food stocks. They made their way to Entilli camp, where they were put up for a few days. They then planned to make for Aleppo in three days and then on to the Palestine front, but after a debate they decided to retrace their steps and make for Adana and Miss Davies. However, when they stumbled into a sentry and were asked who they were, Long's Turkish let him down. He answered "*bashi bazouk*" which he thought meant "civilian" but actually meant "bandit." In order to avoid admitting to being escaped prisoners of war, they kept up a pretence of being Americans making their way to Mamourie station for work, which is where they were sent, and they worked in the coal sheds. For their next break for freedom, they waited for a night train to pass and made a dash into the undergrowth disguised by the noise, towards Adana again.

They entered the village of Osmania, hungry, not expecting it to be a garrison town, but it was, and the pair decided to surrender. Unlike their previous unpleasant encounters, when their surrender was accepted by a colonel, they were offered food and iced water and accommodation:

> To say that we were amazed is to put it very mildly. Here was a Turk of all Turks; kind and considerate, and able to appre-

ciate our condition as unfortunate soldiers. What a pity there were not more of his sort in the Turkey of those days.[38]

The recruits in the barracks were even instructed to be respectful to the "English sergeants." Long wrote to Miss Davies, who replied that she would be in great danger if it was known she was helping escaped prisoners. She also chided him for attempting to escape again.

Corporal Dade succumbed to typhus and went to the hospital. Long was left alone again in a non–English-speaking environment. In his boredom, Long noticed that the bolts of the recruits' rifles were only halfway in and held in place by string. He examined the rifles and bolts and found that they were of Russian origin and the Turks had been unable to decipher the serial numbers to place the correct bolt to rifle. He developed a system so that the bolts and rifles could be relocated if mixed up, and each rifle had its correct place in the rack. The recruits commanding officer held up Long as an example to the recruits:

> This English soldier is our prisoner now, but he has not forgotten that he is still a soldier and his example is a good one for you all to follow.[39]

Then, suddenly, with Corporal Dade recovered, it was announced that they were leaving Osmania. They traveled by rail to Aleppo passing stations associated with the former escape attempts, the Amanus tunnel, "that monument to the British slaves who died in its construction"[40] and then on to Nisbin. The railway had reached Nisbin although the railhead had only advanced 20 miles beyond Ras-el-Ain. At the railhead, by chance Long met a *bimbashi* who had been in the American Mission at Adana which opened up opportunities, including being accommodated with the other "English."

Each station was a blockhouse so that in the event of attack, the garrison could barricade itself inside with loopholed walls and flat-topped, crenulated roofs. All desert stations were planned like this. The attackers were likely to be Arab tribes, and the senior rank there, a sergeant from the Worcesters, had organized the defense of the camp by manning a machine gun from the roof. The Turkish soldiers had looked to him for leadership, and he had been awarded a medal.[41]

At Nisbin, Long and Dade were allocated to the carpenter's shop for the construction of two railway bridges, one over the Jag-Jag River and the second over a canal. Although the company was German, and there was a large German military presence for the forward transport of material from the railhead to the front line, the large number of British and Indian prisoners there allowed a number to rise to positions of some importance. This presented many opportunities to pilfer and sabotage at the enemy's expense. There were also Russian and Romanian prisoners as well as Armenian and Kurdish refugees.[42]

Long and Dade's task to build two bridges required wood of a size which was not available in the country. They planned to sabotage it by carefully sabotaging the timbers. This had to be done in such a way that the bridge would stand, but would not withstand the first train. But it had to be undertaken so that no blame could be attached to them, or they would certainly face death. An unexpected torrential downpour flooded out the camps of the various groups of prisoners and refugees, and also the bridge. Search parties were sent out to recover the timbers for inspection, but they had long since disappeared. No doubt an Arab tribe had pilfered the timbers for their own use.[43]

Long spent a brief period working on a house for a company official and his wife. During this time there were many further adventures with local bandits; they also drew supplies from the company's stores and sold them to the locals, they lived and worked with a party of war-disabled German craftsmen, and they built the coffin for the burial of Sergeant Major Leach, 1/4th Hampshires, and a key figure in the lives of the Kuttites. Long was then summoned back to the Jag-Jag.[44] He and Dade planned another escape. It was now 1918. This time the objective was to reach the British lines north of Baghdad.

This escape attempt was for eight personnel with six weeks food and was properly planned with compasses and water skins. They even acquired pistols and ammunition for the hostile Bedouin they were sure to meet. Food was prepared and dried. The party of four Britons and two Indians set off, but the expedition did not get off to a great start. There was a stream to cross and it rained, so everything and everyone was soaked. The following day they were able to dry out, but finding water became a problem. By marching at night to avoid detection it became more difficult to find water. The ground was rougher than expected which made the going slower than planned. Unfortunately, the first day they changed to daytime marching, they ran into a gang of Arabs, desert rats, which in 1918 meant ragged, dirty Arabs, not Bedouin.

They tried, and failed, to outrun the mounted Arabs. When they were fired upon, the escapees reluctantly drew their revolvers, but the ammunition proved to be duds, probably from the soaking it received early in the escape attempt. Unable to resist, the party were robbed of everything apart from their clothes, water skins and enough food to reach the next village.

After three further days without finding fresh water, the party stumbled upon a Bedouin encampment: if they were not hospitable, at least they did not rob them anymore. Attempts at bribery for taking them to the British lines failed. All they would offer was directions to the Tigris.

After a fight with another group of Arabs, the escapees became separated, so Long and Dade pushed on together until they reached a stream they took to be the Tigris, and then they followed that downstream for three days. They came across an Arab encampment, which now accepted them. At first Long pretended to be a German working for the company, but the sultan had been to Baghdad and knew the difference in the languages. Nevertheless, he lauded all the things that the British possessed in Mesopotamia and decided that the Germans would soon be finished. They traveled with this part of the Shammar tribe for some days but then had to strike out on their own. Several days later they met another group of Arabs who decided that they were deserters and immediately handed them over to the Turkish authorities. They were passed on to a ration depot, which Long recognized as Kalat Shergat near the Tigris. So close, yet so far.[45]

The pair traveled to Mosul with a party of sick *askari*, where they were reunited with the majority of the other escapees. From Mosul, they were allocated a guard. The guard commander, an old *yuzbahsi*, informed them that he had been captured at Qurna in 1914 and had only just been repatriated from India. He wished he was still in India![46] They were able to obtain a lift in a German lorry for the last 35 km to Nisbin where they were harangued by the commandant. At the same time he was dealing with another group of would-be escapees who, inspired by the long absence of Long's group, made a similar attempt, but that lasted just 24 hours.

Long's next "posting" was to Ghir Ghiro, a two-day, 50-mile walk to a camp where there were only 10 other Britons. He worked as a carpenter for two weeks before being recommended for an accountant's job, as he spoke Arabic and could communicate with the Bedouin who brought in the food for the camp. This was an opportunity to exploit the company for the benefit of himself and the Bedouin. In late summer, Spanish flu spread though Turkey, which laid Long low, as was mentioned by Rich in Constantinople.

All of the prisoners from Ghir Ghiro were marched to Mosul where the rumor was that they were to dig trenches. The prisoners decided that they would do no such thing. After a day of inactivity, they were marched back to Ghir Ghiro. Something big was happening, but the prisoners were at a loss to know what it was. They were then marched another two days to Nisbin where they discovered that the Germans were packing up to leave. A trainload of Germans with their possessions was held up by Kurds, ransacked, and the Germans stripped naked. The Turkish commandant made himself scarce, and several of his less pleasant guards were beaten up.

A train was laid on to take the prisoners to Aleppo, but when it ran out of fuel 20 miles short of their destination, they were told to get off and walk. The prisoners had other ideas and ripped off doors and seats to provide the fuel for their journey. They rested in Aleppo for two or three days and received some pay. In the best traditions of the British Army, they went on a "bender." There was a further train journey to Homs, then lorry to Tripoli, steamer to Taranto in Italy and train to Calais, where they had to wait for a channel storm to abate before crossing to Calais, train to Canterbury and finally repatriation to their homes.

No more listening to Turks shouting "Yellah, yellah."

Summary

Of the above abbreviated histories, only Townshend's needs commentary. His position and action in captivity had political implications. His attempts to create a future career and to rewrite his career from his arrival in Mesopotamia need some explanation.

The remainder of the Kuttites survived as best they could while they watched their comrades murdered, abused, neglected and wasting away. Their accounts speak for themselves and I have only commented when one account overlaps with another.

11

Dunsterforce, Late 1917–October 1918

Of all the British imperial adventures, Dunsterforce is arguably the most unusual and bizarre. There were a great many expeditions launched into outlandish parts of the world with limited contact with the Western world. Dunsterforce was launched with the backdrop of the Great War; through a neutral power with an ineffective central government; across lands which had been ravaged by Ottoman and Russian armies, bandits and revolutionaries; through starving civilian populations; into the maelstrom of revolutionary Russia to fight local indifference, Turkish armies and freed German and Austro-Hungarian prisoners of war. The means to achieve these aims would be small military training teams raising local recruits and turning them into forces that could resist the battle-hardened Ottomans, Russians, Germans and Austrians.

The aim of Dunsterforce was to counter a modified version of the pre-war German aim to dominate the Near East. With the fall of Baghdad, any hope of reviving the Berlin-Baghdad scheme was dead. The modified plan was now further north: Berlin-Baku-Bokhara.[1] Baku was an oil-rich port on the western shore of the Caspian Sea which was joined, by rail, to Bantum on the Black Sea. From the Black Sea there were links by sea to the Ottoman and Austro-Hungarian empires. Across the Caspian Sea, the port of Krasnovodsk was the terminus of a railway line heading eastwards towards Bokhara. This city is located in modern-day Uzbekistan, which lies to the north of Afghanistan. This route would have provided the link to the North West Frontier of India which various exponents had failed to establish through Mesopotamia and Persia.

Baku would also have given the Germans access to one of the largest oil deposits being exploited at that time. The Caucasus region was also mineral rich and a large producer of wheat and cotton.

The extent to which these "plans" could be substantiated was slight to say the least. General Marshall in Baghdad called them "bogies." However, there was sufficient momentum to dispatch troops to yet more obscure and remote locations.[2]

Dunsterforce was intended to reach Tiflis, sitting midway between Bantum and Baku on the railway. The town was believed to be defended by only a handful of Armenian troops. The only possible route to this region was via Baghdad, but it was 800 miles to Baku. It was simply not practical to send a force to Baku that could hope to stem the Turko-German advance: it was hoped, however, that a team of specialists would be able to stiffen the resolve of the defenders.

There was, of course, no guarantee that Dunsterforce would be welcomed. Over the winter of 1917-1918, it was still possible that the Germans would win the war. With Russia out of the war, German, Austro-Hungarian and Turkish resources could be turned against Italy, France and Syria/Mesopotamia. How would the Allies fare in the face of this renewed onslaught? Mesopotamia had suffered following the release of Turkish troops form Gallipoli; the British had only been able to fight their way out of Egypt in 1915-1916 with great effort and the support of the Arab Revolt; the Italians had collapsed at Caporetto; the Allies on the Western Front had failed to break the German trenches; and the Americans were not fully in the war yet.

The event which opened up the possibility of this northerly route was the collapse of the Imperial Russian Army throughout late 1917. In the summer, the Russian line extended from South Russia, through the Caucasus, the Caspian and into northwest Persia down to the British in Mesopotamia. Throughout the autumn, the Russian line collapsed as regiments decided, en masse, to go home.[3]

The man selected for this task was Major General Lionel Dunsterville. He had attended the United Service College with Rudyard Kipling and is believed to be the inspiration for Stalky in his 1899 novel, *Stalky & Co.* Although he would ultimately command about 1,000 British, Imperial and Commonwealth troops, in January 1918 when he arrived in Baghdad he commanded just 12 officers and 41 men with which to cover the 300-mile front abandoned by the Russians. Several Imperial Russian officers joined Dunsterforce, and it was hoped that at least some of the Russian forces in Persia could be persuaded to serve in Dunsterforce.[4]

To get to Tiflis, Dunsterforce had to pass through neutral Persia. Nominally neutral but with a weak, ineffectual central

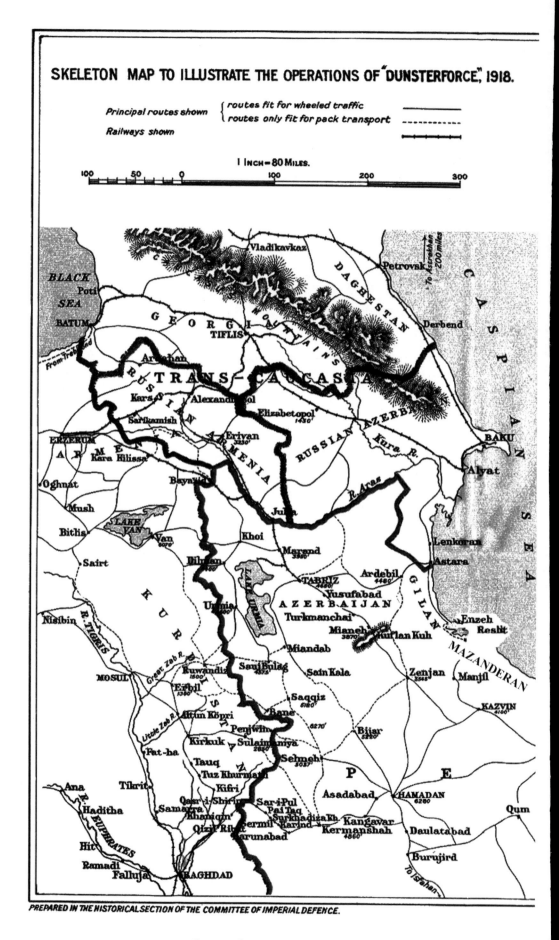

SKELETON MAP TO ILLUSTRATE THE OPERATIONS OF "DUNSTERFORCE", 1918.

PREPARED IN THE HISTORICAL SECTION OF THE COMMITTEE OF IMPERIAL DEFENCE.

Above and opposite: Area of Operations of Dunsterforce — General

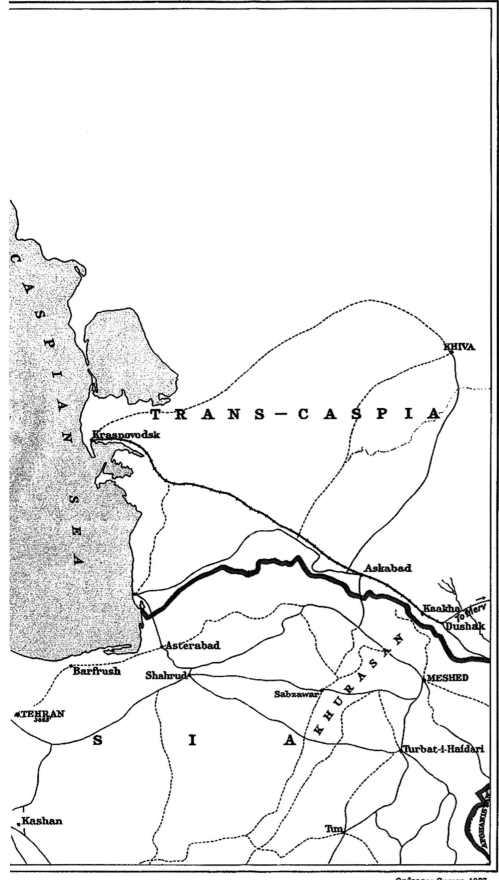

CASPIAN SEA

KHIVA

TRANS-CASPIA

Krasnovodsk

Askabad

Kaakha
To Merv
Dushak

MESHED

Asterabad

Barfrush

Shahrud

Sabzawar

KHURASAN

TEHRAN

S   I   A

Turbat-i-Haidari

Kashan

Tun

Ordnance Survey, 1927.

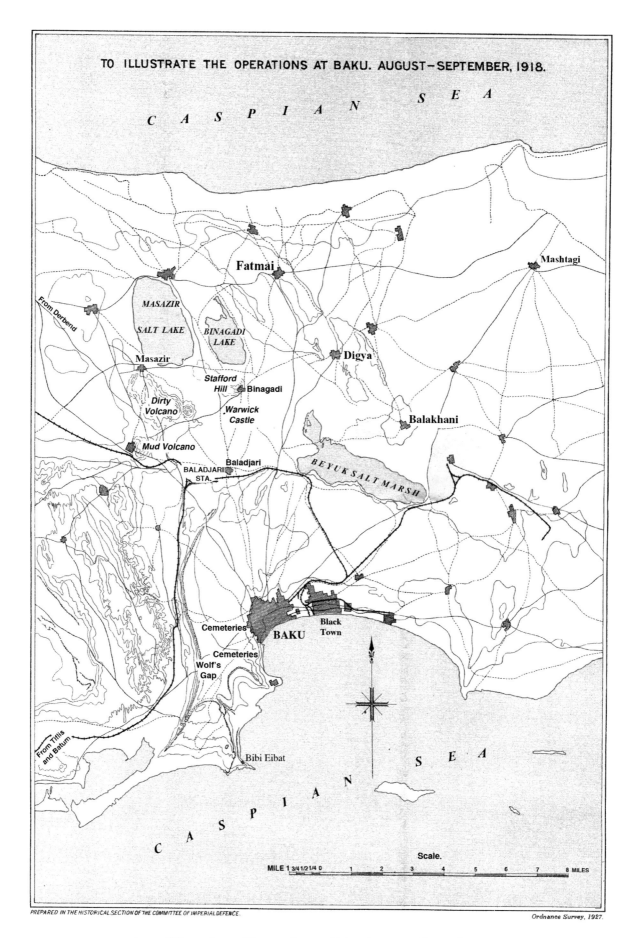

TO ILLUSTRATE THE OPERATIONS AT BAKU. AUGUST—SEPTEMBER, 1918.

C A S P I A N   S E A

From Derbend

Fatmai

Mashtagi

MASAZIR
SALT LAKE

BINAGADI
LAKE

Digya

Masazir

Stafford
Hill

Binagadi

Dirty
Volcano

Warwick
Castle

Balakhani

Mud Volcano

Baladjari

BALADJARI
STA.

BEYUK SALT MARSH

Cemeteries

BAKU

Black
Town

Cemeteries

Wolf's
Gap

From Tiflis
and Batum

Bibi Eibat

C A S P I A N   S E A

C

Scale.

MILE 1 3/4 1/2 1/4 0   1   2   3   4   5   6   7   8 MILES

PREPARED IN THE HISTORICAL SECTION OF THE COMMITTEE OF IMPERIAL DEFENCE.

Ordnance Survey, 1927.

Area of Operations of Dunsterforce — Baku, August to September 1918 government incapable of defending its borders, Persia during the Great War had been fought over by Russian and Ottoman armies in the northwest. Along the Persian Gulf, the British had intervened to secure their interests against German intrigue. In the east, an Anglo-Russian cordon breached Persian neutrality to prevent German agents from reaching Afghanistan. Finally, Persia was the center of much intrigue by Germany as it attempted to destabilize the British position in India and Mesopotamia. In "normal" warfare, breaches of neutrality should be avoided. When a sovereign state is incapable, or unwilling, to secure its territorial integrity from exploitation by a belligerent power, the opposing belligerent power will adopt an appropriate stance to counter the threats.

Entering Persia was no easy task. The mountains were high, the roads difficult, and snow blocked the passes. Dunsterforce had to be self-sufficient. The initial party required four cars and 36 vans. On 24 January 1918, part of Dunsterforce, with an armored car under Lieutenant Singer as escort, set off for Hamadan with Dunsterville, and the remainder left Baghdad three days later. The route was not easy, and a good speed was 10 mph. The convoy reached the village of Pai-Taq three miles below the watershed of the Taq-i-Giri Pass on the Ottoman-Persian border. There, sitting on the edge of a cliff, Dunsterville found a Hampshire on guard. This route, which had seen Medes and his Persians traveling from Persia to Babylon, was now being watched over by a lad "from the kindly Hampshire downs."[5]

Finally, on 3 February, Dunsterville reached Kermanshah, which would be his base for the remainder of the year. In Kermanshah, the British consul, Colonel Kennions, and the manager of the Imperial Bank of Persia, and their wives, were the unsung heroes of the war who had "kept the flag flying" despite provocation from the Turks. There were also French and Russian consulates, the American Mission and a force of Cossacks under Colonel Bicherakoff.[6]

On 7 February, Dunsterville traveled over to Hamadan to meet the British consul and bank manager, and General Baratoff, formerly commander of the Russian forces in Persia and now with the unenviable task of trying to get a revolutionary army out of Persia to Enzeli on the Caspian Sea and then on ships home to Russia. From there, Dunsterville moved on to Karvin, where again the bank manager was hospitable, even if the townspeople were not, and from where it was possible to consult with Sir Charles Marling, the British minister in Tehran. In Karvin, Dunsterville learnt that the local powers were opposed to his further movement. Mirza Kuchik Khan, leader of the Gilanis, working in conjunction with a Bolshevik Committee in Enzeli, did not want Dunsterville's presence in their areas of interest: the Bolsheviks because they thought that the British wanted to prolong the war; the Gilanis (or "Jangali" because they came from the jungles of northwest Persia) because they feared that, having thrown off the Russians, the British would now occupy the area. The "Gilan" movement

was perhaps easiest summed up as "Persia for the Persians" or a militant "Young Persian" movement, although they took advantage of German and Austrian advisors and Turkish equipment. Dunsterville was dismissive of the aims of such revolutionary idealists as Kuchik, but the effect was to derail the Tiflis' plan.[7]

Dunsterville's answer was bluff, and despite Kuchik's threats that they would not pass and the visible presence of his men on the roadside, the column passed on to Resht, the town before Enzeli. At Resht, they met the British and Russian consuls and the bank manager to discuss the situation in Enzeli. They were subsequently taken prisoner by the Gilanis and suffered at their hands until they effected their escape. Such was the price of "flying the flag."[8]

The Bolshevik Committee at Enzali had nationalized everything, with the possible exception of the customs, which were, in common with the whole of Persia, run by the Belgians, in this case a M. Hunin. Mdm. Hunin played the role of the hostess. Everyone knew that Dunsterforce needed shipping to cross to Baku. It became clear from the outset that that was not going to happen. Indeed, Dunsterville was now in the middle of a petty politics game between the revolutionary committees in Enzali and Baku, and Kuckik's Young Persians. While Dunsterville played them at their own game, there was also the risk of being trapped in Enzali without being able to go forwards or backwards. There was the possibility of remaining in Enzali, making friends with the local revolutionary committee and attempting to advance British policy there, but that would mean becoming a Bolshevik and that was a step too far. Before dawn on 20 February, Dunsterforce slipped out of Enzali to run the Gilani gauntlet back to Hamadan.[9]

The retirement of Dunsterforce through northwest Persia was accompanied by rumors of their failure and the reason for it. With access to the telegraph system, Dunsterville was able to obtain instructions from London on what to do now that the route to Tiflis was blocked. The reply was to watch the Persian situation and take advantage of any opportunities which presented themselves.[10]

Dunsterforce then set up an intelligence network. In Baghdad, a camp was established for the "Hush-Hush Army," which would reinforce Dunsterville and provide a more robust formation with which to return to Enzali. At the end of March, thirty rifles of the 1/4 Hampshires arrived, accompanied by the first aircraft from Baghdad. As nobody had seen an aircraft before, this single asset was a great boost to their prestige.[11]

In the meantime, Persia was in the grip of famine. Dunsterville gave three reasons for this. The harvest of 1917 had been a bad one due to the war and weather. The demands of the Turkish and Russians armies had consumed so much extra wheat. Thirdly, the Persian landowners and grain dealers contrived to keep the prices artificially high and so out of the reach of some 30 percent of the population. Cannibalism was suspected, and investigations by the civil authorities uncovered a number of offenders, all female, who were then stoned to death. Rumor was rife that children left unattended were being snatched and eaten. In the absence of any effective civil government, the only agencies trying to provide famine relief were the Imperial Bank of Persia and the American Mission. Into this came the British Army. Dunsterville asked for, and got, £20,000 per month for famine relief. Martin Donohoe, and probably many after him, threw their army biscuits from their vehicles to the starving as they drove past or donated a half tin of potted meat to a starving mother and her child. The British consul in Hamadan calculated that 200 were dying daily, with the dead lying unburied in the street. The Shi'ite imam who buried the paupers recorded 160 daily in the first fortnight of May 1918.[12]

A combination of naivety and lack of experience hampered the best intentions. Tickets were printed with the intention that one laborer would receive a ticket for a day's work for which they were paid three krans. The first problem was crowd control, with some 6,000 laborers all rising at once for a ticket. To get around this problem, the consul and prominent citizens allocated the tickets, but it soon became clear that the tickets were being sold for one kran, so that the laborer only gained two for his day's work. Knowing that an extra £400 per day was entering the local economy from the British, the price of bread went up as those who were able profited at the expense of the poor. The cooperation of the Imperial Bank was essential to maintain the flow of cash. To counter this scam, payment was later made partly in cash and partly through a soup kitchen. One ruse which succeeded was a telegram, sent in clear, informing the British that a large supply of grain had been dispatched from Baghdad for Hamadan. Fearing a collapse in the price, the merchants who had been withholding the grain rushed to release it and normal prices were realized.

Ensuring that work was undertaken was another predicament. Dunsterforce was not large enough to supervise this scheme. On the first day, many men were simply too weak to do anything but pretend to work, and at the end of the day, some lay dead. But with a relief scheme in place, albeit by no means perfect, the means to acquire food was provided, deaths were reduced and the local roads were improved.

Towards the end of April 1918, a squadron of the 14th Hussars arrived, and the appearance of the first blossoms heralded the end of winter and the opening of the passes.[13]

At the same time, news was brought from Baku that suggested that the inhabitants were tiring of the Bolshevik government, lead by an Armenian, Stepan Shaumian. In April, as a result of disarming troops returning from Persia, fighting had broken out in the town resulting in the destruction of part of the Muslim Tartar area of Baku. Not a single significant building remained. The result was to increase the existing animosity between the two groups. In the event that the Turks took Baku, the Armenians could expect to be on the receiving end of revenge attacks. The scheme proposed was for the

British to provide leadership and organization to the defenders of Baku, but no British soldiers. Dunsterville made it clear that he had no troops, nor could he promise that any would be sent from Baghdad. Dunsterforce remained weak, with its forces dissipated across more and more of northwest Persia attempting to fill a void with mostly bluff, discipline, and the judicious application of a handful of modern weapons systems.[14]

Dunsterville left Hamadan for Kasvin on 1 June 1918. The Tiflis plan was now dead (in any case, the British Mission had evacuated Tiflis following the approach of German forces through the Ukraine), but similar aims could be achieved by taking Baku: the rail links from the Caucasus to Central Asia would be blocked and the oil deposits denied to the Turks. He expected to concentrate in Kasvin around the 12th of the month sufficient troops to implement his plan:

- 14th Hussars
- 8 armored cars
- A mobile column of:
  - 1/4th Hampshires
  - 1/2nd Gurkhas
  - 2 mountain guns
  - 500 Ford vans
- No. 8 Battery, Royal Field Artillery

Acquiring sufficient petrol for so many vehicles was problematic, but it was achieved. A far greater problem was keeping so many vehicles on the road after such a long journey over poor roads. By the time they reached Kasvin, less than half of the vehicles were operable.[15]

The first obstacle was Kuchik Khan's Gilani army which had dug in around the Manjil Bridge. He commanded some 2,500 entrenched infantry, lacking artillery but with ample well-sited machine guns, on both sides of the bridge. Theoretically, this was a strong position. Colonel Stokes, Intelligence Department, spent two days at Kuchik Khan's headquarters near Resht trying to persuade him not to oppose Dunsterforce but "finding himself unable to induce the Jangalis to see the folly of their ways," and knowing Dunsterville's timetable, he left and continued on his way to Enzeli.

On 11 June, Dunsterville concentrated some 1,000 Cossacks (artillery, infantry and cavalry) under Bicherakoff, with a squadron of the 14th Hussars, two armored cars and two airplanes. At dawn the following day, Dunsterville and Bicherakoff set off. The airplanes flew over the Gilani positions with orders not to fire on or bomb their positions until the Gilani intent was known—Dunsterville suspected that the whole affair was just for show. He was to be proven wrong when the Gilanis fired, ineffectually, at the airplanes.

Two and a half miles before the bridge was a low spur with a hairpin bend. Although it was not possible to see the bridge—it lay between steep cliffs so was only visible from close up—this position dominated the Gilani positions and should have been held in force. It was not. A few troops were positioned on the spur, but they withdrew without providing any resistance, and the Cossacks took possession — Bicherakoff waved his walking stick at them and they fled.

The German commander, von Passchen, arrived to parley. He offered to let the Cossacks through but not the British. Bicherakoff was "overcome with the impertinence of the proposition," and replied to the effect:

> I do not recognize a German officer as a representative of Kuchik Khan, and I consider your appearing before me in German uniform as a piece of insolence. I want no terms from the Jangalis, and intend to open fire as soon as you get out of the way.

Meanwhile the artillery had deployed on the spur. The Cossack cavalry and Hussars moved forward into the open on the Gilanis' right, the Cossack infantry extended across the plan and the armored cars proceeded down the road against the Gilanis' left. The Gilanis were soon seen evacuating their trenches to cross the bridge, but the armored cars got there first and cut many of them off from their escape. The collapse in morale spread across the bridge. The machine-gunners fled without firing a shot, chased by the cavalry, while the infantry formed up across the bridge. Thus ended the Battle of Menjil Bridge, with "trivial" losses to Dunsterville or Bicherakoff.[16]

This did not mean that the road to Enzeli was open and peaceful. Lieutenant Colonel Matthews of the 1/4th Hampshires commanded a mobile column of 800 rifles from his regiment and the Gurkhas, two mountain guns and the armored cars. With this he had to dominate 50 miles of road through mountains and jungles. They acquitted themselves well but not without loss. On 18 June, for example, a detachment of the Hampshires was ambushed in which Captain Durnford was killed and six others wounded before the attackers were driven off. A month later, a determined attack was made on the British-garrisoned town of Resht. There were 450 Hampshires and Gurkhas, two mountain guns and two armored cars to hold a town with a seven-mile perimeter. The main attack came from the south and was repulsed, but a secondary attack succeeded in reaching the British consulate with a defense force of just 20 rifles. Reinforced, just in time (the narrow streets negated the speed of the armored cars), the consulate was saved and the Gilanis withdrew, but there would be another two days of street fighting before the town was cleared of the attackers. In the aftermath, a military governor was appointed to replace the Persian governor, who had fled the fighting.

The result of this final action at Enzeli was the final opening of the road to the Caspian Sea, five months after Dunsterville first reached Persia. The major towns along the road were also in British hands, with the exception of Enzeli itself. The road itself had been built by the Russian Road Company under a concession from the Persian government, from Hamadan to Enzeli, and from Tehran to Kasvin. There were tollhouses every 30 miles, and the road was accompanied by telephone and telegraph lines. Dunsterforce leased the road from the company. This allowed the road to continue to function as a going concern (including paying salaries to staff and issuing dividends to the shareholders) instead of being nationalized, which, from Dunsterville's experiences in the Caspian Sea area, resulted in a complete collapse of all normal economic and commercial activities.[17]

Dunsterville reached Enzeli on 27 June to discuss further operations with Bicherakoff. The latter had decided to convert to Bolshevikism as this was the only way for him and his army to reach the Caucasus. The Bolsheviks were elated at this conversion, and he was offered command of the Red Army, which he accepted. However, he was cautious enough not to ship his Cossacks into Baku. He sailed instead for Alyat, 50 miles south of Baku, astride the Tiflis railway. From here, he could keep his force separate from the Bolshevik authorities and work in cooperation with those elements of the Red Army actually in the field. This proved to be a wise choice. When Dunsterville reached Baku, he was constantly frustrated by late-night debating and the issuing of countless revolutionary decrees when action was needed to repel the Turks.

The Red Army was supposed to muster 10,000 men. Dunsterville, characteristically dismissive, counted revolutionary soldiers for nothing: "if they really had been soldiers and had had any fight in them the plan evolved by Bicherakoff should have been successful." Opposing the Red Army was the 12,000-strong Turkish Caucasus-Islam Army. This was composed of about half Turkish regulars and half levies from the local Muslim peoples. Their advance from the Tiflis direction towards Baku was hampered by shortages of railway engines, rolling stock and fuel. It was further hampered by Germans in Tiflis who were, according to Dunsterville, opposed to their allies capturing Baku: "They had a private arrangement with Lenin, and through him with the Baku Government, that the town should be peacefully handed over to them. To see the Turks in Baku would be almost as bad as to see the British there." Into this confusion was added the personal attitudes of the Russians themselves. Russian officers fought with the Turks to keep the Germans out of Baku and to fight the Bolsheviks; they also served with Dunsterforce and the Bolsheviks to keep the Germans out of Baku.[18]

On 3 July, Bicherakoff embarked his Cossacks at Enzali for Alyat. Dunsterville allowed him to take the British staff officers and armored cars which had previously been attached to him (now in Russian uniforms). At that point, the Turks had not yet crossed the Kura River over its single bridge at Yeldakh, 150 miles west of Alyat. His plan was to seize the bridge and halt the Turkish advance there or, failing that, to delay their advance by adopting defensive positions in the mountains between the Kura and Baku. Unfortunately, by the time Bicherakoff reached the front, he found that the Red Army had allowed the Turks to take possession of the bridge without any resistance. Furthermore, he found that he could not rely on any troops but his own. His sole option was to retire on Baku, contesting every mile to delay the Turkish advance, to buy time for proper defensive positions to be prepared around the town. Even this action was fraught with difficulties. When a party of Bicherakoff's cavalry with an armored car crossed over a bridge to reconnoiter the Turkish positions, they impressed upon the Red Army commander the importance of his position. On their retirement, they found that the bridge was in Turkish hands. To regain control of the bridge, the cavalry suffered heavy losses and the armored car was lost:

> One cannot help smiling at the idea of troops in action leaving their posts to attend political meetings, but these comic incidents have tragic endings, and in this case the amusing behaviour of the Red Army soldiers meant the lives of many brave men and the loss of the armoured car. When freedom is carried to the extent of permitting men to leave their military duties during the progress of an action, war becomes impossible.[19]

Dunsterville's scathing comments would be prophetic for his own action in Baku. By the end of July, the Turkish army reached the outskirts of Baku but unexpectedly halted when complete victory was almost theirs. Bicherakoff withdrew his men out of Baku to Derbend where he could continue the fight should Baku fall. Although Baku considered his actions to be treasonous, his action was based on the impossibility of working with the Baku authorities, as Dunsterville would find later that year.[20]

Meanwhile, in Enzeli, Dunsterville found the committee far less able to dictate than during his former visit. Then the committee had 2,000 men to back them up. Now there were just 200 Red Guards, while Dunsterville had 100 Hampshires. In Baku, the situation was looking more favorable too. Dunsterville was in daily contact with the Social revolutionaries, Armenian Dashnaks and Mensheviks (collectively they would become known as the Centro-Caspian Dictatorship) who were planning a coup d'état. He was also being reinforced, by lorry, by Lieutenant Colonel Faviell's 39th Infantry Brigade, composed of the 7/Gloucesters, 7/North Staffordshires, 9/Worcesters and 9/Warwicks.[21]

While Dunsterville was contending with the international revolutionary politics of Caucasus oil, yet another of the forgotten tragedies of the Great War in the Middle East was unfolding, and it was only due to the (very limited) presence of Dunsterforce that the tragedy did not evolve into greater proportions. In and around Lake Urumiah were two Christian communities which had suffered from Turkish and Kurdish raids since the beginning of the war. About 80,000 strong, most belonged to either the Christian Armenian or Assyrian churches, the latter being referred to as the Jilus. For a year they had been surrounded by the Turkish 5th and 6th Divisions. Russian officers trained the Jilus and stiffened their resistance.

The Jilus requested aid in the form of arms, ammunition and money, which Dunsterville agreed to provide. The South African Lieutenant Pennington flew into Urumiah with messages, and, being the first airplane ever to land there, he was fortunate not to be shot down or lynched. A further misunderstanding arose from his shorts, which convinced the womenfolk that Britain was short of khaki material, and they fashioned trousers for him from their own skirts, much to his embarrassment. The plan was for a force of Jilus to fight their way through the Turkish positions southwards to the British at Sain-Kaleh where they would receive the aid. Unfortunately, the party's return was delayed and rumors spread that they had all been captured and massacred. An estimated 50,000 people, men, women and children, with their possessions and cattle, panicked. They fled down the Bijar road with Turks and Kurds on their flanks to pillage and massacre. Once the refugees reached the British lines, the British formed a rear guard to halt their pursuers. Subsequently, the Jilus made their way to refugee camps in Mesopotamia where they were rationed and accommodated by the British authorities. There the men were formed into labor corps. After the war, the Jilus were repatriated to their homeland.[22]

In and amongst the slaughter of the Great War, and with all of the demands on the British authorities and taxpayers, both domestic and imperial, it remains amazing that a whole ethno-religious group could be saved. The Persian government had failed in its duty to protect its inhabitants. The judicial application of timely action by a few Britons on the ground prevented another massacre. The willingness of national authorities, already overburdened, to take on yet another responsibility is to be applauded. All of this was undertaken with the minimum of media coverage, and, even if there had been, it is unlikely that there would have been much sympathy for another anonymous, alien people in the midst of the global suffering.

Another small expedition left Hamadan on 21 May for Tabriz which was the railhead for a line crossing into Russia at Julfa and then running towards Tiflis. Fifteen British and one French officer plus 35 British non-commissioned officers (NCOs) were commanded by Major Wagstaff, of the Indian Army but recently attached to the South Persia Rifles. Additional assets were acquired en route, but the force remained less than formidable. The Turkish garrison at Zinjan fled before them and a similar experience was had at Mianeh, but on reaching Tabriz, a city of 20,000 inhabitants, it was felt to be prudent to fall back. Tabriz was a gateway into the Caucasus and, together with Kuchik Khan's attempts to block the British further east, was part of a cordon to keep the British out. The Turks entered Tabriz on 15 June. Despite initial zeal for their co-religionists and encouraging talk of pan-Islamism to drive the British out of Persia, the Turks were poor paymasters. They commandeered what they needed and forgot to pay their local levies, who deserted and went over to the British in Mianeh. Wagstaff requested reinforcement, especially artillery, to counter the expected Turkish offensive from Tabriz. Eventually, he received C Squadron, 14th Hussars, a platoon each of Hampshires and Gurkhas, and a section of howitzers with a couple of mountain guns. Wagstaff's force advanced towards Tabriz but were forced back, a retreat that was precipitated by the fleeing of their Persian levies. Mianeh showed its displeasure at the retreating British. The British made a stand on a ridge at Kuflan Kuh. On 9 September, reinforcements arrived under Colonel Matthews of the Hampshires. There they were attacked by 2,000 Turks who attacked in good order and eventually, despite desperate fighting with bayonets and clubbed rifles, were literally pushed over the ridge. Matthews fell back on Jamalabad, where the situation was saved by the arrival of armored cars from Kasvin. The Turks withdrew to Kuflan Kuh and dug in. The Tabriz expedition was over, as was the idea that a handful of officers and NCOs could take hold of the line with barely trained Persians. In the words of Martin Donohoe, the bubble of Persian fighting efficiency had been pricked.[23]

Back in Enzeli, on 26 July 1918, the Bolshevik government in Baku was deposed by the expected coup d'état and replaced by the five-man Central-Caspian Dictatorship. The Bolshevik leadership attempted to leave for Astrakhan (the only remaining Bolshevik stronghold on the Caspian Sea) by seizing 13 ships. They took with them the bulk of the Red Army and the military stores, without which the defense of Baku would have ceased immediately. The new government controlled some gunboats which were dispatched to order the return of the convoy.[24]

The first British troops arrived on 4 August, consisting of a few officers under Colonel Stokes, Skinner's Horse, and a detachment of the Hampshires. The townspeople were disappointed at the small size of this contingent, but the morale effect was immeasurable. The following day, the Turks attacked, and it appeared that everybody seized a rifle to repel the attackers. Although there were some 600 defenders killed and the front line buckled, it held and the attackers lost even more. The future looked optimistic, although just to be on the safe side, Dunsterforce secured three steamers to assist their escape should the town fall. One of them, the *President Kruger*, became the British headquarters in Baku, with a life-sized portrait of "Oom Paul" in the saloon, under which sat many South African officers wearing South Africa 1899–1902 medals![25]

Furthermore, Dunsterville refused to fly the red revolutionary flag, so he turned the Imperial Russian flag upside down, which happened to become that of the Kingdom of Serbia:

> A British General on the Caspian, the only sea unploughed before by British keels, on board a ship named after a South African Dutch president and whilom enemy, sailing from a Persian port, under the Serbian flag, to relieve from the Turks a body of Armenians in a revolutionary Russian town.[26]

On 15 August, Dunsterville received a military assessment of the situation in Baku. It was not good. The main line of defense was on a stony cliff. Rifle pits were ill sited so that the occupants could only fire into the air, and even if they were moved to better positions, fire would be "plunging" and unsuitable for machine guns. The front was unwired. There were no communication trenches. There were supposed to be 6,000 defenders in 22 battalions, varying from 150 to 500 men strong, for a 21,000-yard-long front line. It was difficult to establish what military stores were available to plan for their best use. There were few officers and little discipline. Units returned to town when they wished. One hundred Staffords held 4,000 yards of trenches while their reserve, the Baku Army, was too far away to be of any use. Ammunition discipline was poor, and a lot was wasted. Sanitation was bad. Transport was inadequate, and cars could not get everywhere, while there was inadequate fodder for the animals. The Turks needed to be pushed 15,000 to 20,000 yards west of Baku to render the docks safe from artillery fire with aerial observation.[27]

The Turks, on the other hand, were proactive in exploiting weaknesses in the Baku line.

British troops were concentrated in two positions, known as the Mud Volcano, near the middle of the line, and the Wolf's Gap, towards the southern end of the line, opposite Baku town. They never amounted to more than about 900 rifles. Number 8 Battery, Royal Field Artillery, provided the only mobile defense for the town. The gunners also sorted through the artillery, and ammunition was recovered from the Bolsheviks. After a great deal of sorting, 30 working guns were assembled and sent to the front.[28]

Behind the British, the town was in turmoil. The new regime was no more effective than its predecessor. The town was full of released German and Austrian prisoners of war, and the Tarter population were regarded as being pro–Turkish. Shelling of the town, ships and the Hotel d'Europe (used for accommodation by the British officers) was accurate. This could only have been obtained by a spotter with a telephone line in the town. When the officers decamped for the Metropole, the shelling followed them. Negotiations with the Bolsheviks were finally concluded, and they were imprisoned until the last day of the siege. When their vessels were at last unloaded, the pretext of taking military supplies with them was discovered to be a cover for general looting. Meanwhile, normal commerce had ceased. All goods in the ports had been nationalized. So had all the shipping. There was therefore no point in private enterprise, while state enterprise had failed. So nothing was moved. Watermelons, for example, were 8 pence in Enzeli but 10 shillings in Baku. The crews of ships passing between the two ports, including Dunsterforce's, purchased as many watermelons as they could in Enzeli and refused to sail until they could take no more. Then they were sold from the ship at Baku, with the ship's committee arranging the sales. Watermelons were clearly not nationalized, so free capitalism reigned, but this one example shows the complexities of life in the new workers' paradise. Fortunately, the supply situation was eased when peace was made with Kuchik Khan, who became the sole contractor of rice for Baku. One foodstuff that was available in large quantities was fresh caviar, but the soldiers had no liking for "herring paste" or "fish jam."[29]

Commodore Norris, RN, and a naval party arrived to take control of the ports. He had the opportunity to observe the revolutionary navy at work. Turkish trains were running along a track south of Baku and within 1,000 yards of the coast. These trains were ideal targets for naval gunnery. However, the gunnery was poor, and nothing was hit. Norris suggested that they would be more likely to hit something by moving closer to the shore. The order was given, but then a spokesman of the committee asked why there was a change. The captain explained and was told to resume the original course while the committee discussed the matter. The new course was discussed. The committee decided that as there was a Turkish battery somewhere on that part of the coast, operating closer to the shore would bring the gunboat under fire. The committee issued new orders, and the gunboat was ordered to return to Baku. Naval operations were over for the day.[30]

The Turks attacked Mud Volcano on 26 August. It was held by "D" Company, North Staffords, under Captain Sparrow, MC. To their rear, at Baladjari Station, a reserve of Baku troops was supposed to be stationed. There was a telephone line from Mud Volcano to the station to call up the reserves.

The Turks attacked at 1030 hours with great vigor and were well supported. One hundred and fifty Staffords and four machine guns of the LAMB held off four attacks, but the fifth attempt overran and annihilated the defenses at Number 1 post. From there, the Turks were able to work their way around the north of the position, bringing fire on the reverse of Number 2 and 3 positions. They were rushed and overrun at about 1330 hours. Only six men escaped uninjured. Eighty men were missing, including all of the officers.

British reinforcements were rushed forward, but too late to save the position. Another company of the Staffords took up positions below the crest of the hill and inflicted severe casualties on the Turkish attackers but were unable to regain the lost positions.

The Staffords had fought with gallantry to hold off the Turkish attack, and had been wiped out almost to a man. Had the attack fallen on local troops, Dunsterville believed that they would have given way with nothing to halt the advance into Baku. The reinforcements in Baladjari Station were missing. They had either refused to move to support the Staffords, or the local staff had failed to transmit the order to move. If the Baku troops to the left (three battalions) and right had turned their flanks to bring their fire to bear on the attacking Turks, it may have saved Mud Volcano. Nothing had been done to save Baku. As it was, the Staffords' sacrifice had only postponed the inevitable.[31]

A further attack was launched on Binagadi Hill (Stafford Hill) on 31 August. Another Staffords company held this position because it was an obvious Turkish target. This time, arrangements were made to support the forward units by other British units. Again, local Baku troops failed to support the British.

At about 0600 hours, some 500 Turks attacked with machine gun and artillery support. In the dark, machine guns protected by large shields had been moved forward and placed in the open to sweep the British positions with enfilading fire. With the company commander, Lieutenant Petty, killed, Binagadi Hill was becoming untenable, and it was evacuated at 0830 hours. They withdrew to the right of the Warwick's position, Warwick Castle. When a Baku battalion to the left of Warwick Castle withdrew, and without support from Baku reserves in Binagadi village, the Warwicks were now in a tenuous position. They too were forced to withdraw to avoid encirclement and capture.

A reserve company of Warwicks moved forward through the oil derricks to cover the retiring company but were insufficient to hold the Turkish advance. Colonel Faviell then ordered a withdrawal to establish a new defensive line which would hold against further Turkish attacks.

British losses were two officers killed or dead of wounds, and 34 four other ranks killed, wounded or missing. Without significant reserves, there was little Faviell could do to preserve those positions. Withdrawal or annihilation were the only options.[32]

Dunsterville wrote to the Baku government to complain about the lack of action by the Baku troops. He was invited to a Council of War, headed by General Dukuchaiev, but also attended by all those who claimed any voice in government: the Armenian National Council; the five dictators who ran the town; delegates from the workers, soldiers and sailors, and peasant deputies. Dukuchaiev outlined his plan, commencing at 2000 hours. Then each of the delegates disagreed. Dunsterville left at 0100 hours, with the debate in full flow but without anything being achieved.[33]

In response, the following day, 1 September, Dunsterville called a meeting with the Baku dignitaries at 1600. He announced that nothing now could save Baku, and he intended to withdraw the British troops. The indignant response of the dictators was to accuse Dunsterville of deserting them after accepting joint responsibility in the defense of Baku. He was accused of bringing just 1,000 soldiers, despite having stated from the beginning that a large expedition was impossible; in response, he stated that he had been informed that Baku had 10,000 troops who just needed training and organization.[34]

Dunsterforce was still in Baku when, on the 12th, an Arab deserter gave information of a large-scale Turkish attack on the 14th, but he was unable to specify where on the 14-mile front it would fall. The indications were that it would fall on the left flank, and this sector was strengthened. The information proved to be accurate, and at 0400 hours firing was heard. The Turkish 5th Caucasian Division attacked around the Wolf's Gap, through the Baku battalion, which should have been holding the line, and occupied the heights just 3,000 yards from the docks. Had there been cavalry with the Turks, they could have raced down the road into Baku. Unexpectedly, they halted, but having secured the heights, reinforcements could now be brought up unimpeded. At dawn, the Turkish 15th Infantry Division attacked along the Baladjari front.

The Staffords were withdrawn to a secondary position, thereby shortening the line and preventing them from being outflanked. The British troops could not be used for a counter-attack, as it was feared that their removal from the front line would have resulted in the Baku troops melting away. Dukuchaiev ordered two counter-attacks from the Baku troops, who advanced with bravery but without skill and achieved nothing. Two airplanes and six armored cars were deployed to good effect. By 0800 hours the situation had stabilized and did not appear as critical as it had been four hours earlier. An effective counter-attack from Baku could have restored the situation and regained the heights from the Turks. Dunsterville visited Dukuchaiev's headquarters and saw for himself the chaos within. He was convinced, if he really needed convincing, that the town was lost. Commodore Norris was ordered to prepare the ships for evacuation.

At 1600 hours, Dunsterville heard that the final counter-attack had failed due to the inability to concentrate the necessary troops. Dunsterforce was ordered to retire from 2000 hours. When a note was delivered to the dictators, they were in such disarray that the reply was "Do what you please." The British withdrawal took place while in contact with the Turks, and although skillfully conducted, it was not without loss, including Major Beresford Havelock, North Staffords, grandson of Sir Henry of Lucknow fame. At last light the fighting died down.

A delegation of the dictators realized what was happening and ordered Dunsterville to return his men to the front line, but he refused to sacrifice his men in their cause. The ships slipped off in the dark, past the guardships and into the open sea. All made landfall at Enzeli.[35]

In six weeks at Baku, 900 men, all of them New Army Battalions from the English Midlands, had held back a Turkish army 10 times their size. Dunsterville himself was the first to admit that British alone had not kept the Turks out of Baku. The Baku artillery had served well alongside the British. Some of the Baku infantry had done well alongside the British.

In the final day's fighting, the Turks had been fought to a standstill. There had been 180, or 20 percent of the fighting force, killed, wounded and missing. Despite this success, only

a counter-attack on the scale which only the Baku troops could provide would have restored the situation. Without that, the Turkish success was inevitable (indeed, some had considered that it was inevitable as soon as Dunsterforce had landed in Baku), and more British lives would have been lost for a cause few at home realized even existed. If the people of Baku were not prepared to save their town, then it was unfair to expect others to do so for them.[36]

The Turkish Caucasus-Islam Army entered Baku. It was sacked for two days with all the horrors that entailed. Estimates of the numbers of Armenians killed varied between 9,000 and 30,000.[37]

Dunsterforce itself soon received orders to be stood down and replaced by the 14th Division — Norperforce — on 14th September. In Persia, Dunsterforce had provided famine relief, offered a notion of government where the Persian government had offered none, "conquered" Hamadan not by the sword but by sound government, rebuilt roads, provided security on roads for travelers, defeated anti–Tehran revolutionaries, prevented genocide, withstood Turkish invasions (although as Persia was neutral, the British were invaders too), had taken over from the Russian armies, and been properly provisioned, unlike the Turks and Russians before them.

It was a truly bizarre expedition to intervene in several extremely complex theaters with limited resources at great distances. Attempts to turn local inhabitants into well-trained soldiers overnight, through the provision of officers, instructors and modern weapons systems, had failed. It also failed to reach Tiflis, but selected a suitable alternative, Baku, which would have achieved the same objectives as Tiflis. Dunsterforce failed to motivate the Baku dictatorship, or even its inhabitants, in their own defense, but then that is not the purpose of foreign military advisors. Baku's defense was its own responsibility. Dunsterforce could, and did, assist, but not replace, their own responsibilities. Dunsterforce also failed to provide a British-controlled stop to the expected Turko-German advance on Central Asia to threaten India.

This policy of sending a small force to strengthen indigenous troops was an understandable approach, given the critical manpower shortages afflicting the allies by late-1917 into 1918. It was not defense on the cheap. Dunsterforce was not starved of material or money, unlike, for example, the old Indian Expeditionary Force "D" back in 1914–1915.

What Dunsterforce did achieve was far more humanitarian in Persia, by stabilizing the situation and bringing a degree of government which was lacking. That, alone, in and amongst the horrors of the Great War, is highly commendable in its own right.

12

The Mesopotamia Commission,
December 1915–May 1917

In the spring of 1916, the British war effort in the Middle East was not going well. Gallipoli had been evacuated and Townshend surrendered at Kut. Losses were immense. The loss to British prestige was also considered to be immense. In a classic case of "something needs to be done," Parliament ordered two special commissions into what had gone so badly wrong. But by the time the Mesopotamia Commission had reported, the army had corrected all of the failings, and Maude's entry into Baghdad two months earlier was being hailed as a great success.

Indian Expeditionary Force "D" had, as we have seen, been short of artillery, modern communications, medical provisions and logistical support when thrust into a theater which lacked the most basic infrastructure. Initially, the small scale of the fighting, limited troop numbers and the short operating distances from Basra meant that these shortcomings could be managed. Even so, Spackman's account of the aftermath of the Battle of Shaiba illustrates the impact on the common soldier:

> Pause to imagine being brought in, with other wounded with broken limbs or massive injuries, on a mule cart without springs, traveling for miles across the rough desert under a burning sun. Imagine the pain and the thirst.[1]

The writing was on the wall. As the distances from Basra grew, so did the problems. By mid–October 1915, despite all of the headline-grabbing successes of Townshend and Gorringe, there were sufficient rumors reaching England for Chamberlain to write to Harding:

> I know that the difficulties must be great, and that it is impossible to foresee every emergency, but I trust that you will impress upon all concerned that in this matter of health they cannot take too many precautions and that we shall not question expenditure required to safeguard the lives of our men.[2]

Harding did not respond.

NacNeese Report

At the end of December, Harding asked Duff to investigate into the constant complaints of insufficient supplies, stores and comforts. Duff's response was to commission a report from a pair of "safe hands," although by selecting non-military men he created the air of impartiality. The pair were Lord Chelmsford, former governor of Queensland and New South Wales and future viceroy, and Surgeon General J.G. MacNeese, director of medical services in India. In the event, Chelmsford was recalled to London in preparation to become viceroy and never acted on the commission. MacNeese visited the medical facilities in Basra and Bombay and pronounced himself satisfied. Duff was able to pronounce that "everything was found to be all right at Basra and from there to India, wherever, in fact, we control matters directly." Whether he realized it or not, Duff's statement precisely identified the problem, which lay not between Bombay and Basra, but above Basra, where they did not control matters directly.[3]

Duff missed the opportunity for a thorough investigation into IEF "D"'s failings. Had he implemented the thorough, impartial investigation which was needed, the government of India could have kept the complaints "in house," rectified those complaints found to be justified and, perhaps most importantly for the government's prestige, avoided embarrassing questions from the home government.

Vincent-Bingley Report

Early in 1916, letters began to appear in the *Times*, and questions were asked in Parliament. More letters were being received in India indicating that all was not well at the front. Duff considered that another inquiry into affairs at the front was required, and Hardinge agreed. This time Sir William Vincent and Major General A.H. Bingley were appointed.

Vincent was a member of the Indian Government Council while Bingley was newly arrived in India, having spent the war so far in Egypt. Hardinge informed Chamberlain of this new inquiry on 25 February, following further questions into the state of medical facilities in Mesopotamia. Hardinge reassured Chamberlain that "medical arrangements in Mesopotamia have constantly occupied the attention of the Commander-in-Chief and myself, but Nixon never reported that all was not well." Nixon was replaced by Lake, who approved of the investigation and indeed wanted to extend the remit to include Townshend's protests against the advance on Baghdad, the early attempts to relieve Kut, the lack of river transport and the shortages which resulted. The remit of the Vincent-Bingley inquiry was expanded to include those suggestions, provided they were related to the medical situation. London added Mr. E.A. Ridsdale of the Red Cross to the inquiry, which Hardinge agreed too.[4]

After eight days in Bombay, Vincent and Bingley traveled to Basra in early March, where they met Ridsdale (unfortunately he would not arrive until mid–April) for two and a half months. They inquired, took written statements from officers now invalided back to Britain, and wrote their report. When it was submitted on 31 March, it was exactly what had been asked for, and what was needed, but not what Hardinge and Duff wanted to read. The report criticized everyone except the medical staff themselves: lack of river transport and hospital ships, shortages of medical staff, the lack of ambulances, and the 3rd and 7th Divisions had deployed with incomplete or without medical services. Worse still, names were named, and both Nixon and Surgeon General G.H. Hathaway, Deputy Director of Medical Services in Mesopotamia, came in for particular criticism. Duff criticized the report by stating that it had deviated from its remit by criticizing the pre-war preparation, yet this was precisely to point. Most of the units sent to Mesopotamia were Indian Army and with their pre-war establishment. Any weaknesses in the Indian divisions' performances in Mesopotamia resulted from incorrect pre-war planning assumptions and a failure to provide additional, theater-specific equipment.

Paul Davis' assessment of the Vincent-Bingley inquiry was that Hardinge and Duff were genuinely ignorant of the reality of front-line conditions in Mesopotamia; otherwise they would never have cooperated so willingly with the inquiry. Duff was stung by the report. Copies were sent to Chamberlain and Robertson, Chief of the Imperial General Staff, in London with Duff's extensive comments into why the report should not be published. At best, it was embarrassing to the government of India; at worst it provided information to the enemy.[5]

Mesopotamia Commission

Hardinge and Duff had little to worry about with the Vincent-Bingley report. Worse was to come. Kut surrendered. Had the 6th Division been relieved, or even broken out, the

clamor for an inquiry in Parliament might have been swept under the table by a wave of national rejoicing. It was not to be. Letters to members of Parliament demanded answers, and Prime Minister Asquith was under pressure. On 11 May he agreed to release papers concerning Townshend's objections to advancing on Baghdad, but they had not been released a month later and there were more questions in Parliament. There were debates in Cabinet, where the War Office opposed their release. A compromise between the full release of all the papers (which was undesirable as it would assist the enemy) and the partial release (which it was feared would provide an incomplete picture) were sought. Parliamentary debates were suggested. Finally, twin commissions were suggested. This did not please everyone either. Those whose role was about to be examined would be distracted from their primary purpose—winning the war—by preparing their own defense. There appeared to be no other avenue to investigate the failings and to appease an appalled public. Parliament passed the "Special Commissions (Dardanelles and Mesopotamia) Act," 1916, on 1 August 1916. The commission was composed of:

- Lord George Hamilton (chairman)—former Secretary of State for India
- The Earl of Donoughmore
- General Sir Neville Lyttelton
- Admiral Sir Cyprian Bridge—former director naval intelligence
- Lord Hugh Cecil, MP
- Sir Archibald Williamson, MP
- John Hodge, MP
- Commander Josiah Wedgewood, MP—recently returned to the Commons from active service.

The commission would meet 60 times in the coming 10 months and would interview over 100 witnesses.[6]

Manpower

Addressing India's attitude towards IEF "D," the War Office had directed India to send the expedition, but, unlike the other IEFs, control remained with India. India had assumed that as they were sending a complete, self-contained division consisting of everything it needed, that was all. India had conformed to the regulations. There was no more to be done. No investigation was undertaken into the special conditions which would be encountered in Basra.

During 1915, when there were almost two whole divisions in Mesopotamia but Townshend was requesting two more to reach Baghdad, there were genuine concerns along India's North West Frontier. There were seven attacks, five of which were serious. India had deployed overseas six and one-third of her nine mobilized divisions. The remaining divisions and 33 volunteer battalions were all that was left to defend the country, which included the modern states of Pakistan and Bangladesh.

The report held that more could have been made of India's manpower reserves. The result of which was, for the 6th Division at least, under-strength units so that every man had to remain in the front line and there were no relief units to bring units out of the front line to rest. In France, no unit had to spend an entire year in the front line. Adequate troop numbers may have allowed Townshend to succeed at Ctesiphon.

When Hardinge wrote to Crewe that "India has done her duty to the Empire" and of "our generosity to His Majesty's Government," the commission commented scathingly that this "was not the attitude of an Englishman but of an Indian Rajah." India, the report concluded, could have done more.[7]

The Port of Basra

The report found that, at least until the end of 1915, the port of Basra was adequate to handle the material needs of IEF "D," despite all of the problems described earlier in this book. In late 1915, there were sufficient material and stores amassed at Basra. The port failed when the massive increases of men and material commenced at the end of 1915 and into 1916.

Even when it became apparent that the port was inadequate in late 1915, Nixon refused to incur the cost of improving the facilities. Sir George Buchanan, who had many years of experience running the port of Rangoon, was appointed Director-General of Port Conservancy. He arrived in mid–December 1915, just as the port was about to collapse under the increased demands. The report noted that Nixon acknowledged its inadequacy, and yet "when the best assistance available is sent, instead of being availed of it is deliberately put aside."

When attempts to make improvements did finally commence, they were too late to materially assist in the relief of Kut.[8]

Riverine Transport

If there were adequate stores in Basra for IEF "D" in late 1915, there were significant difficulties in getting them to the front where they were needed. Sir George Buchanan explained the problem in elementary simplicity:

> (a) the requirements of the army at the front in tons per day, delivered where required, including extra steamers for special services; (b) the tonnage capacity of the river fleet and number of vessels available for all purposes; and if (a) exceeds (b) something unpleasant was bound to happen.

Something unpleasant did happen. In fact, it was not merely the resupply of the 6th Division in particular as it made its way up the Tigris, or of the relief forces, which were severely restricted. Had there been adequate shipping for Townshend in the summer of 1915, it is highly probable that he could have pursued the Turks all the way into Baghdad. Instead, delays were incurred in resupplying his division and also in moving his division forward. This delay allowed the Turks to reinforce their troops and to prepare their defences. The 12th Division's expedition on the Euphrates did not help, and their continued presence at Nasariya added to the shipping demands.

When there had been just the 6th and 12th Divisions in theater, the river fleet was some 600 tons, and this barely met the demands. When the other divisions were arriving, their demand was 12,000 tons, while, until 10 March 1916, there were just 1,760 tons available.

Nixon defended himself by stating, correctly, that he had repeatedly asked India for more shipping. What was sent was often inappropriate, which was even more scandalous because when Basra fell, Barrett was told exactly what type of ships he required for the Tigris and how many. Commander A. Hamilton, Royal Indian Marine, had participated in a 1905–1907 Basra-to-Baghdad river survey and accompanied Barrett to Basra. His advice was ignored.

The question of increasing the river fleet was first raised in August 1915 in preparation for the advance to Kut, but a combination of red tape, questioning the requirements, and passage of messages between departments meant that the required ships would not be available until March 1916. The War Office provided gunboats, essential as we have seen, but unable to relieve the supply problems. Fortunately, the Lynch Brothers made available their three remaining steamers; otherwise the situation would have been even worse.

In January 1916, General Cowper, with the title of Deputy Assistant Quartermaster General (DAQMG) of IEF "D," meaning that he was responsible for transport in Mesopotamia, composed a telegram for Duff. Lake made some alterations before it was transmitted, but the theme was that without adequate transport, attempts to relieve Kut should be halted. Duff's reply was a threat to remove Cowper if he received any more such telegrams.

Given these acknowledged shipping problems, the question was put to Nixon — to which he had no adequate response — why the advance was continued. He replied, "We had these troops up there and we were going on fighting." He denied any responsibility for the shortage — that was India's responsibility. India, however, was accused of failing to adopt the correct "war footing." Several companies operating in India and the Far East offered their services to design, build or otherwise acquire suitable shipping for the Tigris, some of which were at work on the inland Chinese rivers. Their patriotic offers were never taken up.

In the end, though, most additional shipping was acquired after Ctesiphon. By the time this additional shipping arrived, it was too late to materially assist the Relief of Kut: ten Nile steamers traveled 4,000 miles each and only arrived in Basra on 4 March 1916.[9]

Medical Provision

The Indian Medical Service suffered from several problems in Mesopotamia. Firstly, it was unprepared for an overseas war in 1914. Secondly, it was understaffed. Thirdly, there was a shortage of medical supplies, and finally there were inadequate medical evacuation procedures.

Pre-war reforms had been introduced by Surgeon General Sir William Babtie, who had intended to reach full recruitment and improve salaries. When war broke out, though, the service was still understaffed, and 350 "civil subassistant surgeons" available for military service in India could not be compelled to serve overseas, despite the offer of double pay. India had been asked to send her best to Europe, so, according to Sir Havelock Charles, medical advisor to the secretary of state for India, she did. Her second best was sent to Egypt, the third best to East Africa and what was left went to Mesopotamia. The 6th Division, it should be remembered, originally sailed with IEF "A" for France and so was presumably included in "the best." When it sailed, it contained the following:

- Five field ambulances (500 beds)
- One clearing hospital (200 beds)
- Two general hospitals (850 beds)
- One X-ray section
- One stores depot
- 71 medical officers

Gorringe's 12th Division was less complete.

While distances were short and casualties limited, these facilities could cope. From Ctesiphon, the nearest hospital was Al-Amara, then Basra. Chamberlain announced to Parliament in October 1915 that there was a well-equipped hospital in Basra, and he understood that there were other hospitals throughout the theater. He knew no better, as at that point he had only been asked for additional medical supplies, not further hospitals or staff. The following month, Hardinge summed up the underlying problem:

> I am afraid our hospitals in Mesopotamia leave much to be desired.... The great difficulty is to evacuate the wounded from the front to the base which is so far distant, and which can only be done by river, while the river transport is very small.

The solution seems to have been to capture Baghdad and move the medical facilities there, thereby shortening the distance from the front to the base hospitals. This approach, of course, required the capture of Baghdad.

Nixon was accused of not informing London or Delhi of the situation; Nixon responded by stating that he had requested additional transport. Babtie sent additional medical officers in June 1915, but not as many as requested by the deputy director of medical services in Mesopotamia, Surgeon General G.H. Hathaway, and only after Nixon warned of a breakdown if the services were not improved. Babtie's response was that medical personnel could only be released once the internal security and North West Frontier arrangements had been fulfilled. In June 1915, though, the medical services were holding up, and would do so until after Ctesiphon.

Ctesiphon was the watershed. Medical provision was based on the casualties from Kut, about 1,000, so two steamers were allocated. Five more steamers with four days' supplies had to be added, but even these were not adequate, and the casualties remained on board for over a week with inadequate staff to care for them.

When questioned about why he did not call a halt to the advance when the medical services were understood to be inadequate, as with riverine transport in general, Nixon had no adequate response. The answers suggest that until he traveled on one of the steamers from Ctesiphon to Basra following the battle, he simply did not understand how critical the medical situation was. He even refused offers of Red Cross launches which would have assisted.

Lloyd George's wartime memoir summed up the failings: "If the neglect by the military authorities was directly responsible for the failure and defeat of the expedition, their neglect of the medical equipment turned disaster into horror."[10]

The Government of India

The nature of Indian government confused the situation. There was the British government with its own departments, including the War Office, which was responsible for military matters. There was the India Office, part of the British government, with a Military Department, which could give orders but not oversee the running of a campaign. Then there was the Indian government with its own military branch. Since Kitchener's tenure as commander-in-chief in India, in 1906–1910, the post also occupied that of the Military Member of the Council. He was both military head of the army and head of the political army department. Various Council members made it clear that Mesopotamian affairs were not discussed in Council but came from Hardinge and Duff alone. Hardinge's defense was that as the campaign was outside of India, it was not necessary to consult the Council, and in any case the questions required urgent replies, which did not allow time for consultation in Council.

Indian government finances also served to deter any requests for expenditure. The pre-war planners had never seriously considered the Indian Army for fighting a modern European enemy outside its borders. The poverty of the Indian peasantry was given as one reason for light taxation. The military budget for 1913-1914 was £21.266 million; for 1915-1916 it was £23.216 million, an increase of less than £2 million, yet there were now four overseas expeditions to fund. It is little wonder that Sir Percy Cox, chief political officer in Mesopotamia, never considered asking for equivalent funding to the millions in gold guineas, collected from all over the Empire, which were delivered to Lawrence to fund the Arab Revolt. There was a culture of avoiding unnecessary expenditure, which bred a culture of not asking for expenditure, no matter how vital it might be.[11]

Two Reports from the Mesopotamia Commission

The report was published on 17 May 1917, by which time, as has been stated above, Baghdad had been captured, Kut avenged, Maude was a hero, and the logistical shortcomings so evident over the winter of 1915/1916 had been largely addressed by the likes of Lt.-Gen. Sir George MacMunn, Inspector General of Communications in Mesopotamia and Sir George Buchanan.

The report found that the expedition to Mesopotamia was justified but required careful control. All of the advances prior to Baghdad were justifiable as defensive actions, but the Baghdad advance was a political and military mistake undertaken with too few, tired troops and without adequate preparation. Those responsible for the Baghdad advance were, in order of priority, Nixon, Hardinge, Duff, Chamberlain, and the War Committee of the Cabinet. The London connection was included, as they directed military policy. The division of responsibilities between the secretary of state for India and the Indian government was found to be unworkable. The modern expression "mission creep" is applicable, as no strategy or goals were ever established. Supply should have been controlled from the ports, not Indian headquarters, and the commander-in-chief, India, or his representatives, should have visited the theater to familiarize themselves with the circumstances.

Commander Josiah Wedgewood MP dissented from the majority report. He prepared and delivered his own minority report. Davis considers his criticisms to be the more pertinent. Captain Arnold Wilson, writing a decade after the commission was published, considered that the minority report commanded "more general acceptance" than the majority report. Wedgewood disagreed with the blame placed on the London authorities, especially with regards to the Baghdad advance — in October 1915 there would have been more criticism if they had not advanced. It would be a bad day for the Empire, he considered, when risks were declined, and when the opinion of the man on the ground was discounted. Nixon was not the only Indian Army general to lose his job through failure, and he should not be censured in isolation. The blame for this was the poor quality of training for senior Indian Army officers.

He laid the blame for the failure at the foot of the government of India, which was, in effect, Hardinge and Duff:

> I found that the advance to Baghdad failed because the transport was insufficient and the force ill-found.
>
> I find that the troops maintained the best traditions of the Service, that the generalship was fair, but that General Townshend alone inspired his men with that confidence and devo-

tion without which victories such as the first battle for Kut and Ctesiphon are impossible.

Parliamentary Debate

The House of Commons held a three-day debate commencing on 12 July 1917. The opening comments concerned whether or not legal proceedings could, or should, be brought against those named in the report. No conclusion was reached before Chamberlain stood up and, at the end of an hour-long recital of well-known events, offered his resignation. Almost every subsequent speaker was in his favor, but he resigned on the 17th nonetheless. The speakers then swung their attack against the Commission itself, which the commissioners vehemently defended, and they eventually returned to the issue of prosecuting those accused in the report.

Hardinge's tenure as viceroy ended, and he returned to his post as Permanent Undersecretary of State for Foreign Affairs. Ten days before the report was published, he made his maiden speech in the House of Lords. This created uproar for two reasons. Firstly, as a permanent undersecretary, he could not also exercise his rights as a peer of the realm. The prime minister waived this rule for him. Secondly, he used the speech to defend himself. One MP commented that "No Peer — thank God, really, for it — has ever made a maiden speech in defence of himself and in sacrifice of his officials." Although others were less critical, this was nevertheless a damning indictment.

The debates dragged on. The House of Commons did at least agree on two things. Firstly, they roundly criticized sectors of the press who attacked the Commission purely for their own gain, particularly the *Daily Mail*. Audrey Herbert, MP, who had been part of the delegation to arrange the release of the Kut garrison, thought that he had "rarely seen anything meaner than the perversion of that Report by the 'Daily Mail' for its own purposes."

The second factor to be agreed on was the need to reform the Indian administrative system. The report had made a number of recommendations, and Wedgewood agreed. By then there were new men running India — Chelmsford as viceroy, Munro as commander-in-chief, and Montagu as the secretary of state for India — who implemented reforms of the administration and army in the post-war period.

A third day of parliamentary debates was heard on 18 July, but by then, the passion had gone.

The Army Council

The Army Council considered court-martial proceedings but found that there was little prospect. No one could be tried more than three years after the commission of an offense had elapsed, and a section in the Special Commissions Act stated that statements given to the commission could not be used in criminal proceedings. Following a precedent from the South

African War, written statements were requested from those accused. As a result, Hathaway was asked to retire, despite being the most junior of the three surgeon generals named; Babtie and MacNeese (of the MacNeese Report) were exonerated. Duff appears never to have replied.

Of the other figures named, Chamberlain resigned but returned to government as a minister without portfolio the following year. Duff left India to attend the Commission and never returned. He died in 1919.[12]

Conclusion

So, what, if anything, did the Mesopotamia Commission achieve? The Commission has been criticized for many failings, like the absence of a member with current understanding of India, or never going to Mesopotamia. Others criticized it for being a waste of money. The *Official History*, written after the war, was highly critical:

> that the Commission did not always appreciate the true significance of what it learnt, lends force to the criticism often made that, generally speaking the members of the Commission were lacking in the technical and up-to-date knowledge of military operations and military war organization required in an inquiry of this nature. It is undoubtedly true that in a military sense, its report was incomplete and in a few cases inaccurate.[13]

Yet it was also a genuine and conscientious attempt to get to the bottom of what had gone wrong, within the constraints of both time and wartime conditions. It was simply not possible to interview everyone, most notably Townshend and the 6th Division in captivity.

By the time the Commission reported, the criticisms were largely rectified. Indeed, the Vincent-Bingley Report had highlighted the medical shortcomings, and it was this report that deserves the praise for highlighting those particular problems.

Nobody was held to account in any judicial context, be that in Parliament, court-martial or in the civil courts. Hathaway was asked to resign by the army, but his two seniors were not reprimanded in any way. Hardinge was never out of government employment. Chamberlain returned to the government after a period of months. Lake and Nixon had already been removed from Mesopotamia. Of the three commanders-in-chief of India during and before the war who had created the Indian Army which had deployed in 1914, Kitchener was dead; O'Moore Creagh had been censured for resigning in protest at shortcomings instead of attempting to address them; and Duff was relieved to attend the commission and, although he did not return, neither was he formally punished.

If there was a positive outcome, it was the new triumvirate who ran India from 1917: Chelsford the viceroy; Munro the commander-in-chief, India; and Montague, the secretary of state for India, who would be the first holder of that post to visit India. The post–war Montagu-Chelmsford reforms would make significant changes to Anglo-Indian relations. This, however, was not what the commission set out to achieve. The aim of the Commission had been to find out what had gone wrong. For the soldiers still slogging up the Tigris, what mattered was not words but that the earlier failings had largely been put right.

Aftermath

In late 1918, when the war was over and the soldiers began to be demobilized and returned home, the question of what to do with Iraq remained unanswered. There had been plenty of debate, but the needs of winning the war naturally took priority — you cannot divide the spoils of war unless you are confident of winning the war in the first place. This situation was further complicated by developments during the war.

Initially, there had been an agreement between the allies that there would be no permanent acquisition of territory until the war was over. This sensible agreement prevented the creation of inter-allied tensions. In Basra, the downside of this agreement was twofold. Firstly, as it was expected that Basra could be returned to Turkey after the war, India was extremely reluctant to invest in the infrastructure projects which the growing military commitment there desperately required. As we have seen, this policy had disastrous results. Secondly, until the indigenous population were confident that the Turks would not return, they would not cooperate with the British for fear of retributions from returning Turks after the war. In the only town to be recaptured by the Turks from the British, Kut, collaborators were hanged, and the rest of Mesopotamia was only too aware of their fate.[1]

In 1915, the secret Anglo-French Sykes-Picot Agreement divided up the post-war Turkish territories. It envisaged that Basra and Baghdad would fall into a British sphere of influence, while Mosul would become part of a French-dominated Syria. Russia had designs on territory in what is now eastern Turkey as far south as Mosul *vilayet*. Given Anglo-Russian animosity in "the Great Game" which had only been resolved in 1907, there were advantages to having a French "wedge" between British and Russian territory. The infamy of this agreement rests not with its contents but because it was released by Russian revolutionaries to embarrass the western Allies amongst the Arabs, but by the time the agreement was made public, events had moved on and the agreement was already dead.

The Indian officers and officials sent to Basra saw the potential there for an Indian colony, much in the same way that South Africa and Australia would take over former German colonies. The potential of Basra was there for all to see; it just needed a hard-working, industrious population to colonize it, and who better than the ex-soldiers who had fought there? As more and more of Mesopotamia came to be occupied, the ideas developed. An Indian colony in Basra and an Arab protectorate in Baghdad was one idea that was proposed.

By the time of the Armistice, these imperial approaches to the Mesopotamia Question had been overtaken by U.S. President Woodrow Wilson's Fourteen Points. The concept of a mandate was born, whereby new states would develop under the tutelage of the imperial powers until deemed mature enough to exist on their own. To head this fledgling state, Emir Faisal was "elected" king, although in all fairness it was a political fix by the British. Faisal was a war hero, who had fought in the Arab Revolt. He was the son of Ali, the spiritual head of the revolt, and his brother, Abdullah, became king of the Transjordan (modern-day Jordan). Equally importantly, Faisal was not from Iraq, so he was immune to the existing internal factions. With his war record, family connections and neutrality, Faisal was considered the best candidate.

Not all of the administrators in Mesopotamia agreed with the mandate approach. It made for the eventual independence of the new state, but how long would this take? Sir George Buchanan, disparagingly, but not too far from the mark, said that Iraq's sole export was dates.[2] Although there was potential wealth from oil in Mosul, this was a long way in the future. Furthermore, as a British protectorate, funding could be raised for the infrastructure projects which the country needed. As a mandate, this funding was not available.

From the London viewpoint, the overriding question was how to reduce the manpower and expenditure committed to Mesopotamia. In 1920-1921, Britain spent £34 million on the defense and civil administration of Mesopotamia. This was reduced to £4 million by 1925-1926, by which time the army had been replaced by the Royal Air Force and the Iraq Levies. The last British battalion left Iraq in 1927, and the last Indian battalion left the following year. The size of the RAF was also reduced over time, from eight to four squadrons by 1930.[3]

Yet Britain was not able to simply walk away, even if she had wanted too. Writing in the *Sunday Times* of 2 August 1920, T.E. Lawrence summed up Britain's arrival in Mesopotamia: "The people of England have been led in Mesopotamia into a trap from which it will be hard to escape with dignity and honor." Towards the end of the war, Gertrude Bell would write, "We are pledged here. It would be an unthinkable crime to abandon those who have loyally served us." In his preface to the first edition of *Loyalties Mesopotamia 1914–1917*, Wilson established what he thought was the moral obligation upon the British having entered Mesopotamia: "to provide an administration to take the place of the Turkish regime which we have destroyed; and, so far as in us lay, to make good by successive installments the promises of liberty, justice, and prosperity so freely made to the Arab inhabitants at the very outset of the campaign."[4] Promises had been made to the Arabs, and there would have been howls of treachery had the British simply pulled out, as the 1920 rebels desired. It would also have been an abandonment of those who had fought and died in Mesopotamia to leave without at least trying to create a new state worthy of their sacrifice. Finally, there was the expenditure. Britain was entitled to gain some commercial advantage for its expenditure. These same dilemmas were heard again following the 2003 invasion of Iraq.

Despite the enlightened aims of the mandate (compared with the protectorate model), this was anathema to the Iraqis themselves. In July 1920, a rebellion broke out. There were just 29,500 combat troops (many scattered in isolated garrisons), two RAF squadrons and eight Royal Navy gunboats in Iraq to face some 130,000 rebels. Reinforcements were sent.[5] The rebellion was defeated, but there were a further 426 British killed with a similar number "missing," and another Victoria Cross was awarded.[6] One weakness with the rebellion was that it was not a universal uprising. Al-Amara and Kut did not rebel (the later having been rebuilt by the British), and in Basra there were too many vested interests who did not want to jeopardize trade with the empire. In 1922, the Iraqi Army consisted of 250 officers and 3,500 men.[7] This amounted to just 12.5 percent of the infantry combat power which Britain had been able to deploy against the 1920 rebellion and had failed to contain without externally provided reinforcements. Exactly how the new Iraqi state was going to secure itself against internal (let alone external) threats without support from Britain is unclear.

The pressure from the Iraqi government to end the mandate was persistent, until in 1929 Britain announced that it would support Iraq's admission to the League of Nations in 1932, which duly occurred. After 11 years within which to mature, Iraq was an independent nation. Under the 1930 Anglo-Iraqi Treaty, the RAF remained while Britain retained a presence and a "guiding hand" until the 1958 Revolution ended the monarchy. Within a year of admission to the League, however, the writing was on the wall for the future of Iraq. In August 1933, General Bakr Sidqi slaughtered 600 Assyrians, returned to Baghdad seated beside the prime minister, and was promoted. The following month, King Faisal died, and his heir, Ghazi, lacked the personality of his father. Sidqi launched a successful coup d'état in October 1936, only to be assassinated in August 1937. On 1 April 1941, the "Golden Square" of military officers seized power. Britain responded to restore the monarchy, and "Bill" Slim returned to Iraq, now as GOC of the 10th (Indian) Division. The 1958 Revolution, led by General Abdul Karim Qasim, included the murder of the royal family, and so the end of the Hashemite dynasty in Iraq. Qasim himself was overthrown and executed by the Ba'ath Party revolution of 1963, which ruled Iraq until 2003.

Conclusion

The Mesopotamia campaign cost some £350 million and 100,000 casualties.[1] At its peak, there were some 250,000 men employed in the theater. Once the war was over, the United Kingdom maintained a military presence for a further 40 years to support the kingdom of Iraq. While writing this book, the U.S. military is finally pulling out of Iraq following their nine-year presence there.

Following both invasions and the subsequent military operations, the question has been asked, was it worth it?

Britain undertook to reverse their 19th-century policy of supporting the Ottoman Empire and equipped a British Army to defeat the Turks in a minor theater. The loss of Mesopotamia would never have brought down the Ottoman Empire, and it is unlikely that, had Turkey remained in the war for the remainder to the 1918–1919 campaigning season, Britain would have been able to continue the advance from Mosul, across the Tarsus Mountains and on to Constantinople to knock Turkey out of the war. British policy reflected this, so that in 1918 the main effort switched to Syria. The loss of Baghdad was no more fatal to Constantinople than was the loss of Jerusalem, no matter how significant these cities are to the modern reader.

To determine whether or not the British Army was successful, it is necessary to break down the campaign into its different phases.

The 1914 landings and the actions of the 6th (Poona) Division aimed to secure the Persian oil supply and safeguard Britain's position at the head of the Persian Gulf. With limited support from the Royal Navy and whatever local support could be acquired (most importantly from the Lynch Brothers), Indian Expeditionary Force "D" successfully completed its objectives with the minimum of fuss and with losses which were entirely supportable by the original establishment. With an enlarged organization following the piecemeal arrival of the 12th Division, IEF "D" was able to secure Basra "in depth" with outposts at Shaiba and Qurna, and also to launch forays against Turkish troop concentrations along the Euphrates and against anti–British Persian tribes along the Karun. While difficulties were encountered, such as the casualty evacuation

following Shaiba, these did not raise any concerns, as they were well within the pre-war planning assumptions, and the casualties could be absorbed and replaced by the existing system.

With these limited objectives achieved, IEF "D" could (and I believe, should) have dug in to wait out the war, like a number of other garrisons around the globe: Aden, Salonika, and even Egypt for the first part of the war. The loss of Mesopotamia was never going to deliver the killer blow to knock Turkey out of the war; Mesopotamia was a military and strategic backwater. The Gallipoli landings may have removed Turkey from the war and opened up a warm-water port to the Russians. That was not going to be achieved from either Egypt or Mesopotamia. From a base in Basra, though, it was possible to exert a regional influence. Operations could be conducted into Persia to safeguard the oil supply or influence Persian politics (the weakness of the Tehran government remained a concern to Britain and Russia throughout the war). IEF "D" was poised to strike at Baghdad, a threat which Constantinople could not ignore and which would have drawn troops from the other fronts. It also brought to an end the Berlin-Baghdad Railway plan by denying an exit to the sea, and prevented the *Emden* and *Konigsberg* from using Basra as a base to operate against British interests in the Persian Gulf.

The pressure to advance beyond the immediate environs of Basra began almost immediately after Basra was occupied. The combination of Cox's desire to capture Baghdad and Nixon's desire not to maintain a passive defense, coupled with a lack of clearly defined objectives from either London or Delhi, allowed the "men on the ground" to set the agenda, rather than IEF "D" fitting into the imperial war effort. Promises of easy victories (which owed as much to poor Turkish performance as they did to British martial ability) or economies (the argument for capturing Kut was that it was mutually supporting Nasariya and so could be garrisoned by fewer troops than at Nasariya and Al-Amara) from Basra enticed the politicians to authorize advances. Turkish threats from Nasariya could have been held by a combination of an aggressive defense from

186

Shaiba and a Royal Navy blocking force without Gorringe's men having to fight their way through to Nasariya.

However, orders to advance to occupy the whole of Basra *vilayet* were given, and they were inspired by Townshend's unprecedented breakthrough at Qurna and advance on Al-Amara; Townshend deserved all of the credit for planning and (in the latter part) personally leading the advance which netted so many prisoners and advanced so far for so few casualties. Had Townshend been in a position to concentrate his division at Al-Amara and then push on towards Baghdad, it is conceivable that Baghdad could have fallen. This is, of course, conjecture, but by the time the advance resumed, the Turkish defenders had been reinforced and had dug in, whereas Townshend's command was largely the same one which had broken through at Qurna. Nixon was confident that with one division he could take Baghdad, and with two he could hold it. Townshend's one division was under-strength and tired from campaigning without respite. The momentum and the panic that induced in the Turkish defenders at Qurna had been lost. The moment had gone.

One of the recurring problems experienced by British commanders in Mesopotamia was the shortage of transport. Beyond Baghdad, Maude, and then Marshall, were only able to conduct operations on the three axes of advance consecutively, not concurrently, due to transport shortages. The summer of 1915 was the same. Townshend could advance up the Tigris, or Gorringe up the Euphrates, but not at the same time.

The reverse process was equally true for the casualty evacuation procedures, which became increasingly extended as Townshend advanced without any appropriate increase in medical transport capacity or medical provision. When the medical scandal broke, the authorities reluctantly accepted the many offers of assistance. By the time the political storm reached its peak, with the Mesopotamia Commission's report, the failings had been rectified and the repercussions on those named as failing in their duty were minimal. In the winter of 1915 and into 1916, there were just too many disasters to contend with: Gallipoli, the Somme, the Shell Crisis, the loss of the *Hampshire* with the death of Lord Kitchener, and the Siege of Kut.

Townshend's plans for his battles reflected a professional who understood his trade and, furthermore, had combat experience from his career-hopping exploits. Qurna was an innovative approach to a unique problem, which succeeded beyond all expectations. If there was a weakness with his operational planning after Qurna, it was in underestimating the challenges which his attacking columns would encounter. Navigational difficulties and, in particular, failure of communications severely impacted the effectiveness of his plans. His plans were to get part of his force behind the Turkish positions and, by forcing their surrender, prevent them from escaping to reform further defensive positions. It was a far more imaginative use of tactics than those used in attempting to relieve Kut and

would be used to great effect at Ramadi, but the cavalry in particular was ineffective early on in the campaign. Later on, more aggressive cavalry commanders and motorized transport to supply the horses allowed them to operate much more effectively.

The capture of Kut was based on sound assumptions but inaccurate intelligence; Kut and Nasariya would have been mutually supporting if the Shatt-al-Hai was navigable, which unfortunately it was not. The advance on Baghdad was not based on sound assumptions and should not have taken place. Townshend argued against it, but ultimately he had to obey his superior's orders. Nixon (and Cox) should have been well aware of the logistical difficulties Townshend was experiencing. However, there were political pressures due to current or impending military disasters, not least of which was the expected failure at Gallipoli. Baghdad needed to be captured to provide the politicians with good news. Townshend was right to caution against further advance. He also won his final battle: even the Turks acted as if they had lost. Where Townshend made his first (of three) critical mistake was in choosing Kut to make his stand — Kut was a trap which had been identified by Townshend's staff officers in advance. Although it is true that Kut was the last significant supply depot before Al-Amara and there was a risk in continuing the retreat, these factors had to be offset against remaining in such a trap. Occupying Kut did not prevent the Turks from reoccupying hard-won terrain. The position in Kut would not have been so critical had Townshend made an accurate assessment of his food stocks from the beginning. His failure to do this placed unnecessary demands on those charged with relieving him, and as a result new formations were thrown into the battle, ill prepared and unsupported, to achieve premature deadlines. The weather conditions experienced by the relief forces were simply appalling and comparable with, if not worse than, those of the Western Front. Certainly, Allenby's Egyptian Expeditionary Force did not face conditions as bad as those along the Tigris. It is a moot point whether or not Gorringe and Aylmer would have ever been able to break through to relieve Kut, but they deserved to have as full and as accurate information as possible with which to make their battles. Townshend denied them this information, and so although his conduct in the siege was commendable, the responsibility for his ultimate surrender rests on his shoulders.

Townshend's third and final failing was that he lived in luxurious captivity and developed pro–Turkish sentiments while his men were experiencing the worst conditions imaginable. It is unlikely that Townshend alone could have improved his men's conditions, but there are well-documented examples of his officers doing what they could. Townshend should at least have made a nuisance of himself with the Turkish and neutral nations authorities. Whether the Turkish state's actions were part of a deliberate policy or symptomatic of official incompetence, indifference and ineffectiveness is difficult to determine, but only Townshend was in a position to do anything in Constantinople to change the conditions for all of his men.

For his men, unfortunately, it is clear from accounts that by the end of the siege, they were in a greatly weakened state. It is amazing that any of them made it to the work camps at all. A selection of surviving descriptions of their exploits is recounted here. It is clear that they suffered at the hands of indifferent or brutal guards and negligent officials, while at the same time they were saved by the kindness of the enemy and strangers.

With the surrender of Kut, there was a breathing space for Maude to rebuild the shattered army. As with Allenby before the Third Battle of Gaza, Maude benefited from the structural changes and logistical investment commenced by his predecessor. Maude's offensive in the winter of 1916-1917 was hard fought and showed that the Turk was by no means defeated, but by the application of the increasing resources available to him and a methodical approach which included pauses to allow the logistics to catch up, Maude's capture of Baghdad marked the first major enemy city to fall to the allies in the war. Perhaps the most important lesson learned was Slim's experiences gained while watching an army being rebuilt while in contact with the enemy. Slim would repeat the process and save India in the next world war.

Beyond Baghdad, though, the purpose of the massive investment in manpower, material and money becomes more difficult to justify. East along the Diyala, contact was made with the Russians, at last, who, it was hoped, would share the load for the subsequent fighting. The British were disappointed. The Russians refused to participate in offensive operations even before the Revolution. The sole benefit was that, finally, the land route to India was closed and the threat of jihad finally ended. West on the Euphrates, there was initially a threat from the Yilderim, but once this force was redirected against Allenby, the threat to Baghdad retired. Northwards, along the Tigris, the Turks were steadily forced back on Anatolia, but again there were limited strategic gains. The largest, and final, gain was to secure the Mosul oil fields (at the time, unexploited) for the new Iraqi state, which provided a major economic asset to make the new state financially viable. British industry also expected to be able to exploit the opportunities of the newly acquired oil fields around Mosul, which is entirely understandable given the national sacrifice to win the war. However, it was recognized in London that once Baghdad had fallen, the strategic benefits were going to be limited, which is why the 3rd and 7th Divisions were transferred to Palestine where it was believed that there were more gains to be had at less cost.

If the aim of the 1914 Shatt-al-Arab landing was to protect the Persian oil and safeguard Britain's allies in the Gulf, then that was achieved before the end of 1914. What followed for almost three more years alternated between opportunism; the exploitation of the confusion between the political masters in London and Delhi; and a methodical, well-resourced campaign to defeat the enemy in a minor theater.

In comparison with the Palestine campaign (the only other theater which was comparable to Mesopotamia), which is far more well known thanks to the Australian presence and the publicity given to Lawrence of Arabia, Mesopotamia deserves to be far better known. For one thing, the fighting conditions were far worse. There was no opportunity to disengage from the enemy behind the Suez Canal. In the Sinai and Palestine, there were deserts, mountains and intense heat in the Jordan Valley. Mesopotamia also had the marshes around Nasariya and the flooding rivers to contend with. There were no friendly towns in which to relax, like Cairo and Alexandria, in Mesopotamia. The Arabs developed the same unsavory reputation in both theaters, but in Palestine there was at least the Arab Revolt to help. For several reasons, this approach was not adopted in Mesopotamia. In France, for all of the horrors of the Western Front, the trench warfare, gas and mud, there were at least the comforts of a friendly and accommodating native population just a few miles behind the lines, where alcohol, baths and female company could be found. Leave was available to travel home to see friends and family, which was definitely unavailable from Palestine or Mesopotamia.

Despite these additional hardships, Mesopotamia's fighting started from the very outbreak of the war with a naval landing and continued until a few days after the Armistice. Basra was the first enemy town to fall to the Allies, and Baghdad the first major city. Indeed, as Baghdad fell, General Murray in Egypt was still over a fortnight away from launching his unsuccessful First Battle of Gaza, which was, then as now, only just across the Egyptian border. A second, unsuccessful battle would be fought at Gaza the following month, and it would be November before the third, and final, battle of Gaza would finally break into the Ottoman Empire through the Turkish lines at Beersheba. The charge of the Australian Light Horse was recreated in the Australian 1987 film *The Lighthorsemen*. In Mesopotamia, by comparison, two months earlier, Brooking's 15th Division had perfected the 1917 all-arms battle to destroy entirely a Turkish army, at Ramadi. On the Western Front, the five-week-long Battle of Arras was about to commence. Although this offensive included the Canadian success at Vimy Ridge, attritional warfare resumed and the 27 divisions employed suffered over 150,000 casualties for limited gains. The Mesopotamian battle may have been the smallest battle, but in comparison with the Arras and First and Second Gaza, it was by far the most successful. Would a few extra divisions and their resources have made any difference in the mud and slaughter of the Western Front? In the context of reinforcing success, then the Gallipoli campaign and the failed First and Second Battles of Gaza starved Mesopotamia of resources where success was possible. Where was the extra division which Townshend needed to punch through at Ctesiphon and reach Baghdad? Trapped in Gallipoli or guarding the Suez?

The constant exposure to combat in Mesopotamia allowed for tactics to be developed. It would be wrong to imagine that Palestine/Syria and Mesopotamia developed their tactics in isolation from one another. The RFC squadrons, for example, came under the same Middle Eastern Brigade, and there were conversations and transfers of personnel between the two theaters. Armored vehicles were experimented with in Mesopotamia in 1915 and were put to great use especially beyond Baghdad. Armored vehicles were experimented with in the Western Desert of Egypt against the Senussi rebellion over the winter of 1915-1916, but, again, it would not be until Palestine that they were employed to their full potential.

One area in which the Mesopotamian tactics were more developed than in Palestine was with regard to cavalry. The horse in Mesopotamia were cavalry, armed with lance, sword and rifle, but were almost always used as mounted infantry, as at Ramadi or Hadraniya. There were a few cavalry charges, with mixed successes, as at Lajj, Samarra Station and Tikrit, but these were the exceptions. These were not great successes, on the whole. In Palestine, on the other hand, despite there being large formations of mounted rifles, most famously the Australian Light Horse but also the New Zealand Mounted Rifles Brigade, cavalry charges were much more common despite the shorter operational period after Third Gaza. On several occasions, like at Beersheba, mounted rifles drew their bayonets in imitation of swords. Two brigades were armed with swords as real cavalry. As late as 26 October 1918, the 15th (Imperial Service) Brigade launched an unsuccessful charge at Haritan near Aleppo.[2]

In this respect alone, Mesopotamia was proving itself to be at the forefront of innovation. The charge was almost removed and replaced by mobile troops (supported by LAMBs, motorized infantry and lorried resupply) cutting off the enemy's retreat and forcing them to surrender. Townshend was attempting this approach in his 1915 battles (except for Qurna), and this general tactic was used throughout the campaign.

In other aspects, it is more difficult to prove whether or not Mesopotamia was ahead of Palestine, but the large-scale fighting from a much earlier date allowed tactics and procedures to be developed. In Mesopotamia, there was the opportunity to practice these procedures, and there is no better place to perfect skills than "on the job."

In Mesopotamia there was also a desperate need to introduce infrastructure which was already in place in Palestine. Egypt and the Levant coast (to say nothing of France) were well served by ports, like Jaffa. There were some metaled roads and railways already. The almost complete absence of the kinds of infrastructure which were taken for granted in more economically developed parts of the Ottoman Empire and the Middle East meant that it was down to the British Army to introduce these for the first time in Mesopotamia. These developments, such as an adequate, functioning port to facilitate international trade; maps; railways; and roads were essential for modern warfare and also for a modern nation-state. Whatever accusations are laid on the British military and administrators for failing to create a perfect, newly formed, independent and functioning nation-state, British infrastructure investment in the war years far outstripped anything which could have been expected from Constantinople. Similarly, British administrators set about with a genuine desire to improve the newly conquered lands. From the very outset, Sir Percy Cox attempted to make it clear to both the British authorities and the indigenous peoples that the Turks could not and would not be allowed to return. This created an unusual situation where the newly conquered lands, inhabited by aliens, were treated to the sort of facilities which one would expect a modern aid agency to construct in a humanitarian crisis environment. Pragmatism prevailed — Basra's merchants were given permission to trade with the allies; otherwise the local economy would have collapsed. So, from the very beginning, almost by accident, Britain was developing the sort of projects which the kingdom of Iraq would need to survive. Of course, this development was mostly for the benefit of the invaders, but there were also free medical and veterinary facilities. This all sounds like the ideal of 21st-century military intervention into a "failed state."

So, what can be said of the British Army in Mesopotamia during the Great War? It was ultimately successful in driving the enemy from its own possessions, in a minor theater which could not deliver a critical blow to the enemy's war effort. The advances could have been halted years before. The campaign has been largely forgotten despite fighting in far worse conditions than those experienced in comparable theaters. It achieved far more than many of the more famous fronts — the Western Front's inactivity despite more men and material being committed there, or in Egypt which was years behind in capturing an Ottoman town. In Mesopotamia, the British Army was able to develop tactics and hone skills through constant contact with the enemy — some of which were distinctly modern in appearance. It created a modern nation-state with the mineral reserves and invested in infrastructure — although what that nation-state decides to do with what it has been given once the invader/liberator/occupier leaves is outside of the latter's powers. Finally, Mesopotamia provided the training ground for several British field marshals and a unique engineer (Major Hobart), whose effect on the Second World War would be immense.

Chapter Notes

Introduction

1. See also the Marquise of Anglesey's *History of the British Cavalry*, vol. 5, p. xxi, where the author had planned a single volume on the whole of the First World War but then realized that it required three volumes, one each for the Western Front, Palestine and Mesopotamia.

2. For the 1915 Turkish attack on Egypt, see Anglesey, *British Cavalry*, vol. 5, pp. 25–26, where the British defenders were dug in on the west bank of the Canal and defeated the Turks as they attempted to cross. Those Turks who did cross were quickly rounded up. For overviews of the military aspects of the Arab Revolt, see Nicolle, *Lawrence and the Arab Revolts*, and Murphy, *The Arab Revolt 1916–18*. The big problem in Mesopotamia was that there was no single Arab figure to lead a revolt, whereas in Arabia there was Sharif Hussein ibn Ali, although it was his son, Feisal, who would lead the armies and later become king of Iraq; Hussein's descendents still rule Jordan today. There were those amongst the British who favored Sheikh Abdul Aziz ibn Saud over Hussein, and in the 1920s ibn Saud would evict Hussein's Hashemites from the Hejaz to found the Kingdom of Saudi Arabia. Howell, *Daughter of the Desert*, pp. 267, 288–89.

Chapter 1

1. Although it is outside the scope of this book, the high-water mark of the Ottoman Empire was 1683. Constantinople ruled across North Africa, the Sudan, the Arabian Peninsula, the Middle East to Persia, the Balkans and around the Black Sea. In that year, their failure to capture Vienna halted expansion into Europe. With hindsight, we can see 1683 and the Siege of Vienna as the high-water mark; 17th-century Europeans did not know this, and the prospect of Ottoman invasion remained a very real fear.

2. Karsh & Karsh, *Empires of the Sand*, pp. 9–17.

3. Ibid., pp. 18–26.

4. McMeekin, *Berlin-Baghdad Express*, p. 101.

5. Satia, "The Defense of Inhumanity," pp. 16–25; Winstone, *Captain Shakespear*; Howell, *Daughter of the Desert*, pp. xix–xxii, for maps of her travels, pp. ix, 99–134, 256, 257, 259, 287; Lawrence, *Seven Pillars*, p. 266; Townsend, *Proconsul*, p. 70.

6. Harvey, *War of Wars*, pp. 249–329; McMeekin, *Berlin-Baghdad Express*, pp. 12, 101.

7. Karsh & Karsh, *Empires of the Sand*, pp. 27–41, 80–83; Catherwood, *Churchill's Folly*, p. 28.

8. Ford, *Eden to Armageddon*, pp. 1–2. While attempting to escape from Turkey, Long thought that "*bashi bazouk*" meant "peasant," which brought to an end one of his escape attempts. Towards the end of the war it mean a bandit or "guerrilla fighter of sanguinary reputation"; Long, *Other Ranks of Kut*, p. 220.

9. Karsh & Karsh, *Empires of the Sand*, pp. 42–68.

10. McMeekin, *Berlin-Baghdad Express*, pp. 70, 72, 80, 102–4. For a recent summary of the confusion of the various campaigns and alliances in the two Balkan Wars, see Jowett, *Armies of the Balkan Wars*.

11. Ibid., pp. 80–82.

12. Ibid., p. 35.

13. Hopkirk, *On Secret Service*, p. 19; McMeekin, *Berlin-Baghdad Express*, p. 57.

14. Karsh & Karsh, *Empires of the Sand*, pp. 94–101; McMeekin, *Berlin-Baghdad Express*, p. 75.

15. Von Sanders, *Five Years in Turkey*, pp. 1–18.

16. Quoted in Catherwood, *Churchill's Folly*, p. 94.

17. Hopkirk, *On Secret Service*, pp. 21–23; McMeekin, *Berlin-Baghdad Express*, pp. 3, 14, 23, 65.

18. Buchan, *The Complete Richard Hannay*, pp. 112–17, 231–32.

19. Hopkirk, *On Secret Service*, p. 19; McMeekin, *Berlin-Baghdad Express*, pp. 17–31; for Gertrude Bell, see G. Howell's *Daughter of the Desert*.

20. Hopkirk, *On Secret Service*, pp. 30–31; McMeekin, *Berlin-Baghdad Express*, pp. 89, 90.

21. Hopkirk, *On Secret Service*, pp. 63, 108.

22. McMeekin, *Berlin-Baghdad Express*, pp. 3–10.

23. Ibid., p. 12; Hopkirk, *On Secret Service*, p. 23.

24. Quoted in McMeekin, *Berlin-Baghdad Express*, p. 85; Hopkins, *On Secret Service*, p. 1. This is reminiscent of Napoleon's insult: "*L'Angleterre est une nation de boutiquiers.*" Both lost to Britain in the end.

25. While not wanting to be accused of overly simplifying the Sunni-Shia Muslim divide, for a Christian audience the Catholic-Protestant divide has parallels. Shias are unlikely to recognize the Caliph, like a Protestant will not recognise the pope's authority. See, for example, Catherwood, *Churchill's Folly*, pp. 23–28; see Eleanor Egan quoted in Bernstein, *Mesopotamia Mess*, p. 27.

26. McMeekin, *Berlin-Baghdad Express*, p. 67.

27. Quoted in Bernstein, *Mesopotamia Mess*, p. 122.

28. Hopkirk, *On Secret Service*, p. 159.

29. McMeekin, *Berlin-Baghdad Express*, p. 89.

30. Hopkirk, *On Secret Service*, pp. 41–43, 49.

31. Ibid., pp. 44–48.

32. Ibid., pp. 48–52.

33. *Official History*, vol. 1, p. 90n.

34. Hopkirk, *On Secret Service*, p. 79; Melotte, *Mons, ANZAC and Kut*, pp. 41–42.

35. *Official History*, vol. 1, pp. 21–24; McMeekin, *Berlin-Baghdad Express*, p. 62.

36. Hopkirk, *On Secret Service*, p. 29. Colonel Malcolm Meade, political resident of the Gulf, was sent to Kuwait on a shooting trip, the cover for political activity.

37. McMeekin, *Berlin-Baghdad Express*, p. 34.

38. Ibid., pp. 22, 34.

39. Algeria in 1881. McMeekin, *Berlin-Baghdad Express*, p. 56.

40. McMeekin, *Berlin-Baghdad Express*, pp. 37–43.

41. *Official History*, vol. 1, pp. 40–42; Carver, *Turkish Front*, pp. 1–2.

42. Wilson, *Loyalties*, pp. 1–2.

43. Hubbard, *Gulf to Ararat*, pp. 30, 37, 44; Wilson, *Loyalties*, p. 42.

44. Catherwood, *Churchill's Folly*, pp. 64, 66–67, 68, 75. Catherwood's assessment was that although Britain did not enter Mesopotamia for oil, Britain would remain for the oil, p. 205.

45. Wilcox, *Battles on the Tigris*, p. 2. The British government remained a major shareholder until privatization under Margaret Thatcher in the 1980s, of which the author took advantage.

46. *Official History*, vol. 1, pp. 81–82.

47. Karsh & Karsh, *Empires of the Sand*, pp. 105–12.

48. Ibid., p. 112; *Official History*, vol. 1, p. 97.

49. Ibid., pp. 112–13; McMeekin, *Berlin-Baghdad Express*, pp. 91, 107–8, 112; Butler, *Sultan's Realm*, p. 69.

50. *Official History*, vol. 1, pp. 75, 76–77; Karsh & Karsh, *Empires of the Sand*, pp. 114–16; McMeekin, *Berlin-Baghdad Express*, pp. 109–13; Butler, *Sultan's Realm*, pp. 70–72.

51. Nunn, *Tigris Gunboats*, pp. 19–25, 26–27.

52. Wilcox, *Battles on the Tigris*, pp. 4–5.

53. Karsh & Karsh, *Empires of the Sand*, pp. 115–17.

54. McMeekin, *Berlin-Baghdad Express*, p. 122.

Chapter 2

1. *Official History*, vol. 1, pp. 1–10.

2. McNab, *Bravo Two Zero*.

3. "India" in 1914 included modern-day India, Pakistan, Bangladesh and Sri Lanka.

4. Tennant, *Clouds Above Baghdad*, pp. 5–11; Townshend, *My Campaign*, p. 41; *Official History*, vol. 1, p. 129; Howell, *Daughter of the Desert*, p. 292.

5. Wilson, *Loyalties*, p. 14. See also Townsend, *Proconsul*, p. 105.

6. Lyman, *First Victory*, p. 7.

7. Tennant, *Clouds Above Baghdad*, p. 7.

8. *Official History*, vol. 1, p. 28; Townshend, *When God Made Hell*, pp. 28–29; Ford, *Eden to Armageddon*, p. 24; Townshend, *My Campaign*, pp. 34–35. This work is not intended to be a study of the Turkish Army. The following short works by Nicolle will introduce the topic: *The Ottoman Army 1914–18*; *Ottoman Infantryman 1914–18*; Jowett, *Armies of the Balkan Wars 1912–13*; Anglesey, *British Cavalry*, vol. 5, pp. 21–25.

9. *Official History*, vol. 1, p. 56n; Wilcox, *Battles on the Tigris*, pp. 4–5.

10. *Official History*, vol. 1, p. 59; Davis, *Ends and Means*, p. 184; Wilcox, *Battles on the Tigris*, pp. 6–7; Bernstein, *Mesopotamia Mess*, p. 44.

11. Wilcox, *Battles on the Tigris*, p. 5.

12. Anglesey, *British Cavalry*, vol. 5, pp. 2–3, 187.

13. *Official History*, vol. 1, pp. 57–58. See also Bernstein, *Mesopotamia Mess*, p. 44.

14. *Official History*, vol. 1, p. 63n; Townshend, *When God Made Hell*, pp. 24–5.

15. *Official History*, vol. 1, pp. 59, 63–64, 65, 102; Strong & Marble, *Artillery in the Great War*, p. 55; Wilcox, *Battles on the Tigris*, pp. 6, 16.

16. Davies, *Ends and Means*, p. 49.

17. Ibid., p. 50; Sumner, *The Indian Army*, pp. 7, 9; Chappell, *British Army*, pp. 4–5.

18. Wilcox, *Battles on the Tigris*, p. 3; Nunn, *Tigris Gunboats*, p. 20; Wilson, *Loyalties*, p. 4.

19. Nunn, *Tigris Gunboats*, p. 21; Wilcox, *Battles on the Tigris*, pp. 3–4.

20. Wilcox, *Battles on the Tigris*, p. 10.

21. Nunn, *Tigris Gunboats*, pp. 20, 21; *Official History*, vol. 1, p. 44. The Lynch Brothers' connection with the Tigris extended back to the 1840s.

22. Nunn, *Tigris Gunboats*, pp. 24–26; Buchanan, *Tragedy of Mesopotamia*, p. 3.

23. Quoted in Nunn, *Tigris Gunboats*, p. 19.

24. Buchanan, *Tragedy of Mesopotamia*, pp. 5–7; Tennant, *Clouds Above Baghdad*, pp. 13–14.

25. Nunn, *Tigris Gunboats*, p. 22.

26. Ibid., p. 24.

27. Ibid., pp. 27, 28.

28. Ibid., pp. 30–31.

29. Wilcox, *Battles on the Tigris*, p. 5.

30. *Official History*, vol. 1, p. 99; Wilcox, *Battles on the Tigris*, pp. 7–8.

31. *Official History*, vol. 1, p. 103; Townshend, *When God Made Hell*, pp. 4–5.

32. *Official History*, vol. 1, pp. 100, 106; Nunn, *Tigris Gunboats*, p. 32; for the characteristics of the Maxim machine gun, see Anglesey, *British Cavalry*, vol. 5, p. 16. The biggest drawback with this weapon (and the Vickers which replaced it) was that the gallon of cooling water would boil after 90 seconds of continuous firing, about 600 rounds. The steam gave away the position and had to be replaced (with the obvious problems when operating in the desert) until a condenser to collect and recycle the water was issued.

33. *Official History*, vol. 1, p. 108; Nunn, *Tigris Gunboats*, pp. 32–34.

34. Davies, *Ends and Means*, p. 53.

35. Nunn, *Tigris Gunboats*, pp. 36–37. *Official History*, vol. 1, p. 109, adds two guns from the 23rd Mountain Battery.

36. Nunn, *Tigris Gunboats*, 37; Wilcox, *Battles on the Tigris*, pp. 9–10. *Official History*, vol. 1, p.

110, adds that the 18th and 17th brigades were following on, although it would be late November before the 17th arrived, p. 140.

37. Wilcox, *Battles on the Tigris*, pp. 24–26.

38. Nunn, *Tigris Gunboats*, pp. 38–40; *Official History*, vol. 1, pp. 115–16.

39. Ibid., p. 38.

40. See *Official History*, vol. 1, pp. 117–18, for the effects of the mirage; Satia, "The Defense of Inhumanity," p. 19; Bernstein, *Mesopotamia Mess*, p. 49.

41. Carver, *Turkish Front*, p. 12; Nunn, *Tigris Gunboats*, p. 40; Wilcox, *Battles on the Tigris*, p. 10.

42. Spackman, *Captured at Kut*, pp. 2–3; *Official History*, vol. 1, pp. 120–23.

43. Nunn, *Tigris Gunboats*, pp. 40–41; *Official History*, vol. 1, p. 125.

44. Nunn, *Tigris Gunboats*, pp. 42, 62; *Official History*, vol. 1, p. 128; Wilcox, *Battles on the Tigris*, p. 11.

45. Nunn, *Tigris Gunboats*, pp. 42–45; *Official History*, vol. 1, pp. 127, 128; Wilcox, *Battles on the Tigris*, p. 11.

46. For the full version, see *Official History*, vol. 1, pp. 130–31; Wilson, *Loyalties*, p. 13.

47. Spackman, *Captured at Kut*, p. 5.

48. Wilson, *Loyalties*, p. 35; Wilcox, *Battles on the Tigris*, p. 11.

49. Wilcox, *Battles on the Tigris*, pp. 15–16; Townshend, *My Campaign*, p. 50; Wilson, *Loyalties*, p. 14; *Official History*, vol. 1, pp. 132–33, 172.

50. Davies, *Ends and Means*, pp. 54–55; Wilcox, *Battles on the Tigris*, pp. 12–13.

51. Ibid.. The full telegram is in *Official History*, vol. 1, pp. 133–34.

52. Ibid., p. 56.

53. Ibid., pp. 56–57.

54. Nunn, *Tigris Gunboats*, pp. 46–49.

55. Ibid., pp. 49–51; *Official History*, vol. 1, p. 141.

56. See Wilcox, *Battles on the Tigris*, p. 10, for the effects.

57. Nunn, *Tigris Gunboats*, pp. 51–54; *Official History*, vol. 1, pp. 142–44.

58. *Official History*, vol. 1, pp. 146–48.

59. Nunn, *Tigris Gunboats*, pp. 54–60; *Official History*, vol. 1, pp. 148–51.

60. Carver, *Turkish Front*, p. 13; Nunn, *Tigris Gunboats*, pp. 58–61; Wilcox, *Battles on the Tigris*, pp. 17–19; *Official History*, vol. 1, p. 151.

61. Spackman, *Captured at Kut*, p. 9; *Official History*, vol. 1, pp. 242–43.

62. Carver, *Turkish Front*, pp. 13; Davies, *Ends and Means*, pp. 63–64; Wilcox, *Battles on the Tigris*, p. 19.

63. Spackman, *Captured at Kut*, p. 10; Hubbard, *From the Gulf to Ararat*, p. 162.

64. Spackman, *Captured at Kut*, pp. 11, 14.

65. *Official History*, vol. 1, pp. 179, 192–93; Wilcox, *Battles on the Tigris*, pp. 20–24.

66. Carver, *Turkish Front*, pp. 102–5; *Official History*, vol. 1, pp. 174, 179, 183–85; Davies, *Ends and Means*, p. 67; Wilcox, *Battles on the Tigris*, p. 27.

67. Quoted in Carver, *Turkish Front*, pp. 102–5.

68. Lyman, *First Victory*; Lyman, *Iraq, 1941*.

69. Spackman, *Captured at Kut*, pp. 13–16. See also *Official History*, vol. 1, p. 176.

70. Carver, *Turkish Front*, p. 102; Wilcox, *Battles on the Tigris*, p. 28.

71. *Official History*, vol. 1, p. 200.

72. Wilcox, *Battles on the Tigris*, p. 28; *Official History*, vol. 1, pp. 181–83.

73. 1/4th Hampshire Regiment, 11th Rajputs, 66th and 67th Punjabis with the 1/5th Hampshire Howitzer Battery commanded by Major General Gorringe. Davies, *Ends and Means*, pp. 69–71; Wilcox,

Battles on the Tigris, pp. 28–29; *Official History*, vol. 1, pp. 194. When questioned before the Mesopotamia Commission, Duff considered the Baghdad plan to be "prudent," whereas Nixon considered that this indicated a change of policy.

75. Gliddon, *VCs*, p. 49; Wilcox, *Battles on the Tigris*, pp. 29–30.

76. Gliddon, *VCs*, pp. 49–50; *Official History*, vol. 1, p. 199.

77. Gliddon, *VCs*, p. 50.

78. Ibid., pp. 50–51; *Official History*, vol. 1, p. 203.

79. Gliddon, *VCs*, pp. 50–52; *Official History*, vol. 1, pp. 200, 201–2, 205–6.

80. Gliddon, *VCs*, pp. 50–52; *Official History*, vol. 1, pp. 206, 207–8.

81. Townshend, *When God Made Hell*, p. 87.

82. Spackman, *Captured at Kut*, pp. 16–18.

83. *Official History*, vol. 1, p. 205.

84. Spackman, *Captured at Kut*, p. 19.

85. Carver, *Turkish Front*, p. 106; Crowley, *Kut 1916*, p. 19; Wilcox, *Battles on the Tigris*, p. 30.

86. *Official History*, vol. 1, pp. 214–16. Melliss is quoted from Townshend, *When God Made Hell*, p. 86.

87. Spackman, *Captured at Kut*, pp. 20–21.

88. Wilson, *Loyalties*, p. 34.

89. Davies, *Ends and Means*, p. 73.

90. Tennant, *Clouds Above Baghdad*, p. 7.

91. Wilcox, *Battles on the Tigris*, p. 30.

92. Davies, *Ends and Means*, pp. 76–77.

93. Wilcox, *Battles on the Tigris*, pp. 30–31.

94. Davies, *Ends and Means*, pp. 76–78; Wilcox, *Battles on the Tigris*, p. 32.

95. See, for example, Townshend, *When God Made Hell*, pp. 72–73.

Chapter 3

1. Braddon, *The Siege*, clearly dislikes Townshend (and, indeed, just about everyone else), but he has to concede that "Townshend the Thruster's" battle of Qurna was "brilliantly successful," conducted by a "general ... of unusual flexibility." Braddon also sees Townshend as the most "brilliant" general in Mesopotamia early in the war, although towards the end "unbalanced" from heatstroke which he never fully recovered from and nervous exhaustion. He was also a "moral coward"; pp. 9, 30, 38, 39, 66, 143, 153, 167.

2. General Sir Redvers Buller (1839–1908) won the Victoria Cross in the 1879 Zulu War. He had commanded a brigade in Wolseley's campaign and was promoted to major general. He would, however, fail miserably in the Boer War.

3. Nash, *Chitral Charlie*, p. 91.

4. Nunn, *Tigris Gunboats*, p. 102.

5. Townshend, *When God Made Hell*, p. 95.

6. Townshend, *My Campaign*, pp. 42–44; *Official History*, vol. 1, p. 190.

7. Townshend, *My Campaign*, p. 48; Nash, *Chitral Charlie*, p. 172; Townshend, *When God Made Hell*, p. 99.

8. Townshend, *My Campaign*, p. 65; Nash, *Chitral Charlie*, p. 170; Nunn, *Tigris Gunboats*, p. 100. Townshend, *When God Made Hell*, p. 98, and *Official History*, vol. 1, pp. 246–47, 249, say 372 *bellums* were collected.

9. Nash, *Chitral Charlie*, pp. 170–72; Nunn, *Tigris Gunboats*, pp. 100–101; *Official History*, vol. 1, p. 249.

10. Townshend, *My Campaign*, pp. 44, 45, 46, 47, 61; Townshend, *When God Made Hell*, pp. 96–97, 99, 101; *Official History*, vol. 1, p. 243.

11. Townshend, *My Campaign*, pp. 61–66; Nash, *Chitral Charlie*, p. 173; *Official History*, vol. 1, pp. 254–56.

12. Nunn, *Tigris Gunboats*, pp. 104–5; *Official History*, vol. 1, pp. 254–57.

13. Townshend, *My Campaign*, p. 66; Anon., *30 Squadron*, pp. 1–2; *Official History*, vol. 1, pp. 158, 255; Satia, "The Defense of Inhumanity," n45. These airplanes had been requested on 9 January 1915.

14. Nunn, *Tigris Gunboats*, pp. 106–7.

15. Ibid., p. 105; *Official History*, vol. 1, p. 258.

16. *Official History*, vol. 1, pp. 258–59.

17. Nunn, *Tigris Gunboats*, p. 111.

18. Townshend, *My Campaign*, p. 70; Nunn says that this "secret" was given to the principal citizens of Qualat Salih, "a well-built little town for those parts, with a few decently verandaed houses facing the busy street on the river" on the afternoon of 2 June 1915. Whenever and wherever the information was given, Townshend was sowing panic amongst the Turks and ensuring that the Arab inhabitants remained passive. Nunn, *Tigris Gunboats*, pp. 113–14; *Official History*, vol. 1, p. 260.

19. Nunn, *Tigris Gunboats*, p. 97, says 20,000.

20. Ibid., pp. 115–17; *Official History*, vol. 1, pp. 262–63.

21. *Official History*, vol. 1, p. 264.

22. Ibid., vol. 1, p. 265.

23. Townshend, *My Campaign*, pp. 70–72; *Official History*, vol. 1, p. 262.

24. Anglesey, *British Cavalry*, vol. 5, p. 206.

25. Wilson, *Loyalties*, p. 49.

26. Nunn, *Tigris Gunboats*, p. 117; Wilcox, *Battles on the Tigris*, p. 44. Braddon, *The Siege*, found nothing to recommend Al-Amara, but then this book finds little positive to say about anything or anyone, pp. 47–48. Candler gives a more positive description in *Long Road to Baghdad*, vol. 1, pp. 36–37.

27. Tennant, *In the Clouds*, pp. 15–16.

28. Beharry, *Barefoot Soldier*; Mills, *Sniper One*.

Chapter 4

1. Davis, *Ends and Means*, p. 84.

2. Wilson, *Loyalties*, p. 52.

3. Ibid., p. 207, wrote that the "energetic punitive measures" around Nasariya "were remarkably barren of practical results."

4. Nunn, *Tigris Gunboats*, pp. 93–95; Wilson, *Loyalties*, p. 53; *Official History*, vol. 1, pp. 244–45.

5. *Official History*, vol. 1, p. 138.

6. Nunn, *Tigris Gunboats*, p. 143; Tennant, *Clouds Above Baghdad*, pp. 40–45.

7. *Official History*, vol. 1, p. 270.

8. Ibid., vol. 1, p. 226.

9. Quoted from Townshend, *When God Made Hell*, pp. 109–10.

10. Braddon, *The Siege*, p. 51.

11. Nunn, *Tigris Gunboats*, pp. 131–32, 149.

12. Ibid., pp. 132–33.

13. Ibid., pp. 134.

14. Wilcox, *Battles on the Tigris*, p. 45; Birch-Reynardson, *Mesopotamia 1914–15*, pp. 164, 182.

15. Nunn, *Tigris Gunboats*, pp. 134–35; *Official History*, vol. 1, pp. 277–78.

16. Quoted from Carver, *Turkish Front*, p. 111.

17. Nunn, *Tigris Gunboats*, pp. 135–36; Wilson, *Loyalties*, p. 53.

18. Nunn, *Tigris Gunboats*, pp. 137–38; *Official History*, vol. 1, p. 278.

19. Nunn, *Tigris Gunboats*, p. 138; *Official History*, vol. 1, pp. 278–79.

20. Nunn, *Tigris Gunboats*, pp. 139–40; *Official History*, vol. 1, pp. 279–80.

21. *Official History*, vol. 1, pp. 280–81.

22. Nunn, *Tigris Gunboats*, p. 140; *Official History*, vol. 1, p. 282.

23. Wilcox, *Battles*, p. 48; Nunn, *Tigris Gunboats*, p. 142; *Official History*, vol. 1, p. 283.

24. Nunn, *Tigris Gunboats*, pp. 142–43; *Official History*, vol. 1, p. 283.

25. Ibid.

26. Nunn, *Tigris Gunboats*, pp. 143–44; Buchanan, *Tragedy of Mesopotamia*, p. 18; *Official History*, vol. 1, pp. 283–84.

27. Nunn, *Tigris Gunboats*, pp. 144–45.

28. Ibid., p. 145.

29. Wilson, *Loyalties*, p. 54.

30. Quoted from Townshend, *When God Made Hell*, pp. 112.

31. Townshend, *When God Made Hell*, p. 112; Wilson, *Loyalties*, p. 59; *Official History*, vol. 1, p. 166; the 12th Brigade left India for Basra on 1 February consisting of the 2/West Kents, 4th Rajput, 44th Merwara and 90th Punjabis.

32. Nunn, *Tigris Gunboats*, p. 145; *Official History*, vol. 1, pp. 287–89.

33. Quoted from Carver, *Turkish Front*, pp. 112–14.

34. Nunn, *Tigris Gunboats*, p. 146.

35. Ibid., pp. 145–46; *Official History*, vol. 1, p. 289.

36. Nunn, *Tigris Gunboats*, p. 146; *Official History*, vol. 1, p. 291.

37. See also Atkinson, *The Queen's Own*, pp. 106–7. *Official History*, vol. 1, pp. 291–92, says the attack started at 0530 hours.

38. Nunn, *Tigris Gunboats*, pp. 147–48; *Official History*, vol. 1, pp. 293–94.

39. Wilson, *Loyalties*, pp. 58–59.

40. Nunn, *Tigris Gunboats*, p. 148; Barker, *First Iraq War*, p. 71; *Official History*, vol. 1, p. 294.

41. Nunn, *Tigris Gunboats*, pp. 148–49; *Official History*, vol. 1, pp. 294–95.

42. Townshend, *When God Made Hell*, p. 116; Nunn, *Tigris Gunboats*, p. 148; *Official History*, vol. 1, p. 295.

43. Nunn, *Tigris Gunboats*, pp. 149–51; *Official History*, vol. 1, pp. 276n, 296–97.

44. Quoted from Davis, *Ends and Means*, p. 84; *Official History*, vol. 1, p. 298.

45. Nunn, *Tigris Gunboats*, p. 133; *Official History*, vol. 1, p. 298.

46. Wilson, *Loyalties*, p. 60.

47. Quoted in Davis, *Ends and Means*, p. 84.

48. Nunn, *Tigris Gunboats*, pp. 154–55.

49. Quoted from Townshend, *When God Made Hell*, pp. 117–18.

Chapter 5

1. Townshend, *My Campaign*, p. 133.

2. Wilcox, *Battles on the Tigris*, p. 51; Townshend, *My Campaign*, pp. 72–73; *Official History*, vol. 1, pp. 301n, 302–7, 312.

3. Carver, *Turkish Front*, p. 116; Townshend, *When God Made Hell*, p. 122; *Official History*, vol. 1, pp. 311–12, 314–16.

4. Wilcox, *Battles on the Tigris*, p. 53; Crowley, *Kut 1916*, p. 28; Townshend, *When God Made Hell*, p. 123.

5. Townshend, *When God Made Hell*, pp. 122–23; *Official History*, vol. 1, pp. 316–18.

6. Townshend, *When God Made Hell*, p. 126; *Official History*, vol. 1, pp. 319–20.

7. *Official History*, vol. 1, pp. 329–30. The armored cars were supplied as an experiment. They proved their worth and were used following the battle for casualty evacuation. Unfortunately, their construction was too light for the terrain, and they were soon out of action due to mechanical failures. As with aviation at this point, they were the forerunners of major changes which would be implemented by 1918.

8. *Official History*, vol. 1, pp. 323–24.

9. Carver, *Turkish Front*, p. 116; *Official History*, vol. 1, pp. 325–30.

10. Nunn, *Tigris Gunboats*, pp. 161–63; *Official History*, vol. 1, p. 335.

11. Townshend, *My Campaign*, p. 121.

12. Spackman, *Captured at Kut*, p. 39.

13. Nunn, *Tigris Gunboats*, p. 163.

14. *Official History*, vol. 1, pp. 335–37.

15. *Official History*, vol. 2, pp. 4–33.

16. Townshend *My Campaign*, p. 143; Wilson, *Loyalties*, p. 84; *Official History*, vol. 2, p. 37. This was especially so for the 16th Brigade, which had been in country longest.

17. Townshend, *When God Made Hell*, pp. 144–45.

18. Quoted from Wilcox, *Battles on the Tigris*, pp. 59–60.

19. *Official History*, vol. 2, pp. 48–49.

20. Ibid., pp. 45n, 50n, 63.

21. Ibid., 58–60, 7; Anon., *30 Squadron*, p. 6.

22. Quoted from Wilcox, *Battles on the Tigris*, p. 60.

23. *Official History*, vol. 2, pp. 65–66. Two battalions of the 51st Division did not arrive on the battlefield until the 23rd.

24. Wilcox, *Battles on the Tigris*, p. 62.

25. Quoted from Wilcox, *Tigris Battles*, p. 63; *Official History*, vol. 2, pp. 67–69.

26. Spackman, *Captured at Kut*, pp. 38–50; *Official History*, vol. 2, pp. 72–91; Braddon, *The Siege*, p. 96.

27. Nunn said, "It seldom took less than nine or ten days to reach Lajj from Basra; but frequently considerably longer, depending on the amount of time the ship spent aground in the shallow reaches." *Tigris Gunboats*, p. 177; Townshend, *My Campaign*, p. 179; *Official History*, vol. 2, p. 54n.

28. Townshend, *When God Made Hell*, pp. 161–62; *Official History*, vol. 2, p. 91.

29. *Official History*, vol. 2, pp. 92–97; Townshend, *When God Made Hell*, pp. 162–63.

30. *Official History*, vol. 2, pp. 100–101.

31. Townshend, *My Campaign*, p. 182.

32. *Official History*, vol. 2, pp. 100–101.

33. Ibid., p. 101.

34. Ibid., p. 107.

35. Nunn, *Tigris Gunboats*, pp. 178–79; Townshend, *My Campaign*, p. 191.

36. Nunn, *Tigris Gunboats*, p. 180; Buchanan, *Tragedy of Mesopotamia*, p. 48.

37. Nunn, *Tigris Gunboats*, p. 183.

38. Spackman, *Captured at Kut*, p. 54; Townshend, *My Campaign*, p. 195.

39. Nunn, *Tigris Gunboats*, pp. 182, 185.

40. Ibid., pp. 169, 176; Wilcox, *Battles on the Tigris*, p. 78; Spackman, *Captured at Kut*, p. 41.

41. Spackman, *Captured at Kut*, p. 57.

Chapter 6

1. Braddon, *The Siege*, pp. 283–84.

2. Quoted in Cowley, *Kut 1916*, p. 35.

3. Townshend, *My Campaign*, p. 198; Buchanan, *Tragedy of Mesopotamia*, p. 48; Rimmington, "Kut-ul-Amara," p. 21.

4. Rimmington, "Kut-ul-Amara," p. 23.

5. Quoted in Crowley, *Kut 1916*, p. 38.

6. Davis, *Ends and Means*, p. 140; see also Rimmington, "Kut-ul-Amara," p. 22.

7. Nash, *Chitral Charlie*, p. 230.

8. Townshend, *My Campaign*, p. 212.

9. Ibid., pp. 212–13.

10. Ibid., pp. 218–19.

11. Davis, *Ends and Means*, p. 141.

12. See also Barker, *The First Iraq War*, pp. 114–15.

13. Nunn, *Tigris Gunboats*, p. 189.

14. *Official History*, vol. 2, p. 157; *Mesopotamia Commission Report*, p. 169, quoted in Crowley, *Kut 1916*, p. 38. Nunn, *Tigris Gunboats*, also quotes Hehir on p. 190.

15. Barker, *First Iraq War*, p. 119.

16. Townshend, *My Campaign*, p. 230; quoted in Crowley, *Kut 1916*, pp. 39–40; Spackman, *Captured at Kut*, p. 60; Townshend, *When God Made Hell*, pp. 181–82.

17. Crowley, *Kut 1916*, p. 44.

18. *Mesopotamia Commission Report*, p. 169.

19. Townshend, *My Campaign*, pp. 221–22.

20. Quoted in Crowley, *Kut 1916*, p. 52.

21. Crowley, *Kut 1916*, p. 89.

22. Spackman, *Captured at Kut*, pp. 61–62; Barker, *First Iraq War*, pp. 121–22; Townshend, *My Campaign*, p. 223.

23. Crowley, *Kut 1916*, p. 53.

24. *Official History*, vol. 2, p. 174; Crowley, *Kut 1916*, p. 54.

25. Quoted in Crowley, *Kut 1916*, pp. 54–55.

26. Ibid., p. 58.

27. Spackman, *Captured at Kut*, p. 64.

28. Townshend, *My Campaign*, pp. 231–33.

29. Quoted in Crowley, *Kut 1916*, p. 59.

30. Barker, *First Iraq War*, pp. 123–25; Townshend, *When God Made Hell*, pp. 189–91.

31. Quoted in Crowley, *Kut 1916*, p. 62.

32. Ibid.

33. Townshend, *My Campaign*, p. 237; Crowley, *Kut 1916*, p. 70.

34. Townshend, *When God Made Hell*, p. 215.

35. Townshend, *My Campaign*, pp. 265–66.

36. Spackman, *Captured at Kut*, p. 71.

37. Ibid., pp. 58–59.

38. Quoted in Crowley, *Kut 1916*, p. 102.

39. Spackman, *Captured at Kut*, p. 71, mentions scurvy at the end of February.

40. Hopkirk, *On Secret Service*, pp. 201–2; Buchan, *Greenmantle*.

41. Townshend, *My Campaign*, p. 283; Townshend, *When God Made Hell*, p. 213.

42. Townshend, *My Campaign*, pp. 233, 236, 237, 283.

43. Ibid., p. 286; Spackman, *Captured at Kut*, pp. 72–73.

44. Townshend, *My Campaign*, p. 286.

45. Ibid., p. 287; Townshend, *When God Made Hell*, p. 216.

46. Townshend, *My Campaign*, p. 288.

47. Spackman, *Captured at Kut*, p. 74.

48. Townshend, *My Campaign*, pp. 299–301.

49. Ibid., pp. 294–95.

50. Davis, *Ends and Means*, p. 163.

51. Crowley, *Kut 1916*, pp. 126–27; Spackman, *Captured at Kut*, p. 71.

52. Townshend, *My Campaign*, p. 299.

53. Quoted in Crowley, *Kut 1916*, p. 129.

54. Townshend, *When God Made Hell*, p. 222.

55. Sanders, *Five Years in Turkey*, p. 133.

56. Townshend, *My Campaign*, p. 313.

57. Ibid., p. 321.

58. Ibid., p. 321, Crowley, *Kut 1916*, p. 146.

59. Townshend, *My Campaign*, p. 320; Crowley, *Kut 1916*, pp. 131, 149; Melotte, *Mons, ANZAC and Kut*, pp. 180–81; Spackman, *Captured at Kut*, pp. 70, 76; Townshend, *When God Made Hell*, pp. 243–44; Barker, *First Iraq War*, pp. 217–18; Davis, *Ends and Means*, pp. 159–60, 164–65.

60. Crowley, *Kut 1916*, p. 151; Spackman, *Captured at Kut*, pp. 76–77; Townshend, *When God Made Hell*, p. 245; Anon., *30 Squadron*, pp. 10, 46; Braddon, *The Siege*, p. 226.

61. Crowley, *Kut 1916*, p. 152.

62. Howell, *Daughter of the Desert*, p. 283.

63. Spackman, *Captured at Kut*, pp. 77–78; Nunn, *Tigris Gunboats*, pp. 227–28; *Official History*, vol. 2, pp. 435–36; Braddon, *The Siege*, p. 249; Wilson, *Loyalties*, p. 96.

64. Lawrence, *Seven Pillars*, p. 59; Howell, *Daughter of the Desert*, pp. 283–84; Brown, *Letters of T.E. Lawrence*, p. 82, 18 May 1916.

65. Vice Admiral Sir Rosslyn Wemyss, commander-in-chief East Indies Squadron who was visiting Mesopotamia at the time.

66. Crowley, *Kut 1916*, pp. 163–64.

67. Spackman, *Captured at Kut*, p. 84.

68. Quoted in Crowley, *Kut 1916*, pp, 164–65.

69. Braddon, *The Siege*, p. 261; Wilson, *Loyalties*, pp. 99–100; Anglesey, *British Cavalry*, vol. 5, p. 272.

Chapter 7

1. Crowley, *Kut 1916*, p. 53.

2. Wilcox, *Battles on the Tigris*, pp. 93–97.

3. The 35th Brigade would be replace by the 21st, consisting of an English Composite Battalion of the 2/Norfolks and 2/Dorsets, 6th Jats, 9th Bhopals, Composite Mahratta Battalion.

4. Wilcox, *Battles on the Tigris*, pp. 119–20.

5. Ibid., p. 88.

6. Quoted from Crowley, *Kut 1916*, pp. 67–68.

7. Ibid., p. 66.

8. Anon., *Highland Regiment*, p. 17.

9. Quoted in Wilcox, *Battles on the Tigris*, p. 92.

10. Quoted from Gliddon, *VCs*, p. 55.

11. Gliddon, *VCs*, pp. 53–57.

12. Anon., *Highland Regiment*, pp. 20–21.

13. Gliddon, *VCs*, pp. 58–62; Anglesey, *British Cavalry*, vol. 5, pp. 332–34.

14. Gliddon, *VCs*, pp. 63–68.

15. Wilcox, *Battles on the Tigris*, p. 103.

16. Buchanan, *Tragedy of Mesopotamia*, p. 50.

17. Quoted from Wilcox, *Battles on the Tigris*, p. 105.

18. Ibid., p. 106.

19. Gliddon, *VCs*, pp. 69–72.

20. Townshend, *My Campaign*, p. 268; Wilson, *Loyalties*, p. 120.

21. Wilcox, *Battles on the Tigris*, pp. 163–64.

22. Quoted from Wilcox, *Battles on the Tigris*, p. 88.

23. Wilcox, *Battles on the Tigris*, p. 116.

24. http://www.st-dunstans.org.uk.

25. Gliddon, *VCs*, pp. 73–78.

26. Ibid., pp. 79–80.

27. Wilson, *Loyalties*, p. 121.

28. Gliddon, *VCs*, pp. 81–85.

29. Ibid., pp. 86–90.

30. Ibid., pp. 91–95.

31. Ibid., pp. 96–98.

Chapter 8

1. Quoted from Wilcox, *Battles on the Tigris*, p. 143.

2. Tennant, *Clouds Above Baghdad*, pp. 8, 10, 13.

3. Ibid., pp. 13, 15, 17.

4. Ibid., pp. 16–17.

5. Ibid., pp. 28–30.

6. Ibid., p. 21.

7. Quoted in Anglesey, *British Cavalry*, vol. 5, p. 121n.

8. Tennant, *Clouds Above Baghdad*, pp. 22–23, 40; Anon., *30 Squadron*, p. 13.

9. Tennant, *Clouds Above Baghdad*, pp. 48–49.

10. Ibid., p. 49.

11. Satia, "The Defense of Inhumanity," pp. 32–34.

12. Tennant, *Clouds Above Baghdad*, p. 50.

13. Ibid., p. 35; Anon., *30 Squadron*, pp. 13, 14, 28.

14. Tennant, *Clouds Above Baghdad*, p. 39.

15. Ibid., pp. 34, 35, 41.

16. Ibid., pp. 30–32.

17. Ibid., p. 48.

18. Ibid., pp. 40–45.

19. Ibid., pp. 50–51.

20. Bernstein, *Mesopotamia Mess*, p. 107.

21. Tennant, *Clouds Above Baghdad*, p. 23; Neave, D., quoted in Crowley, *Kut 1916*, p. 20.

22. Tennant, *Clouds Above Baghdad*, pp. 26, 27.

23. Horne, *The Lonely Leader*, p. 14.

24. Tennant, *Clouds Above Baghdad*, p. 51.

25. Wilcox, *Battles on the Tigris*, pp. 148, 161–66.

26. Tennant, *Clouds Above Baghdad*, pp. 56–58, 62–63.

27. Ibid., pp. 58–59, 61, 64.

28. Ibid., pp. 59–60.

29. Ibid., pp. 67–68, 75–76.

30. Ibid., pp. 69–70.

31. Gliddon, *VCs*, pp. 99–102; Lyman, *Bill Slim*, pp. 8–11.

32. Gliddon, *VCs*, pp. 107–10.

33. Ibid., pp. 111–14.

34. Tennant, *Clouds Above Baghdad*, pp. 81, 83; Anon., *30 Squadron*, p. 18.

35. Tennant, *Clouds Above Baghdad*, p. 89.

36. Holland, *With a 14th Hussar*, pp. 6–7.

37. Gliddon, *VCs*, pp. 115–18.

38. Tennant, *Clouds Above Baghdad*, pp. 84, 85; Anon., *30 Squadron*, pp. 19–20.

39. Tennant, *Clouds Above Baghdad*, p. 91.

40. Ibid., pp. 96–97.

41. Gliddon, *VCs*, pp. 119–23.

42. Ibid., pp. 124–29.

43. Tennant, *Clouds Above Baghdad*, pp. 99–100.

44. Ibid., p. 102.

45. Buchanan, *Tragedy of Mesopotamia*, pp. 166–67.

Chapter 9

1. *Blackwood Magazine*, August 1917, quoted in Anon., *Highland Regiment*, p. 64.

2. Downham, *Old Contemptible*, pp. 250–51.

3. Ibid., p. 252.

4. *Official History*, vol. 3, p. 248.

5. Wilson, *Loyalties*, p. 234; Roosevelt, *Armoured Cars in Eden*, pp. 26–27.

6. Townshend, *When God Made Hell*, p. 387.

7. Roosevelt, *Armoured Cars in Eden*, pp. 60, 62, 77, 83.

8. Downham, *Old Contemptible*, p. 253.

9. Barker, *First Iraq War*, pp. 318–19.

10. Ibid., p. 320.

11. Ibid., pp. 320–21; Townshend, *When God Made Hell*, p. 388; Anglesey, *British Cavalry*, vol. 6, p. 104.

12. Nunn, *Tigris Gunboats*, pp. 276–79.

13. Thompson, *Tigers*, p. 25.

14. Ibid., p. 26.

15. Townshend, *When God Made Hell*, p. 391.

16. Anon., *Highland Regiment*, p. 71.

17. Howell, *Daughter of the Desert*, pp. 296–97.

18. Roosevelt, *Armoured Cars in Eden*, pp. 78, 106.

19. Thompson, *Tigers*, p. 21.

20. Ibid., p. 48.

21. Ibid., p. 24.

22. Ibid., p. 31.

23. Downham, *Old Contemptible*, p. 253.

24. Thompson, *Tigers*, p. 53.

25. Barker, *First Iraq War*, p. 328.

26. Ibid., pp. 323, 327–28, 340.

27. Ibid., pp. 324–25.

28. Anglesey, *British Cavalry*, vol. 6, p. 99.

29. Wilcox, *Battles on the Tigris*, p. 170; Carver, *Turkish Front*, p. 177; Barker, *First Iraq War*, pp. 323–26, 327–28; Townshend, *When God Made Hell*, p. 393.

30. Anglesey, *British Cavalry*, vol. 6, p. 100.

31. Anon., *Highland Regiment*, p. 68.

32. Barker, *First Iraq War*, pp. 321–22; Tennant, *Clouds Above Baghdad*, pp. 118–19; Wylly, *Leicesters*, pp. 173–74; Anon., *Highland Regiment*, pp. 73–81; Thompson, *Tigers*, p. 59.

33. Anon., *Highland Regiment*, p. 82.

34. Thompson, *Tigers*, p. 20; Wylly, *Leicesters*, p. 174.

35. Thompson, *Tigers*, pp. 26–37; Wylly, *Leicesters*, p. 175.

36. Thompson, *Tigers*, pp. 41–42.

37. Ibid., pp. 40, 45.

38. Downham, *Old Contemptible*, p. 259.

39. Thompson, *Tigers*, pp. 45–46.

40. Barker, *First Iraq War*, pp. 326–27; Townshend, *When God Made Hell*, p. 392, cites Burnes, *Mesopotamia*, p. 30, who says that the staff could not understand why the 39th Brigade halted.

41. Downham, *Old Contemptible*, p. 253.

42. Barker, *First Iraq War*, p. 328; Anglesey, *British Cavalry*, vol. 6, p. 100; Downham, *Old Contemptible*, p. 255.

43. Downham, *Old Contemptible*, p. 256.

44. Wilcox, *Battles on the Tigris*, p. 171.

45. Downham, *Old Contemptible*, pp. 256–58.

46. Wilcox, *Battles on the Tigris*, p. 171; Carver, *Turkish Front*, p. 179; Barker, *First Iraq War*, pp. 329–31; Downham, *Old Contemptible*, pp. 257–58; Anglesey, *British Cavalry*, vol. 6, pp. 101–2.

47. Anon., *Highland Regiment*, pp. 84–87.

48. Ibid., pp. 87–89.

49. Thompson, *Tigers*, pp. 50, 57–58, 66.

50. Ibid., pp. 58–59.

51. Ibid., pp. 56, 59.

52. Wilcox, *Battle on the Tigris*, p. 171; Gliddon, *VCs*, pp. 130–34; Barker, *First Iraq War*, pp. 331–32; Anon., *Highland Regiment*, pp. 84–100; Thompson, *Tigers*, pp. 59, 60, 65.

53. Thompson, *Tigers*, pp. 67, 92.

54. Ibid., pp. 76–77.

55. Ibid., pp. 79–80.

56. Wylly, *Leicesters*, p. 179.

57. Wilcox, *Battle on the Tigris*, pp. 171–72; Carver, *Turkish Front*, pp. 180–81; Barker, *First Iraq War*, pp. 332–34; Wylly, *Leicesters*, pp. 177–79; Thompson, *Tigers*, pp. 73, 80–84.

58. Ibid., pp. 84, 87.

59. Gliddon, *VCs*, pp. 135–38; Thompson, *Tigers*, p. 78.

60. Barker, *First Iraq War*, pp. 333–34; Tennant, *Clouds Above Baghdad*, p. 150; Anglesey, *British Cavalry*, vol. 6, pp. 102–3; Thompson, *Tigers*, p. 95; *Official History*, vol. 3, p. 326.

61. Wilcox, *Battle on the Tigris*, p. 172; Ford, *Eden to Armageddon*, pp. 85–86; Thompson, *Tigers*, pp. 93–94, 96–97; Downham, *Old Contemptible*, p. 260.

62. Barker, *First Iraq War*, pp. 328–29.

63. Downham, *Old Contemptible*, pp. 259–60, n62.

64. Wilcox, *Battle on the Tigris*, pp. 172–73; Carver, *Turkish Front*, pp. 181–82; Barker, *First Iraq War*, pp. 335–36; Downham, *Old Contemptible*, pp. 260–62, n76–80; Ford, *Eden to Armageddon*, pp. 88–90.

65. Downham, *Old Contemptible*, p. 278.

66. Wilcox, *Battle on the Tigris*, p. 177; Barker, *First Iraq War*, pp. 319–20, 322; Townshend, *When God Made Hell*, pp. 387–88.

67. Townshend, *When God Made Hell*, pp. 389–90.

68. Barker, *First Iraq War*, p. 337.

69. Tennant, *Clouds Above Baghdad*, pp. 181–82.

70. Wilcox, *Battle on the Tigris*, p. 177; Carver, *Turkish Front*, p. 182; Barker, *First Iraq War*, pp. 341–42; Tennant, *Clouds Above Baghdad*, pp. 183–84.

71. Downham, *Old Contemptible*, pp. 273–74.

72. Quoted from Anglesey, *British Cavalry*, vol. 6, p. 106.

73. Ibid., pp. 105–6.

74. Ibid., pp. 106–7; Roosevelt, *Armoured Cars in Eden*, p. 102.

75. Downham, *Old Contemptible*, pp. 278–95.

76. Wilcox, *Battle on the Tigris*, p. 177; Barker, *First Iraq War*, pp. 342–43; Roosevelt, *Armoured Cars in Eden*, p. 111; Tennant, *Clouds Above Baghdad*, pp. 126–27, 187, 191; Ford, *Eden to Armageddon*, p. 103; Anon., *30 Squadron*, pp. 32, 36. 72 Squadron was formed at Upavon, England, on 2 July 1917 and arrive in Basra on 2 March 1918.

77. Roosevelt, *Armoured Cars in Eden*, pp. 85–86.

78. Townshend, *When God Made Hell*, p. 397.

79. Anglesey, *British Cavalry*, vol. 6, pp. 131–32.

80. Atkinson, *The Queen's Own*, p. 337.

81. Fanshaw, *18th (Indian) Division*, pp. 1–3.

82. Barker, *First Iraq War*, pp. 338–39; Anglesey, *British Cavalry*, vol. 5, p. 159; vol. 6, p. 109.

83. Tennant, *Clouds Above Baghdad*, p. 190; Anglesey, *British Cavalry*, vol. 5, p. 243; vol. 6, pp. 108, 154; Howell, *Daughter of the Desert*, pp. 282, 298–99, 300, 301, 309, 311, 314–15, 317, 324; Townshend, *When God Made Hell*, pp. 409, 410–11; Downham, *Old Contemptible*, pp. 274, 297; Roosevelt, *Armoured Cars in Eden*, pp. 23, 54; Thompson, *Tigers*, pp. 52, 106; Barker, *First Iraq War*, pp. 343–44; Wilson, *Loyalties*, pp. 257, 271; Bernstein, *Mesopotamia Mess*, pp. 155–56, 164, 165–70.

84. Roosevelt, *Armoured Cars in Eden*, pp. 16–19.

85. Ibid., p. 76.

86. Holland, *Hussar Through Mesopotamia*, pp. 36–37; Barker, *First Iraq War*, pp. 344, 345; Tennant, *Clouds Above Baghdad*, p. 200; Anglesey, *British Cavalry*, vol. 6, pp. 117, 118.

87. Anglesey, *British Cavalry*, vol. 6, pp. 113–14.

88. Wilcox, *Battle on the Tigris*, pp. 178–79; Holland, *Hussar Through Mesopotamia*, p. 37; Barker, *First Iraq War*, pp. 345–47; Tennant, *Clouds Above Baghdad*, p. 204; Anglesey, *British Cavalry*, vol. 6, pp. 111–18.

89. Quoted from Anglesey, *British Cavalry*, vol. 6, p. 111.

90. Anglesey, *British Cavalry*, vol. 5, pp. 57, 72, 80–81, 130–31, 223, 318–21, 336–39.

91. Thompson, *Tigers*, pp. 110–13.

92. Roosevelt, *Armoured Cars in Eden*, pp. 38, 76.

93. Thompson, *Tigers*, pp. 114–18.

94. Anglesey, *British Cavalry*, vol. 6, p. 122.

95. Barker, *First Iraq War*, pp. 349–51; Roosevelt, *Armoured Cars in Eden*, p. 33; Anglesey, *British Cavalry*, vol. 6, pp. 119–23; Wylly, *Leicesters*, pp. 183–84; Thompson, *Tigers*, p. 120.

96. Roosevelt, *Armoured Cars in Eden*, p. 41.

97. Thompson, *Tigers*, p. 124.

98. Tennant, *Clouds Above Baghdad*, p. 225.

99. Barker, *First Iraq War*, pp. 350–52; Roosevelt, *Armoured Cars in Eden*, pp. 43–48, 53; Anglesey, *British Cavalry*, vol. 6, pp. 123–29; Thompson, *Tigers*, pp. 125–26.

100. Roosevelt, *Armoured Cars in Eden*, pp. 45–46.

101. Thompson, *Tigers*, pp. 129–31.

102. Roosevelt, *Armoured Cars in Eden*, pp. 49–50.

103. Barker, *First Iraq War*, pp. 348–50.

104. Ibid., p. 350.

105. Ibid., pp. 352–53; Wilson, *Loyalties*, pp. 275–77.

106. Wilcox, *Battle on the Tigris*, pp. 180–82; Carver, *Turkish Front*, p. 182; Barker, *First Iraq War*, pp. 352–55; Roosevelt, *Armoured Cars in Eden*, pp. 52–53; Anglesey, *British Cavalry*, vol. 6, p. 134; Townshend, *When God Made Hell*, p. 401.

107. Barker, *First Iraq War*, pp. 347–48.

108. Ibid., p. 362; Roosevelt, *Armoured Cars in Eden*, p. 79; Roosevelt served in a LAMB accompanying the cavalry.

109. Anglesey, *British Cavalry*, vol. 6, pp. 138–39.

110. Evans, *The Years Between*, pp. 57–58, quoted in Anglesey, *British Cavalry*, vol. 6, p. 143.

111. Anglesey, *British Cavalry*, vol. 6, p. 144.

112. Barker, *First Iraq War*, pp. 361–64; Roosevelt, *Armoured Cars in Eden*, pp. 79–81, 89; Anglesey, *British Cavalry*, vol. 6, pp. 136–44.

113. Wilcox, *Battle on the Tigris*, p. 209; Carver, *Turkish Front*, p. 184; Barker, *First Iraq War*, pp. 362–63; Roosevelt, *Armoured Cars in Eden*, pp. 80, 83–84, 89; Tennant, *Clouds Above Baghdad*, pp. 269–84, 288.

114. Wilcox, *Battle on the Tigris*, pp. 209–11.

115. Quoted from Carver, *Turkish Front*, pp. 184–85.

116. Tennant, *Clouds Above Baghdad*, p. 288.

117. Wilcox, *Battle on the Tigris*, p. 211; Candler, *The Long Road to Baghdad*, vol. 2, p. 20; Barker, *First Iraq War*, pp. 363–64.

118. Barker, *First Iraq War*, p. 364.

119. Wilcox, *Battle on the Tigris*, pp. 211–12; Roosevelt, *Armoured Cars in Eden*, pp. 109–14; Anglesey, *British Cavalry*, vol. 6, pp. 145–52; Ford, *Eden to Armageddon*, pp. 106–10.

120. Wilcox, *Battle on the Tigris*, p. 212; Downham, *Old Contemptible*, p. 297.

121. Anglesey, *British Cavalry*, vol. 6, p. 154.

122. Ford, *Eden to Armageddon*, p. 111.

123. Anglesey, *British Cavalry*, vol. 6, p. 156.

124. Ibid..

125. The 18th Division replaced the 3rd Division, which was sent to Palestine. The 17th Division replaced the 7th Division, which was sent to Egypt. Fanshaw, *18th (Indian) Division*, p. 4; Wilcox, *Battles on the Tigris*, p. 182; Barker, *First Iraq War*, pp. 359–60; Anglesey, *British Cavalry*, vol. 6, p. 157.

126. Anglesey, *British Cavalry*, vol. 6, pp. 157–58.

127. Ibid., p. 158.

128. Ibid., pp. 158–59.

129. Ibid., pp. 159–60.

130. Ibid., p. 160.

131. Ibid., pp. 160–1.

132. Wilson-Johnston, *18th (Indian) Division*, pp. 26–27, 28–30, 31, 33–35; Anglesey, *British Cavalry*, vol. 6, pp. 155–63.

133. Anglesey, *British Cavalry*, vol. 6, pp. 163–64.

134. Ibid., p. 164.

135. Ibid., pp. 165–66.

136. Ibid., pp. 166–67.

137. Wilson-Johnston, *18th (Indian) Division*, pp. 32–33; Anglesey, *British Cavalry*, vol. 6, pp. 162–70.

138. Anglesey, *British Cavalry*, vol. 6, pp. 172–73.

139. Wilcox, *Battle on the Tigris*, p. 217.

140. At Megiddo there was also naval gunfire support from the Mediterranean. In Mesopotamia, as we have seen, naval cooperation was being used to great effect but the Tigris was no longer navigable by the Fly-class gunboats. Tanks were also used in Palestine but not in Mesopotamia.

141. For Megiddo, see Perrett, *Megiddo 1918*.
142. *Official History*, vol. 4, p. 319; Barker, *First Iraq War*, p. 372; Townshend, *When God Made Hell*, p. 435; Atkinson, *The Queen's Own*, pp. 461–69; Anglesey, *British Cavalry*, vol. 6, pp. 172–73.
143. Wilson-Johnston, *18th (Indian) Division*, pp. 36–41.
144. Downham, *Old Contemptible*, p. 298.
145. Wilson-Johnston, *18th (Indian) Division*, p. 41; Barker, *First Iraq War*, pp. 372–73; Ford, *Eden to Armageddon*, pp. 116–17.
146. Downham, *Old Contemptible*, pp. 301–15.

Chapter 10

1. Carver, *Turkish Front*, pp. 154–55; Nash, *Chitral Charlie*, p. 281.
2. Nash, *Chitral Charlie*, p. 271.
3. Original reproduced in Nash, *Chitral Charlie*, p. 266.
4. His ADC, Captain Moreland; Lieutenant Colonel Parr, a staff officer; an Indian servant; a Portuguese cook; two soldier orderlies; and his dog; Nash, *Chitral Charlie*, p. 271.
5. Nash, *Chitral Charlie*, p. 272; Townshend, *When God Made Hell*, p. 310.
6. Nash, *Chitral Charlie*, p. 273.
7. Ibid., pp. 273–74; Townshend, *When God Made Hell*, p. 319.
8. Nash, *Chitral Charlie*, p. 274.
9. Ibid., p. 276.
10. Ibid., p. 277 for a summary of the debate on this letter to Melliss; Crowley, *Kut 1916*, p. 204.
11. Ibid., pp. 278–81; Ford, *Eden to Armageddon*, p. 397; Townshend, *When God Made Hell*, pp. 432–33.
12. Spackman was a lieutenant throughout the fighting until his capture at Kut. During his captivity he became eligible for promotion to captain and adopted that rank.
13. Spackman, *Captured at Kut*, p. 108.
14. Ibid., p. 129.
15. Ibid., pp. 121–22.
16. Ibid., p. 125.
17. Ibid., p. 161.
18. See E.H. Keeling, *Adventures in Turkey and Russia* (1924).
19. "Major-General Henry H Rich CB," in P. Liddle, ed., *Captured Memories 1900–1918*, pp. 159–83.
20. Jones, *The Road to En-Dor*, p. 70.
21. Ibid., p. 77.
22. Ibid., pp. 158–59.
23. Long, *Other Ranks of Kut*, p. 24.
24. Ibid., pp. 24–25.
25. Ibid., p. 32.
26. Ibid., pp. 51–52.
27. Ibid., p. 85.
28. Ibid., pp. 94–95, 101.
29. Ibid., pp. 107–9.
30. Ibid., p. 112.
31. Ibid. p. 117.
32. Ibid., pp. 142–43.
33. Ibid. pp. 149–51.
34. Ibid. pp. 151–53.
35. Ibid. pp. 162–78.
36. Ibid., p. 194.
37. Ibid., p. 198.
38. Ibid., p. 232.
39. Ibid., p. 246.

40. Ibid., p. 255.
41. Ibid., pp. 269–70.
42. Ibid., pp. 275, 276, 284–86.
43. Ibid., pp. 283–84, 290–92, 307–8.
44. Ibid., pp. 311–22.
45. Ibid., pp. 322–52.
46. Ibid., pp. 357–58.

Chapter 11

1. Dunsterville, *Dunsterforce*, p. 1.
2. Townshend, *When God Made Hell*, p. 418.
3. Dunsterville, *Dunsterforce*, p. 2.
4. Ibid., pp. 3, 10; Ford, *Eden to Armageddon*, pp. 191–92.
5. Dunsterville, *Dunsterforce*, pp. 12, 16, 17–18.
6. Ibid., pp. 20–22.
7. Ibid., pp. 24–29; Donohoe, *Persian Expedition*, pp. 72–73.
8. Dunsterville, *Dunsterforce*, p. 36.
9. Ibid., pp. 37–50.
10. Ibid., p. 58.
11. Ibid., pp. 66, 82–83.
12. Ibid., pp. 102–3, 110; Donohoe, *Persian Expedition*, pp. 76–77, 117–18; Ford, *Eden to Armageddon*, p. 192; Townshend, *When God Made Hell*, p. 421.
13. Dunsterville, *Dunsterforce*, pp. 113, 115; Donohoe, *Persian Expedition*, pp. 123–26, 127–28.
14. Dunsterville, *Dunsterforce*, p. 115; Hopkirk, *East of Constantinople*, pp. 282–87.
15. Dunsterville, *Dunsterforce*, p. 156; Hopkirk, *East of Constantinople*, p. 271.
16. Dunsterville, *Dunsterforce*, pp. 157–63; Donohoe, *Persian Expedition*, pp. 204–6.
17. Dunsterville, *Dunsterforce*, pp. 164–66, 201–4, 207; Donohoe, *Persian Expedition*, pp. 210–11.
18. Ford, *Eden to Armageddon*, p. 198.
19. Dunsterville, *Dunsterforce*, p. 196.
20. Ibid., pp. 166–68, 196–98, 199; Donohoe, *Persian Expedition*, p. 206; Ford, *Eden to Armageddon*, p. 194.
21. Dunsterville, *Dunsterforce*, pp. 169, 182; Donohoe, *Persian Expedition*, pp. 211–14; Ford, *Eden to Armageddon*, pp. 194, 425.
22. Dunsterville, *Dunsterforce*, pp. 179–81; Donohoe, *Persian Expedition*, pp. 136–37, 165–69, 219–24; Townshend, *When God Made Hell*, p. 427.
23. Donohoe, *Persian Expedition*, pp. 140–65, 169–95; Ford, *Eden to Armageddon*, p. 199.
24. Dunsterville, *Dunsterforce*, pp. 207–8; Hopkirk, *East of Constantinople*, pp. 320–29.
25. Dunsterville, *Dunsterforce*, pp. 208–9, 218; Ford, *Eden to Armageddon*, p. 196.
26. Dunsterville, *Dunsterforce*, p. 291.
27. Ibid., pp. 222–25; Ford, *Eden to Armageddon*, p. 194.
28. Dunsterville, *Dunsterforce*, pp. 230–31, 255.
29. Ibid., pp. 235, 244–45, 249–50, 255, 257–58, 268; Hopkirk, *East of Constantinople*, p. 336.
30. Dunsterville, *Dunsterforce*, p. 262.
31. Ibid., pp. 264–67; Donohoe, *Persian Expedition*, pp. 215–16; Ford, *Eden to Armageddon*, p. 196.
32. Dunsterville, *Dunsterforce*, pp. 270–73; Ford, *Eden to Armageddon*, p. 196.
33. Dunsterville, *Dunsterforce*, pp. 277–78.
34. Ibid., pp. 273–90.
35. Ibid., pp. 291–92, 297–313; Donohoe, *Persian Expedition*, pp. 217–18.

36. Dunsterville, *Dunsterforce*, pp. 312–13; Ford, *Eden to Armageddon*, pp. 198–99.
37. Townshend, *When God Made Hell*, pp. 430–31; Anglesey, *British Cavalry*, vol. 5, p. 243.

Chapter 12

1. Spackman, *Captured at Kut*, p. 20.
2. Quoted in Davis, *Ends and Means*, p. 173.
3. Ibid., p. 174; Townshend, *When God Made Hell*, pp. 324–25.
4. Davis, *Ends and Means*, p. 175.
5. Ibid., pp. 175–77; Townshend, *When God Made Hell*, pp. 325–28; Wilson, *Loyalties*, pp. 170–71.
6. Davis, *Ends and Means*, pp. 177–81; Townshend, *When God Made Hell*, pp. 327–29; Wilson, *Loyalties*, pp. 171–72.
7. Davis, *Ends and Means*, pp. 181–85.
8. Ibid., pp. 185–87.
9. Ibid., pp. 187–94; Townshend, *When God Made Hell*, pp. 331–32.
10. Davis, *Ends and Means*, pp. 194–99; for the Red Cross contribution, see Cox, *The Red Cross Launch Wessex on the River Tigris—1916*; George, *War Memoirs*, vol. 2, p. 816.
11. Davis, *Ends and Means*, pp. 199–207; Townshend, *Proconsul*, p. xl, Townshend, *When God Made Hell*, pp. 329, 330–31; see Wilson, *Loyalties*, pp. 174–75, for a ban on India making plans for an expedition to Mesopotamia on the grounds of economy, pp. 176–77.
12. Davis, *Ends and Means*, pp. 211–22; Hansard, 95, 2336, 13 July 1917; Hansard, 95, 2320, 13 July 1917; Ford, *Eden to Armageddon*, pp. 93–94; Townshend, *When God Made Hell*, pp. 333–35; Wilson, *Loyalties*, pp. 173–74, 177, 177–82.
13. *Official History*, vol. 4, p. 30.

Aftermath

1. Barker, *First Iraq War*, pp. 226–27; Wilson, *Loyalties*, p. 241.
2. Buchanan, *Tragedy of Mesopotamia*, p. 267.
3. Satia, "The Defence of Inhumanity," p. 32; Browne, *Iraq Levies*; Bernstein, *Mesopotamia Mess*, pp. 143–44.
4. *Sunday Times*, 2 August 1920; Wilson, *Loyalties*, pp. xi–xii; Bell quoted in Bernstein, *Mesopotamia Mess*, p. 155.
5. Clayton, *British Empire as a Superpower*, pp. 120–24; Bernstein, *Mesopotamia Mess*, pp. 132–33.
6. Captain George Henderson, 2/Manchesters, on 24 July 1920 near Hilla, was fatally wounded while leading his company in a bayonet charge against an attack by Arabs. The rebellion arose from "a population writhing under protracted military occupation"; Satia, "The Defense of Inhumanity," p. 25.
7. Bernstein, *Mesopotamia Mess*, p. 143.

Conclusion

1. Buchanan, *Tragedy of Mesopotamia*, p. 260.
2. Anglesey, *British Cavalry*, vol. 5, pp. 223, 334–39.

Bibliography

Anglesey. *A History of the British Cavalry 1816–1919*. Vol. 5, *1914–1919 Egypt, Palestine & Syria*. Barnsley: Leo Cooper, 1994.

_____. *A History of the British Cavalry 1816–1918*. Vol. 6, *1914–1918 Mesopotamia*. Barnsley: Leo Cooper, 1995.

Anon. *History of No. 30 Squadron: Egypt and Mesopotamia 1914 to 1919*. Uckfield: Naval and Military Press facsimile.

_____. *With a Highland Regiment in Mesopotamia*. Uckfield: Naval and Military Press facsimile of Bombay: The Time Press, 1918.

Atkinson, C. *The Queen's Own Royal West Kent Regiment, 1914–1919*. Uckfield: Naval and Military Press reprint of London: Simpkin, Marshall, Hamilton, Kent & Co., 1925.

Barker, A.J. *The First Iraq War 1914–1918: Britain's Mesopotamia Campaign*. New York: Enigma Books, 2009. Originally published, 1967, as *The Neglected War* (UK) and *The Bastard War* (U.S.).

Beharry, J. *Barefoot Soldier*. London: Sphere, 2006.

Bernstein, J. *The Mesopotamia Mess: The British Invasion of Iraq in 1914*. California: InterLingua Publishing, 2008.

Birch-Reynardson, H. *Mesopotamia 1914–1915*. London: Andrew Melrose, 1919.

Braddon, R. *The Siege*. London: Jonathan Cape, 1969.

Brown, M., ed. *The Letters of T.E. Lawrence*. London: J.M. Dent & Sons, 1988.

Browne, J.G. *The Iraq Levies, 1915–1932*. Uckfield: Naval and Military Press facsimile of London: Royal United Services Institute, 1932.

Buchan, J. *The Complete Richard Hannay*. London: Penguin, 1992.

Buchanan, G. *The Tragedy of Mesopotamia*. London: William Blackwood & Sons, 1938.

Butler, D.A. *In the Shadow of the Sultan's Realm: The Destruction of the Ottoman Empire and the Creation of the Modern Middle East*. Dulles, VA: Potomac Books, 2011.

Candler, E. *Long Road to Baghdad*. Vol. 1. Nabu Public Domain Reprints facsimile of London: Cassel & Co., 1919.

_____. *Long Road to Baghdad*. Vol. 2. Charleston, SC: BiblioLife facsimile of London: Cassel & Co., 1919.

Carver, Lord. *The National Army Museum Book of the Turkish Front 1914–1918*. London: Pan Books, 2003.

Catherwood, C. *Churchill's Folly: How Winston Churchill Created Modern Iraq*. New York: Barnes & Noble, 2007.

Chappell, M. *The British Army in World War I*. 3 vols. Oxford: Osprey Publishing, 2005.

Childers, E. *The Riddle of the Sands*. London: Penguin, 1995.

Claytons, A. *The British Empire as a Superpower*. London: Macmillan, 1986.

Cox, H., ed. *The Red Cross Launch Wessex on the River Tigris—1916: The Diary of Sydney Cox M.B.E.* Christchurch: Natula Publications, 2002.

Crowley, P. *Kut 1916: Courage and Failure in Iraq*. Stroud: History Press, 2009.

Davis, P.K. *Ends and Means: The British Mesopotamian Campaign and Commission*. London: Associated University Presses, 1994.

Donohoe, M.H. *With the Persian Expedition*. Charleston, SC: BiblioLife facsimile of London: Edward Arnold, 1919.

Downham, P., ed. *Diary of an Old Contemptible: From Mons to Baghdad 1914–1919*. Barnsley: Pen and Sword Military, 2004.

Dunsterville, L.C. *The Adventures of Dunsterforce*. Uckfield: Naval and Military Press facsimile of London: Edward Arnold, 1920.

Falls, C. *History of the Great War Based on Official Documents: Military Operations in Egypt and Palestine, 1914–1918*. Vol. 2. London: His Majesty's Stationery Office, 1930.

Ford, R. *Eden to Armageddon: World War I in the Middle East*. London: Phoenix Paperback, 2010.

Gliddon, G. *VCs of the First World War: The Sideshows*. Stroud: Sutton Publishing, 2005.

Hansard. London: His Majesty's Stationery Office, 13 July 1917.

Harvey, R. *The War of Wars: The Epic Struggle Between Britain and France: 1789–1815*. London: Constable and Robinson, 2007.

Holland, R.E. *With a 14th Hussar Through Mesopotamia 1916–1918*. The Armourer Magazine, n.d.

Hopkirk, P. *On Secret Service East of Constantinople: The Plot to Bring Down the British Empire*. London: John Murray, 2006.

Horne, A. *The Lonely Leader: Montgomery 1944–1945*. London: Pan Military Classics, 2009.

Howell, G. *Daughter of the Desert: The Remarkable Life of Gertrude Bell*. London: Macmillan, 2006.

Hubbard, G.E. *From the Gulf to Ararat: An Expedition Through Mesopotamia and Kurdistan*. New Delhi: Asian Educational Services, 2003; reprint of London: William Blackwood and Sons, 1917.

Jones, E.H. *The Road to En-Dor: Being an Account of How Two Prisoners of War at Yozgad in Turkey Won Their Way to Freedom*. Nabu Public Domain Reprints facsimile of London: John Lane, 1920.

Jowett, P. *Armies of the Balkan Wars 1912–13: The Priming Charge for the Great War*. Oxford: Osprey Publishing, 2011.

Karsh, E., and I. Karsh. *Empires of the Sand: The Struggle for Mastery in the Middle East, 1789–1923*. Cambridge, MA: Harvard University Press, 2001.

Keeling, E.H. *Adventures in Turkey and Russia*. London: J. Murray, 1924.

Lawrence, T.E. *Seven Pillars of Wisdom*. Reprinted London: Penguin Classics, 2000.

Liddle, P., ed. *Captured Memories 1900–1918: Across the Threshold of War*. Barnsley: Pen and Sword Military, 2010.

Lloyd George, D. *War Memoirs of David Lloyd George*. Vol. 2. London: Ivor Nicholson & Watson, 1933.

Long, P. *Other Ranks of Kut*. Uckfield: Naval and Military Press facsimile of London: Williams & Norgate, 1938.

Lyman, R. *Bill Slim*. Oxford: Osprey Publishing, 2011.

_____. *First Victory: Britain's Forgotten Struggle in the Middle East, 1941*. London: Constable & Robinson, 2006.

Lyman, R. *Iraq 1941: The Battles for Basra, Habbaniya, Fallujah and Baghdad*. Oxford: Osprey Publishing, 2005.

McMeekin, S. *The Berlin-Baghdad Express: The Ottoman Empire and Germany's Bid for World Power, 1898–1918*. London: Allen Lane, 2010.

McNab, A. *Bravo Two Zero*. London: Corgi Books, 1993.

Melotte, E., ed. *Mons, ANZAC and Kut by an MP*. Barnsley: Pen and Sword Military, 2009.

Mesopotamia Commission Report. London: His Majesty's Stationery Office, 1917.

Mills, D. *Sniper One: The Blistering True Story of a British Battlegroup Under Siege*. London: Penguin, 2008.

Moberly, F. *History of The Great War Based on Official Documents: The Campaign in Mesopotamia 1914–1918*. Vol. 1. London: His Majesty's Stationery Office, 1923.

_____. *History of The Great War Based on Official Documents: The Campaign in Mesopotamia 1914–1918*. Vol. 2. London: His Majesty's Stationery Office, 1924.

_____. *History of The Great War Based on Official Documents: The Campaign in Mesopotamia 1914–1918*. Vol. 3. London: His Majesty's Stationery Office, 1925.

_____. *History of The Great War Based on Official Documents: The Campaign in Mesopotamia 1914–1918*. Vol. 4. London: His Majesty's Stationery Office, 1927.

Murphy, D. *The Arab Revolt 1916–18: Lawrence Sets Arabia Ablaze*. Oxford: Osprey Publishing, 2008.

Nash, N.S. *Chitral Charlie: The Rise and Fall of Major General Charles Townshend*. Barnsley: Pen and Sword Military, 2010.

Nicolle, D. *Lawrence and the Arab Revolts*. Oxford: Osprey Publishing, 1989.

_____. *The Ottoman Army 1914–1918*. Oxford: Osprey Publishing, 1994.

_____. *Ottoman Infantryman 1914–1918*. Oxford: Osprey Publishing, 2010.

Nunn, W. *Tigris Gunboats: The Forgotten War in Iraq 1914–1917*. London: Chatham Publishing, 2007; reprint of London: Andrew Melrose, 1932.

Perrett, B. *Megiddo 1918: The Last Great Cavalry Victory*. Oxford: Osprey Publishing, 1999.

Rimmington, J. "Kut-ul-Amarah" *Army Quarterly*, 1923.

Roosevelt, K. *Armoured Cars in Eden*. Leonaur, 2006. Reprint of *War in the Garden of Eden*. New York: Scribner, 1919.

Satia, P. "The Defense of Inhumanity: Air Control and the British Idea of Arabia." *American Historical Review*, February, 2006.

Sluglett, P. *Britain in Iraq: Contriving King and Country*. London: I.B. Tauris, 2007.

Snelling, S. *VCs of the First World War: The Naval VCs*. Stroud: Sutton Publishing, 2002.

Spackman, T., ed. *Captured at Kut, Prisoner of the Turks*. Barnsley: Pen and Sword Military, 2008.

Strong, P., and S. Marble. *Artillery in the Great War*. Barnsley: Pen and Sword Military, 2011.

Sumner, I. *The Indian Army 1914–1947*. Oxford: Osprey Publishing, 2001.

Sunday Times (London), 2 August 1920.

Tennant, J.E. *In the Clouds Above Baghdad*. Uckfield: Naval and Military Press reprint of London: Cecil Palmer, 1920.

Thompson, E.J. *Tigers Along the Tigris: The Leicestershire Regiment in Mesopotamia During the First World War*. Leonaur, 2007. Originally published as *Beyond Baghdad with the Leicestershires*. London: Elpworth Press, 1919.

Townshend, C. *My Campaign in Mesopotamia*. London: Thornton Butterworth, 1920.

_____. *When God Made Hell: The British Invasion of Mesopotamia and the Creation of Iraq*. London: Faber & Faber, 2010.

Townsend, J. *Proconsul to the Middle East: Sir Percy Cox and the End of Empire*. London: I.B. Tauris, 2010.

Von Sanders, L. *Five Years in Turkey*. Uckfield: Naval and Military Press facsimile of Annapolis, MD: United States Naval Institute, 1927.

Wilcox, R. *Battles on the Tigris: The Mesopotamian Campaign of the First World War*. Barnsley: Pen and Sword Military, 2006.

Wilson, A. *Loyalties: Mesopotamia 1914–1917*. Oxford: Oxford University Press, 1931.

Wilson-Johnston, W.E. *An Account of the Operations of the 18th (Indian) Division in Mesopotamia*. Uckfield: Naval and Military Press facsimile of London: Finden Brown & Co, 1920.

Winstone, H.V.F. *Captain Shakespear*. London: Jonathan Cape, 1976.

Wylly, H.C. *History of the 1st and 2nd Battalions: The Leicestershire Regiment in the Great War*. Uckfield: Naval and Military Press reprint of Aldershot: Gale and Polden, 1929.

General Index

Abadan Island 9, 14; Battle of (1914) 15
Abdul Hamid II, Sultan 5, 6, 8
Abu Gharaib 145
Abu Jisr 119
Addison, the Rev. W.R.F., VC RAChD 93
Aden 13, 47, 52, 186
Adena Hospital 164
Adhaim 128
Afghanistan 7, 13, 50, 51, 57, 61, 70, 87, 117–118, 167, 171
Afion Kora Camp 160, 164
HMS *Agamemnon* 156
HMS *Agincourt* 10
Ahmed Bey 135
Ain Leilah 116
Ain Nukhaila pass 147–148
Akaika Channel 36, 38
Al-Amara 1, 34, 59, 181, 186; capture of 33–34, 62
Al-Fao 12, 14, 15, 46, 147
Al-Huwair river 32
Al-Kutuniya 53
Alcock, Capt. J., RFC 159
Aleppo 135, 136, 143–144, 147, 158, 164–166, 197
Alexandretta 8, 161
Ali-Al-Gharbi 46, 61–62, 80, 82; RFC aerodrome 97
Ali Ihsan Bey 115–116, 118, 119, 123, 129, 140, 147, 152–153
Allenby, E., Field Marshall 1, 30, 86, 97, 115, 132, 136, 144, 147, 152, 156, 187–188; enters Jerusalem 6, 112
Alyat 173
Amanus Tunnel 165
American Express 158
Ana 115, 144
Anglo-Persian Oil Company (APOC) 9, 152; supply army with fuel 133
Anglo-Russian Persian Cordon 118, 171
Aq-Su 145
Aqaba Crisis (1906) 8
Arab Labour Corps 135
Arab relations with British Army 1, 20, 43, 51, 57, 58, 60, 82, 100, 121, 130, 143, 158, 162, 163, 165; Army market for produce 133; employment of 133, 135; siege of Kut 63, 78; *see also* Beni Lam; Dulain; Shammar
The Arab Revolt *see* Lawrence, T.E. (of Arabia)

Arabic official language 1
Armenia 164, 165; massacres 154
Arras, Battle of (1917) 188
Artillery 1–2, 12–15, 17, 19, 23–24, 31, 37, 40, 42–43, 44–45, 47, 48, 52–55, 57–59, 82, 83, 89, 91–92, 94, 95, 99, 102–103, 106, 108, 111, 116, 119, 120, 123, 125–130, 131, 137, 139–140, 145, 147–148, 150–152, 154, 159–160, 162; Artillery formation 121; with Dunsterforce 172–177; markers for the infantry 123; Mesopotamia Commission 178; RHA guns re-allocated 140; Siege of Kut 62, 65–67, 69–73, 75, 78; tractors 99, 139
Asquith, H.: Mesopotamia Commission 179; on Townshend 52
Assani Anchorage 42
Astrakhan 174
AT (Army Transport) Carts 25, 56, 91, 117
Ataba Marsh 48
Atabiya Creek 44
Atatürk *see* Mustafa Kemal
Ati's House 40
Auchinleck, C., Maj. 62nd Punjabis 120
Auqaf *see* Dept. of Pious Bequests
Australia 1, 7, 9, 36, 60, 93, 99, 159, 163, 183, 188; Australian Light Horse 136, 188; pilots 32; prisoners of war 164
Austro-Hungary 157, 158, 167, 171, 175
Aylmer Lt.-Gen. Sir Fenton, VC 28, 109; dismissed 90; Relief of Kut 66, 69–83, 87, 89–90, 187
Az-Zubair 23–24
Aziziyeh 51, 53, 57, 58, 108, 161; RFC aerodrome 109

Ba'ath Party 185
Babi Bend 120
Babylon 36
Baden-Powell, Sir R. 152
Baghdad 113–115, 130, 155, 157–158, 184, 188; advance on 1, 18, 23, 33, 47, 51–52, 59, 181, 186; evacuated by Axis 11, 158; improvements 133; second advance on 96, 102, 109
Baghdad Archaeological Museum 133
Bagtchi Camp 163, 164

Bahrain 6, 10, 14
Baku 152, 167, 172, 173; collapse of commerce 175; oil-fields 167; sacked 177; Turkish army reaches 174–176
Balad Canal 119, 140
Balad Ruz *see* Balad Canal
Baladjari Station 176–177
Balkan Wars 4
Baquba 115, 119
Baratoff, Gen. 73, 96, 103, 106, 109, 117–118
Barjisiya Woods 23–24
Barrett, Lt.-Gen. Sir A. 15, 17, 21; replaced by Townshend 26
Basra 8, 9, 11, 18, 181, 184, 186; logistics to front line 52, 87; looting 17; need to garrison 46; port facilities 1, 87, 96, 99, 135, 178; trade 6
Basra 108
Bastadio 157, 164
Beharry, Pvt. J., VC PWRR 34
Beit Aieesa 93, 95
Bekir Sami, Kaimakam 67
Beled Station, Battle of (1917) 120–122
Bell, G., Maj. Miss 1, 3, 6, 11, 34, 116, 185; development of Iraq 135; Siege of Kut 77
Bellum 9, 20, 30–32, 35, 37–38, 40, 46, 99
Beni Lam 33–34, 36
Berlin-Baghdad Railway 8–9, 14, 17, 109, 157–158, 186; Arab attacks on 165; sabotage 165
Bersheeba, Battle of (1917) 152, 188
Bhistie 24, 65
Bicherakoff 172–173
Bingley *see* Vincent-Bingley Report
Bisereria 162
Black Sea 10, 15, 158, 167
Blosse Lynch 31, 37
Bolchara 167
Bolsheviks 171–175
Bonham-Carter, E. *see* Infrastructure
Boot, Battle of the (1917) 128–129
Breslau 9–10, 15
British Cavalry: cavalry vs. cavalry action 135; charge at Tirkrit 139; improved performance 119, 136; issued bayonets 147; need to water horses 56; poor perform-

ance 25, 53, 90–91; tactics 136, 189; where wheeled vehicles cannot go 145
British Naval Mission to Turkey 5; Anglo-Russian Convention (1907) 7
British Petroleum (BP) *see* Anglo-Persian Oil Company
Brooking, Maj.-Gen. H.: after Ramadi 143, 144; Nasariya 99; Ramadi 2, 135–136, 188
Buchan, J.: *Greenmantle* 6, 72; *The 39 Steps* 8
Buchanan, A., Lt. VC South Wales Borderers 91, 93
Buchanan, Sir G. 99, 180, 182, 184
Bulbul 32
Bulgaria 51, 147
Bushire 6, 11, 20
Bustan 55
Butterfly 58, 107

Camp Abu Naji *see* Al-Amara
Canada 188
Carmsir 15
Caspian Sea 167, 173
Cassels, Col. 119, 123–124, 128, 147, 152
Central-Caspian Dictatorship 175
Ceylon 46
Chamberlain, A. 36, 47, 51–52, 178, 181, 183
Chandler E. 116
Chatta Singh, Sepoy, VC 9th Bhopals 83
Childers, E.: *The Riddle in the Sands* 9
Christie, Dame A. 36, 37; *Murder on the Orient Express* 8
Churchill, Sir W.: oil 9, 26; post-war settlement 6, 11; support for Turkey 4
Climo, Col., 24th Punjabis 43, 55–56
Clio 31, 36, 46
Cobbe Lt.-Gen. A. 136, 147, 152
Comet 31–33, 58
Commonwealth War Graves: Al-Amara, 91, 103; Basra 26, 93
Communications (Army): Telephone cable length 48; Wireless 50; *see also* Royal Navy
Constantinople 155, 161
Cookson, Lt.-Cmdr. E., VC RN 35, 47, 50
Cornwallis, K. 34

199

Military Units Index

British Army and British Army in India

I Indian Army Corps 100, 103, 106, 108, 109, 143, 147
II (Indian) Corps 23, 26, 30
III Indian Army Corps 102, 103, 106, 108–109, 119, 128, 137, 140, 147
Indian Expeditionary Force "D" 10, 14–15, 18, 26, 143, 178–180, 186
Indian Expeditionary Forces 13, 181
Tigris Corps 1, 79, 81–82, 87, 89, 95, 96, 100, 102, 103, 106, 109, 111, 140, 143

Brigades

6th Cavalry Brigade 23, 58, 62, 136; Battle of Ramadi 135; Relief of Kut 80, 82–83
7th Cavalry Brigade: Mosul 147, 150, 152; north of Baghdad 119, 136, 140
11th Cavalry Brigade 143; Mosul 147–148, 152
7th Brigade: Mosul 147; Ramadi 129–130; Relief of Kut 94
8th Brigade: advance on Baghdad 103; north of Baghdad 119, 139; Relief of Kut 94
9th Brigade: advance on Baghdad 103; north of Baghdad 119; Relief of Kut 83, 95
12th Brigade 44–45; Battle of Ramadi 135
16th Brigade 10, 14, 15, 24, 32–33; Kut 48–51; Siege of Kut 65
17th Brigade 31–32; Ctesiphon 55; Kut 48–51; Mosul 147–148, 150, 152; Siege of Kut 65
18th Brigade 15–16, 18, 24; capture of Nasariya 44; garrisoning Dirhamiyeh 31; Kut 48–51; Mosul 147; Siege of Kut 65
19th Brigade: advance on Baghdad 106; north of Baghdad 120–121, 123, 125, 127; Relief of Kut 83, 92, 95
20th Brigade 123
21st Brigade: advance on Baghdad 106; north of Baghdad 120–121, 124; Relief of Kut 80, 83, 95
28th Brigade 47, 61; "Mobile Column" 120; north of Baghdad 120, 125; only force between Kut and Basra 62; Relief of Kut 82–83, 91–92
29th Brigade 91
30th Brigade: Ctesiphon 55, 58; Nasariya 36–46, 50; Siege of Kut 62, 65
33rd Brigade 23
35th Brigade: north of Baghdad 140; Relief of Kut 83
36th Brigade: north of Baghdad 140
37th Brigade: north of Baghdad 140, 145
38th Brigade: advance on Baghdad 108; crossing the Diyala 110–111; north of Baghdad 123, 128–129; Relief of Kut 91, 93
39th Brigade: advance on Baghdad 103; Dunsterforce 174; north of Baghdad 121, 123, 128; Relief of Kut 91, 93
40th Brigade: north of Baghdad 121, 123, 127–129, 140; Relief of Kut 91–93
42nd Brigade 135, 143
50th Brigade 143
53rd Brigade 150

British Cavalry and Yeomanry Regiments

7th Hussars 148, 150
13th Hussars 139, 145, 150; charge at Richardson's Bluff 150–152
14th Hussars 58, 119, 135, 170, 172
Dorsetshire Yeomanry 143
Hertfordshire Yeomanry 112, 119; north of Baghdad 119

British Infantry Regiments

2/Black Watch: enter Baghdad 112; north of Baghdad 120, 125; Relief of Kut 82–83, 85–86
8/Cheshire 91, 128–129
1/Connaught Rangers: Relief of Kut 81, 93–94
2/Dorset 20–21, 24, 33, 119, 157–158; weak strength 52
6/East Lancashire 110–111, 121, 123, 128–130, 147, 153
7/Gloucestershire 174
1/4 Hampshire 33, 47, 107, 111, 171–173; Dunsterforce 171–175;

Nasariya 36–46; prisoners of war 165; Shumran Bend 107
1/1 Kent Cyclist Battalion 132
King's (Liverpool) Regiment 111
6/King's Own 110, 123, 128–129
Lancashire Fusiliers 111
1/Manchester 89, 139
2/Norfolk 19, 23, 24; Shumran Bend 107; Siege of Kut 67
6/North Lancashire 93, 110–111
7/North Staffordshire: advance on Baghdad 103; Dunsterforce 174, 175, 176
1/Oxfordshire and Buckinghamshire Light Infantry 31, 35; Relief of Kut 91; Siege of Kut 67
2/Queen's Own Royal West Kent 33, 128, 132, 143
2/Royal Leicester: Baghdad station bell 112; north of Baghdad 120, 125–127, 137; Relief of Kut 82, 91
9/Royal Warwickshire: advance on Baghdad 103; Dunsterforce 174
8/Royal Welsh Fusiliers: missed 128, 129
1/Seaforth Highlander 106
6/South Lancashire 108, 110, 123, 128–129
4/South Wales Border 91
5/Wiltshire 123, 129
9/Worcester: advance on Baghdad 103; Dunsterforce 174

Divisions

Cavalry Division 106, 109, 111, 123, 128, 130, 136, 137; disbanded 140
✗ 3rd (Lahore) Division 74, 179, 188; advance on Baghdad 103; expected in theatre 62; north of Baghdad 119, 147*c9n*125; Relief of Kut 91–93
6th (Poona) Division 4, 11, 14, 15, 27, 30, 31, 46, 47, 52, 53, 78, 115, 162, 179–181, 183, 186; battle of Kut 47–51; in captivity 154, 162; Ctesiphon 54–57; retire to Kut 57–59; Siege of Kut 60–78
7th (Meerut) Division 74, 98, 179, 188; advance on Baghdad 106–108, 111; expected in theatre 62; north of Baghdad 120, 123, 136, 137, 147*c9n*125; Relief of Kut 69, 80, 82–83, 91–94
12th Division 26, 31, 33, 36, 42,

51, 53, 74, 78, 180–181, 186; Capture of Nasariya 36–46; Line of Communications 50–51
13th (Western) Division 100; advance on Baghdad 106, 108, 110, 111; expected in theatre 75; north of Baghdad 121–123, 140, 144, 145; Relief of Kut 87, 90–91, 93
14th (Indian) Division: advance on Baghdad 103, 106–107; north of Baghdad 128, 140; relieves Dunsterforce 177   *from March 1918*
15th (Indian) Division: arrived in theatre 99; Ramadi 135–136, 143, 144, 188
17th (Indian) Division 147–148, 147*c9n*125, 150, 152
18th (Indian) Division: arrived in theatre 131–132, 152, 147*c9n*125

Gurkha Regiments

1/1st Gurkhas 119
1/2nd Gurkhas: Dunsterforce 172; Shumran Bend 107
2/7th Gurkhas 40, 43, 45; Ctesiphon 55, 57; Siege of Kut 66
1/8th Gurkhas 120, 125, 139
2/9th Gurkhas 107

Indian Cavalry Regiments

1st Guides 125, 148
7th Hariana Lancers: at Ctesiphon 56; at Shaiba 23–24; Siege of Kut 65
10th Lancers 130, 132
13th Lancers 139, 150
14th Lancers 144, 150
21st Cavalry 119, 145
22nd Cavalry 135, 145
23rd Cavalry 150
32nd Lancers: charge at Samarra Station 127; enter Baghdad 112; Mosul 147–148; north of Baghdad 119, 120–121
33rd Queen Victoria's Light Cavalry 15, 20–21; Siege of Kut 65

Indian Infantry Regiments

1/1st Mahrattas 119
4th Rajputs 120
6th Jats 82–83
7th Rajputs 19, 20–21, 23
9th Bhopals: north of Baghdad 120, 125; Relief of Kut 83